DESTINATION WEMBLEY

The History of the Rugby League Challenge Cup

Graham Morris

To Tom,
Who shares my passion for
Wembley,
Graham Morris

VERTICAL EDITIONS

www.verticaleditions.com

First published in the United Kingdom in 2009 by Vertical Editions, Unit 4a, Snaygill Industrial Estate, Skipton, North Yorkshire BD23 2QR

www.verticaleditions.com

A CIP catalogue record for this book is available from the British Library

ISBN 978-1-904091-37-0

Cover design and typeset by HBA, York

Printed and bound by the The MPG Group, Bodmin

CONTENTS

Introduction............5
The Way to
Wembley.................7
1897......................9
1898......................12
1899......................14
1900......................16
1901......................18
1902......................20
1903......................22
1904......................24
1905......................26
1906......................28
1907......................30
1908......................32
1909......................34
1910......................36
1911......................39
1912......................41
1913......................43
1914......................45
1915......................47
1920......................49
1921......................51
1922......................53
1923......................56
1924......................58
1925......................61
1926......................63
Radio coverage 65
1927......................66
1928......................68
Empire Stadium ...70
1929......................71
1930......................74
1931......................76
1932......................78
1933......................80

1934......................82
1935......................84
1936......................86
1937......................88
1938......................90
1939......................92
Second
World War............94
1941......................95
1942......................97
1943......................98
1944......................100
1945......................102
1946......................104
1947......................107
1948......................109
1949......................111
1950......................113
1951......................115
1952......................117
1953......................119
1954......................121
1955......................124
1956......................126
1957......................128
1958......................130
1959......................132
1960......................134
1961......................136
1962......................138
1963......................140
1964......................142
1965......................144
1966......................146
Royalty 148
1967......................149
1968......................151
1969......................153

1970......................155
1971......................157
1972......................159
1973......................161
1974......................163
Schools 165
1975......................166
1976......................168
1977......................170
1978......................172
1979......................174
1980......................176
1981......................178
1982......................180
1983......................183
1984......................185
TV Coverage 187
1985......................188
1986......................191
1987......................193
1988......................195
1989......................197
1990......................199
1991......................201
1992......................203
1993......................205
1994......................207
1995......................209
Entertainment 212
1996......................214
1997......................217
1998......................219
1999......................221
Venues................224
2000......................226
2001......................228
2002......................230
2003......................232

2004......................235
2005......................238
2006......................241
New Wembley 243
2007......................244
2008......................247
2009......................250
Still great............253
Summary
of results.............254
Club facts and
figures.................255
Players facts and
figures.................256
Coaches/referees/
attendance facts and
figures.................257
Index of
players 258
Index of
coaches...............271
Index of
referees 272

ACKNOWLEDGEMENTS

I am indebted to others whose support has helped make this publication possible. In particular Richard Bailey, Steve Calline, Phil Caplan, Tony Collins, Bill Dalton, Harry Edgar, John Edwards, Paul English, Ray Fletcher, Mike Flynn, Simon Foster, Steve Fox, Ray French, Robert Gate, Derek Hallas, Don Hammond (Kiwis Association), Tony Hannan, Andrew Hardcastle, Andy Harland, Phil Hodgson, Steven Elliott James (who provided the front cover photograph of the new Wembley Stadium), Sig Kasatkin and Dave Williams (www.RLPhotos.com), John Lindley, Peter Lush, Bruce Montgomerie (New Zealand journalist), Keith Nutter, Neil Ormston, Chris Park, Stuart Portman, Ian Proctor, John Riding, Emma Rosewarne (Rugby Football League), Mike Rylance, Alex Service, Gary Slater, Carmen Taplin (New Zealand Rugby League), Mike Turner, Brian Walker and Harry Waring.

Also the University of Huddersfield Archive (Hilary Haigh and colleagues), British Library Newspapers (London), plus the staff of the following main/central libraries: Barrow, Batley, Bradford, Castleford, Dewsbury, Edinburgh, Halifax, Huddersfield, Hull, Keighley, Leeds, Leigh, Manchester, Oldham, Rochdale, St Helens, Salford, Scarborough, Wakefield, Warrington, Widnes, Wigan, Workington and York.

During my research, the following books and periodicals have been consulted: *Rugby League Record Keepers' Club* publications (editor Irvin Saxton, 1972-94), *Rothmans Rugby League Yearbooks* (1981/82-99), *Code 13* (editor Trevor Delaney, 1986-91), *League Publications Limited/Gillette Rugby League Yearbooks* (1996-2008/09), *50 Greats: Castleford RL Club* (by David Smart/Andy Howard, 2002), *100 Greats: Cumberland Rugby League* (Robert Gate, 2002), *100 Greats: Featherstone Rovers RLFC* (Ron Bailey, 2002), *100 Greats: Huddersfield RLFC* (David Gronow, 2008), *100 Greats: Hull RL Club* (Raymond Fletcher, 2002), *100 Greats: Leeds RL Club* (Phil Caplan/Peter Smith, 2001), *100 Greats: St Helens RLFC* (Alex Service, 2006), *100 Greats: Thrum Hallers 1945-1998* (Robert Gate, 2004), *100 Greats: Warrington RLFC* (Eddie Fuller/Gary Slater, 2002), *100 Years of Rugby* (John C. Lindley, 1973), *Being*

Eddie Waring (Tony Hannan, 2008), *The Complete Who's Who of England Rugby Union Internationals* (Raymond Maule, 1992), *The Encyclopaedia of Rugby League Players* (Alan Whiticker/Glen Hudson, 1999), *The Football Grounds of England and Wales* (Simon Inglis, 1985), *Trevor Foster: The Life of a Rugby League Legend* (Simon Foster/ Robert Gate/Peter Lush, 2005), *Neil Fox – Rugby League's Greatest Point Scorer* (Robert Gate, 2005), *The Grounds of Rugby League* (Trevor Delaney, 1991), *Guinness Rugby League Fact Book* (Robert Gate, 1991), *Halifax RL: The First 100 Years* (Andrew Hardcastle, 1999), *The Headingley Story 1890-1955* (Ken Dalby, 1955), *The Headingley Story 1955-1979* (Ken Dalby, 1979), *The International Grounds of Rugby League* (Trevor Delaney, 1995), *Oldham RLFC: The Complete History* (Michael Turner, 1997), *Rugby League Hall of Fame* (Robert Gate, 2003), *Rugby League in Twentieth Century Britain* (Tony Collins, 2006), *Saints v Wigan* (Robert Gate, 1990), *So Close to Glory* (Eddie Fuller/Gary Slater, 2008), *The Story of Rugby League* (Keith Macklin, 1984), *Thrum Hall Greats* (Andrew Hardcastle, 1994), *The Thrum Hall Story* (Andrew Hardcastle, 1986), *A Ton Full of Memories* (Brian F. Cartwright, 1986), *The Eddie Waring Book of Rugby League* (Eddie Waring, 1966), *Wembley 1923-1973* (various authors, 1973), *Who's Who of Welsh International Rugby Players* (John M. Jenkins/Duncan Pierce/Timothy Auty, 1991), Willie (Mike Gardner, 1995). I have also researched many newspapers and endeavoured to acknowledge them within the main text where appropriate.

INTRODUCTION

Eighty years ago, on 4 May 1929, Wembley hosted its first Rugby League Challenge Cup Final when Dewsbury met Wigan in a classic 'Battle of the Roses' confrontation. From that moment the very mention of 'Wembley' has had a magical ring about it amongst the rugby league fraternity and it has become the ambition of every supporter, player or club official that their team sample its special atmosphere. Its unique twin towers provided the backdrop to Challenge Cup Finals for the next 70 years until, like so many of Britain's historic rugby and soccer grounds, it was decided that the tired old stadium had to be laid to rest and replaced by a new 'state of the art' facility. So it was, with some sadness, that rugby league bade a fond, almost tearful, farewell after the 1999 finale and waited with bated breath for its replacement and the next instalment of the 'Wembley weekend'. That wait, for varying reasons, was slightly longer than anticipated, but, in 2007, the gleaming, magnificent new Wembley Stadium was again open for business and St Helens and Catalans Dragons took centre stage on yet another memorable day out.

During its enforced absence, the rugby union strongholds of Twickenham, Murrayfield and the Millennium Stadium provided more than adequate substitutes, allowing the 'away-day' tradition for the many thousands who enjoy the annual jaunt to continue. However, with all due respect to those three excellent venues—Cardiff's Millennium Stadium in particular earning plaudits—it was not quite the same as a trip to Wembley with dinner and a beer or two in the West End and the obligatory walk and photo-shoot around Trafalgar Square. One Bradford Bulls player, interviewed after the 2000 event at Murrayfield and obviously delighted at gaining his first Challenge Cup winners medal, nonetheless expressed a tinge of disappointment that he had been unable to fulfil his dream at Wembley Stadium.

My personal Wembley experience began in 1964. The fact that it made a big impression is supported by the knowledge that, even after all the years, I can still visualise Alan Burwell's breakaway try for Hull Kingston Rovers and Frank Collier's late clincher for Widnes. I recall being told beforehand that, as it was

my first visit, I would probably spend the first half of the game absorbing the Wembley scene and its incredible atmosphere, and that was certainly how it turned out. Having entered the stadium and climbed its stairways, I emerged through an opening to see the famed lush-green turf 'in the flesh' for the first time. Everything seemed to me to be on a colossal scale compared to what I had previously experienced 'up north' and, with the enclosure being oval—rather than rectangle—I was conscious of the many thousands sharing the experience with me.

And, of course, before the match I took part, for the first time, in the traditional 'community singing', led on that occasion by Bill Scott-Coomber who was accompanied by the Band of the Welsh Guards in their splendid red tunics and bearskins. It climaxed, as ever, with the singing of 'Abide With Me' and—still in my teens—I believe it was the first time I witnessed grown men shedding tears. With so much going on around me it is small wonder that the two tries I remember both came towards the end of the match, the rest having now become a blur of colour and razzamatazz! But those feelings, I am sure, are no different to those of so many other supporters as they savour the occasion for the first time, either as a one-off visit or for the start of what, for many, becomes a compelling yearly outing.

Players too, crave to reach Wembley but it can be an over-powering experience that often unnerves the best of them. Many years ago, during an interview I conducted for the *Open Rugby* magazine, Andy Gregory, who appeared in eight Challenge Cup Finals at Wembley, reflecting on his first in 1981, told me: 'When we were getting changed before the game a few of my team-mates had a word with me. They said: "When you walk out, whatever you do keep your eyes on the pitch. If you look at the crowd your mind will go off the game." As I walked out I started to look round and then I remembered what they said. I pretended I was playing for (my former amateur team) St Patrick's or for the school in front of a few people!'

Although Wembley was to become the 'Holy Grail' for both players and their supporters it should also be realised that the Challenge Cup Final was held in high esteem long before that first occasion in 1929, the *Huddersfield Daily Examiner* describing it, in 1920, as 'the most coveted trophy in the Northern Union game'. Crowd fervour in those earlier years was no less intense and, although fans did not sport the replica jerseys associated with today's followers, they wore almost any manner of things bearing their club colours, be it hats, badges, scarves and, often, more bizarre items by modern standards. In 1900 when Salford met Swinton at Fallowfield, 'medal badges' depicting the cup were in great demand 'with its accompanying bit of ribbon, blue or red, according to the predilection of the purchaser.' The various modes of public transport, too, were usually bedecked in the appropriate team colours including the railway steam engines that transported players and supporters to and from the final.

The completion of the new 90,000 all-seated Wembley Stadium with its colossal 315 metre archway—an iconic image that is certain to become as famous around the world as the former twin towers—signals the start of a new era for the Rugby League's most famous trophy. Once again everyone connected with the sport can relish their weekend break in the capital whether numbered amongst the many thousands who make the pilgrimage annually or those who live for the day when they can journey to London and see their team lift the cup, their destination, once more, being Wembley.

Graham Morris
September 2009

NOTES ON FACTS AND FIGURES

The following should be noted when referring to the statistical records associated with each final:

Drop-goals: For consistency, I have referred to drop-goals as exactly that throughout the book, although commonly known as field-goals since the late 1990s.

Head-to-head form guide: Matches are listed in chronological order and refer to that season only. Any matches subsequent to the Challenge Cup Final are not included.

Progressive score: In some instances, the time ('min') shown against a score may differ slightly to previous publications I have been involved in, due to updated research and the increased availability of video and dvd recordings.

Receipts: From 1999 onwards no receipts have been published by the RFL.

Route to the final: When referring to semi-final venues, note that Odsal Stadium, Bradford, is the same as the Grattan Stadium, the McAlpine Stadium, Huddersfield, is the same as the Galpharm Stadium, and the Halton Stadium, Widnes, is the same as the Stobart Stadium.

Substitutes: From 1965 onwards, 'dnp' indicates did not play.

Video referee: From 1999 onwards, an asterisk (*) against a try indicates it was referred to the video referee.

(*Additional note:* In the main text, from 1990 onwards, I have referred to field distances in metres, rather than the previous measure of yards to reflect rule changes to the 'Field of Play' introduced at that time.)

THE WAY TO WEMBLEY

The Challenge Cup—the Rugby League's oldest surviving competition—had been around for 31 years before the revolutionary suggestion of taking its deciding match into London was first mooted. Although essentially a northern-based tournament, forward thinking minds had no doubt noted the impact of the Football Association Cup since its first Wembley final in 1923. Indeed, one well-known rugby league referee of the time, the Reverend Frank Chambers, at a meeting of the Yorkshire Society of Referees on 15 March 1928, was possibly the first to float the idea of using Wembley. As a resident of Huddersfield, his thoughts must have been influenced by the local euphoria attached to Huddersfield Town's appearance in the 1926 FA Cup Final. He may also have been mindful of the fact that the Rugby League needed a larger venue to stage its own event having himself had charge of the 1924 Oldham-Wigan Challenge Cup Final at Rochdale Hornets' Athletic Grounds. The largest crowd to date—41,831—overflowed on to the pitch making some passages of play almost farcical and it was by no means the first time the occasion had experienced crowd congestion difficulties.

The problem was that the Rugby League did not, in itself, have possession of a large-capacity ground. The earliest finals of The Northern Rugby Football Union Challenge Cup—to give it its full title at that time—took place at Headingley, which could then accommodate just over 30,000. However, when it went west of the Pennines there were limited options and, at the turn of the century, the destination of the trophy was twice resolved at Fallowfield Stadium, Manchester. Although able to house larger crowds it did not cope well with such gatherings, a conclusion the soccer authorities had already arrived at after staging an FA Cup Final and semi-final there. During the 1920s the numbers wishing to attend what became known as the Rugby League Challenge Cup from 1923 steadily grew but there was still no venue within the sport that could comfortably accept a 40,000 attendance. British rugby league's largest ever club ground, Bradford Northern's Odsal Stadium—scene of the historic 1954 Challenge Cup Final replay—did not exist until 1934. Even then, the sport turned to Leeds

United's Elland Road and Manchester City's Maine Road soccer grounds in the late 1930s when it was realised the Northern Rugby League Championship Final required greater capacity for its audience.

Whether the Reverend Chambers' words carried any influence is unclear, but, during the Rugby League 1928 Annual Conference, held at Llandudno's seafront Marine Hotel, his idea resurfaced. For the morning of Monday 25 June, during the second day of discussions—the first being on Saturday—the following item appears in the Minute Book: 'Mr John Leake moved that it be a recommendation to the Council that the Final Tie for the Challenge Cup be played each year in London.' Further down the page another entry tells use: 'Mr Walter Waide seconded, and after a number of members had spoken for and against, the recommendation was carried by 13 votes to 10.' Leake—a Yorkshireman from Pontefract—was Chairman of the Rugby League's Welsh Commission, the sport having gained a foothold in south Wales on the back of the short-lived Pontypridd club that competed in the Northern Rugby League but had recently demised. For the record, the remaining 34 council members consisted of representatives of the 28 professional clubs (including Waide for Hunslet), the Cumberland Commission, Millom, West Yorkshire, East Yorkshire, West Lancashire and East Lancashire.

The idea was moved forward through a succession of council meetings and, on 3 October, it was agreed the final would, indeed, go to London, either at the Crystal Palace or Wembley. In the interim, White City (Manchester), which had just opened as a 40,000 capacity greyhound-cum-speedway venue, and Wigan, bidding to stage their third consecutive final, had both put themselves forward but were rejected. As a consequence, the current Rugby Football League Chairman Fred Kennedy (of Broughton Rangers) and Secretary John Wilson were mandated to visit London to inspect the two venues and discuss terms. Meantime, a circular letter was issued to all clubs, district associations and supporters organisations under the heading 'Cup Final in London' stating: 'For the first time in the history of The Rugby League, the Final Tie of the Challenge Cup will be played in

London, on May 4th 1929. The intention is to make this an annual event in the sporting calendar, and to make it a success in this and following years, the Council desires to enlist the services and goodwill of every organisation and individual interested in the Game. The two main objects to be aimed at are (1) to create a desire in as many people as possible to attend the match, and (2) to make it easy in a financial sense, and convenient from a travelling point of view to get there.'

It was on 25 October 1928 that the morning press reported: 'The Rugby League Challenge Cup final will this season be played at Wembley Stadium,' the momentous decision to take the 13-a-side code's biggest day to the famous setting being taken at a meeting in the Stratford Arms Hotel, Wakefield, the previous evening. The committee unanimously decided on Wembley, although no specific reason is documented in the minutes. In *The Eddie Waring Book of Rugby League* (published in 1966) the author claims Wilson told him Crystal Palace asked for a prohibitive 33% of the gate. What is clear from subsequent Rugby League accounts and correspondence with Wembley's authorities was that the latter took 15%. The Rugby Football League were determined to make the event a success and arranged to have 'Sandwich (Board) Men' advertising it on the approaches to Twickenham for England's rugby union clashes with Wales and Ireland, played, respectively, during January and February 1929, 15,000 leaflets being distributed.

The RFL prepared a VIP guest list that included Lord Daresbury (who was invited to present the cup), Sir Granville Pyne (The High Commissioner for Australia), Sir Joseph Turner, Sir Edwin Airey, Brigadier General Kentish, Lord Cozens Hardy and Sir George Holden. Meanwhile, with the FA Cup Final being held one week ahead of the Challenge Cup Final, the rugby posts were erected on Tuesday, the Wembley ground staff, reportedly, taking 'all week' to remove the soccer markings.

The Australian rugby league authorities sent the RFL a cablegram that said: 'Send greetings and best wishes for the success of your venture at Wembley. Hope forerunner of Australian fixture.' The latter comment, effectively suggesting a Test match at Wembley during the visit of the Australian tourists later that year, hit a stumbling block. The Rugby League council made plans to stage the opening Test at Wembley during October but a letter received from Wembley's Managing Director, Arthur J. Elvin, that was put before a Council Meeting in June 1929 caused

a rethink. In it, Elvin stated that the agreement reached for the 1929 final 'was in the nature of a missionary effort, and did not provide a reasonable profit to the stadium company.' He asked that the terms be raised to 25% for the first match in any one year and 20% for subsequent matches the same year. As a result the Test match was rescheduled for Craven Park, Hull. Thankfully, and mercifully for the generations that have followed the sport ever since, an agreement was ironed out to stage the Wales-Australia match at Wembley in January 1930 followed by the next Challenge Cup Final four months later. The rest, as they say, is history.

WEMBLEY INDISPOSED

The Rugby Football League wanted to bring the 1932 Challenge Cup Final forward to 9 April due to the upcoming tour to Australia and New Zealand but, realising that the date clashed with the England-Scotland soccer international at Wembley, decided on 16 April instead. However, with the FA Cup Final scheduled for the stadium on 23 April, confirmation depended on the co-operation of the Football Association whose arrangement with Wembley dictated no game be played there in the week before an FA Cup Final. The idea was rejected and the RFL chose Wigan's Central Park for 9 April. Almost a half-century later, during May 1981, the Rugby Football League reached agreement with Wembley's authorities that Challenge Cup Final replays over the following three years would take place at Wembley. However, when the 1982 final ended in a draw, Wembley was unavailable for the rematch of Hull and Widnes due to the visit of Pope John Paul II, and it was staged at Elland Road, Leeds.

1897 NORTHERN UNION CHALLENGE CUP FINAL
Batley v St Helens

The Batley and St Helens teams pose for the camera in front of Headingley's main stand prior to the first Northern Union Challenge Cup Final. Smart looking Batley, on the left, in white jerseys with club badges contrast with the varying blue and white tops of the Saints players, most of whom retained fading kit worn in earlier rounds for good luck. Note the Challenge Cup on display at the front of the stand

Batley and St Helens were pitted against each other in the first Northern Union Challenge Cup Final, although contemporary reports viewed it more as a confrontation between Yorkshire and Lancashire. When St Helens were the first to emerge onto the Headingley pitch—where they were subsequently photographed for posterity—the reception from the crowd was muted, the *St Helens Reporter* saying 'few of them gave the sturdy Lancashire lads a welcoming cheer' whereas when Batley went through the same routine, minutes later, 'a cheer of rousing dimensions' greeted them. In fairness, many of the 920 Saints' supporters that, reportedly, made the journey across the Pennines from the glass-manufacturing town did not arrive until midway through the first half, two special trains taking three hours to complete the journey.

Batley supporters wore 'favours' in cerise and fawn—the club's traditional colours—although their team played in smart looking white jerseys. St Helens' dress sense, meanwhile, was contradictory, wearing eye-catching black-leaded boots but, in most cases, faded blue and white hooped jerseys, their players superstitiously retaining the kit that saw them through the previous rounds. The Yorkshire team—known as 'The Gallant Youths'—looked the bigger, more imposing outfit, their success based on a 'phenomenal' pack. St Helens were without three-quarter T. Sutton who broke a collarbone in the semi-final meeting with Swinton the previous Monday.

Shortly after the kick-off Batley's Joe Oakland made a great run and kick downfield, placing St Helens under immediate pressure, the Yorkshire side's forwards 'carrying scrum after scrum like clockwork' at a time when a scrum-down quickly followed each tackle. The siege temporarily abated after Batley were penalised and David Traynor booted the ball into Batley's quarters. The Yorkshire side, though, worked their way back and Oakland dropped a goal—then worth four points—which just 'skimmed' over the crossbar. After 15 minutes play they increased their lead when Wattie Davies directed a cross-field kick towards the Saints' goal, Jack Goodall obligingly scooping the ball up to go beneath the posts for the opening try. Davies missed the easy conversion, hitting a post, the score standing at 7–0.

St Helens, finding some composure after a hectic opening, then came near to scoring themselves on several occasions; Freddie Little was hauled down two yards short of Batley's goal, Richard O'Hara's drop-goal

THE 1897 SEMI-FINALS

Atrocious weather on the Saturday before the 1897 Challenge Cup Final caused the St Helens-Swinton semi-final to be postponed until Monday. The Batley-Warrington tie went ahead, but Warrington, who had objected to playing, subsequently registered a protest (apparently, it was so muddy players could not recognise each other), also claiming the match ended several minutes short. Their appeal, heard in Manchester on Monday, was turned down.

The first Challenge Cup winners Batley show off their trophy. Standing: Gath, Munns, Lowrie, Wilby, J. Goodall, Stubley, H. Goodall, Barraclough, Fisher. Seated: Shackleton, Oakland, Naylor, Littlewood. On ground: Wilson (asst. trainer), Shaw, Garner, Spurr, Main, Bennett (trainer)

effort failed to lift, and Billy Jacques was just wide with a penalty attempt. Play developed into a state of fluctuation as St Helens' backs continually sent the ball

REPORTING THE FIRST NORTHERN UNION CUP FINAL

Although the Challenge Cup Final would soon capture the imagination with in-depth newspaper coverage, the inaugural 1897 competition was rather low key in comparison with neither the Batley nor St Helens newspapers going 'overboard' in their reporting. The *Batley News* correspondent, who caught an early train, said: 'At two o'clock when I suppose most Batley people were struggling for seats in the train, yours truly was basking in the radiant smiles of two Headingley officials,' adding 'their pride was pardonable. This was the first Northern Union Cup final, and, after their experience of football finals in general, they were anxious to know what the gate would be like. Although the season was far advanced, and one of the contesting teams hailed from the extreme portion of Lancashire, there was a very gratifying attendance.'

downfield with some big kicks, helping their forwards conserve energy. Before half-time Oakland attempted another drop-goal but this time it was a poor effort.

St Helens suffered a severe jolt after the interval, Little quitting when his 'weak knee' failed him. Billy Briers was moved from the pack to cover him at halfback, leaving their forward strength depleted. Batley attempted further drop-goals through Ike Shaw and Jack Goodall. Whilst Shaw's was just wide of the post, the latter's attempt skewered towards the corner, leading to what was acknowledged by both camps as the most spectacular moment of the match. Saints winger Bob Doherty caught the ball a few yards from his own try-line and, after looking set to kick, sped away at pace. As Davies tackled him, he transferred the ball to the supporting Traynor, who shot down the touchline, handing off several opponents as they attempted to push him out of bounds before crossing the try-line near the corner flag. He then veered inside to complete the touchdown, the only one conceded by Batley in that year's competition, Jacques missing the goal.

David Traynor of St Helens—scorer of the game's outstanding try

STATS

Batley 10 St Helens 3

Saturday 24 April at Headingley, Leeds (3.30 pm)

Batley (white): Garner, Davies, J. Goodall (captain), Fitzgerald, Shaw, Oakland, H. Goodall, Shackleton, Gath, Maine, Spurr, Fisher, Stubley, Littlewood, Munns. Trainer: F. Bennett

St Helens (blue and white narrow hoops): Foulkes (captain), Doherty, Traynor, Barnes, Jacques, O'Hara, Little, T. Winstanley, Briers, W. Winstanley, Reynolds, Thompson, Dale, Rimmer, Whiteley. Trainer: R.K. Forsyth

Referee: J.H. Smith

Touch-judges: E. Gresty, H. Hutchinson

Half-time: 7–0   Attendance: 13,492   Receipts: £624

Weather: sunny with chill wind

Cup presentation:
Mrs H.H. Waller, wife of Northern Union president

Progressive score:

Batley	score (min)	St Helens
Oakland drop-goal	4–0 (4)	
J. Goodall try	7–0 (15)	
	7–3 (55)	Traynor try
Munns try	10–3 (65)	

Route to the final:

First round:
Batley (bye), St Helens 58 Lees (Oldham) 0

Second round:
Bramley 0 Batley 11, St Helens 17 Castleford 3

Third round:
Batley 6 Brighouse Rangers 0, St Helens 11 Wigan 0

Fourth round:
Batley 10 Widnes 0, St Helens 12 Tyldesley 0

Semi-finals:
Batley 6 Warrington 0 (Fartown, Huddersfield, 5,500),

St Helens 7 Swinton 0 (Wheater's Field, Broughton, 20,000)

Head-to-head form guide:

No previous meetings during season

The try brought the match to life, the excitement around the ground reaching 'fever pitch'. Little returned to the fray but, unable to make a meaningful contribution, positioned himself out wide. Batley sealed their win when Paudy Munns forced his way over following a scrum near the corner. Davies' kick was just wide, the Batley players, who initially thought he had found the target, 'indulged in somersaults'. But, at 10–3, it proved a winning score.

As soon as referee Jack Smith sounded the final whistle, hordes of supporters rushed towards the grandstand where the trophy had stood gleaming in the sunshine throughout the match, members of the Northern Union Committee and club representatives seated alongside. There was such a crush of people that it took a while for the players to reach the temporary platform that had been set up.

The *Batley News*, rejoicing in the success of their team, said: 'The style of play adopted by the winners was little short of a novelty to a large number of the spectators, Lancashire folk especially. Every man in the pack played football as football should be played, and, what is more, appeared to do it by instinct, rather than through any effort.'

The Batley team arrived back by train in the early evening to find 160 'fog signals' placed on the railway line on the approach to the station that sounded 'like the discharge of a field battery'. As they pulled alongside the platform, the Batley Old Band played 'See the Conquering Hero Comes' whilst an exited crowd yelled and shouted at the sight of their heroes, sticks and hats being held aloft in salute. It was a scene to be repeated at various railway stations around the north over the next few decades as victorious teams returned home with their prize.

In additional to the winners' medals already presented to the 15 players that took part, Batley club president David Burnley announced a subscription list had been opened to raise £40 to provide them with commemorative caps, plus additional medals for the reserves.

1898 NORTHERN UNION CHALLENGE CUP FINAL
Batley v Bradford

Pre-match favourites Batley retained their prize in the first all-Yorkshire Challenge Cup Final, again played at Headingley, beating Bradford 7–0 in front of 27,941 spectators, claimed at the time as the largest to date in either code of rugby. For Bradford—who had four former England rugby union internationals in their ranks—the result ended an unbeaten run of 22 matches stretching back to early December.

Bradford could have got off to a flying start but, unfortunately for them, Fred Cooper was off-target with two early penalties, *The Bradford Daily Telegraph* saying 'the Batley supporters shouted with delight at the failure.' The 'Park Avenuites', as they were known, were undaunted and, with their backs receiving plenty of the ball, attacked vigorously, Batley's defence containing them. The Bradford forwards made a 'rush' towards the Batley try-line, kicking the ball into the in-goal area, Arthur Garner managing to kick it dead. At length, Batley began to mount their own pressure and won a penalty kick,

Wattie Davies being wide with his shot. Further scoring chances for Bradford came through B. Patrick, almost succeeding with an ambitious drop-goal from halfway, and E. Kelsey, crossing the whitewash from a scrum but having his touchdown claim rejected, half-time arriving without a score.

The second 40-minute spell opened with Batley's Joe Oakland obtaining the ball from a scrum and racing around the opposition before placing it over the try-line, but the touchdown was overturned due to an 'irregularity'. Davies then missed a goal attempt after Bradford were penalised at the succeeding scrum. Batley, though, had the bit between their teeth and were bombarding the opposition's line. Davies had another crack at goal—this time from a 'mark'—but, having been struck from some distance, the ball sailed well wide. Eventually, following a lengthy assault, Batley scored after Davies was held on the line following a break by Oakland. Clever passing by brothers Jack and Harry Goodall quickly followed, Dai

Batley retain their prize! Players only are, standing (third row): Fisher, Phillips, Fitzgerald, Shackleton, Gath, Rodgers, Munns. Seated: Spurr, Garner, J. Goodall, Oakland, H. Goodall. On ground: Fozzard, Davies, Stubley, Main

12

Fitzgerald obtaining possession and passing to Davies who scored a tremendous drop-goal 'amidst a scene of great excitement', spectators 'cheering lustily'. From the restart Davies had another goal opportunity, his penalty going wide. Bradford, meanwhile, faded as their forwards began to look 'worn out and demoralised', halfbacks Bob Wood and Harry Prole struggling to obtain possession.

A kick towards Bradford's try-line by Davies saw Charlie Stubley grab the ball and claim a touchdown for Batley but it was 'ruled back'. Towards the end, Bradford—still only two points adrift—mounted a last desperate challenge but Batley repelled them and

Bradford captain Tom Broadley

Stubley, Jim Gath and Mark Shackleton dribbled the ball away to the centre of the field, subsequent play taking them to Bradford's line where Harry Goodall's 'clever dribble' through an opening enabled brother Jack to score under the posts despite Cooper's tackle. Davies missed the easy conversion but, from the restart, Bradford were again under the cosh, Oakland getting the ball to Jack Goodall whose drop-goal concluded the scoring.

The *Batley News* correspondent 'Raven' was asked by fellow journalists in the press box as to how Batley were 'in such splendid condition' so late in the season. Sharing his response with his readers he said: 'The men conduct themselves in the cup-ties as they do all through the season. There is no change in their mode of living. They follow their usual occupations regularly, take care of themselves, and are careful not to over-train', adding that 'Salford's holiday at Southport did them more harm than good', a reference to the preparation undertaken by their semi-final opponents.

STATS

Batley 7 Bradford 0

Saturday 23 April at Headingley, Leeds (3.30 pm)

Batley (white): Garner, Davies, J. Goodall (captain), Fitzgerald, Fozzard, Oakland, H. Goodall, Shackleton, Gath, Maine, Spurr, Fisher, Stubley, Munns, Rodgers. Trainer: F. Bennett

Bradford (red, amber and black hoops): Patrick, Dobson, Cooper, W. Murgatroyd, F. Murgatroyd, Wood, Prole, Broadley (captain), Fearnley, Robertson, Holden, Kelsey, Holt, McLoughlin, Toothill. Trainer: H.J. Knutton

Referee: J.H. Smith   Touch-judges: H. Hutchinson, E. Gresty

Half-time: 0–0   Attendance: 27,941   Receipts: £1,586

Weather: sunny and warm

Cup presentation:
Mrs J.E. Warren, wife of Northern Union president

Progressive score:

Batley	score (min)	Bradford
Davies drop-goal	2–0 (56)	
J. Goodall try	5–0 (73)	
J. Goodall drop-goal	7–0 (75)	

Route to the final:

First round:
Batley 12 St Helens 7, Bradford 7 Swinton 2

Second round:
Batley 8 Walkden 0, Birkenhead Wanderers 0 Bradford 5

Third round:
Castleford 4 Batley 10, Hull 2 Bradford 6

Fourth round:
Batley 3 Oldham 0, Bradford 7 Broughton Rangers 5

Semi-finals:
Batley 5 Salford 0 (Watersheddings, Oldham, 15,000),

Bradford 13 Widnes 0 (Thrum Hall, Halifax, 14,000)

Head-to-head form guide:

Bradford 10 Batley 10 (League)

Batley 3 Bradford 8 (League)

WINNING CAPTAIN

Jack Goodall (Batley 1897, 1898)

Jack Goodall made his Batley debut in 1891 during the club's rugby union era. Noted as a steady centre with reliability in defence, he made over 290 appearances for his local club from the time they joined the Northern Union in 1895 until his retirement in 1905. With the famed 'Gallant Youths' he won the Northern Union Challenge Cup (1897, 1898, 1901) and Yorkshire League (1898/99), and represented Yorkshire once (1902). His brothers Harry (who shared his Challenge Cup success) and Percy also played for Batley, their father, James, being club president.

1899 NORTHERN UNION CHALLENGE CUP FINAL
Oldham v Hunslet

The first Challenge Cup Final held in Lancashire took place at Fallowfield Stadium, home of Manchester Athletic Club, Oldham taking on Hunslet. There had been concerns about the venue for, although it could accommodate a sizeable crowd, it had poor vantage points, a recent mid-week FA Cup semi-final being abandoned at half-time after spectators encroached the playing area. With a larger police presence and more turnstiles operating, the Northern Union experienced no real problems although the 15,763 turnout fell below expectation.

Oldham conceded an early penalty for 'informality in a scrimmage', Albert Goldthorpe obliging with the two points via a drop-goal for Hunslet. From the restart Oldham's forwards pushed deep into Hunslet's half and, with defenders Jack Mitchell and Walter Goldthorpe indecisive, Sam Lees hoofed the ball underneath the posts before dropping on it, adding the conversion himself for a 5–2 lead. Hunslet fought back; Albert Goldthorpe just missed a goal from a mark, and, later, severe pressure on Oldham's line forced Dicky Thomas to kick the ball dead.

Play became more even, although Oldham received a setback when Jim Telfer was carried off midway through the half after colliding with a colleague. Albert Goldthorpe fell short of the target with a penalty chance but achieved a better result after intercepting

Oldham strike a theatrical pose after winning their first Challenge Cup competition. Standing: Edwards, Moffatt, Bonser, Ellis, A. Lees, Broome, J. Lees, Frater. Seated: Fletcher, Sellars, Thomas, S. Lees, Davies. On ground: Martin, Williams, Lawton, Barnes

Joe Lawton's pass. Racing away, he drew full back Thomas before sending brother Walter into the clear, the latter dropping over the line for a try as Sam Williams tackled him. The *Oldham Standard* said 'hats, caps, handkerchiefs, etc., were waved in the air', Albert Goldthorpe's goal placing Hunslet 7–5 ahead.

Encouraged, Hunslet's forwards began playing with greater enthusiasm. Oldham defended well but, when they conceded a penalty through another scrum infringement, Albert Goldthorpe succeeded with a magnificent drop-goal from the centre of the field. The Lancashire side received a boost when Telfer returned to action just before half-time.

Hunslet merited their 9–5 interval lead having had most of the play but the quick pace had taken its toll, pre-match favourites Oldham looking sharper after the break as the contest turned firmly in their favour. Hunslet moved Owen Walsh from their pack to assist an under pressure back line—a common ploy during this era—but the *Leeds Mercury* was unforgiving, saying 'this was a tactical confession of inferiority' and, with Oldham adding four second half tries without reply, concluded 'it was a conspicuous failure.' In fact, Owen Walsh later returned to the forwards in an effort to tighten the game with Hunslet handicapped through Walter Goldthorpe departing after just over one hour's play through a broken collarbone.

WINNING CAPTAIN

Arthur Lees (Oldham 1899)

Halfback Arthur Lees joined Oldham in 1892 from Leesfield Trinity during the club's rugby union era. Raised in nearby Lees, he helped Oldham win the Lancashire Club Championship of 1893/94 and, following the formation of the Northern Union, enjoyed further success, winning the Northern Union Challenge Cup (1899), Championship (1904/05) and Lancashire League (1897/98, 1900/01). An astute, tactically aware player, he took over as club captain during the 1898/99 campaign and also led the Lancashire county side, with whom he made 15 appearances (3 Rugby Union, 12 Northern Union). His last Oldham match was in 1907 having played for the club 356 times since 1895 under Northern Union rules alone. He subsequently coached the club's 'A' (reserve) team and was elected to their committee.

Oldham fans, meanwhile, rejoiced in a quartet of excellent touchdowns from Williams (bursting through the defence after receiving the ball from Sam Lees), James Moffatt (accepting a pass on the try-line from Tom Fletcher who had followed up a kick before brushing Mitchell aside and picking up the ball), Joe Lees (catching the ball after it rebounded off an opponent before dropping over the try-line) and Williams again (after good work by Sam Lees and Fletcher). With Sam Lees missing the first three conversions, Thomas had better luck with the latter to complete a 19–9 score-line.

The 1899 competition was tarnished through Salford having five players sent off in their semi-final meeting with Hunslet, the dismissal of Parksiders halfback Tom Gillings costing him his place in the final. Meanwhile, Salford and Swinton officials, upset at neither being allocated the final, organised a counter attraction between their clubs for the same day, posters advertising the match. An appeal from the Lancashire Northern Union Committee resulted in it taking place the previous evening.

Oldham's skipper as captured by The Athletic News artist

STATS

Oldham 19 Hunslet 9

Saturday 29 April at Fallowfield Stadium, Manchester (3.30 pm)

Oldham (red and white hoops): Thomas, Williams, S. Lees, Fletcher, Davies, A. Lees (captain), Lawton, Telfer, Barnes, Frayter, Ellis, Bonser, Moffatt, J. Lees, Broome. Trainer: H. Varley

Hunslet (white): Mitchell, Hannah, A. Goldthorpe (captain), W. Goldthorpe, Wright, Robinson, Fletcher, Leach, Young, Wilson, Rubrey, O. Walsh, T. Walsh, Ramage, Harrison. Trainer: unknown

Referee: T.H. Marshall
Touch-judges: H.H. Waller, J.H. Houghton

Half-time: 5–9 Attendance: 15,763 Receipts: £946

Weather: mostly sunny, ground wet due to earlier rain

Cup presentation:
Mrs D.F. Burnley, wife of Northern Union president

Progressive score:

Oldham	score (min)	Hunslet
	0–2 (3)	A. Goldthorpe penalty
S. Lees try, S. Lees goal	5–2 (6)	
	5–7 (29)	W. Goldthorpe try, A. Goldthorpe goal
	5–9 (33)	A. Goldthorpe penalty
Williams try	8–9 (55)	
Moffatt try	11–9 (60)	
J. Lees try	14–9 (63)	
Williams try, Thomas goal	19–9 (80)	

Route to the final:

First round:
Oldham 63 Goole 0, Hunslet 11 Maryport 2

Second round:
Oldham 14 Warrington 0, Swinton 0 Hunslet 2

Third round:
Bradford 3 Oldham 23, Hunslet 16 Castleford 0

Fourth round:
Oldham 20 Widnes 0, Hunslet 9 Hull 0

Semi-finals:
Oldham 16 Leigh 2 (Wheater's Field, Broughton, 20,000), Hunslet 15 Salford 8 (Park Avenue, Bradford, 7,000)

Head-to-head form guide:
No previous meetings during season

1900 NORTHERN UNION CHALLENGE CUP FINAL
Swinton v Salford

Swinton and Salford met in the first all-Lancashire Challenge Cup Final, in 1900, the Lions triumphing after assuming control in the second half. The interest in the clash of the derby rivals caused the match to be switched from Broughton Rangers' Wheater's Field (another club in close proximity) to the more spacious Fallowfield Stadium for a second year, a decision meeting with overall approval. Paying spectators were officially given as 17,864, although Swinton's local paper, *The Journal*, estimated 25,000–30,000 were present. Salford were missing centre Radcliffe 'Radley' Thomas, their two-try semi-final hero against Widnes, suffering from blood poisoning in a foot.

Ben Griffiths failed with an early penalty strike for Salford but, following near misses at both ends, the Reds went ahead when, having won a scrum in the corner, skipper Tom Williams sidestepped over the try-line, Griffiths—who added the conversion—delivering the pass after receiving from Ivor Grey. It only took a few minutes for Swinton to respond, Dai Davies instigating a passing move, the ball travelling via Joe Morgan and Bob Valentine to the speedy Bob Messer who scored the afternoon's best try, dummying a pass to Jack Lewis as he raced from midfield. Jim Valentine's kick tied the score at 5–5.

Grey spoilt a chance with a forward pass near the Lions' try-line but, following Swinton pressure inside Salford's 25-yard area, the Reds' forwards broke away after Davies failed to recover the ball from a scrum, dribbling downfield before Arthur Pearson hacked it over the whitewash and scored. Griffiths missed the goal. Swinton again replied quickly, a sustained attack in Salford territory being climaxed by excellent passing from Morgan, Davies, Bob Valentine and Messer, the latter sending Lewis flying in for the score. A disappointing goal attempt from Jim Valentine left the teams level at 8–8, the Swinton skipper suffering worse distress through dislocating his shoulder after 30 minutes' play. He retired for attention, bravely returning just before half-time as

an 'extra' three-quarter. It left the Lions with a seven-man pack, the numbers upfront equal again when Salford's Billy Brown was dismissed after touch-judge Billy McCutcheon spotted him kicking Lewis during a tackle.

The victorious Swinton squad. Players only (wearing caps and playing kit) are, back row: Jones. Third row: Evans, Preston, Vigors, Pollit, Murphy. Second row: Tickle, Hampson, R. Valentine, J. Valentine, Messer, Lewis, Chorley, Harris. Front (seated): Morgan, Davies. Their trainer, Cooper, is on the third row, second from left

Swinton's star backs sparkled in the second half, Lewis being denied three times; once through a forward pass, twice by stepping over the touchline. Eventually, poor control from Pearson enabled Messer to dribble the ball towards the Reds' line before

---

STATS

Swinton 16 Salford 8

Saturday 28 April at Fallowfield Stadium, Manchester (3.30 pm)

Swinton (navy blue): Chorley, Lewis, Messer, R. Valentine, Hampson, Davies, Morgan, Vigors, Harris, Preston, Jones, J. Valentine (captain), Pollitt, Evans, Murphy. Trainer: J. Cooper

Salford (red): Smith, Pearson, T. Williams (captain), Harter, Hadwen, Griffiths, Grey, Shore, Shaw, Tunney, Gledhill, Brown, Fisher, J. Williams, Rhapps. Trainer: J. Roberts

Referee: F. Renton

Touch-judges: W. McCutcheon, J. Bruckshaw

Half-time: 8–8   Attendance: 17,864   Receipts: £1,100

Weather: sunny

Cup presentation:
Mrs J.H. Smith, wife of Northern Union president

Progressive score:

Swinton	score (min)	Salford
	0–5 (7)	T. Williams try, Griffiths goal
Messer try, J. Valentine goal	5–5 (9)	
	5–8 (22)	Pearson try
Lewis try	8–8 (25)	
R. Valentine try, J. Valentine goal	13–8 (60)	
Davies try	16–8 (65)	

Route to the final:

First round:
Swinton 53 Eastmoor (Wakefield) 0, Salford 9 York 0

Second round:
Holbeck 8 Swinton 17, Leigh 2 Salford 9

Third round:
Swinton 14 Oldham 2, Salford 6 Huddersfield 5

Fourth round:
Swinton 9 Broughton Rangers 0, Salford 11 Rochdale Hornets 3

Semi-finals:
Swinton 8 Leeds Parish Church 0 (Fartown, Huddersfield, 15,500),
Salford 11 Widnes 0 (Watersheddings, Oldham, 14,000)

Head-to-head form guide:

Salford 6 Swinton 11 (League)

Swinton 25 Salford 5 (League)

---

picking up and sending Bob Valentine over behind the posts, Jim Valentine's extra two points placing the Lions 13–8 ahead. Swinton's Alf Chorley made two disappointing drop-goal attempts, redeeming himself in between those efforts by tackling Herbert Hadwen when he looked set to score. Swinton confirmed their superiority with a fourth try, Davies crossing from a scrum near the line, Jim Valentine's conversion falling short.

At this point, *The Journal's* correspondent observed that 'it was interesting to note the exodus of spectators', adding 'the red favours (of Salford) dwindled considerably'. The defectors missed a desperate late Salford rally; Grey having a try disallowed through an earlier infringement, Ezekiel Harter and Pearson both held near the try-line. But it was too late and Swinton held on for a deserved 16–8 success.

Apart from Brown's dismissal—whose resultant sine die suspension was later reduced to eight months—the match was described as 'well contested', the *Salford Reporter* observing 'it was the cleverness and speed of the (Swinton) backs that sealed the fate of the (Salford) borough representatives.'

The Swinton Lion bares its teeth to Salford after defeating their local rivals at Fallowfield, an image published in The Athletic News

1901 NORTHERN UNION CHALLENGE CUP FINAL
Batley v Warrington

Batley made it three wins from three Challenge Cup Finals, sinking Warrington 6–0 in 1901 with two early tries in a disappointing contest. The Gallant Youths' experienced, but aging team was expected to face a stern test against a younger, energetic Warrington outfit in the forward battle, but, as the *Batley News* remarked, 'the youthful Warringtonians found the excitement too much for them, and their nervous condition was quite pitiful to behold.'

Warrington had early opportunities, Jack Fish missed a penalty and J. Duckworth had a try chance, fumbling the ball as he attempted to ground it after Batley's Wattie Davies lost possession. Davies tried to redeem himself with a penalty from near halfway but the ball hardly lifted. The players were struggling with a ball that was 'very light' and 'almost as difficult to catch as an eel'. This excuse was used for Batley not claiming a try after Warrington's Jack Hallam kicked the ball skyward and the wind blew it back, Bob Spurr, with an open line, being unable to get hold as it bounced haphazardly. But their opening score soon followed, Jack Goodall snatching the ball from Warrington's George Dickenson as he tried to pass out of a tackle, the Batley centre breaking away and, as Hallam moved in, delivering the ball to the speeding Davies who shot over near the posts. Surprisingly Davies missed the goal, blaming a crack across the centre of his kicking boot!

He then missed another penalty but a second try soon followed. Joe Oakland, from a scrum near

Warrington's line, brought the ball away for Batley but collided with one of the posts in attempting to score. From the resulting scrum, Oakland again grabbed possession, firing the ball out to Dai Fitzgerald, who drew Danny Isherwood and Fish before sending Wilf Auty haring over the try-line. Davies' boot again failed to raise the ball above ground level, but Batley led 6–0. Fish missed with a penalty and Batley's Paddy Judge—a late

---

STATS

Batley 6 Warrington 0

Saturday 27 April at Headingley, Leeds (3.30 pm)

Batley (white): Garner, Davies, Fitzgerald, J. Goodall, Auty, Oakland (captain), J. Midgley, Fisher, Judge, Rodgers, Stubley, Spurr, Maine, Fozzard, Hollingworth. Trainer: M. Shackleton

Warrington (primrose and blue): Hallam, Fish, Isherwood (captain), Dickenson, Harris, Bate, Duckworth, Boardman, Fell, Edmondson, Scholtze, Eden, Cunningham, Morrison, J. Swift. Trainer: unknown

Referee: J. Kidd   Touch-judges: J. Oakland, J. Bruckshaw

Half-time: 6–0   Attendance: 29,563   Receipts: £1,644

Weather: sunny and windy, ground wet from earlier rain

Cup presentation:
Mrs H. Hutchinson, wife of Northern Union president

Progressive score:

Batley	score (min)	Warrington
Davies try	3–0 (13)	
Auty try	6–0 (18)	

Route to the final:

First round:
Batley (bye), Leeds 0 Warrington 19

Second round:
Batley 6 Huddersfield 2, Warrington 19 Heckmondwike 2

Third round:
St Helens 5 Batley 7, Warrington 11 Leeds Parish Church 0

Fourth round:
Batley 5 Runcorn 2, Warrington 10 Bradford 8

Semi-finals:
Batley 9 Oldham 2 (Fartown, Huddersfield, 16,000),
Warrington 21 Castleford 5 (Wheater's Field, Broughton, 9,000)

Head-to-head form guide:
No previous meetings during season

WINNING CAPTAIN

Joe Oakland (Batley 1901)

Joe Oakland's Batley debut was during the 1894/95 season, the club's last as a rugby union outfit, and he then went on to notch over 430 appearances with them under the Northern Union code, his final match being in 1911. Described as 'one of the trickiest halfbacks in the (Yorkshire) county', his successes with Batley include the Northern Union Challenge Cup (1897, 1898, 1901) and Yorkshire League (1898/99). He represented Yorkshire twice and created a club record of five tries in a match (against Bramley, 1908), since equalled but not beaten. Born at Cross Bank, Batley, he played for Callinghow Rangers and Healey Albion prior to joining Batley.

A Batley player prepares to take a penalty kick. In all probability it is Wattie Davies who missed all six of his attempts (two conversions and four penalties) despite being the Northern Union's third-highest goal scorer that season with 38

replacement for foot-injury victim Ike Carroll—saw the ball hit an upright and bounce back in a similar attempt at the other end. Dickenson intercepted a pass and almost scored for Warrington but was tackled just short of the try-line by Arthur Garner. Another penalty award provided Davies with his fifth kick at goal, his best effort so far, although the wind sent it wide. As the interval drew near, opposing wingers Fish and Auty were cautioned for fighting following a touch-judge's intervention.

After the break, Fish was off-target with two further penalty kicks (the second in front of the posts), sandwiching a run by colleague Elliott Harris who was brought down a yard from Batley's try-line by Garner. Ten minutes into the half Batley forward George Maine was dismissed following his contribution to a tackle on Isherwood, and subsequently banned until December. Then Davies, despatched on a touchline run by Oakland, created a try opportunity after kicking the ball over Hallam's head, the pair—plus Isherwood—racing after it. Davies, though, was obstructed but failed to add the resultant penalty. Towards the end, Harris damaged a rib and was carried off, the last move of note being a break from Fish, Goodall apprehending him.

The *Warrington Guardian* conceded: 'Both fore and aft, the Tykes were immeasurably the superior team.' The official paid attendance was 29,563 and, with members of the Leeds club and other invites, the total was reported as just short of 35,000, which 'exceeded expectations'. After about five minutes' play,

barriers on the terrace gave way through congestion and spectators spilled onto the pitch, no one being injured. The *Batley News* suggested better crowd distribution could have avoided the incident because, despite an excellent attendance (some spectators sat on top of the pavilion and stand roofs), 'the resources of the ground were by no means over-taxed'.

Another Batley triumph! Back row: Cairns (asst. trainer), Nelson, Shackleton (trainer). Third row: Hollingsworth, Spurr, Fitzgerald, Carroll, Judge, Midgley. Seated: Fozzard, Maine, Rodgers, Oakland, Auty, Lloyd, Wolstenholme. On ground: Stubley, Davies, Garner, J. Goodall

1902 NORTHERN UNION CHALLENGE CUP FINAL
Broughton Rangers v Salford

Broughton Rangers captain Bob Wilson was feted as a hero following his side's 25–0 demolition of neighbours Salford (both being based in what was then the Royal Borough of Salford). Having scored three tries he was later presented with the match ball after it had been 'embellished' by Rangers officials, the club being the first to achieve a Challenge Cup and Championship 'double'. Salford lost to a superior, faster back division, despite holding their own territorially in the forwards.

Willie James just missed a penalty for Rangers before they demonstrated their cutting edge when, from a scrum, his brother Sam got Wilson and Andy Hogg away, the latter's kick towards Salford's line nullified through one of their forwards being given offside. Shortly after, Sam James repeated the exercise, transferring the ball to Wilson who roared towards lone defender Dan Smith, his dummy pass to the supporting Hogg enabling him to bypass the full back for the first try. The pressure continued, and Willie James—having intercepted Tom Williams' pass to Dai Davies—was held just short, Sam James and Wilson

also getting close.

A second try came when Tom Williams' pass to Davies was again cut off, this time by Wilson who raced downfield before passing to Hogg for a simple run in. Salford's attacks were coming to nought with only James Lomas looking dangerous amongst their backs. Willie James missed a goal from a mark by Wilson 10 yards inside the Reds' half, before another Broughton try was initiated by Sam James' pass to Wilson from a scrum. The skipper sent the ball out to Hogg who raced a few yards before returning inside for Wilson to score under the posts. Willie James' third conversion made it 15–0 at the break.

Backed by a strong second half wind, Salford hoped for a revival, Tom Williams being overhauled after being put through by Lomas. Sam James put his shoulder out but, after attention, courageously returned, George Whitehead vacating the pack as an extra back to cover him. Lomas then made a tremendous run, handing off five players before being held. Salford were experiencing their best moments of

Broughton Rangers—the first side to complete a Challenge Cup and Championship double. Players only (in playing kit) are, back row: Thompson, Trotter, Winskill. Third row: Widdeson, Stead, Ruddick, S. James, Fielding, Harry. Seated: Garrity, Hogg, Wilson, Whitehead, Oram. On floor: W. James, Barrett. Trainer Royle is on the back row, extreme left (next to Thompson)

Bob Wilson, captain and three-try hero of Broughton Rangers

the match, Ernie Bone being just held and then having another opportunity after recovering a loose ball, was chased down by Billy Oram when he had a clear run. Ben Griffiths was wide with a drop-goal and Bone made another tremendous break, Arthur Widdeson catching him from behind. After that it was all Broughton, who proved their superiority with two quick tries. From a scrum near the Reds' line the ball went out to Wilson who raced through an opening, fending off Smith as he crossed the whitewash, Oram appending the goal. From the restart, Sam James got possession and passed to Widdeson, who covered half the length of the field before placing the ball beneath the posts. Willie James added the extras to complete the scoring.

The Rangers won without injured forward George Ruddick, Charlie Thompson replacing him, whilst veteran halfback, Alf Barrett, missed out when Willie

WINNING CAPTAIN

Bob Wilson (Broughton Rangers 1902)

Bob Wilson joined Broughton Rangers in 1900 from Morecambe Northern Union club where he had been captain, previously playing for hometown team, Carnforth. Noted for his speed, natural 'swerve' and ability to deliver a dummy pass, he was respected for 'high conduct' on and off the field, qualities that earned him the Rangers captaincy. He led them to the 'double' of Northern Union Challenge Cup and Championship in 1901/02, scoring a club record 33 tries that season, and Lancashire Cup success in 1906. He represented England (once—in 1905) and Lancashire (16 times—captain on several occasions). A broken collarbone during a match in 1908 virtually ended his career. He made several more appearances but his form deserted him, his last Rangers match being in 1909 after 256 appearances. After retirement, his health declined and he passed away in 1916, aged only 38.

STATS

Broughton Rangers 25 Salford 0

Saturday 26 April at The Athletic Grounds, Rochdale (3.30 pm)

Broughton Rangers (navy blue and white hoops): Fielding, Hogg, Wilson (captain), Harry, Widdeson, W. James, S. James, Woodhead, Whitehead, Winskill, Stead, Oram, Trotter, Garrity, Thompson. Trainer: T. Royle

Salford (red): Smith, Bone, T. Williams (captain), Davies, Price, Lomas, Griffiths, Rhapps, Tunney, Heath, Brown, Buckler, Shaw, J. Williams, Gledhill. Trainer: G. Cook

Referee: W. Robinson

Touch-judges: J.H. Smith, B. Ashton

Half-time: 15–0   Attendance: 15,006   Receipts: £846

Weather: sunny, strong wind

Cup presentation:
Mrs J.H. Houghton, wife of Northern Union president

Progressive score:

Broughton Rangers	score (min)	Salford
Wilson try, W. James goal	5–0 (-)	
Hogg try, W. James goal	10–0 (-)	
Wilson try, W. James goal	15–0 (38)	
Wilson try, Oram goal	20–0 (70)	
Widdeson try, W. James goal	25–0 (72)	

Route to the final:

First round:
Keighley 7 Broughton R 15, Salford 28 Pontefract 2

Second round:
Broughton R 5 Stockport 0, Dewsbury 0 Salford 2

Third round:
Broughton R 13 Hull 2, Salford 67 Goole 0

Fourth round:
Broughton R 13 Swinton 0, Huddersfield 6 Salford 9

Semi-finals:
Broughton R 9 Hunslet 5 (Belle Vue, Wakefield, 10,500),
Salford 8 Batley 0 (Watersheddings, Oldham, 13,000)

Head-to-head form guide:

Broughton R 3 Salford 2 (League)

Salford 0 Broughton R 3 (League)

James recovered from six weeks in bed with a fever. The final began 25 minutes after its scheduled 3.30 pm, Salford's special train labouring for one and a half hours to make the short journey from Salford Station to Rochdale. The final was played in front of a deserted 'railway side' stand (excepting a lone policeman), a late surveyor's inspection declaring it unsafe (it was replaced a few years later), a consequence of Glasgow's 'Ibrox Disaster' earlier that month when 26 were killed and 500 injured as a stand collapsed at the Scotland-England soccer international.

1903 NORTHERN UNION CHALLENGE CUP FINAL
Halifax v Salford

Halifax celebrated their first Challenge Cup Final appearance with a 7–0 win over Salford, condemning the Reds to a third runners-up slot in four years. It was a day that caught the imagination of Halifax's residents, many being on the streets as early as 6.00 am, an estimated 6,000—bedecked in various blue and white favours from the 'many vendors' in Horton Street—heading for the railway station for the two hour journey to Leeds. Further opportunities awaited supporters outside Headingley, the *Halifax Evening Courier* noting that cries of 'colours of the winning teams "all a penny" came from numerous mouths, and if you purchased both kinds you were sure of getting the right one.' The same newspaper revealed that: 'Both teams had luncheon at The Great Northern Hotel (Leeds) and we had the remarkable sight of the rival teams rubbing shoulders together in a friendly spirit before hostilities commenced.'

Halifax trotted onto the Headingley pitch eight minutes after Salford, led by Archie Rigg, club skipper George Kitson's 'indisposition' sidelining him since February. Rigg was called upon in the early stages to tackle Salford's Thomas Bell when the latter almost crossed Halifax's try-line. Shortly after, play was held up for some minutes when a barrier gave way at the pavilion corner. Supporters in the vicinity were shepherded by police onto the ground where they 'swarmed along the touchline', the *Halifax Evening Courier* saying: 'It looked like a big county cricket match to see people seated on the grass.' After play resumed, Halifax came close to scoring a couple of times; William Wedgewood kicking towards the corner and sending Billy Williams away before he was tackled, Billy Bulmer almost forcing his way across the whitewash. Salford full back Dan Smith found himself in the wars, lying flat out after a collision with Joe Riley before he eventually 'came round'. As a scoreless first half—described as a 'grim struggle'—headed towards its close, Herbert Hadwen (Halifax) and James Lomas (Salford) both made poor penalty goal attempts, whilst Rigg lost the ball to spoil a promising Halifax raid.

Halifax wasted little time in the second half, scoring the game's only try after three minutes, following a Johnny Morley break. The halfback passed to Billy

Williams who kicked the ball towards Salford's in-goal, his forwards rushing up in support, Ike Bartle taking possession to score behind the posts. Former Salford

---

STATS

Halifax 7 Salford 0

Saturday 25 April at Headingley, Leeds (3.30 pm)

Halifax (blue and white hoops): Little, Wedgewood, W. Williams, Rigg (captain), Hadwen, Morley, Joe Riley, Jack Riley, Bartle, Mallinson, Swinbank, Morton, Hammond, Bulmer, Winskill. Trainer: J. Midgley

Salford (red): Smith, Norris, Messer, Lomas (captain), Bell, Harter, Griffiths, J. Williams, Rhapps, Tunney, Heath, Brown, Buckler, Shaw, Shore. Trainer: G. Cook

Referee: J. Bruckshaw

Touch-judges: J.H. Smith, H. Sewell

Half-time: 0–0   Attendance: 32,507   Receipts: £1,834

Weather: sunny and windy

Cup presentation:
Mrs J. Clifford, wife of Northern Union president

Progressive score:

Halifax	score (min)	Salford
Bartle try, Hadwen goal	5–0 (43)	
Hadwen penalty	7–0 (55)	

Route to the final:

First round:
Halifax 34 Salterhebble (Halifax) 0, Salford (bye)

Second round:
Castleford 0 Halifax 0, Salford 11 Leigh 0

Second round replay: Halifax 10 Castleford 3

Third round:
Halifax 0 Brighouse Rangers 0, Rochdale Hornets 0 Salford 15

Third Round replay: Brighouse R 2 Halifax 8

Fourth Round: Runcorn 0 Halifax 2, York 2 Salford 25

Semi-finals:
Halifax 8 Hull 5 (Fartown, Huddersfield, 17,500),
Salford 0 Oldham 0 (Wheater's Field, Broughton, 19,000)

Semi-final replay:
Salford 8 Oldham 0 (Wheater's Field, Broughton, 12,000)

Head-to-head form guide:

Salford 12 Halifax 0 (League)

Halifax 5 Salford 5 (League)

---

player Hadwen added the goal. The Reds tried to respond, increasing the pressure, but Halifax's defence proved too strong, their forwards taking command over Salford's octet. Joe Riley made a mark for Halifax after fielding the ball, earning a goal attempt for Billy Little, but it was off-target. Hadwen, having temporarily retired with an injury, was back in time to land a penalty after a Salford forward put a hand on the ball during a scrum. It increased Halifax's lead to 7–0 and was the last score of the afternoon although Smith later excited the Reds fans with a 75-yard run, and

The verdict, as given by The Athletic News cartoonist, was concise

Hadwen was unsuccessful with a drop-goal.

The match had been a forward dominated war of attrition, the *Halifax Guardian* remarking: 'It was not by any means a great final,' although it was certainly a memorable occasion for their supporters, whose team emulated Broughton Rangers' feat of securing a Challenge Cup and Championship double, watched by a, reportedly, record Northern Union crowd of 32,507.

WINNING CAPTAIN

Archie Rigg (Halifax 1903)

James Arthur 'Archie' Rigg signed for Halifax in 1891 from the Halifax Gymnasium club. A halfback or centre, he was in the side that twice won the Yorkshire Challenge Cup (1893, 1894) whilst still a rugby union club. He remained with them following the Northern Union breakaway in 1895, being the first captain under the new code. In the 1902/03 season he shared in the 'double' of Northern Union Challenge Cup and First Division Championship, having regained the captaincy midway through the campaign due to the unavailability of the incumbent George Kitson. He retired in 1905 but was tempted back by Bradford Northern, where he played from 1908 to 1912. Returning to Halifax, he played one match during 1912 and then—having become team trainer—a further three wartime 'friendly' games in 1915 when he was almost 44. In total, he made 333 appearances for the club under both codes. He represented Yorkshire 32 times (19 Rugby Union, 13 Northern Union) being captain on several occasions.

Halifax captain Archie Rigg tosses the coin before kick-off as Salford opposite James Lomas (right) makes the call. Referee J. Bruckshaw (in 'plus fours') seems pre-occupied with other matters!

23

1904 NORTHERN UNION CHALLENGE CUP FINAL
Halifax v Warrington

The successful Halifax team, standing: Naylor, Jack Riley, Spencer, Langhorn, Hammond, Ricketts (secretary), Little, Winskill, Joe Riley. Seated: Mallinson, Bartle, J. Morley, Rigg, Bulmer, Wedgwood, Morton. On ground: Midgley (trainer), Nettleton, Gledhill, Hadwen, Hartley, Morris (asst. trainer)

Halifax retained the Challenge Cup in 1904, being the first club to win it outside their own county thanks to an 8–3 triumph over Warrington at The Willows, Salford. Due to their closer proximity to the venue, slight favourites Warrington claimed the majority of support inside the ground, the Northern Union officials, as per usual, being seated in the centre of the main stand fronted by the trophy. It was noted that their accompanying wives in 'smart dresses lent lustre to the proceedings', the *Warrington Guardian* correspondent commenting: 'A football crowd is generally a sombre one, and this introduction of the gentler sex was by no means out of place despite the fact that their ideas of the vigorous pastime must be at an elementary stage.'

Halifax—whose late selection saw Herbert Hadwen picked on the wing ahead of William Wedgewood—emerged 10 minutes after their opponents, Warrington no doubt glad they were able to await them in bright sunshine! The Yorkshire team adopted an early policy of 'kick and rush', keeping it tight amongst their pack. Warrington, though, had an early chance when star winger Jack Fish was pushed into touch near the corner flag. Halifax made several efforts to open their

account; Billy Little's lengthy drop-goal attempt missing the target, Johnny Morley almost burrowing his way through a packed defence to cross the Wires' try-line, and Little again missing the goal after one of his forwards made a mark.

Although Halifax had looked the more likely, Warrington appealed for the first try when George Dickenson got the ball over the whitewash after following up an angled kick, referee Jack Smith disallowing the score, awarding a five-yard scrum instead. Eventually Halifax got their reward, pressure by their forwards on the Wires' line saw Arnold

---

WINNING CAPTAIN

Johnny Morley (Halifax 1904)

Halfback Johnny Morley signed for Halifax at the start of the 1899/1900 season from the Sowerby Bridge rugby union club. He was to play just 130 times for Halifax, the last of which was five appearances during early 1905 when he briefly returned, having retired for 'business reasons' following the 1903/04 campaign. With Halifax he won the Northern Union Challenge Cup (1903, 1904) and Championship (1902/03). He represented England and Yorkshire once each.

Nettleton almost get over before Morley got the ball away to Joe Riley who charged past Danny Isherwood to score near the posts 'amidst a hurricane of cheers'. Hadwen added the goal, missing a penalty shortly after, the Yorkshiremen turning around with a 5–0 advantage.

At the start of the second half Halifax tackled in determined fashion but, on the hour, Warrington worked their way downfield and, when Dai Davies got the ball out to Fish, the latter sped down the touchline before kicking the ball clear of full back Little. Davies was on hand to recover possession and score in the corner after a race with Little, Fish missing the conversion. The score motivated the Wilderspool outfit and they put together their best spell of the game. An excellent round of passing got Isherwood within a yard of the Halifax line but, with the defence split, his pass to the supporting Elliott Harris was low and the winger stumbled as he reached down for it. From Warrington's viewpoint, it was a crucial miss.

Halifax regained the upper hand, their forwards again pummelling the opposition, who began to look a spent force. The match was now played almost exclusively in Warrington territory, Joe Riley nearly getting over the try-line but for the combined resistance of Isherwood and Davies holding him off.

Five minutes from the end, Morley wriggled his way though the defence for a try, Little's goal attempt hitting the post.

Although the match had followed a similar pattern to Halifax's win over Salford the previous year, their forwards taking centre stage throughout, the *Halifax Guardian* opined of the match: 'It was an exceedingly good one for a cup final, and much better than last year's from a spectator's point of view.' The *Yorkshire Post* said, perceptively, of Warrington: 'We trust they will be able to keep their fine set of backs together for the next season, and to infuse a little more weight into the front rank. If that should be so, a third appearance in the final tie, with victory as the crowning point, is not an extravagant forecast.'

Halifax emulated Batley's feat in keeping possession of the trophy

---

STATS

Halifax 8 Warrington 3

Saturday 30 April at The Willows, Salford (3.30 pm)

Halifax (blue and white hoops): Little, Hartley, Joe Riley, Williams, Hadwen, Nettleton, Morley (captain), Bartle, Bulmer, Langhorn, Mallinson, Jack Riley, Morton, Swinbank, Winskill. Trainer: J. Midgley

Warrington (primrose and blue hoops): Hallam, Fish, Isherwood (captain), Dickenson, Harris, Davies, Hockenhall, Thomas, Boardman, Morrison, Lunt, Cook, Jolley, Edmondson, Naylor. Trainer: unknown

Referee: J.H. Smith

Touch-judges: J. Priestley, E.H. Smirk

Half-time: 5–0   Attendance: 17,041   Receipts: £936

Weather: sunny

Cup presentation:
Mr F. Lister, Northern Union vice-president

Progressive score:

Halifax	score (min)	Warrington
Joe Riley try, Hadwen goal	5–0 (30)	
	5–3 (60)	Davies try
Morley try	8–3 (75)	

Route to the final:

First round: Halifax 15 St Helens 0, Swinton 0 Warrington 0

First round replay: Warrington 20 Swinton 0

Second round: Barrow 6 Halifax 11, Warrington 3 Wigan 0

Third round: Halifax 8 Leeds 2, Pontefract 4 Warrington 10

Semi-finals:
Halifax 7 Hunslet 2 (Belle Vue, Wakefield, 21,000),
Warrington 3 Bradford 3 (Wheater's Field, Broughton, 13,000)

Semi-final replay: Warrington 8 Bradford 0 (Fartown, Huddersfield, 10,000)

Head-to-head form guide:

Halifax 2 Warrington 0 (League)

Warrington 10 Halifax 4 (League)

1905 NORTHERN UNION CHALLENGE CUP FINAL
Warrington v Hull Kingston Rovers

Warrington came up trumps during their third Challenge Cup Final in five seasons, defeating Hull Kingston Rovers 6–0 in 1905 following a determined struggle at Headingley. The Lancashire side were without influential forward Jack Preston—who shared

---

STATS

Warrington 6 Hull Kingston Rovers 0

Saturday 29 April at Headingley, Leeds (3.30 pm)

Warrington (primrose and blue hoops): Hallam (captain), Fish, Isherwood, Dickenson, Kenyon, Davies, Brooks, Thomas, Boardman, Shugars, Jolley, Belton, Naylor, W. Swift, Harmer. Trainer: I. Hackett

Hull Kingston Rovers (white): Sinclair, Madley, Robinson, Phipps, West, Barry, Gordon, Starks (captain), Kemp, Osborne, Spackman, Windle, Ellis, Gorman, Reed. Trainer: H. Shann

Referee: J. Bruckshaw

Touch-judges: W. Robinson, J.H. Smith

Half-time: 0–0   Attendance: 19,638   Receipts: £1,271

Weather:
mostly rain with some sunshine, ground wet and slippery

Cup presentation:
Mrs F. Lister, wife of Northern Union president

Progressive score:

Warrington	score (min)	Hull Kingston Rovers
Fish try	3–0 (44)	
Fish try	6–0 (54)	

Route to the final:

First round:
Warrington 30 Morecambe 0, Hull KR 73 Brookland Rovers (Maryport) 5 (Brookland gave up home advantage)

Second round: Warrington 3 Keighley 3, Hull KR 3 Leeds 0

Second round replay: Keighley 0 Warrington 7

Third round: Warrington 13 Wigan 0, Hull KR 8 Hunslet 2

Semi-finals:
Warrington 7 Bradford 2 (The Athletic Grounds, Rochdale, 15,000),

Hull KR 10 Broughton Rangers 6 (Belle Vue, Wakefield, 12,000)

Head-to-head form guide:

Hull Kingston Rovers 13 Warrington 0 (League)

Warrington 4 Hull Kingston Rovers 2 (League)

---

the goal-kicking duties with Jack Fish—following a leg injury two weeks earlier, whilst Bill Harmer was 'a surprise selection' ahead of D. Morrison in the pack. For Rovers, forward Richard Townsley, having played in the previous rounds, fell foul of the 'working clause' rule then operating in the sport, not qualifying to play following several weeks of unemployment.

WARRINGTON'S FULL-BACK.

J. HALLAM.

Warrington captain Jack Hallam

Warrington applied early pressure but it was the Rovers that produced the first real passing move, Jim Barry and Jimmy Gordon creating an opening for Billy Phipps, who sent 'Tich' West on his way as the Yorkshire contingent in the crowd 'shouted themselves hoarse', Fish's tackle rescuing the situation.

Warrington's forwards, though, were in rampant mood and their backs reaped the benefit, good bouts of passing carving out openings for George Dickenson and Fish. Eventually, Fish, following a 25th-minute penalty award, tried a difficult shot at goal but it did not carry enough.

Two minutes later, an unusual occurrence (by today's standards at least) happened when Barry passed to West, and Warrington's Danny Isherwood intervened by heading the ball away 'in Association (Football) style'. An alert Fish raced up to grab possession before flying past Phipps and West in a spectacular run. But the showery weather had made the pitch greasy and handling conditions difficult and he slipped near the touchline trying to negotiate Herbert Sinclair, the Robins' full back. In doing so, he wrenched his knee, resuming to 'a hearty cheer' after a few minutes' attention. Towards the latter stages of the half the Hull outfit looked dangerous; Barry made a spectacular touchline run before kicking to the Warrington goal (Jack Hallam and Fish saving the situation after an 'exciting scramble'), whilst Sinclair and A. Robinson both failed with drop-goal attempts.

Warrington resumed control after the interval as Rovers showed signs of tiredness. Fish made a break that was defused but, a few minutes later, from a scrum near the Rovers' try-line, the ball came out to Warrington. Dai Davies broke away and passed to Isherwood who despatched Fish on a run, the winger grounding the ball over the whitewash after wriggling free of Sinclair and West. Fish made a poor effort to convert, the ball not rising, but Warrington led 3–0. They soon increased their tally when, from a midfield position, Davies got the ball to Ernie Brooks who burst through an opening in Rovers' defence. As he reached Sinclair he transferred to the supporting Fish who sprinted over near the posts. This time Hallam attempted the goal but his easy looking shot hit an upright and bounced back, Warrington leading 6–0. The Robins made a valiant effort to pull the match out of the fire, West—scorer of a record 53 points (11 tries and 10 goals) in the first round against Brookland Rovers—twice being apprehended by Fish whilst, at the opposite end, T. Kenyon (twice) and Fish came close but there was no further score.

At that evening's reception at Warrington Town Hall, the Borough Band welcomed the team with the obligatory 'See the Conquering Hero Comes' and, following a speech by Warrington skipper Hallam, who told the crowd he was 'about as proud as anyone', they closed proceedings with a rendition of 'Poor Cock Robin'. Runners-up Rovers had travelled to Headingley with style, the 'monster engine' provided by the North-Eastern Railway and manned by a driver and stoker wearing club jerseys, having been used for the 1900 World Exhibition in Paris.

WINNING CAPTAIN

Jack Hallam (Warrington 1905)

Jack Hallam—described as a 'sturdy' full back with a 'judicious kick'—was an unlikely candidate to become a leading rugby player. Born and bred in Stoke-on-Trent he played soccer at school and cricket after the family moved to Huddersfield. Further relocation to Warrington saw him take up the Northern Union code with local juniors Latchford Rangers, joining the town's senior club in 1895. His Warrington first team debut was in 1897, playing in 217 matches for them until his last in November 1905. He was appointed club captain for 1904/05, leading them to Northern Union Challenge Cup victory in 1905 and a member of the team beaten in the 1901 and 1904 finals. He played in Lancashire county trials in 1901 and 1904 but failed to gain selection.

Warrington—winners of the Challenge Cup for the first time. Standing: Hackett (trainer), Harmer, Shugars, Preston, Boardman, Belton, Jolley, Heeson (asst. trainer). Seated: Swift, Kenyon, Dickenson, Hallam, Isherwood, Fish, Jenkins. On ground: Thomas, Davies, Brooks, Naylor

1906 NORTHERN UNION CHALLENGE CUP FINAL
Bradford v Salford

Bradford conjured up a late, late show to condemn Salford to a fourth Challenge Cup Final defeat from four appearances, sparked by a brilliant piece of individual skill from scrum half Sammy Brear. With just 15 minutes remaining of what had been a disappointing final—hindered through miserable weather—Bradford's Benny Smales was held up just short of the Salford try-line. A scrum quickly followed, the Yorkshire side winning the heel and Brear grabbing possession before shooting across the whitewash in a flash. Although George Marsden missed the conversion, the 'Park Avenueites' spirits were lifted and their supporters—sensing victory—burst into song!

With the Challenge Cup having become the most sought after trophy in the Northern Union, it was not surprising to read that 'nothing else is spoken of in Bradford' in the week leading to the final. Both teams were depleted; Bradford unable to include three-quarter J. Dunbavin (sprained ankle), Salford without forward Arthur Buckler (knee injury). Early play see-sawed from one end of the pitch to the other before Salford captain James Lomas attempted a long-distance penalty shot, but the ball did not carry far enough. A Bradford attacking run from Jimmy Dechan gave his colleague Bill Sinton an opportunity but John Cochrane hauled him down near Salford's try-line. The signs did not look too good for the Reds when, firstly,

BIRTH OF THE NORTHERN UNION CHALLENGE CUP COMPETITION

The decision to instigate a 'Northern Union Cup' was taken at the Northern Union committee meeting on 5 March 1896. It was created as a replacement for the first Northern Rugby League Championship that had taken place during the 1895/96 term. The latter competition (played during the inaugural campaign following the breakaway of leading Lancashire and Yorkshire clubs from the Rugby Union) had proved unwieldy. The 22 clubs had 42 fixtures each and, taking the amount of cross-Pennine travelling into account, was replaced by separate Lancashire and Yorkshire competitions, the Challenge Cup being seen as a means of retaining inter-county rivalries.

Lomas missed an easy 25-yard penalty eight minutes before the interval after Bradford had obstructed and then, a few minutes later, his co-centre Willie Thomas

STATS

Bradford 5 Salford 0

Saturday 28 April at Headingley, Leeds (3.30 pm)

Bradford (red, amber and black broad hoops): Gunn, Sinton, Dechan, Heseltine, Connell, Marsden (captain), Brear, Feather, Laidlaw, Francis, Smales, Grayson, Greenwood, Sharratt, Turner. Trainer: J. Farrell

Salford (red): Cochrane, McWhirter, W.S. Thomas, Lomas (captain), Hampson, John, Preston, Rhapps, E.J. Thomas, Rees, Brown, Spencer, Warwick, Lewis, Foster. Trainer: J. White

Referee: W. McCutcheon

Touch-judges: W. Taylor, W. Jones

Half-time: 0–0   Attendance: 15,834   Receipts: £920

Weather: mostly rainy and dull, some hailstone, brief sunshine, cold wind

Cup presentation:
Miss Smith, daughter of Northern Union president

Progressive score:

Bradford	score (min)	Salford
Brear try	3–0 (65)	
Laidlaw penalty	5–0 (78)	

Route to the final:

First round: Wakefield Trinity 0 Bradford 5, Rochdale Hornets 0, Salford 6

Second round: Bradford 15 Leigh 0, Salford 38 Egerton (Salford) 5

Third round: Bradford 0 Halifax 0, Salford 2 Broughton Rangers 2

Third round replays: Halifax 2 Bradford 8, Broughton Rangers 3 Salford 3

Third round second replay:
Salford 5 Broughton R 3 (Central Park, Wigan)

Semi-finals:
Bradford 11 Batley 3 (Fartown, Huddersfield, 15,707),
Salford 6 Keighley 3 (Wilderspool, Warrington, 8,500)

Head-to-head form guide:

Salford 13 Bradford 0 (League)

Bradford 33 Salford 0 (League)

Bradford 1906. Standing: Hoyle (secretary), Greenwood, Connell, Feather, Smales, Francis, Grayson, Walton, Mosby, Surman, Rees, Farrell (trainer). Seated: Gunn, Sharratt, Dechan, Marsden, Turner, Laidlaw, Mann. On ground: Dunbavin, Heseltine, Brear

G. H. Marsden,
Yorkshire.

Bradford skipper George Marsden, as featured on a 1902 cigarette card

failed with a drop-goal that hit the lower section of an upright.

After a scoreless first period during which, according to the *Yorkshire Daily Observer*, Bradford 'had done exceptionally well in keeping out their opponents', the game ebbed and flowed more in the second half as play slowly opened up before the tide turned firmly in the Yorkshire side's favour. Unfortunately, an otherwise cleanly fought game was tarnished midway through the half when Harry Feather of Bradford and Salford's Silas Warwick came to blows, referee Billy McCutcheon despatching them to the changing rooms. Two minutes later, Salford were penalised in front of their own posts for offside. Marsden appeared to have found the target and cheers rang out around the ground in celebration but were silenced when the ball was ruled to have sailed 'inches' wide. But, with Bradford keeping Salford hemmed into their own territory, it was not long before those same voices roared again after Brear struck for his try. The pressure continued and J. Francis almost dribbled the ball over

Salford's line for another touchdown. At the following scrum the Reds were pulled up for an infringement and Alex Laidlaw landed a straightforward goal to complete a 5–0 victory.

Although it took the Yorkshire team over an hour to break the deadlock, the *Leeds Mercury* declared, 'Bradford never looked like losing the match'. Having enjoyed the euphoria of capturing the trophy for the first time it is difficult to believe that, following the 1906/07 season, the club withdrew from the Northern Union to take up Association Football as Bradford Park Avenue, Bradford Northern being born out of the ashes.

WINNING CAPTAIN

George Marsden (Bradford 1906)

Born in Morley, near Leeds, George Marsden initially played rugby union for Morley Red Rose, Morley Wanderers and Morley. During this period he represented England (3 times), the North of England (2) and Yorkshire (11). In 1900, he switched codes, joining Bradford, playing in 173 matches and winning the Northern Union Challenge Cup (1906), Championship (1903/04) and Yorkshire League (1900/01). Rated one of the finest Northern Union halfbacks of his day, he was a strong player, noted for his surging breaks from the scrum. Under Northern Union rules he played for England (once—in 1905) and Yorkshire (12 times). He retired in 1906 but made a comeback in 1910 for Bradford Northern, founded in 1907 to replace his former Bradford club. He played his 65th and last game for Northern in 1913.

1907 NORTHERN UNION CHALLENGE CUP FINAL
Warrington v Oldham

The first 13-a-side Challenge Cup Final had a sensational climax when Warrington wingman Jack Fish, like all great players, produced a moment of genius when it mattered most to put rivals Oldham out of contention. The under-pressure Wires were protecting a 7–3 lead with eight minutes remaining when Oldham centre Sam Irvin took possession from Arthur Lees following a scrum in Warrington's half but, when he attempted to pass the ball along the line, the predatory Fish interjected. Dribbling past George Tyson, he took hold of the ball on the bounce, swerving past Dicky Thomas and into open territory for a sensational try. Fish added the goal for a nine-point lead as a cornet player who attended all Warrington's matches sounded 'The Last Post'.

Minutes later, Warrington were through again, quick passing inside Oldham's 25-yard area saw Sammy Lees and Ernie Brooks get the better of Michael Yewlett and Arthur Lees. Tom Hockenhull then dribbled the ball forward, propelling it past Tom White and Thomas before picking up and crossing the whitewash. Fish augmented to underline a 17–3 triumph, Warrington's late blitz providing a memorable end to what was hitherto described by the *Liverpool Echo* as 'not a great game by any means.'

Fish had been presented with chances at the start of the match, well-intentioned kicks to the flank from Brooks and Ike Taylor both deceiving him as the ball bounced out of reach. Fish and Oldham's Joe Ferguson (twice) failed with penalty attempts before excellent passing from the Roughyeds' Arthur Lees, Tyson and Bert Avery almost got Irvin over, Danny Isherwood forcing him into the corner flag.

Oldham continued to press and, as half-time approached, Arthur Lees beat two opponents before passing to Avery who, although confronted by Isherwood, managed to score, Ferguson failing the conversion. White had a chance to extend Oldham's lead, missing from in front of the posts following a mark. Warrington then began to have more of a say, Fish being successful with the second of two further penalty shots, narrowing the score to 3–2 in Oldham's favour. Warrington fans thought their side had the lead when Brooks kicked the ball towards Oldham's goal, George Heath catching it and touching down over the try-line but, as the *Warrington Guardian* pointed out, the 'cheers were a trifle too premature', referee Frank Renton ruling him offside.

Warrington made a tactical change amongst their backs for the second half; Brooks exchanging places with Hockenhull to operate closer to the pack. For Oldham, Yewlett almost found a way through but for Jimmy Tilley's timely tackle, and Ferguson was off-target with a penalty. Again Warrington came back into it, Sammy Lees grounding short of the try-line. But they suffered a setback when Frank Shugars and Taylor collided, both retiring to the touchline for attention. Despite their absence Warrington continued to knock on Oldham's door, and, after Sammy Lees, Brooks and Isherwood had combined, Fish was held near the try-line but somehow got the ball back to Sammy Lees who dodged two defenders before scoring against his former club to claim the lead. Fish appended the extras.

Four points ahead, Warrington were boosted by the return of Shugars and Taylor—albeit with heads bandaged—but 20 minutes still remained as Oldham desperately tried to break the Wires' defensive resolve, aiming a succession of high kicks towards their try-line

The 1907 Warrington team with the Challenge Cup.
Standing: Hackett (trainer), Shugars, Boardman, Belton, Heath, Harmer, Heesom (asst. trainer). Seated: Brooks, Taylor, Isherwood, Fish, Tilley, Jordan. On ground: Naylor (kneeling), Hockenhull, Lees, Thomas (kneeling)

before Fish intervened with his match-winner. In actual fact, Fish had not enjoyed one of his better games until that moment, the *Athletic News* saying: 'He gave one the impression he had lost some of his speed and a little of his pluck until that brilliant effort and magnificent piece of opportunism put a gilt-edged halo on his head.'

The Wires won without halfback Jack Jenkins (knee problem) whilst Oldham, as in the previous weekend's Championship Final, competed without injured three-quarters Tommy Cash (knee cartilage) and 'Birdie' Dixon (leg).

Jack Fish—Warrington's legendary winger and captain who scored a crucial try

STATS

Warrington 17 Oldham 3

Saturday 27 April at Wheater's Field, Broughton (3.30 pm)

Warrington (primrose and blue hoops): Tilley, Fish (captain), Taylor, Isherwood, Brooks, S. Lees, Hockenhull, Heath, Boardman, Thomas, Shugars, Belton, Naylor. Trainer: I. Hackett

Oldham (red and white hoops): Thomas, White, Irvin, Billy Dixon, Tyson, A. Lees (captain), Yewlett, Ferguson, Topham, A. Smith, Vowles, Avery, Wilkinson. Trainer: unknown

Referee: F. Renton
Touch-judges: J. Priestley, J. McGowan

Half-time: 2–3   Attendance: 18,500   Receipts: £1,010

Weather: showery rain

Cup presentation:
Mrs J.B. Cooke, wife of Northern Union president

Progressive score:

Warrington	score (min)	Oldham
	0–3 (-)	Avery try
Fish penalty	2–3 (-)	
S. Lees try, Fish goal	7–3 (58)	
Fish try, Fish goal	12–3 (72)	
Hockenhull try, Fish goal	17–3 (80)	

Route to the final:

First round: Warrington 34 Batley 9, Oldham 5 Runcorn 0

Second round: Warrington 16 Hull 0, Halifax 5 Oldham 10

Third round: Huddersfield 9 Warrington 15, Wakefield Trinity 10 Oldham 14

Semi-finals:
Warrington 21 Swinton 0 (Central Park, Wigan, 12,000),
Oldham 6 Salford 0 (The Athletic Grounds, Rochdale, 16,000)

Head-to-head form guide:

Warrington 10 Oldham 2 (Lancashire Cup)
Oldham 17 Warrington 8 (League)
Warrington 5 Oldham 14 (League)

WINNING CAPTAIN

Jack Fish (Warrington 1907)

Jack Fish is one of the celebrated names in the Warrington club's history, often mentioned in the same breath as their other immortal wingman, Brian Bevan. Described as a 'flying' winger whose pace often took him past opponents with ease, Fish originated from Runcorn, joining Warrington in 1898 from Lostock Gralam (near Northwich, Cheshire). He went on to make 321 appearances (215 tries, 262 goals) for Warrington until 1911. Twice a winner of the Northern Union Challenge Cup (1905, 1907), he represented England (3 times) and Lancashire (16). He later took on the role of Warrington trainer.

1908 NORTHERN UNION CHALLENGE CUP FINAL
Hunslet v Hull

Hunslet won the 1908 Challenge Cup Final in near-Artic conditions, courtesy of their 14–0 victory over Hull. Having already won the Yorkshire League and Yorkshire Cup, they subsequently claimed the Northern Rugby League Championship to become the first of only three teams to boast an 'All Four Cups' campaign. The final was not considered outstanding, the players hindered by the heavy pitch, snow having fallen early in the day, reappearing at half-time and continuing throughout the second half.

Harry Fulton almost drew first blood for Hull when, having taken a pass from Harry Wallace close to Hunslet's try-line, he was just stopped 'in the nick of time' from getting over by Herbert Place. Understandably, given the conditions, the game developed into a pattern of end-to-end kicking. Eventually, Hunslet went looking for points; Walter Goldthorpe's attempted drop-goal fell short, then Billy Batten almost got in for a try following a neat passing move, Ned Rogers producing a great tackle. From the ensuing play, the ball found its way to Walter Goldthorpe who transferred to Billy Eagers, the centre opening the scoring with a drop-goal after 22 minutes.

Hull's pack tried to lift themselves and William Carroll came close to entering Hunslet's in-goal area but subsequent erratic play twice gifted opportunities to the Parkside club, Jack Randall (after fumbling by the Hull backs) and Walter Goldthorpe (having charged down Carroll's kick) both having touchdowns disallowed through earlier transgressions. Just before

CLUB BADGES

At one time teams only wore their club badge on special occasions, for Wembley in particular. They first appeared at the stadium in 1935, Castleford and Huddersfield setting a trend only Widnes (1937) and Barrow (1938) defaulted on prior to the Second World War. Since the war, just four teams have competed at Wembley without badges, Leeds being the last in 1957, the fashion for permanently incorporating them into jersey design gaining momentum during the 1980s. Instances when teams wore badges for Challenge Cup Finals in pre-Wembley years include Batley (their three early triumphs), Hunslet (1908) and Swinton (the 1920s, and 1932 when the final temporarily left Wembley).

WINNING CAPTAIN

Albert Goldthorpe (Hunslet 1908)

Albert Edward Goldthorpe is, arguably, the most famous name in Hunslet's proud history. Raised in Stourton, on the outskirts of Leeds, and one of five brothers who played for the club, he made his debut aged 16 during 1888. A model sportsman, he turned out for them until 1910. Initially a centre, he moved to stand-off in 1901 where his skilful ball handling and awareness made him a pivotal figure. An excellent tactical kicker, he landed almost 1,000 goals for Hunslet. During the club's successful 1907/08 'Four Cups' campaign, he set a, then, club record of 101 goals in a season, the first Northern Union player to register a century. Affectionately known as 'Ahr Albert', his first club honour came under rugby union rules, defeating Huddersfield in the 1892 Yorkshire Cup Final. After Hunslet left the RU in 1895, Goldthorpe gained further successes in Northern Union, winning the Northern Union Challenge Cup (1908), Championship (1907/08), Yorkshire Cup (1905, 1907) and Yorkshire League (1897/98, 1907/08). He represented Yorkshire six times, including their 1898/99 county championship success, adding to three previous titles with the white rose (1891/92, 1892/93, 1893/94) under RU rules.

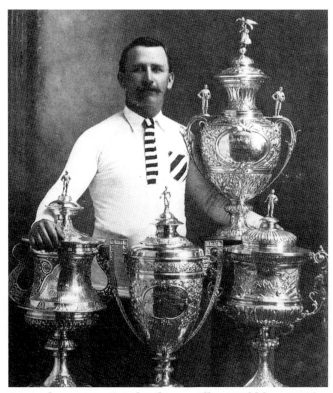

A proud moment—Hunslet skipper Albert Goldthorpe with his team's phenomenal trophy haul

Hunslet with 'All Four Cups' in 1908. Players only (in playing kit) are, third row (standing): J. Wray, W. Goldthorpe, Smales, Cappleman, Randall, Jukes. Second row: W. Wray, C. Ward, W. Ward, A. Goldthorpe, Batten, Place, Brooks, Higson. Front row: Hoyle, Whittaker, Smith, Eagers. The trainer, Hannah, is in the third row (centre)

STATS

Hunslet 14 Hull 0

Saturday 25 April at Fartown, Huddersfield (3.30 pm)

Hunslet (white): Place, Farrar, Eagers, W. Goldthorpe, Batten, A. Goldthorpe (captain), F. Smith, Wilson, Brookes, Jukes, Randall, Higson, Walsh. Trainer: W. Hannah

Hull (black and white hoops): W.H. Taylor (captain), Parry, Cottrell, Cook, E. Rogers, Wallace, Anderson, Herridge, Owen, Kilburn, Carroll, Fulton, Holder. Trainer: T. Coates

Referee: J.H. Smith

Touch-judges: W. Emmott, J. Priestley

Half-time: 7–0   Attendance: 18,000   Receipts: £903

Weather: overcast, heavy snow throughout second half, ground muddy

Cup presentation: Mr H. Ashton, Northern Union president

Progressive score:

Hunslet	score (min)	Hull
Eagers drop-goal	2–0 (22)	
Smith try, A. Goldthorpe goal	7–0 (35)	
A. Goldthorpe goal from mark	9–0 (60)	
Farrar try, A. Goldthorpe goal	14–0 (78)	

Route to the final:

First round: Leeds 5 Hunslet 14, Hull 9 Swinton 5

Second round: Hunslet 15 Oldham 8, Hull 15 Salford 9

Third round: Barrow 0 Hunslet 8, Hull 19 Wakefield Trinity 0

Semi-finals:

Hunslet 16 Broughton Rangers 2 (Central Park, Wigan, 16,000), Hull 7 Leigh 0 (Thrum Hall, Halifax, 8,296)

Head-to-head form guide:

Hull 8 Hunslet 9 (League)

Hunslet 17 Hull 3 (League)

the interval, Hunslet increased their lead to 7–0 when, from a scrum near Hull's try-line, Albert Goldthorpe—who subsequently appended the goal—passed the ball to Fred Smith, the halfback sprinting around George Cottrell for an excellent try near the posts.

Despite the terrible weather, Hull began the second half determined to get back on terms, Frank Cook's pass sending Rogers heading for the Hunslet try-line, Fred Farrar managing to tackle him just in time. Rogers again made a break but once more Farrar halted his progress. Midway through the half Albert Goldthorpe added another two points to Hunslet's score, kicking a goal after Smith had made a mark from a poor clearance by Wallace. Both packs were finding it a tortuous experience to make any headway and it was not until the closing minutes that Hunslet wrapped up matters with a second try, Farrar scoring near the posts off Eagers' pass, the latter having latched on to Walter Goldthorpe's cross-kick. Albert Goldthorpe augmented.

Despite his lack of pace in what was his 20th season with the club, Albert Goldthorpe stood out as the chief architect of Hunslet's victory. Their famed pack, known as 'The Terrible Six' seemed, according to the *Leeds Mercury*, 'to be feeling the strain of their heavy season' and 'had periods when they were by no means terrible'. Their below-par form allowed Hull's forwards to introduce their backs into the game spasmodically, although they were not a match for Hunslet's on the day.

1909 NORTHERN UNION CHALLENGE CUP FINAL
Wakefield Trinity v Hull

Wakefield Trinity 1909, standing: unidentified (in jacket), J. Taylor, Bennett, Lynch, Unsworth, Mr J.B. Cooke (club president), Crosland, Beaumont, Walton, G. Taylor. Seated: Kershaw, Metcalfe, Slater, Auton, Parkes. On ground: Holmes, Simpson, Newbould, Sidwell

Wakefield Trinity made their Challenge Cup Final debut in 1909 where they faced the previous year's runners-up Hull. Despite the Humberside club finishing 13th in the League—seven places below Trinity—they were installed as slight favourites but, in the event, had their hopes dashed by a determined Wakefield side that adapted better to a rain-lashed, soggy Headingley pitch. Heavy overnight and morning rain had flooded the playing area and, as it abated, ground staff worked hard to clear the water before kick-off, removing it in buckets and laying sawdust in the slushiest areas. But it was in vain as the rain, accompanied by the sound of thunder, lashed down again midway through the first half, the ground turning into a quagmire as the crowd, according to the *Hull Times*, 'looked pitiful as they received their soaking'.

It was also disappointing for referee, Ted Smirk, who earlier told the same newspaper that he hoped 'the game will be particularly fast' as he was in 'good form' having completed his own training schedule of

walks between the Lancashire seaside resorts of Lytham and St Annes! The Hull players, meanwhile, had their own pre-match preparation on the day of the final. Arriving in Leeds on an early train they were promptly despatched to bed for several hours in rooms reserved at the Grand Central Hotel!

The weather did not dampen the supporters' enthusiasm, one Wakefield fan decked out in red and blue, who had 'imbibed too freely', climbing the railings to join a contortionist entertaining the crowd on the pitch. He was hastily tackled by a police constable and duly escorted to a stand!

Wakefield dominated the opening; Ernest Bennett made a terrific break, followed later by an excellent passing move that terminated when Billie Simpson knocked-on, and then Jimmy Metcalfe's attempted drop-goal fell short. Eventually the pressure told, Tommy Newbould, receiving the ball from a scrum, outwitting the opposing halfbacks with a dummy pass before forcing himself through a group of Hull forwards

Three Wakefield Trinity tries and the terrible weather are depicted in this drawing!

and placing the ball over the whitewash for a try. Hull, inspired by Billy Anderson, began to have more of the play but it soon developed into a battle of attrition.

The Airlie Birds eventually gave some hint of their capability, Jimmy Dechan ending a bout of passing with a breathtaking run as he beat 'man after man' before Harry Slater brought him down. Wakefield, though, still held the edge, and, from a scrum near Hull's line, Billie Lynch managed to touch down, the score being disallowed through a forward pass. A minute later, Slater's wide transfer from a scrum enabled E. Sidwell to draw opposition winger Ned Rogers before sending Bennett over for a second try. In the latter stages of the half, Wakefield's forwards almost succeeded, on a couple of occasions, in dribbling the ball over Hull's try-line. As half-time approached, Metcalfe made a poor goal attempt from a mark, but there was no further scoring before the break, Wakefield leading 6–0.

After the resumption Ned Rogers missed two fairly simple penalty shots for Hull but Wakefield looked the more likely to gain a try, a Bennett break being foiled by Harry Taylor, and Simpson being stopped from getting over by Anderson. Eventually, with Wakefield

WINNING CAPTAIN

Harry Slater (Wakefield Trinity 1909)

The whippet-like speed of Wakefield Trinity's Harry Slater made him a dangerous opponent, eager to exploit any gap created by long-term halfback partner Tommy Newbould. Previously with Wakefield's Balne Lane rugby union club—one of that code's top Yorkshire outfits at the time—he made the first of 180 appearances for Trinity in 1904, winning the Northern Union Challenge Cup (1905) and Yorkshire League (1909/10, 1910/11). He represented Yorkshire three times, his last Wakefield match being in 1913.

dominating scrum possession, the pressure paid off, three more tries accruing from Nealy Crosland (a simple 'walk in' after taking a pass from Jimmy Auton who had scooped up the ball after charging down Taylor's kick), Bennett (receiving the ball from Slater after he went down the 'blind side' of a scrum) and Simpson (beating Dechan to Newbould's cross-kick for the best try of the afternoon). Although Metcalfe succeeded from just one of his five conversion attempts, Trinity still celebrated a comfortable 17–0 victory.

The growing importance attached to Challenge Cup success was illustrated by Wigan and Hull fielding 'reserve' teams in League fixtures ahead of their respective semi-finals with each being fined £25.

STATS

Wakefield Trinity 17 Hull 0
Saturday 24 April at Headingley, Leeds (3.30 pm)
Wakefield Trinity (blue with red band): Metcalfe, Bennett, Sidwell, Lynch, Simpson, Newbould, Slater (captain), Crosland, Auton, G. Taylor, Beaumont, Walton, Kershaw. Trainer: E. Hayley

Hull (black and white irregular hoops): W.H. Taylor (captain), Dechan, Connell, Cottrell, E. Rogers, Wallace, Anderson, Herridge, Holder, Boylen, Britton, Havelock, Carroll. Trainer: J. Lewis

Referee: E.H. Smirk   Touch-judges. W. Emmott, W. Taylor

Half-time: 6–0 Attendance: 23,587 Receipts: £1,490

Weather: heavy rain, some thunder, ground muddy

Cup presentation:
Mrs J. Nicholl, wife of Northern Union president

Progressive score:

Wakefield Trinity	score (min)	Hull
Newbould try	3–0 (6)	
Bennett try	6–0 (-)	
Crosland try, Metcalfe goal	11–0 (-)	
Bennett try	14–0 (-)	
Simpson try	17–0 (-)	

Route to the final:

First round: Bradford Northern 3 Wakefield T 13, Normanton 10 Hull 20

Second round: Leigh 3 Wakefield T 9, Runcorn 9 Hull 11

Third round: Wakefield T 19 Hunslet 0, Oldham 6 Hull 13

Semi-finals:
Wakefield T 14 Wigan 2 (Wheater's Field, Broughton, 18,000), Hull 10 Halifax 4 (Fartown, Huddersfield, 21,800)

Head-to-head form guide:

Hull 17 Wakefield Trinity 6 (League)

Wakefield Trinity 24 Hull 8 (League)

1910 NORTHERN UNION CHALLENGE CUP FINAL
Leeds v Hull

Leeds' runaway win over Hull during the first ever Challenge Cup Final replay contrasted their tightly fought, dour opening match in which the Airlie Birds had, at one time, looked on course to capture the trophy themselves. Played in wet, muddy conditions, that first meeting was delayed because the Leeds to Huddersfield train transporting both teams took two and a half hours to complete the 17-mile journey. At 3.50 pm—20 minutes after the scheduled kick-off time—a chalkboard was carried around Huddersfield's Fartown ground advising spectators: 'Both teams arrived, start at 4 o'clock,' although it was actually 4.20 pm when it did so.

A Frank Young penalty for offside gave Leeds an early lead, Ned Rogers twice failing to respond (from a penalty and a mark) before Harry Wallace levelled the scores with a drop-goal after fielding Young's clearance kick. Hull swept into a 7–2 lead after just 11 minutes when Wallace beat an opponent before delivering a perfect kick to the right corner for George Cottrell to take the ball and race over for a try. Ned Rogers added an excellent conversion, later missing another goal attempt following a mark.

Fifteen minutes before the break, Leeds' first decent passing move ended disastrously, halfback Jimmy Sanders receiving a kick to the lower part of his body. With his departure reducing them to 12 men for the remainder of the match, C.L. Gillie moved to halfback, Fred Webster to the three-quarters. A minute from half-time a Ned Rogers drop-goal attempt landed short.

With Hull having dominated much of the play, Leeds discovered some self-belief during the second half. When Wallace fumbled, Walter Goldthorpe recovered possession near halfway and raced towards Hull's try-line and, with Cottrell moving in to tackle, transferred to Jimmy Fawcett. Cottrell redirected his attention to Fawcett who duly returned the ball to Goldthorpe, the latter going over in the corner. Hull claimed he grounded short but the try stood. Young was wide with the conversion, subsequently missing with a penalty and also from a mark, the latter being charged down.

With 10 minutes left, controversy raged when Hull captain Billy Anderson was penalised for offside as he grabbed the ball, being kicked on the knee by William Biggs in doing so. Young's resultant goal tied the scores at 7–7 but Hull felt the penalty should have been theirs for the 'foul' on Anderson (referee Joseph Priestley later explained he ruled Anderson offside before the kicking incident). Anderson was carried to the touchline for treatment and later returned, although in pain. Both sides tried to secure victory towards the end, Ned Rogers going over with two Leeds players clinging on, but the corner flag was knocked over and the score disallowed, whilst Young missed with two drop-kicks (from a mark and a penalty).

A hastily convened Northern Union Committee meeting took place in the pavilion after the match, the replay being fixed for the same venue next Monday afternoon. In the case of a further draw, there was to be extra 10-minute periods until a result was reached. The early replay decision was influenced through players from both sides departing with the tourists the following Tuesday.

Played on a much drier pitch, the rematch was a more one-sided affair, Hull—already without forward Stanley Britton after he broke a collarbone in the semi-final—losing leg injury victims Anderson and Harry Taylor from the first meeting whilst Leeds were forced to leave out Sanders whose injuries included a broken nose that required an operation.

WINNING CAPTAIN

Fred Webster (Leeds 1910)

Industrious forward Fred Webster was signed by Leeds in 1902 from the Brotherton club, near Castleford. His playing career at Headingley lasted until 1920 and, despite the disruption of the First World War, he still managed 453 official appearances. Remarkably for a forward, his 76 tries for Leeds included eight in one match against the short-lived Coventry side in 1913, a club record since equalled but not surpassed. His only winners' medal with Leeds was for the Northern Union Challenge Cup (1910), being a runner-up in the Championship (1915) and Yorkshire Cup (1919). A member of the first Northern Union touring side in 1910, he made all three of his Test appearances on that trip. He also represented England (4 times) and Yorkshire (6).

Fawcett missed an early drop-goal for Leeds before Young notched a penalty for offside. There was little in it until the 28th minute when the momentum swung to Leeds after Young fielded Ned Rogers' kick and landed a drop-goal. Leeds set up camp in Hull territory, Webster eventually picking up the ball to force his way over near the corner, Young's magnificent goal making it 9–0. Shortly after, a hasty clearance kick from a pressured Hull defence was charged down, resulting in Harry Topham going in for a try virtually untouched, Young again augmenting. Another Hull punt—by Wallace—was caught by Gillie, the centre making a mark, enabling Young to kick his fifth goal, the interval score being 16–0.

Hull made a couple of exciting breaks after the resumption but both floundered. Leeds responded with two quick tries, a Ned Rogers fumble in his in-goal area allowed Goldthorpe to fall on the ball for a touchdown and, two minutes later, Ernest Ware and Gillie set up Harold Rowe who sped past brothers Ned and Greg Rogers before placing the ball behind the posts. Young added both goals, the score rising to 26–0.

Hull, having looked jaded, staged a mini-recovery. Ned Rogers landed a penalty (which went in off the upright) for obstruction and, despite losing Greg Rogers through a knee injury, they added two tries;

Cottrell's cross-kick was collected by Harry Walton who raced 30 yards to score and, three minutes later, George Connell pushed through several defenders to

Ned Rogers—almost won it for Hull but for a disallowed try late in the first encounter

A Challenge Cup win at last for Leeds. Standing: Morn (trainer), Goldthorpe, Barron, Topham, Ward, Biggs. Seated: Sanders, Ware, Webster, Harrison, Whitaker, Rowe. On ground: Fawcett, Young, Gillie, Jarman

STATS

Leeds 7 Hull 7

Saturday 16 April at Fartown, Huddersfield (3.30 pm)

Leeds: Young, Fawcett, Goldthorpe, Gillie, Barron, Ware, Sanders, Biggs, Jarman, Harrison, Topham, Webster (captain), Ward. Trainer: W. Morn

Hull: W.H. Taylor, Cottrell, Devereux, Morton, E. Rogers, Wallace, Anderson (captain), Herridge, Osborne, R. Taylor, Holder, Connell, Walton. Trainer: J. Lewis

Referee: J. Priestley   Touch-judges: F. Farrer, J. Kennedy

Half-time: 2–7   Attendance: 19,413   Receipts: £1,102

Weather: overcast and damp, ground very wet from earlier heavy rain

Progressive score:

Leeds	score (min)	Hull
Young penalty	2–0 (2)	
	2–2 (8)	Wallace drop goal
	2–7 (11)	Cottrell try, E. Rogers goal
Goldthorpe try	5–7 (-)	
Young penalty	7–7 (70)	

Replay: Leeds 26 Hull 12

Monday 18 April at Fartown, Huddersfield (3.30 pm)

Leeds: unchanged except Rowe for Fawcett, Fawcett for Sanders, Whitaker for Biggs

Hull: unchanged except E. Rogers for W.H. Taylor, Atkinson for E. Rogers, G. Rogers for Anderson (the captaincy passed to Wallace)

Referee: J. Priestley   Touch-judges: F. Farrer, J. Kennedy

Half-time: 16–0   Attendance: 11,608   Receipts: £657

Weather: fine and warm, strong wind

Cup presentation:
Mrs J.H. Houghton, wife of Northern Union chairman

Progressive score:

Leeds	score (min)	Hull
Young penalty	2–0 (5)	
Young drop-goal	4–0 (28)	
Webster try, Young goal	9–0 (-)	
Topham try, Young goal	14–0 (-)	
Young goal from mark	16–0 (38)	
Goldthorpe try, Young goal	21–0 (45)	
Rowe try, Young goal	26–0 (47)	
	26–2 (60)	E. Rogers penalty
	26–7 (65)	Walton try, E. Rogers goal
	26–12 (68)	Connell try, E. Rogers goal

Route to the final:

First round:
Hull Kingston Rovers 3 Leeds 5, Hull 10 Leigh 7

Second round:
Leeds 13 Rochdale Hornets 3, Batley 0 Hull 8

Third round: Keighley 4 Leeds 7, Hull 13 Halifax 7

Semi-finals: Leeds 11 Warrington 10 (Wheater's Field, Broughton, 14,959),

Hull 20 Salford 6 (Belle Vue, Wakefield, 11,000)

Head-to-head form guide:

Hull 8 Leeds 10 (League)

Leeds 19 Hull 0 (League)

touch down near the posts. Ned Rogers converted both for a more respectable 26–12 score-line. In the closing minutes Fawcett broke his collarbone.

There were unsavoury scenes near the end when some spectators came onto the field, threatening referee Priestley. Police ran over to quell the incident as the official blew for full-time but he was, reportedly, hit twice as he attempted to leave the field. Running away he fell as he neared the changing rooms and, according to the *Hull Daily Mail*, 'received further unsportsmanlike treatment'.

On a lighter note, Young's seven goals in the replay was a record for the final whilst Leeds' 26 points surpassed Broughton's 25 of 1902.

Leeds' Frank Young set a Challenge Cup Final record with seven goals in the replay

1911 NORTHERN UNION CHALLENGE CUP FINAL
Broughton Rangers v Wigan

Broughton Rangers—18th in the League—produced a shock 4–0 win over table-toppers Wigan in the 1911 Challenge Cup Final. Whilst the Cherry and Whites had to contend with a powerful performance from Rangers' forwards they also had atrocious weather to cope with. The Willows pitch, saturated by persistent rain that began falling the previous evening and continued throughout the match, was described as 'a series of small lakes', the playing area—reduced to a slimy bog—not at all the type of surface suited to Wigan's speedy backs. The *Wigan Examiner* said 'it was palpable to every follower of the game that the ground was in an altogether unfit state for a Cup Final.' Wigan appealed for a postponement but, although there was a brief impromptu meeting of Northern Union officials before the match, their request went unheeded.

Once the match was underway, Wigan captain Jimmy Leytham made a couple of early threats, thwarted both times by George Davidson, the Rangers full back booting the ball dead after the flying winger kicked towards the in-goal, and later pushing him into touch a few yards short of the try-line. Although conditions were difficult, the kicking and fielding of both teams was deemed 'remarkably' good but there were few attempts at open play. Broughton's bustling forwards began gaining valuable yardage, keeping Wigan pinned inside their own half. In the 14th minute Billy Harris put the Rangers ahead with a long-

Billy Barlow almost scored a second half try for Broughton Rangers

---

WINNING CAPTAIN

Jim Clampitt (Broughton Rangers 1911)

James Leslie 'Jim' Clampitt joined Broughton Rangers in 1906. He became club captain in 1910/11, leading them to victory in the Northern Union Challenge Cup that season, having been a member of their 1906 Lancashire Cup winning side. Described as 'strong and vigorous', he was an all-action forward who generally took the hooking role in the pack. A tourist in 1914, he appeared in three Test matches, and represented England (6 times) and Cumberland (24). He played the last of 269 matches for Broughton in 1921, subsequently becoming a director of the club. He was joined at the Rangers by younger brother Dick—another forward—both having transferred from their hometown Millom club.

Broughton Rangers—winners of the Challenge Cup for a second time! Players only (in playing kit) are, back row: Heys, Bouch. Third row: Hirst, Gorry, Winskill, R. Clampitt, Robinson. Second row (seated): Wild, J. Clampitt, Harris, Ruddick. On floor: Davidson, Jones, Barlow, Scott

STATS

Broughton Rangers 4 Wigan 0

Saturday 29 April at The Willows, Salford (3.30 pm)

Broughton Rangers (white with narrow navy blue hoops): Davidson, Bouch, Wild, Harris, Scott, Barlow, Jones, Gorry, Hirst, Winskill, Ruddick, J. Clampitt (captain), R. Clampitt. Trainer: H. Taylor

Wigan (cherry and white hoops): Sharrock, Miller, Todd, Jenkins, Leytham (captain), Thomas, Gleave, Ramsdale, Whittaker, Silcock, Williams, Cheetham, Seeling. Trainer: J. Hesketh

Referee: J.F. May   Touch-judges: W. Emmott, W.H. Hall

Half-time: 4–0   Attendance: 8,000   Receipts: £376

Weather: heavy rain, ground waterlogged

Cup presentation: Lord Derby, Northern Union president

Progressive score:

Broughton Rangers	score (min)	Wigan
Harris penalty	2–0 (14)	
Harris penalty	4–0 (40)	

Route to the final:

First round: Normanton St John's 6 Broughton R 10, Wigan 18 Huddersfield 13

Second round: Broughton R 9 Dewsbury 0, Wigan 21 Warrington 2

Third round: Broughton R 10 Bradford Northern 0, Leeds 4 Wigan 13

Semi-finals: Broughton R 12 Rochdale Hornets 0 (The Willows, Salford, 18,000),

Wigan 4 Batley 2 (Fartown, Huddersfield, 17,578)

Head-to-head form guide:

Broughton Rangers 0 Wigan 15 (League)

Wigan 37 Broughton Rangers 0 (League)

distance penalty after Lance Todd was ruled offside at a scrum. Later, when Todd lost possession, the Rangers—led by Harris and Walter Scott—dribbled it towards Wigan's in-goal, Jim Sharrock and Joe Miller saving the situation as they went 'sliding over the dead ball line on all fours'. Sharrock had a chance to level the score, being wide with a penalty following obstruction by Hilderick Bouch and Alfred Wild whilst, at the other end, Davidson made a poor effort with a drop-goal. Wigan worked an opening when Fred Gleave, Bert Jenkins and Leytham constructed a move, but the latter's inside pass to Charlie Seeling saw the ball go loose. Just on half-time, Broughton doubled their lead to 4–0 through a second Harris penalty, Walter Cheetham fouling Billy Barlow after he kicked the ball.

Following the interval Leytham managed to cross Broughton's try-line but lost the ball in a pool of water as he tried to ground it. Sharrock attempted another, more ambitious, penalty goal from the touchline, awarded after Broughton's Ned Jones failed to play the ball correctly, but it dropped short. Wild—who temporarily left the field with an injury shortly after—and Dick Clampitt dribbled the ball from halfway to the corner flag, where colleague Barlow almost scored. Such were the conditions referee Jimmy May stopped the game whilst mud was removed from his eye. With time running out, Leytham made another good break before kicking towards the Rangers' posts but Tom Whittaker was unable to reach it, Harris kicking dead. Minutes before the end, Harris missed with a penalty attempt after George Ruddick was obstructed.

Perhaps Broughton's success in the first try-less Challenge Cup Final was preordained, contemporary reports pointing out their previous 1902 victory was in the 'Coronation Year' of King Edward VII, and, likewise, 1911 was the year his successor King George V was Crowned. The *Athletic News* said: 'Wigan did not relish the conditions. They tried hard, but could not break through the rare defence of the Rangers.' Broughton's pack included Jim Gorry, believed to be the first Irish player to win the Challenge Cup, the medical student from Tullamore having played for the club in his previous debut season as 'Gerry Michael'. The heavy rain resulted in a disappointing 8,000 crowd, the £376 receipts producing a financial loss.

Graham Morris

1912 NORTHERN UNION CHALLENGE CUP FINAL
Dewsbury v Oldham

Dewsbury stunned Oldham in the 1912 Challenge Cup Final, winning 8–5 after an incident packed conclusion to a contest that was both thrilling and controversial. Odds-on favourites Oldham led 5–2 when, with 15 minutes remaining, their forward Bert Avery received 'marching orders' for dissent towards referee Ben Ennion. Seven minutes later, Dewsbury were level. Oldham won a scrum near their own try-line, halfback George Anlezark taking possession but his attempted clearance did not travel far, Dewsbury's Billy Rhodes catching the ball and racing over for a try in the right corner, Ernest Ware missing the conversion.

From the restart, further drama unfolded after Oldham worked the ball into Dewsbury territory. A clearance kick from Dewsbury's J. Nearey fell to Oldham's Evan Davies who made a mark in front of goal. Alf Wood took the resultant goal-shot, a touch-judge raising his flag as Oldham players 'jumped for joy' believing they had regained the lead, but the referee ruled it wide. A relieved Dewsbury attacked the Roughyeds' line, Tommy Milner transferring the ball to Rhodes who charged through a group of defenders into the in-goal area. Uncertain as to whether the ball was grounded, Ennion consulted touch-judge H. Schofield, before signalling a try. The *Oldham Standard* journalist—who expressed dissatisfaction at several refereeing decisions—argued Rhodes was in touch. Either way, it was a cup-winning moment and 'a great shout of triumph from lusty Yorkshire throats' burst forth. Ware missed the goal but Dewsbury held on.

In the opening minutes of the match, Dewsbury full back Edward Jackett had been forced to save his line after Milner's pass to Ernest Ward went astray. This led to 'fierce scrimmaging' near their try-line, offside by skipper Cosh Richardson conceding a penalty that enabled Joe Ferguson to push Oldham 2–0 ahead from a difficult shot. Dewsbury's forwards responded quickly, taking play near Oldham's in-goal and, from the base of a scrum, Milner transferred to Nearey, whose quickly taken drop-goal levelled the score. Shortly afterwards, Ferguson had another penalty strike at goal but was wide. Dewsbury, ably led

Dewsbury commemorate their only peacetime Challenge Cup success. Standing: Atkinson (physio), Abbishaw, Garnett, O'Neill, Hamill, Davies (trainer). Seated: Evans, Ward, Rhodes, Richardson, Sharples, Ware, Jackett. On ground: Milner, Nearey

by their pack, continued to press; George Sharples being pushed into touch when he threatened, Rhodes' cross-kick into Oldham's in-goal forcing Sid Deane to punch the ball clear as G.A. Garnett and Richardson bore down.

With 20 minutes played, Oldham obtained their anticipated opening try, a brilliant effort after Anlezark gained possession from a scrum in Dewsbury's 25-yard area and passed to Jimmy Lomas. The stand-off evaded Milner, the ball travelling across field, via Davies and Deane, to George Cook, who darted into the right corner. Wood missed the conversion but Oldham led 5–2, although Cook was injured in the process and unable to play a significant role thereafter. Undaunted, Dewsbury continued to show spirit, Ware

WINNING CAPTAIN

Fred Richardson (Dewsbury 1912)

Long-serving Dewsbury forward Alfred Hargreaves 'Fred' Richardson—otherwise known as 'Cosh' due to his all-action style—played the first of 303 games for the club in 1902, his last being in 1915. With Dewsbury he won the Northern Union Challenge Cup (1912) and Second Division Championship (1904/05). Representative honours eluded him, although he twice had trials for Yorkshire (1906 and 1907). Born in Dewsbury, he previously played for Dewsbury Clarence Juniors and Dewsbury Mashers.

(penalty) and Jackett (drop) both missing shots at goal, and Sharples being tackled as he was about to cross Oldham's try-line, but there was no further scoring before the interval.

After the break, Sharples retired for several minutes whilst stitches were inserted in a cut above an eye. Ferguson missed another penalty but Dewsbury's forwards were getting the better of Oldham's six despite being reduced to 12 men after Joe Hammill was carried off with a knee injury. Ward found a chink in Oldham's armour, delivering the ball to Sharples who dived into the corner but was pushed into the flag. Personnel numbers evened up through Avery's dismissal, contemporary reports differing as to the nature of his angst, one suggesting he was upset at the

referee ignoring a claim for a mark.

In one of the greatest days in Dewsbury's history, news of victory 'spread like wildfire' through their town, the main streets overflowing with excited people who headed for the railway station to await their heroes. The *Daily Dispatch* concluded that 'taking the game all through, the honours went to the better side, for Dewsbury had much more of the play.' Both fielded strong sides, Oldham's New Zealand three-quarter George Smith (ankle injury) being the most notable absentee.

STATS

Dewsbury 8 Oldham 5

Saturday 27 April at Headingley, Leeds (3.30 pm)

Dewsbury (red, amber and black hoops): Jackett, Rhodes, Ware, Ward, Sharples, Milner, Nearey, Richardson (captain), O'Neill, Garnett, Hammill, Abbishaw, Evans. Trainer: J.E. Davies

Oldham (red and white hoops): Wood, Cook, Deane, Davies, Williams, Lomas, Anlezark (captain), Ferguson, Avery, Smith, Wright, Wise, Wiltshire. Trainer: J. Mallalieu

Referee: B.R. Ennion

Touch-judges: J.C. Lumley, H. Schofield

Half-time: 2–5   Attendance: 15,271   Receipts: £853

Weather: fine and dry, ground hard

Cup presentation: Mr A.H. Marshall, MP for Wakefield

Progressive score:

Dewsbury	score (min)	Oldham
	0–2 (6)	Ferguson penalty
Nearey drop-goal	2–2 (8)	
	2–5 (20)	Cook try
Rhodes try	5–5 (72)	
Rhodes try	8–5 (76)	

Route to the final:

First round: Dewsbury 36 Lane End United (Leeds) 9, Coventry 3 Oldham 21

Second round: Salford 8 Dewsbury 9, Oldham 12 Wigan 8

Third round: Dewsbury 5 Batley 2, Oldham 2 Huddersfield 0

Semi-finals:
Dewsbury 8 Halifax 5 (Fartown, Huddersfield, 18,271),
Oldham 17 Wakefield Trinity 0 (Wheater's Field, Broughton, 11,000)

Head-to-head form guide:

No previous meetings during season

Billy Rhodes won the match for Dewsbury with his two tries in the second half

Graham Morris

1913 NORTHERN UNION CHALLENGE CUP FINAL
Huddersfield v Warrington

Huddersfield display their 1912/13 trophy cache. Players only (in playing kit) are, standing: Lee, Clark, Swinden, Wrigley, Longstaff, Higson, Chilcott, Gronow. Seated: Holland, Davies, Wagstaff, Gleeson, Todd, Moorhouse. On ground: Rosenfeld, Rogers

Stanley Moorhouse—a local product in the midst of Huddersfield's cosmopolitan 'Team of All the Talents'—was the hero of his club's first Challenge

WINNING CAPTAIN

Harold Wagstaff (Huddersfield 1913, 1915, 1920)

Harold Wagstaff—dubbed 'The Prince of Centres'—is one of the Northern Union's most revered names. A member of Huddersfield's 'Team of All the Talents', he was born in Holmfirth and played for local sides Pump Hole Rangers and Underbank before joining the Fartown set up in 1906, his 436th—and last—match for the club being in 1925. A gifted centre, he became Huddersfield captain in 1911 when still only 19 years old, leading them to success three times each in the Northern Union Challenge Cup (1913, 1915, 1920) and Championship (1911/12, 1912/13, 1914/15). Other club honours included the Yorkshire Cup (1911, 1914, 1919—May, 1919—November) and Yorkshire League (1911/12, 1912/13, 1913/14, 1914/15, 1919/20, 1921/22). A knee infection cost him his 1910 tour place, but he was in the 1914 and 1920 squads, both as captain. He made 12 Test appearances (10 as captain) and represented England (9 times) and Yorkshire (15). He became player-coach of Huddersfield (1924–25), subsequently coaching Halifax (1925–26) and Broughton Rangers (1935–36). In 1988, he was inducted into the Rugby League Hall of Fame.

Cup Final appearance in 1913 with three well-taken second half tries. With 30 minutes remaining and Warrington clinging to an unexpected 5–0 lead, he scored in the corner despite being tackled. It was not a straightforward decision for referee Jimmy May as the winger—given the ball by Harold Wagstaff after he, in turn, received it from Ben Gronow following a 'wheeled' scrum—knocked the corner flag over. After consulting a touch-judge the official indicated the try. With Huddersfield now dominating the forward battle, their skilful backs found space to display their artistry, Warrington taking a calculated risk by withdrawing Jack Chesters from the pack to assist their harassed backs.

But the Lancashire side's luck was out when Huddersfield's Duggie Clark was placed onside after the ball rebounded towards him from a Warrington player, the forward picking up and passing to Moorhouse, who obliged with his second touchdown to put his team one point ahead. His concluding try—equalling the Challenge Cup Final record—resulted from a break by Tommy Gleeson who sent Major Holland racing across the field where he transferred the ball to Wagstaff. In a mesmerising passage of play, the centre passed to Moorhouse who sent it back inside, Wagstaff returning the compliment to send Moorhouse racing over in the corner. With Holland missing the first two conversions, Fred Longstaff faring no better with the third, difficult shot, Huddersfield leading 9–5. As the minutes ticked away, Warrington tried unsuccessfully to rally, Jim Fearnley almost breaking through but Gleeson bringing him down. When the Wires strayed offside, Longstaff missed a late penalty attempt.

Hot favourites Huddersfield found Warrington a handful in the opening half, the Wires forwards subduing the Yorkshire side's pack, denying their danger men the chance to become too involved. Bert Bradshaw had an early opportunity to score for Warrington but Clark pushed him into touch two yards from the try-line. Then, from a scrum near Warrington's line, Clark appeared to get over for a touchdown, but the ball was ruled to have gone dead. A foul by Huddersfield's Jim Davies on Jim Dainteth resulted in the latter being carried off, although he soon returned, Warrington's Bert Renwick falling short with the resulting penalty attempt. Then Wagstaff and Gleeson created an opening but, on this occasion, Moorhouse dropped the latter's pass. Warrington took a 25th minute lead when Syd Nicholas, from a scrum, transferred the ball to Dainteth who handed on to Jimmy Tranter, Bradshaw being the next recipient, arcing around Moorhouse for the try despite Holland's tackle. Ben Jolley added the extras and, with end-to-end kicking dominating the remainder of the half, Warrington led 5–0 at the interval.

Huddersfield took control in the second half, their speedsters making inroads into Warrington's defence.

Stanley Moorhouse—scored all Huddersfield's points through three excellent tries

Albert Rosenfeld looked set to score but was apprehended at the last moment and then a dazzling run from a scrum by Tommy Grey saw him beat three opponents before being tackled. From the ensuing play, the ball found its way to Moorhouse who kicked to the in-goal before diving on it. The referee, though, ruled the ball dead, but his moment of glory was minutes away.

Huddersfield—without centre Edgar Wrigley who injured his knee 17 days earlier—were the first to win the Challenge Cup without playing a home tie. They achieved their reward after a final described by the *Huddersfield Examiner* as 'one of the most strenuous games ever fought under the Northern Union code.'

STATS

Huddersfield 9 Warrington 5

Saturday 26 April at Headingley, Leeds (3.30 pm)

Huddersfield (claret and gold hoops): Holland, Rosenfeld, Gleeson, Wagstaff (captain), Moorhouse, Davies, Grey, Clark, Chilcott, Gronow, Higson, Lee, Longstaff. Trainer: A. Bennett

Warrington (primrose and blue hoops): Jolley, Brooks, Renwick (captain), Tranter, Bradshaw, Dainteth, Nicholas, G. Thomas, Chesters, Skelhorne, Fearnley, R. Thomas, Cox. Trainer: I. Hackett

Referee: J.F. May   Touch-judges: W.O. Smart, J. McGowan

Half-time: 0–5   Attendance: 22,754   Receipts: £1,446

Weather: mostly heavy rain, windy

Cup presentation: Mr A. Sherwell, MP for Huddersfield

Progressive score:

Huddersfield	score (min)	Warrington
	0–5 (25)	Bradshaw try, Jolley goal
Moorhouse try	3–5 (50)	
Moorhouse try	6–5 (66)	
Moorhouse try	9–5 (75)	

Route to the final:

First round:
St Helens 0 Huddersfield 19, Keighley 0 Warrington 8

Second round: Batley 2 Huddersfield 8, Warrington 13 Hull Kingston Rovers 6

Third round:
Wigan 5 Huddersfield 14, Salford 4 Warrington 7

Semi-finals: Huddersfield 35 Wakefield Trinity 2 (Thrum Hall, Halifax, 22,000), Warrington 17 Dewsbury 5 (Watersheddings, Oldham, 15,000)

Head-to-head form guide:

Huddersfield 18 Warrington 3 (League)

Warrington 6 Huddersfield 21 (League)

1914 NORTHERN UNION CHALLENGE CUP FINAL
Hull v Wakefield Trinity

At the fourth time of asking Hull finally got their hands on the Northern Union Challenge Cup, defeating Wakefield Trinity 6–0 in the 1914 finale at Thrum Hall, Halifax, with a sensational two-try blitz in the closing minutes. The hero of the hour for Hull was undoubtedly legendary centre Billy Batten who was a constant thorn in the side of Wakefield, particularly during the second half. With the match still scoreless, he made the critical opening just four minutes from the end, supplying his wingman Jack Harrison with the vital pass to go over at the corner and break Wakefield hearts. Having done his job, and in true 'Boys Own' style, he was carried from the field, moments from the end, with an injured knee, colleague Alf Francis then adding a last-second try off a Bert Gilbert pass to rubber-stamp their triumph, Ned Rogers missing both conversions.

Wakefield's fate seemed destined in the opening stages when nothing went right for them. A brilliant cross-field kick from their centre Tommy Poynton put B. Johnson in the clear only for the wing to trip, enabling Francis to tackle him and this was followed by a trio of poor drop-goal attempts from Jonty Parkin, Billie Lynch and Leonard Land and a woeful penalty

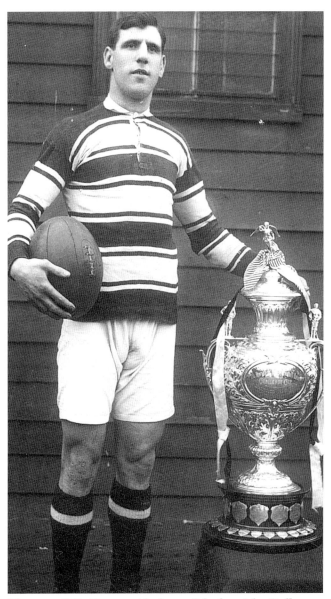

The great Billy Batten—'the hero of the hour' for Hull

strike by William Beattie. Hull produced the first worthwhile move of the match when Billy Anderson passed to Gilbert, the ball continuing through Steve Darmody, Jimmy Devereux and Batten to reach Harrison, although a try was not forthcoming on that occasion. Another scoring chance was presented to the Boulevard outfit when Gilbert charged down Poynton's kick and sped away with the ball, drawing full back Land before passing to the supporting Dick Taylor, the forward being overhauled with the line in

WINNING CAPTAIN

Bert Gilbert (Hull 1914)

Australian Test centre Bert Gilbert—known as 'Herb' in his homeland—was a major signing for Hull in 1912, joining the Humberside club at the conclusion of the 1911/12 Kangaroos tour of England and Wales. The powerfully built three-quarter, who cost a then world record £450 fee, was a product of Souths rugby union club (Sydney) and represented his country in three rugby union Tests against the All Blacks in 1910. Switching codes, he played 13-a-side for South Sydney in 1911 and 1912. His time in England—during which he won the Northern Union Challenge Cup in 1914—was cut short by the outbreak of the First World War, his last match for Hull being in 1915. Returning home he again played for South Sydney (1915) followed by Eastern Suburbs (1916), Western Suburbs (1917–20) and St George (1921), being player-coach at the latter. He made seven Test appearances for Australia and represented New South Wales three times. In addition to the aforementioned United Kingdom tour he was in Australia's party to New Zealand in 1919.

his sights. At the opposite end, Trinity's Bruce Howarth charged down Rogers' kick but Herbert Kershaw spoilt the try-scoring chance with a knock-on. As half-time drew near Harrison broke away down the flank but was eventually pushed into touch, Rogers and W. Millican then missing with goal attempts—both from marks—for Hull and Wakefield respectively.

At the commencement of the second period, Batten raced halfway down the field but when he tried to leap over Land, the Trinity player produced a wonderful try-saving tackle. Disaster hit Wakefield four minutes later when captain Kershaw was dismissed by referee Jimmy May, touch-judge G. Fowler reporting him for kicking Francis during a tackle. Batten went on another exciting run, weaving his way past defenders only for his pass to go astray. Wakefield's five remaining forwards, meanwhile, were putting on a brave show, Beattie missing with a penalty that could have raised their spirits further. But Hull sensed victory; Harrison went close before being pushed into touch at the last moment following a sensational run from Joe Hamill who evaded several would-be tacklers and, moments later, Rogers was wide with a drop-goal. Next up, Taylor crossed the whitewash for a touchdown claim, but a forward pass was the referee's verdict and then Francis was stopped a yard short following another burst from Batten.

After Harrison's break-through try, Poynton joined Batten on the sidelines with an injury, the match finishing with Hull's 12 men opposing Wakefield's 11. *Hull Daily Mail* writer 'Orion' said: 'Without the slightest hesitation, I say Batten won Hull the coveted trophy. The mastermind was ever working.' The outcome reversed the 1909 result between the two clubs, Hull's Australian captain Gilbert becoming the first overseas player to receive the trophy.

STATS

Hull 6 Wakefield Trinity 0

Saturday 18 April at Thrum Hall, Halifax (3.30 pm)

Hull (black and white irregular hoops): E. Rogers, Harrison, Batten, Gilbert (captain), Francis, Devereux, Anderson, Herridge, Holder, R. Taylor, Hammill, Grice, Darmody. Trainer: S. Melville

Wakefield Trinity (blue with red band): Land, Johnson, Lynch, Poynton, Howarth, J. Parkin, Millican, Dixon, Crosland, Beattie, Kershaw (captain), E. Parkin, Burton. Trainer: unknown

Referee: J.F. May
Touch-judges: J.E. Greenwood, G. Fowler

Half-time: 0–0   Attendance: 19,000   Receipts: £1,035

Weather: sunny and windy

Cup presentation: Alderman W.H. Ingham, Mayor of Halifax

Progressive score:

Hull	score (min)	Wakefield Trinity
Harrison try	3–0 (76)	
Francis try	6–0 (80)	

Route to the final:

First round: Hull 8 Salford 5, Wakefield T 2 Swinton 0
Second round:
Featherstone Rovers 3 Hull 27, Wakefield T 9 Leeds 8
Third round: Halifax 0 Hull 13, Wakefield T 9 Wigan 6
Semi-finals:
Hull 11 Huddersfield 3 (Headingley, Leeds, 30,000),
Wakefield T 3 Broughton R 3 (The Athletic Grounds, Rochdale, 10,000)
Semi-final replay:
Wakefield T 5 Broughton R 0 (Fartown, Huddersfield, 7,656)

Head-to-head form guide:

Wakefield Trinity 8 Hull 0 (Yorkshire Cup)
Wakefield Trinity 4 Hull 9 (League)
Hull 18 Wakefield Trinity 5 (League)

It's ours at last! Hull with the Challenge Cup in 1914, standing: Milner, Darmody, Hammill, R. Taylor, Herridge, Holder, Oldham, Melville (trainer). Seated: Devereux, Anderson, Gilbert, Batten, E. Rogers, Harrison. On ground: Francis, G. Rogers

Graham Morris

1915 NORTHERN UNION CHALLENGE CUP FINAL
Huddersfield v St Helens

Huddersfield—possessors of four major trophies! Standing: A. Bennett (trainer), Lee, Higson, Banks, Jones, Heyes, Longstaff, Clark, Swinden, H. Bennett (asst. trainer). Seated: Habron, Holland, Moorhouse, Wagstaff, Gleeson, Todd, Gronow. On ground: Ganley, Rosenfeld, Rogers

Huddersfield won the 1915 Challenge Cup competition to complete a clean sweep of the four major trophies open to them, thereby emulating Hunslet's achievement seven years earlier. Their comprehensive 37–3 victory over St Helens proved beyond doubt they were the code's top combination, coming one week after an equally emphatic 35–2 score-line against Leeds in the Championship Final. In the opening quarter underdogs St Helens, for whom forward Harry Heaton was a late withdrawal after being taken ill, gave as good as they got. But, once the Yorkshire side got their second try on 23 minutes, the rout began as their backs put on a virtuoso performance, the *St Helens Reporter*, in their match report, being moved to comment: 'What was that? A streak of lightening? No, just Huddersfield's backs on the move.'

The match had an unusual start when the ball burst as St Helens' full back Bert Roberts tackled Huddersfield's Stanley Moorhouse. Soon afterwards, crisp passing by Huddersfield led to Tommy Gleeson claiming the opening score, using his wingman Albert Rosenfeld as a foil to dart over. For the next 20 minutes both teams scorned scoring chances, including the usually reliable Harold Wagstaff who spilt a Gleeson pass with a clear path ahead of him. The Huddersfield skipper made amends by obtaining the second try when, having received the ball from Bert Ganley, he exchanged passes with Moorhouse before going behind the posts. The try came against a 12-man St Helens, Roberts having departed for attention shortly before, although he soon returned.

Huddersfield were on a roll, three more tries following before half-time from Rosenfeld (after quick handling by Ben Gronow, Johnny Rogers, Wagstaff and Gleeson), Wagstaff (Rosenfeld, Ganley and Rogers combining to work the opening) and Gleeson (following an excellent break by Moorhouse). St Helens could have broken their 'duck' after 32 minutes, but William Myers failed to retain possession with the Huddersfield try-line open.

The Fartowners continued in the same vein after the interval, Rosenfeld running the ball deep into St Helens territory, Major Holland linking up to take his pass and outmanoeuvre Tom Barton and Matt Creevey to score. Huddersfield were completely in command, missing as many opportunities as they were taking. Eventually they

47

added three further tries in a 12-minute burst through Moorhouse (off Wagstaff's pass to end another polished move), Gronow (breaking away from a scrum outside St Helens' 25-yard line and exchanging passes with Fred Longstaff), and Rogers (racing from halfway to go under the posts following another sizzling raid). Finally St

Ben Gronow contributed 13 points to Huddersfield's score

Albert Rosenfeld's try was his 55th of the season for Huddersfield

STATS

Huddersfield 37 St Helens 3

Saturday 1 May at Watersheddings, Oldham (3.30 pm)

Huddersfield (claret with narrow gold hoops): Holland, Rosenfeld, Gleeson, Wagstaff (captain), Moorhouse, Rogers, Ganley, Banks, Clark, Gronow, Higson, Lee, Longstaff. Trainer: A. Bennett

St Helens (blue and white hoops): Roberts, Barton (captain), Flanagan, White, Greenall, Trenwith, Creevey, Daniels, Durkin, Farrimond, Myers, Jackson, Shallcross. Trainer: A. Glover

Referee: R. Robinson   Touch-judges: F. Mills, A. Roscoe

Half-time: 21–0   Attendance: 8,000   Receipts: £472

Weather: rain and strong wind, ground slippery

Cup presentation: Mr J.H. Smith, Northern Union chairman

Progressive score:

Huddersfield	score (min)	St Helens
Gleeson try	3–0 (3)	
Wagstaff try, Gronow goal	8–0 (23)	
Rosenfeld try, Gronow goal	13–0 (29)	
Wagstaff try	16–0 (31)	
Gleeson try, Gronow goal	21–0 (35)	
Holland try	24–0 (43)	
Moorhouse try, Gronow	29–0 (60)	
Gronow try, Gronow goal	34–0 (66)	
Rogers try	37–0 (71)	
	37–3 (74)	Daniels try

Route to the final:

First round:
Leigh 0 Huddersfield 3, Featherstone Rovers 0 St Helens 6

Second round:
Widnes 3 Huddersfield 29, Swinton 0 St Helens 5

Third round:
Huddersfield 33 Salford 0, Keighley 2 St Helens 3

Semi-finals:
Huddersfield 27 Wigan 2 (Parkside, Hunslet, 18,000),
St Helens 5 Rochdale Hornets 5 (Wilderspool, Warrington, 10,000)

Semi-final replay:
St Helens 9 Rochdale Hornets 2 (Central Park, Wigan, 10,000)

Head-to-head form guide:

No previous meetings during season

Helens—who had lost Tom Durkin through a rib injury—registered a try to conclude the scoring, Sam Daniels crossing the whitewash following a scrum near Huddersfield's line, Barton missing the kick.

Gronow, who succeeded with five of his nine conversion attempts, brought his season's tally to 136 goals for the season, a new record for the code, surpassing colleague Holland who notched 131 in the previous campaign.

THE FIRST WORLD WAR

Great Britain declared war on Germany on 4 August 1914 as the First World War escalated. Seven days later, the Northern Union committee, like other sporting bodies, including the Football League, decided to go ahead with the 1914/15 season (which began in September), the popular view being the war would be a brief affair. Those thoughts diminished as the scale and horror of the conflict intensified and, at the Northern Union's Annual General Meeting on 8 June 1915, their chairman J.H. (Jack) Smith declared: 'The time has arrived when all the forces of the nation should be concentrated on the defeat of the enemy.' The code suspended competitive play 'for the duration of the war' with only friendly matches without pay, excepting expenses, allowed. Conscription was introduced in January 1916 and many Northern Union players were called to arms. Not all of them survived, two of the 1915 Challenge Cup finalists, Fred Longstaff (Huddersfield) and Jimmy Flanagan (St Helens), losing their lives in France during July 1916 and May 1918, respectively. Peace returned in November 1918, the Challenge Cup resuming in 1920.

1920 NORTHERN UNION CHALLENGE CUP FINAL
Huddersfield v Wigan

Following an enforced five-year break due to the First World War, the Challenge Cup competition resumed, Huddersfield picking up from where they had left off with another convincing victory in the final, this time by 21–10 over Wigan. In truth, the score-line was deceptive as the Cherry and Whites were competitive for most of the encounter, and led 13 minutes from the end before the Fartowners cut loose with three irresistible tries to retain their prize. Just as the map of Europe had changed in the interim so, inevitably, had the personnel at many clubs, although Huddersfield still lined up with six of the players that overcame St Helens in 1915. It could have been eight had wingers Albert Rosenfeld (George Todd being 'preferred' to the 34-year-old) and Stanley Moorhouse (who broke an arm two months earlier) also played. Another absentee was their ex-Wigan full back Gwyn Thomas after spraining his leg during training. For Wigan, centre Bert Jenkins, with a hand injury, made way for Frank Prescott.

Unfortunately the weather was poor, the dull, damp day being blamed for the 'disappointing' 14,000 attendance. Continual rain turned the playing surface into a mud heap and it soon became difficult to distinguish the jerseys, the colours 'running' in some cases. Nonetheless, the predicted forward slog did not materialise with both packs prepared to employ their backs, who moved the ball about frequently despite the conditions, the *Huddersfield Daily Examiner* noting that 'rarely have players faced difficulties in such a resolute manner'.

Huddersfield were first to attack and players were soon 'sliding about' on the 'greasy surface' but Wigan, as they would until midway through the second half, defended resolutely. Ben Gronow missed a drop-goal for Huddersfield (the ball hardly lifting), Bill Jolley failing with a penalty at the opposite end. Meanwhile, Wigan's Harry Hall took a

severe blow on his nose and was absent for seven minutes. His luck changed when he was awarded a controversial penalty-try, the *Wigan Observer* correspondent acknowledging 'the referee was rather kind to Wigan'. It occurred when Hall kicked the ball towards the in-goal over Johnny Rogers' head, but was brought down by Hubert Pogson as he pursued it, Huddersfield arguing both Major Holland and Harold Wagstaff were closer to the try-line. Jolley added the goal and Wigan led 5–0.

Eight minutes later Huddersfield were level when a Rogers break, continued by Pogson

Sid Jerram put Wigan ahead with his second half touchdown

and Wagstaff, led to a Duggie Clark try by the posts, Gronow converting. The Fartowners continued to apply pressure, Rogers, Robert Habron, Tommy Gleeson and Wagstaff combining to get Pogson over in the corner, Gronow being just wide with his goal attempt, the Yorkshire side leading 8–5 at the break.

Huddersfield looked dangerous at the beginning of the second half, creating several close calls. But it was Wigan—with 19 minutes left—that got the next try, Ernie Shaw taking possession and kicking into the corner where Sid Jerram beat Pogson to the touch. Jolley's difficult kick just curled inside the near upright giving Wigan an unexpected 10–8 lead. Wigan, though, were tiring and, with George Hesketh limping badly following a knock to the knee (Danny Hurcombe eventually moving to stand-off), Huddersfield dominated the remainder of the match. Rogers was held close to Wigan's try-line and, from a scrum moments later, he got the ball out to Habron who shot over in the corner. Gronow was just wide with the kick but, at 11–10, Huddersfield had regained the lead. Disaster followed for Wigan when Vince Smith tried to boot the ball away, only for Todd to charge it down and go over for another try, Gronow augmenting. Tom Fenwick then crossed the whitewash for Huddersfield

but lost possession in attempting to get closer to the posts and then, with three minutes remaining, Pogson got custody, brushing aside four defenders on his way to the touchdown. Gronow added the goal to complete the scoring.

The *Wigan Examiner* endorsed Huddersfield's success, saying they were 'speedier, bigger and cleverer than the Wiganers'. Wagstaff, a doubtful starter after spending three days ill in bed during the week, became the first to captain three Challenge Cup winning teams.

Huddersfield centre Harold Wagstaff became the first player to captain three Challenge Cup winning sides

---

STATS

Huddersfield 21 Wigan 10

Saturday 10 April at Headingley, Leeds (3.30 pm)

Huddersfield: Holland, Todd, Gleeson, Wagstaff (captain), Pogson, Rogers, Habron, Swinden, Sherwood, Gronow, Fenwick, Naylor, Clark. Trainer: unknown

Wigan: Jolley, Smith, F. Prescott, Hurcombe, Hall, Hesketh, Jerram, Ramsdale, Lowe, Shaw, Coldrick, T. Prescott, Seeling (captain). Trainer: T. McCarty

Referee: F. Mills   Touch-judges: J.C. Lumley, J. Speight

Half-time: 8–5 Attendance: 14,000 Receipts: £1,936

Weather: overcast with frequent showers, ground muddy

Cup presentation: Mr J.H. Smith, Northern Union chairman

Progressive score:

Huddersfield	score (min)	Wigan
	0–5 (26)	Hall penalty-try, Jolley goal
Clark try, Gronow goal	5–5 (34)	
Pogson try	8–5 (37)	
	8–10 (61)	Jerram try, Jolley goal
Habron try	11–10 (67)	
Todd try, Gronow goal	16–10 (72)	
Pogson try, Gronow goal	21–10 (77)	

Route to the final:

First round: Huddersfield 19 Swinton 0, Wigan 64 Healey Street Adults (Oldham) 3

Second round: Wakefield Trinity 2 Huddersfield 3, Wigan 35 York 5

Third round: Huddersfield 2 St Helens Recreation 2, Bramley 0 Wigan 10

Third round replay: St Helens Recreation 6 Huddersfield 8

Semi-finals: Huddersfield 17 Oldham 0 (Thrum Hall, Halifax, 20,000), Wigan 12 Hull 5 (The Willows, Salford, 22,000)

Head-to-head form guide:

Huddersfield 12 Wigan 8 (League)

Wigan 12 Huddersfield 8 (League)

1921 NORTHERN UNION CHALLENGE CUP FINAL
Leigh v Halifax

The small Lancashire coal-mining town of Leigh celebrated its moment of glory in 1921 when their team upset favourites Halifax 13–0 to win the Challenge Cup. It was an unexpected triumph for Leigh, so often in the shadows of near-neighbours Wigan and placed 20th in the League that season, against a team 17 positions higher in the table. Their route to the final opened up after a surprise 8–3 second round replay win at Warrington, watched by 19,364. Despite a miners' strike over pay, the *Leigh Journal* said local 'cup-tie fever was infectious' with just about every mode of transport including 'shank's pony' (walking in other words) conveying supporters to the match.

The venue—Broughton Rangers' ground at The Cliff—had recently enhanced its accommodation, club officials claiming a 35,000 capacity, a 'big application' for tickets being made. Although almost 50 police officers—many mounted—were on duty, two gates were forced open, 'hundreds' gaining free entry, others breaking down crush barriers and perimeter boarding.

Full back Tom Clarkson landed two goals for Leigh

STATS

Leigh 13 Halifax 0

Saturday 30 April at The Cliff, Broughton (3.30 pm)

Leigh (cherry and white hoops): Clarkson, Hurst, Heaton, Thomas, Braund, Parkinson, Mooney (captain), Winstanley, Cartwright, J. Prosser, Darwell, Coffey, Boardman. Trainer: J. Briscoe

Halifax (blue and white hoops): Garforth (captain), Turnbull, Akroyd, Stacey, Todd, Lloyd, S. Prosser, Gibson, Milnes, Broadbent, Beames, Whiteley, Schofield. Trainer: unknown

Referee: F. Renton   Touch-judges: F. Mills, A. Brown

Half-time: 11–0 Attendance: 25,000 Receipts: £2,700

Weather: sunny and hot

Cup presentation:
Mrs W. Fillan, wife of Northern Union chairman

Progressive score:

Leigh	score (min)	Halifax
Thomas try	3–0 (10)	
Parkinson try, Clarkson goal	8–0 (14)	
Thomas try	11–0 (33)	
Clarkson penalty	13–0 (65)	

Route to the final:

First round: Leigh 0 York 0, Halifax 5 Batley 0

First round replay: York 0 Leigh 3

Second round: Leigh 10 Warrington 10, Bramley 4 Halifax 13

Second round replay: Warrington 3 Leigh 8

Third round:
Leigh 7 Bradford Northern 0, Halifax 5 Widnes 2

Semi-finals: Leigh 10 Rochdale Hornets 0 (Central Park, Wigan, 20,000),

Halifax 2 Huddersfield 0 (Headingley, Leeds, 23,500)

Head-to-head form guide:

Leigh 5 Halifax 3 (League)

Halifax 11 Leigh 0 (League)

Leigh were without Welsh centre Wyndham Emery (shoulder injury), Halifax minus veteran forward and captain, Asa Robinson (broken collarbone), both succumbing earlier that month.

Opening play saw several goal attempts; Tom Clarkson (Leigh) and Clem Garforth (Halifax) missing penalties, Cyril Braund's drop-goal effort for Leigh going wide. But it did not take long for Leigh to claim the first score, captain Walt Mooney, having gained possession from a scrum, passing to centre Emlyn Thomas who turned inside three defenders to go behind the posts after just 10 minutes. Surprisingly Clarkson just missed the goal. Leigh had their tails up and, a few minutes later, forced a scrum five yards from Halifax's try-line. Mooney—later described as 'the hero of the afternoon'—again got the ball quickly away, finding halfback colleague Billy Parkinson who raced towards the left before cutting inside an opponent for a 'gem of a try'. Clarkson atoned for his earlier misses, landing the tricky conversion for an 8–0 lead. Shortly afterwards, he was injured when tackled into touch, resuming after several minutes off-field attention.

Thomas, having arrested Cyril Stacey on the try-line when the Halifax centre looked set to score, was Leigh's champion again five minutes later when the ball ricocheted off his knees to frustrate Garforth's clearance kick. As the ball rebounded towards the Halifax in-goal, Thomas picked it up and placed it over the line for another try with two opponents clinging on, Clarkson being just wide with the goal. A few minutes before half-time Braund and Thomas broke away down the left, the chance being lost when the latter dropped the ball.

Immediately after the interval, Halifax centre Albert Akroyd tried to revive his team, almost scoring but for a desperate tackle from Peter Heaton, and then, two minutes later, attempting a drop-goal, although it hardly rose above pitch level. Further drop-goal efforts from Clarkson and Jim Winstanley for Leigh also proved unsuccessful. The former—having almost scored a try two minutes earlier—eventually landed an excellent penalty for the only score of the half after Parkinson was obstructed. The Yorkshire side tried to get back into it with some adventurous passing, Akroyd again being hauled up short of the whitewash, but Leigh stood firm.

Following what was generally considered a memorable match, Northern Union chairman Mr W. Fillan—whose wife presented the trophy—declared afterwards 'you get a better game with two teams from different counties'.

BROUGHTON RANGERS FOOTBALL CLUB CO., LIMITED.

Northern Union Challenge Cup,

HALIFAX v. LEIGH,

FINAL TIE.

Referee - Mr. F. RENTON, Hunslet.

Linesmen - {Mr. F. MILLS, Oldham.
{Mr. A. BROWN, Wakefield.

OFFICIAL PROGRAMME,

TWOPENCE.

BESSES-O'TH'-BARN BAND IN ATTENDANCE.

A. & S. WALKER LTD., MANCHESTER.

WINNING CAPTAIN

Walt Mooney (Leigh 1921)

Scrum half Walt Mooney made 207 appearances for Leigh before a knee injury forced him to quit in 1926. Most of that tally was logged up during the 1920s, the stocky scrum half who at 5 feet 5 inches was described as 'powerful and untiring', managing just 12 outings prior to the First World War. Originating from nearby Hindsford, he played soccer for local St James' Sunday School when he was 15, before turning to the 13-a-side game with Tyldesley Emmets. He joined Leigh, making his debut in 1912, but unable to retain his first team place returned to the amateur ranks with Wardley Rangers. During the First World War he made guest appearances for Broughton Rangers and Bradford Northern, resuming with Leigh in 1919 after hostilities ended. Appointed captain he led them to victory in the Northern Union Challenge Cup (1921) and runners-up slot in the Lancashire Cup (1922). He appeared in two Test matches (both against New Zealand with the 1924 tourists) and played twice for Lancashire (both in 1919—plus a wartime match in 1918 against Yorkshire).

Graham Morris

1922 NORTHERN UNION CHALLENGE CUP FINAL
Rochdale Hornets v Hull

Rochdale Hornets 1922, standing: Bennett, Carter, Jones, J. Corsi, Woods. Paddon, Powell, Edwards, L. Corsi. Seated: Harris, Fitton, Kynan, McLoughlin, Wild, Prescott, Heaton. Trainer Hodgkinson (wearing hat) is at the back, right, his assistant Barker (cap) on the left

Rochdale Hornets won the Challenge Cup in 1922 for the only time in their history after an exhilarating contest with Hull, that was then rated by many pundits as the best final so far. Played at a furious pace before 34,827 spectators—reportedly the most to date for the code in Britain—the Lancashire side triumphed 10–9 after hanging on during a nerve-racking last 10 minutes. The *Hull Daily Mail* claimed 'a more exciting match would be difficult to imagine' adding 'the closing stages of the game beggared description, the excitement being intense.' Rochdale were without their international halfback Ernest Jones due to a thigh injury, whilst, for Hull supporters, news that star three-quarter Billy Batten had been declared fit created 'great rejoicing' inside the ground, although an 'unsound' Ned Rogers had to be replaced at full back by Jack Holdsworth.

Rochdale had an early opportunity to settle any nerves when Tommy Woods charged down Batten's kick near Hull's try-line, but a great chance was lost through a subsequent knock-on. Hull then began attacking with vigour; Eddie Caswell was apprehended by Dai Edwards as he attempted to cross the try-line,

and William Charles actually got over the whitewash but dropped the ball. But the Boulevard team eventually posted the opening points in the eighth minute after Jim Kennedy charged down Jack Heaton's clearance kick. The ball rebounded towards Rochdale's in-goal area, Kennedy getting the touch just before it rolled dead, although his follow-up conversion attempt struck the crossbar.

The Hornets hit back inside 10 minutes to take a 4–3 lead through two penalty goals from Dicky Paddon, the first following an indiscretion during a tackle on Dicky Kynan near the touchline, the second for a foul on Eddie McLoughlin by Jack Beasty. Between those efforts, Paddon could have increased his goal count, missing three attempts; two from penalties, another from a mark (that was charged down) after Tommy Harris fielded Holdsworth's clearance in front of Hull's goal.

An invigorated Hornets seemed unstoppable at this point and, after a forward rush was halted near Hull's try-line by Holdsworth, Louis Corsi took possession and made a charge for glory. Although held up he somehow squeezed the ball out to Tommy Fitton, who waltzed past Billy Stone and Batten before diving over the try-line. Paddon's goal attempt was just wide. The match was unfolding as a 'thriller' as Hull rallied and play was end-to-end. The Airlie Birds almost scored when Stone cut inside and passed to Edgar Morgan, the forward showing great pace before Hughie Wild saved the day for Rochdale with a superb tackle.

Stone was again involved when he roared down the touchline and, arrested by Fitton, managed to off-load with an inside ball to Batten 10 yards from Hornets' try-line. As Frank Prescott dived low to make the tackle, Batten produced his famous leap, going over the full back and planting the ball down for a try near the corner. Rochdale's players argued the centre had gone into touch but, after consulting a touch-judge, the referee confirmed the score. Kennedy missed the goal to trail 7–6. Rochdale tried unsuccessfully to extend their slender lead before the break; Louis Corsi was tackled on the try-line, Kynan had a try disallowed, and Paddon missed a drop-goal from a mark he made himself.

Excitement was at 'fever pitch' as the match recommenced after the break, Hull beginning with a determined assault by their powerful pack, Kynan being forced to save his line as Charles blasted his way through. At the other end, Joe Corsi's touchline run was ended by Stone's tackle when he looked like scoring and, in another burst, the same player beat four men before sending brother Louis away, the latter eventually being forced into touch.

WINNING CAPTAIN

Jack Bennett (Rochdale Hornets 1922)

Versatile hooker Jack Bennett joined Rochdale Hornets as an 18-year-old in 1912 for a reported £10 signing-on fee from Wigan based amateurs Pemberton Rovers. As captain, he had led the Rovers to four trophies during 1911/12, having previously played for the exotically named Wigan Maoris club. Due to travelling restrictions imposed through the intervention of the First World War it was January 1919 before he made his senior debut for Rochdale, appearing meantime as a guest in 41 wartime friendly fixtures for Wigan, his first in March 1917. At Rochdale, his ability as a ball-distributor and dribbler in loose play contributed to one of Hornets' most productive periods, winning the Lancashire Cup (1919) and Lancashire League (1918/19). Appointed captain, he subsequently led them to Challenge Cup success in 1922. After 229 matches for Hornets he transferred to hometown Wigan during 1925, winning the Challenge Cup (1929), Championship (1925/26), Lancashire Cup (1928) and Lancashire League (1925/26). Following 210 matches with Wigan, he returned to Rochdale, playing seven times during 1931. A tourist in 1924, he appeared in seven Tests and represented England (4 times) and Lancashire (8).

Both teams were creating half-chances. For Hull, Batten attempted to drive his way over from 'close quarters' and Bob Taylor made 'one of his famous charges' before Louis Corsi brought him down. Then Kennedy intercepted a Joe Corsi pass before transferring to Morgan who roared towards the corner, Prescott forcing him into touch. Rochdale almost scored when a charge by the forwards nearly got, first, Edwards, and then, Jack Bennett in, both being tackled on the line. The breakthrough for the Hornets occurred in the 63rd minute when, from a scrum near Hull's try-line, Heaton got the ball and quick hands saw it transported through Kynan and Wild to Fitton who then sidestepped Kennedy before diving spectacularly over in the corner for his second try. The *Rochdale Observer* said 'Fitton and his colleagues went delirious with joy', Paddon's goal attempt hitting a post below crossbar level, the Hornets stretching their lead to 10–6.

Hull's skipper Billy Stone

Jack Bennett—the only Rochdale Hornets captain to lift the Challenge Cup

But it was not over! In the 70th minute Hull's Taylor and Pete Garrett broke away on a dribbling run, Kynan managing to cover the ball only for Caswell to retrieve it and send Taylor over at the corner. Kennedy—having missed a penalty midway through the second half—was off-target with the conversion. Down by just one point, Hull exerted tremendous pressure on the Hornets defence as the remaining minutes ticked away but, somehow, the Lancashire side held on much to the relief and delight of their chairman, J.R. Hartley. He confessed afterwards that 'during the last ten minutes of the game, I may say I, along with hundreds of others, was in a state of great perspiration.'

STATS

Rochdale Hornets 10 Hull 9

Saturday 29 April at Headingley, Leeds (3.30 pm)

Rochdale Hornets (white with alternate red and blue hoops): Prescott, Fitton, Wild, McLoughlin, J. Corsi, Kynan, Heaton, Harris, Bennett (captain), Paddon, Woods, Edwards, L. Corsi. Trainer: J. Hodgkinson

Hull (black and white irregular hoops): Holdsworth, Stone (captain), Kennedy, Batten, Gwynne, Caswell, Charles, Beasty, Oliver, Wyburn, Morgan, Taylor, Garrett. Trainer: S. Melville

Referee: R. Jones   Touch-judges: W. Bogg, A. Hestford

Half-time: 7-6   Attendance: 34,827   Receipts: £2,964

Weather: sunny with cool wind

Cup presentation: Mrs W. Fillan, wife of Northern Union chairman

Progressive score:

Rochdale Hornets	score (min)	Hull
	0-3 (8)	Kennedy try
Paddon penalty	2-3 (10)	
Paddon penalty	4-3 (18)	
Fitton try	7-3 (20)	
	7-6 (30)	Batten try
Fitton try	10-6 (63)	
	10-9 (70)	Taylor try

Route to the final:

First round: Rochdale H 54 Broughton Moor (Cumberland) 2, Hull 24 Halifax 10

Second round: Rochdale H 15 Leeds 7, Hull Kingston Rovers 0 Hull 10

Third round: Rochdale H 5 Oldham 2, Dewsbury 4 Hull 9

Semi-finals: Rochdale H 23 Widnes 3 (The Willows, Salford, 10,000),

Hull 18 Wigan 5 (Headingley, Leeds, 16, 685)

Head-to-head form guide:

No previous meetings during season

MARKS AND DRIBBLES!

Some of the earlier match descriptions in this compilation refer to 'marks' and forward 'dribbles' (or 'rushes'), both unfamiliar to the modern game. A mark was a practice whereby a player 'marked' the spot on the ground with his heel after catching the ball on the full from an opponent's kick. It allowed his side a 'free kick', although attempts at kicking a goal from a mark were outlawed after the 1921/22 season. The art of dribbling was once a prominent feature of forward play, the pack—usually breaking from a scrum—charging at their opposition as a unit with the ball at their feet.

1923 RUGBY LEAGUE CHALLENGE CUP FINAL
Leeds v Hull

After a 13-year gap, Leeds acclaimed a second Challenge Cup success, their victims again being Hull. Whereas the Headingley side required a replay to overcome their East Yorkshire rivals in the 1910 decider, they found the task much easier in 1923,

STATS

Leeds 28 Hull 3

Saturday 28 April at Belle Vue, Wakefield (3.30 pm)

Leeds (white): Walmsley, Buck, Bowen, Bacon (captain), Lyons, Binks, Brittain, Dixon, Jackson, Trusler, Davis, Thompson, Ashton. Trainer: A. Hannah

Hull (black and white broad hoops): Samuel, Holdsworth, Whitty, Kennedy, Stone (captain), Caswell, Gwynne, Oliver, Bowman, Beasty, Morgan, Taylor, Garrett. Trainer: S. Melville

Referee: F. Mills   Touch-judges: A. Brown, A. Holbrook

Half-time: 10–0 Attendance: 29,335 Receipts: £2,390

Weather: fine and dry, slight breeze

Cup presentation: Mr G. Ellis, MP for Wakefield

Progressive score:

Leeds	score (min)	Hull
Buck try, Thompson goal	5–0 (22)	
Bowen try, Thompson goal	10–0 (35)	
Davis try, Thompson goal	15–0 (60)	
Brittain try, Thompson goal	20–0 (63)	
Ashton try	23–0 (70)	
	23–3 (78)	Kennedy try
Walmsley try, Thompson goal	28–3 (80)	

Route to the final:

First round: Leigh 5 Leeds 11, Broughton Rangers 0 Hull 13

Second round: Leeds 19 Huddersfield 8, Swinton 5 Hull 13

Third round: York 2 Leeds 10, Salford 0 Hull 24

Semi-finals:

Leeds 0 Barrow 0 (The Cliff, Broughton, 11,187),

Hull 13 Wigan 9 (Fartown, Huddersfield, 22,107)

Semi-final replay:

Leeds 10 Barrow 0 (The Willows, Salford, 9,000)

Head-to-head form guide:

Hull 5 Leeds 11 (League)

Leeds 8 Hull 12 (League)

accumulating a comfortable 28–3 score-line. The first final under the title of The Rugby League Challenge Cup and the only one staged at Wakefield Trinity's Belle Vue ground, it was reported every seat was occupied an hour before kick-off as fans eagerly awaited the game. Leeds selected their 'strongest side', but Hull were missing key players in full back Ned Rogers and centre Billy Batten, both through knee injuries.

The opening 15 minutes were reportedly uninspiring, the sides indulging in a 'kicking duel' from one end of the field to the other to gain territory. The only highlights were provided by Hull's Billy Stone, who almost got over for a try in the opening minutes, and Leeds' Arthur Binks, who came close to scoring following a scrum near Hull's line. Joe Thompson was also short with two penalty attempts for the Headingley side. Abandoning their kicking policy, Leeds started opening out play, and were almost rewarded on 21 minutes when Harold Buck claimed a touchdown, but it was wiped out through a forward pass. A minute later, though, another Leeds attack, orchestrated by Binks, saw the ball travel through the hands of Joe Brittain and Billy Bowen before Buck burst through the defence for the opening try, Thompson adding the goal.

Hull tried to respond, Eddie Caswell extracting the ball from Syd Walmsley's hands before dribbling it towards Leeds' try-line. Walmsley recovered the situation, although the Airlie Birds claimed their

Leeds earned their second Challenge Cup success in 1923. Standing: Hannah (trainer), Ashton, Jackson, Dixon, Davis, Trusler, Thompson, Morn (asst. trainer). Seated: Bowen, Walmsley, Bacon, Lyons, Buck. On ground: Brittain, Binks

player was obstructed. A few minutes before half-time Leeds skipper Jim Bacon took the ball to within a few yards of Hull's in-goal before passing to Jack Ashton, the missive finding its way, via Brittain, to Bowen who scored under posts. Thompson's goal made it 10–0 to Leeds at half-time.

Hull were the first to apply pressure after the interval but it soon fizzled out and Bowen had a try for Leeds disallowed due to a forward pass. Then, with an hour played, the Loiners scored again, Bill Davis picking up the ball during loose play before racing through the defence to finish under the posts. Thompson's goal made it 15–0 and, with Leeds growing stronger by the minute and Hull's tackles falling off, three more tries followed through Brittain (racing over from a scrum), Ashton (despite Edgar Morgan's tackle after accepting Buck's inside pass) and Walmsley (in the corner having taken possession in his own half before passing and re-passing with Buck in a thrilling run for the try-line). Excepting Ashton's try (when he struck a post), Thompson added the extra points. Prior to Walmsley's touchdown, Hull earned a

late consolation when Stone picked up a misfielded ball and delivered a scoring pass to Jim Kennedy, the centre failing to convert his own try.

After a day that also generated front page sports news through the huge crowd that 'invaded' Wembley's first ever FA Cup Final, the *Leeds Mercury* concluded 'It is scarcely conceivable that any team could have matched the Leeds spirit on Saturday, but Leeds found fewer difficulties than anyone expected.' It was a disappointing outcome for the Hull fans following the previous year's failure, and marked their side's fifth defeat in six Challenge Cup Finals.

Harold Buck opened the scoring for Leeds

1924 RUGBY LEAGUE CHALLENGE CUP FINAL
Wigan v Oldham

Aside from Wigan winning the competition for the first time following a 21–4 triumph over Oldham, the biggest talking point of the 1924 Challenge Cup Final was the unprecedented crowd scenes. It led to some amazing incidents with players scoring tries at the feet of spectators and Wigan's South African wingman Attie van Heerden registering a touchdown that has since entered rugby league folklore.

Rochdale Hornets' Athletic Grounds, reputed to hold 50,000, was jammed solid with every conceivable vantage point—and many other positions that offered little or no view—taken up. The official paid attendance was reported at 41,831, setting a new British record for rugby league. The interest ahead of the match had been phenomenal with all the grandstand tickets sold within one day. The activity outside the ground in the hours leading to kick-off had barely been witnessed for a rugby league fixture. All roads from places such as Bolton, Oldham and Manchester were heavily congested with cars and coaches, whilst six special trains from Wigan and two

from Oldham also transported supporters. Additionally, there was a huge influx from Yorkshire despite the county not being represented and even visitors from Wales.

Reportedly, several thousand people were locked out whilst other more determined souls clambered over the outside fence. Inside, the crowd began spilling over the surrounding track and on to the pitch. At first it was a trickle as a few, situated in front of a crammed main stand, began climbing over the rails, but it quickly became a 'general invasion' that soon got out of control as five mounted policemen, assisted by ambulance men and officials tried against almost impossible odds to ease the crowd back outside the playing area. The *Wigan Observer* likened it to the previous year's inaugural Wembley FA Cup Final when mounted police faced a similar predicament. Other spectators climbed on top of the stands, one falling 30 feet and severely damaging his ribs but surviving. Reportedly, and miraculously, there were no other casualties. Apart from helping control the crowd,

Wigan's successful 1924 Challenge Cup squad, standing: McCarty (trainer), Coldrick, Hodder, Roffey, Jerram (behind Challenge Cup), van Rooyen, Hurst, Brown, Fishwick (asst. trainer). Seated: van Heerden, Ring, Owens, Parker, Howley, Sullivan, Webster, Banks. Inset: Price (left), Hurcombe (right)

the ambulance men were busy throughout the afternoon dealing with fainting cases.

When the match began, it was difficult for the players to see either the touch or dead-ball lines, the *Wigan Examiner* saying 'it was not an unusual sight to see members of the contesting teams dive amongst the spectators and disappear from view'. One out of the ordinary incident occurred when players collided with a man on crutches, breaking one of them (they subsequently made a collection for a replacement).

Many believed Wigan's chances of success depended on them overcoming Oldham's mighty pack, something they accomplished with aplomb. It set the platform for their backs to mesmerise their opposition on the way to a comprehensive victory. Initially the two sets of forwards adopted a risk-free policy, effectively tackling each other out of the game. Jim Sullivan failed with an early penalty attempt for Wigan, the ball blown

STATS

Wigan 21 Oldham 4

Saturday 12 April at The Athletic Grounds, Rochdale (3.30 pm)

Wigan (blue): Sullivan, Ring, Howley, Parker, van Heerden, Jerram, Hurcombe, Banks, Brown, Webster, van Rooyen, Roffey, Price (captain). Trainer: T. McCarty

Oldham (white): Knapman, Rix, Hall, Woodward, Corsi, Hesketh, Bates, Collins, Baker, Tomkins, Sloman, Brough, Hilton (captain). Trainer: C.R. Marsden

Referee: Revd F.H. Chambers
Touch-judges: H. Horsfall, J. Lynch

Half-time: 8–4 Attendance: 41,831 Receipts: £3,712

Weather: cloudy, some sunny periods, strong wind

Cup presentation:
Mrs J.H. Dannatt, wife of Rugby League chairman

Progressive score:

Wigan	score (min)	Oldham
	0–2 (15)	Knapman penalty
Roffey try	3–2 (17)	
van Heerden try, Sullivan goal	8–2 (30)	
	8–4 (38)	Brough penalty
Parker try	11–4 (47)	
Price try	14–4 (55)	
Sullivan penalty	16–4 (60)	
Ring try, Sullivan goal	21–4 (70)	

Route to the final:

First round: Wigan 7 Leigh 5, Oldham 5 Rochdale Hornets 0

Second round:
Wigan 49 Broughton Rangers 0, Oldham 18 Dewsbury 0

Third round:
Hunslet 8 Wigan 13, Oldham 24 Wakefield Trinity 10

Semi-finals:
Wigan 30 Barrow 5 (The Willows, Salford, 20,400),
Oldham 9 Huddersfield 5 (Thrum Hall, Halifax, 20,000)

Head-to-head form guide:

Oldham 15 Wigan 5 (Lancashire Cup)

Oldham 10 Wigan 2 (League)

Wigan 20 Oldham 3 (League)

Wigan captain and loose forward Jack Price

WINNING CAPTAIN

Jack Price (Wigan 1924)

Swinton-born Jack Price was noted in his time as one of the fastest loose forwards around and on par with most three-quarters. Broughton Rangers snapped him up from Deans Rovers (of the Manchester and District League) in 1915, but the First World War delayed his 'official' debut until the club's first peacetime fixture in January 1919. Having won the 1920 Lancashire Cup with the Rangers, he transferred to Wigan for £400 in 1922, adding further silverware with the Rugby League Challenge Cup (1924), Championship (1925/26) and Lancashire League (1922/23, 1923/24, 1925/26). He earned six Test appearances, was a tourist in 1924, and represented England (3 times) and Lancashire (14). He was forced to retire after dislocating his knee playing for Wigan on Christmas Eve, 1927.

wide by the wind, before Oldham's Ernie Knapman opened the scoring with a difficult penalty kick after a scrum infringement. Just two minutes later, Fred Roffey claimed the first of Wigan's five tries, Fred Brown having dribbled the ball towards the try-line before picking up and delivering the scoring pass. The wind again thwarted Sullivan in his goal attempt, but the touchdown pepped Wigan and they began to move the ball around more freely.

With half an hour gone van Heerden scored one of the sport's most bizarre tries. Tommy Parker received possession from Jack Price and, with little room to manoeuvre, managed to kick the ball on the turn, van Heerden winning the race against Joe Corsi to collect the ball and cross the try-line at the corner. With a mounted policeman situated in the in-goal area he ran around the back of his horse and headed towards the rear of the posts before placing the ball down! Sullivan added the goal, referee Reverend Frank Chambers then holding up the restart for a couple of minutes whilst attempts were made to move the excited crowd back. Shortly before half-time, Billy Hall broke through for Oldham but, when he got within 10 yards of Wigan's line, he kicked the ball forward and van Heerden recovered it. Moments later and following a scrum offence, Albert Brough landed a penalty for Oldham, Wigan leading 8–4 at half-time.

Due to the continuing encroachment of the crowd, Chambers decided to turn around without a break rather than risk further disturbance. All the second half points went into Wigan's account who, after several promising raids, cut loose with two tries. Firstly, Parker sprinted into the corner to touch down 'practically amongst the spectators' after Danny Hurcombe made the break. Next, Tommy Howley burst through but lost the ball, Oldham's George Hesketh picking up but then fumbling it himself, Howley gratefully recovering possession before transferring to Price who 'disappeared from view' as he scored in the corner. Sullivan, having failed with two

The game as depicted by the pen of Jim Gannon in the Wigan Examiner

penalties since half-time—one before each try—was off-target with both conversions. He made amends on the hour with a tremendous penalty struck from just inside Oldham's half, making it 16–4.

Wigan continued to boss the show and Johnny Ring, having intercepted a Corsi pass, shot past Sid Rix and Knapman to go over by the posts, Sullivan adding the goal. Oldham had their best try-scoring chance soon afterwards, Knapman, in following up a kick, being just beaten to the touchdown by a defender as they dived amongst the spectators. Another incredulous incident occurred after Howley made a run through the opposition and passed to the supporting Bert Webster who was then tackled close to Oldham's try-line. Playing the ball forward he re-gathered and dived over the try-line between a police horse's hoofs! The score, though, was disallowed and the final whistle sounded minutes later, Wigan returning home that evening to scenes 'unparalleled in the history of the borough'.

1925 RUGBY LEAGUE CHALLENGE CUP FINAL
Oldham v Hull Kingston Rovers

Oldham's victory over Hull Kingston Rovers in the 1925 Challenge Cup Final took the famous trophy back to Watersheddings following a 26-year wait. However, they did not have the most ideal start to their afternoon, a delayed train journey to Leeds resulting in them not entering Headingley's changing rooms until 20 minutes before kick-off. Meanwhile, the atmosphere and sense of occasion was building inside the ground on a sunlit afternoon as press and 'cinema photographers' recorded events. The *Oldham Evening Chronicle* declared that 'altogether the scene was one to thrill the sporting public' and, as the teams emerged, the *Hull Daily Mail* noted: 'Bells, rattles and other noise makers were used, whilst some enthusiasts threw miniature balloons on the enclosure.' Oldham produced a selection surprise, Sid Rix moving to centre to the exclusion of Alan Woodward, allowing

Action from the 1925 final at Headingley—Bob Sloman of Oldham in possession

Joe Corsi to return on the wing following injury.

The Robins almost scored early on, their forwards dribbling the ball over Oldham's try-line, Evan Davies managing to touch it down safely at the last moment after the bounce tricked Ernie Knapman. Knapman, having caught a clearance kick by Laurie Osbourne, nearly put Oldham ahead with a sensational wind-assisted drop-goal attempt from 10 yards inside his own half. It just dipped under the crossbar, deceiving several colleagues who 'jumped with joy' thinking he had scored. The match had begun at a terrific pace and Oldham attacked with force, excellent passing finding

Rix racing into space and he, in turn, sent Davies away. But with Rix and Reg Farrar supporting on either side, Davies took on Jimmy Cook and was stopped short of the try-line.

Oldham continued to threaten, Farrar and Albert Brough both missing penalty shots whilst Rix was proving a danger to Rovers, but his scything breaks

---

STATS

Oldham 16 Hull Kingston Rovers 3

Saturday 25 April at Headingley, Leeds (3.30 pm)

Oldham (red and white hoops): Knapman, Farrar, Rix, Davies, Corsi, Hesketh, Beynon, Tomkins, Marlor, Collins, Sloman, Brough, Hilton (captain). Trainer: C.R. Marsden

Hull Kingston Rovers (white with red band): Osbourne (captain), Harris, Cook, Hoult, Austin, McIntyre, Raynor, J.H. 'Jack' Wilkinson, F. Boagey, J.R. 'Bob' Wilkinson, Westerdale, Bielby, Camichael. Trainer: W. Jacques

Referee: R. Jones   Touch-judges: F. Fairhurst, W.K. Hirst

Half-time: 5–0   Attendance: 28,335   Receipts: £2,879

Weather: sunny with chill wind

Cup presentation: Mrs R. Gale, wife of Rugby League chairman

Progressive score:

Oldham	score (min)	Hull Kingston Rovers
Farrar try, Farrar goal	5–0 (33)	
Brough try	8–0 (47)	
Corsi try, Farrar goal	13–0 (59)	
	13–3 (64)	J.H. Wilkinson try
Davies try	16–3 (75)	

Route to the final:

First round: Leigh 0 Oldham 5, Hull KR 9 Bramley 0

Second round:
Oldham 12 Warrington 7, Hull KR 13 Wigan Highfield 5

Third round:
Oldham 26 Featherstone Rovers 0, Keighley 0 Hull KR 5

Semi-finals:
Oldham 9 Rochdale Hornets 0 (Central Park, Wigan, 26,208),

Hull KR 7 Leeds 6 (Belle Vue, Wakefield, 25,263)

Head-to-head form guide:

No previous meetings during season

often lacked support. Eventually George Hesketh and Davies worked an opening on halfway to despatch Farrar, the centre scoring at the corner despite Osbourne and Paddy McIntyre trying to force him into touch. Farrar added a great goal. The Rovers tried to rally, Gilbert Austin and Alf Carmichael both making valiant efforts to get over Oldham's try-line and Lou Harris missing a penalty, but the Lancashire side reached half-time with their 5–0 lead intact.

After the restart Oldham's Bob Sloman and Jack Collins led a forward dash towards the Rovers line, Alf Tomkins almost forcing his way over the whitewash. The Roughyeds' pressure was rewarded when Hesketh, with his backs 'well strung out' delivered a cross-field kick. Farrar retrieved the bouncing ball ahead of Harris before sprinting towards the try-line where he passed to Brough, the forward pushing his way over for the try. Farrar hit the far upright with his conversion attempt, Oldham leading 8–0. Osbourne and Cook both failed with drop-goals (the former following a penalty award) as Rovers struggled to mount a recovery. Meanwhile, with Oldham's forwards winning the battle upfront, Brough was withdrawn from their pack to act as a fifth three-quarter, further exploiting holes appearing in Rovers' defence.

Oldham had command and, after Hesketh had a try disallowed for an earlier infringement, the same player—following a scrum on the Rovers' try-line—sent Corsi charging over for the touchdown, Farrar adding the goal despite a strong wind. To their credit, the Rovers responded five minutes later, Carmichael and Frank Bielby combining to send a wide pass to Jack Wilkinson for a consolation try, Osbourne missing the goal. A further assault, led by Carmichael, almost produced a second, the ball rolling dead before Austin could reach it. Oldham, though, made several late forays before a move by Farrar and Brough got Davies over for an unconverted try, rounding off the scoring at 16–3.

WINNING CAPTAIN

Herman Hilton (Oldham 1925)

Considered one of Oldham's finest ever forwards, Herman Hilton was a local recruit from the Healey Street club in 1913. A tough opponent with a fair turn of speed he began in the back row, moving in later years to prop. At Oldham he won the Rugby League Challenge Cup (1925), Lancashire Cup (1919, 1924) and Lancashire League (1921/22). In the close season following the 1925 Challenge Cup success he became ill and, although returning for several matches at the start of the following season, it curtailed his career. He appeared in 253 matches for Oldham, was a tourist in 1920, played in seven Tests, and represented England (3 times) and Lancashire (2).

Oldham players and officials with the Challenge Cup and other trophies after their 1925 victory. Players only (in playing kit) are, third row, standing: Marlor, Rix, Carter, Collins, Sloman, Baker, Brough, Knapman. Seated: Tomkins, Corsi, Woodward, Hesketh, Hilton, Davies, Farrar, Hall. On ground: Fisher, Beynon, Comm, Hurtley. Seated centre is club president W. McCutcheon

Graham Morris

1926 RUGBY LEAGUE CHALLENGE CUP FINAL
Swinton v Oldham

The Challenge Cup takes centre stage amongst Swinton's 1925/26 trophy collection. Players only (in playing kit) are, back row: Turner, Beswick, Leigh. Third row: Sulway, Fairhurst, Strong, Morris, Entwistle, Blewer, Halliwell. Seated: F. Evans, Pearson, J. Evans, Halsall, Brockbank, B. Evans, Pardon. On ground: Atkinson, Rees

Swinton gave a brilliant display in difficult playing conditions to beat holders Oldham 9–3 in the 1926 Challenge Cup Final. The Lions won the crucial pre-match coin toss, forcing Oldham to face a near-gale force wind in the opening half that, allied to the wet, miserable weather, made passing and kicking difficult. The *Oldham Evening Chronicle* said: 'With almost every gust of wind, hats could be seen flying about' and hosts Rochdale Hornets' match day flag became detached from its flagpole and blew away!

The Lions were bearing down into Oldham territory early on, a loose George Hesketh pass

The Critic. OFFICIAL PROGRAMME, Price 2d.

ROCHDALE HORNETS FOOTBALL CLUB.
SEASON 1925-6.

Rugby League Challenge Cup.

FINAL TIE.

OLDHAM v. SWINTON
AT THE
ATHLETIC GROUNDS, ROCHDALE,
MAY 1st, 1926. - Kick-off 3-30.

CALL AT THE JUNCTION HOTEL.
OLDHAM ROAD,

10 minutes from Grounds.
5 minutes from Station.

A Welcome to Old and New Friends.

Large and Small Parties Catered for.

'Phone Rochdale 1261.

JOE BOWERS,
The Old ROCHDALE HORNETS,
AND LANCASHIRE COUNTY PLAYER,
AND NORTHERN UNION TOURIST.

following a scrum resulting in a Swinton charge, Ernie Knapman being forced to 'save' just short of the try-line. The Lions continued to press, Jack Evans beating a couple of opponents before he was pushed into touch as he tried to get over. Penalty attempts by Swinton's Bert Morris (twice) and Knapman all failed, Jack Pearson producing a futile drop-goal effort for the Lions. Eventually Morris found the target when Alf Higgs was penalised for an incorrect play-the-ball. The elements were contributing to some 'scrappy' play, Swinton looking the more dangerous combination by somehow stringing together several excellent passing moves. One such thrust ended with winger Chris Brockbank being stopped on the Oldham try-line by Rod Marlor.

The crucial breakthrough came when Billo Rees made a terrific burst for Swinton before attempting a drop-goal that rebounded back off the crossbar. The bounce favoured colleague Henry Blewer who gathered the ball as Swinton's eager forwards rushed up, going beneath the posts for a try. Offside appeals were dismissed by referee Arthur Brown, Morris adding the goal, plus a magnificent penalty from halfway three minutes later—Percy Carter being ruled offside at a scrum—for a healthy 9–0 lead. Just before half-time Swinton broke away in midfield, Rees kicking the ball forwards and looking a scorer until Higgs got across, defusing the situation.

Oldham were quick out of the blocks following the interval, a raid ending with Albert Brough being pushed into touch as he tried to place the ball at the corner. Soon afterwards quick handling resulted in Joe Corsi, having kicked the ball over Pearson's head before retrieving it, scoring for the Roughyeds. Knapman missed the conversion although, at 9–3 with the wind in their favour and time remaining, there were expectations of an Oldham comeback. But it was Swinton—having moved Fred Beswick out of the pack as an extra three-quarter to counter Oldham's backs—that gained the upper hand. Oldham did threaten again, Brough being once more shunted into touch as he looked a potential scorer, but Swinton could not be

STATS

Swinton 9 Oldham 3

Saturday 1 May at The Athletic Grounds, Rochdale (3.30 pm)

Swinton (navy blue): Pearson, F. Evans, Sulway, J. Evans (captain), Brockbank, Rees, B. Evans, Strong, Blewer, Morris, Halliwell, Entwistle, Beswick. Trainer: W. Kearns

Oldham (red and white hoops): Knapman, Corsi, Higgs, Rix, Brough, Hesketh, Jones, Marlor, Lister, Read, Baker, Carter, Sloman (captain). Trainer: C.R. Marsden

Referee: A. Brown   Touch-judges: H. Horsfall, J. Thomas

Half-time: 9–0   Attendance: 26,566   Receipts: £2,551

Weather: persistent rain, blustery wind

Cup presentation:
Mrs J.F. Whitaker, wife of Rugby League chairman

Progressive score:

Swinton	score (min)	Oldham
Morris penalty	2–0 (12)	
Blewer try, Morris goal	7–0 (22)	
Morris penalty	9–0 (25)	
	9–3 (45)	Corsi try

Route to the final:

First round: Swinton 19 Batley 9, Leigh 6 Oldham 18

Second round: Swinton 8 Broughton Rangers 8, Oldham 12 Rochdale Hornets 3

Second round replay: Broughton Rangers 3 Swinton 20

Third round:
Swinton 24 Hull Kingston Rovers 3, Oldham 8 Halifax 5

Semi-finals: Swinton 13 Hull 2 (Thrum Hall, Halifax, 17,693), Oldham 15 Wigan Highfield 6 (The Willows, Salford, 18,290)

Head-to-head form guide:

Oldham 8 Swinton 4 (League)

Swinton 12 Oldham 5 (League)

WINNING CAPTAIN

Jack Evans (Swinton 1926)

Intelligent, quick thinking centre Evan John 'Jack' Evans was the eldest of three talented brothers (the others being Bryn and Harold) who played for their local club, Swinton, during the 1920s and 1930s. Their father, also Jack, was a former Wales rugby union international, signed from Llwynypia by Swinton in 1897 and a member of their 1900 Challenge Cup winning side. Like his father, Jack junior was born in Wales, his mother residing there for his birth. He signed for the Lions in 1919 from Swinton Park Rangers, making his debut in 1921. With Swinton he won the Rugby League Challenge Cup (1926, 1928), Championship (1926/27, 1927/28—missing the final of the latter through tour commitments), Lancashire Cup (1925, 1927), and Lancashire League (1924/25, 1927/28). He toured once (1928), made three Test appearances and represented England (5 times) and Lancashire (11). Dogged by health problems following an appendicitis operation, he made the last of 276 Swinton appearances (99 tries) in 1932. He was subsequently Broughton Rangers' team manager, playing twice (in 1934 and 1935) before rejoining Swinton on the coaching staff.

denied. The Lions' back division, ably led by Bryn Evans, Jack Evans and Rees, called most of the shots during the second half, passing the ball with 'amazing accuracy' despite not registering further points.

Swinton repeated Oldham's feat of the previous year in reclaiming the trophy after a 26-year break. The Roughyeds made a late change through centre Abe Johnson failing to recover from a leg injury, Sid Rix moving inside from the flank to occupy his position, Brough transferring from the pack to the wing. Jack Evans lifted the trophy owing to the Lions' team captain and centre, Hector Halsall, being injured the previous week, although the latter at least had the 'honour' of being chaired into the club's headquarters, the Bulls Head Hotel, that evening by his players.

Graham Morris

RADIO COVERAGE

The first radio coverage of a rugby league match was the 1927 Challenge Cup Final from Wigan's Central Park, Oldham meeting Swinton two weeks after the BBC aired its first FA Cup Final. Broadcast to the Manchester region from the Trafford Park-based 2ZY station, Ernest G. Blackwell's commentary was, according to the *Radio Times*, 'preceded by community singing.' *Oldham Evening Chronicle* writer 'Pax' gave an amusing account of that first broadcast under the headline 'Hearing Oldham win', his opening remarks being repeated here: 'I didn't see Oldham win the cup, I heard them win it. In these days of wireless such a phenomenon is easily explained. About twenty-five minutes past three on Saturday afternoon I switched on my three-valver, determined to hear the Oldham-Swinton Cup Final, even if I couldn't see it. What a row, what a hullabaloo of noises came through the loud speaker! What with the medley of whistling, cheering, yelling, community singing, and a thousand and one other noises all mixed up in one glorious symphony, it sounded like a super-pandemonium. Above the roar and the surging storm, or rather behind it, sounded the voice of the announcer, trying heroically to make himself heard.'

The first Wembley final in 1929 was relayed to London and most other regions, as was the 1930 event. Thereafter transmission varied depending on the whim of each region, some taking the 1931 broadcast (not London or the Midlands), whilst the 1932 decider (from Wigan) and that of 1933 was covered only in the north. Then, in 1934, virtually all the regions (including London) took the broadcast. For the remaining pre-war years (1935–39), the north continued to receive the full match, while most other regions that took it did so only for the second half. This resulted in 1938 and 1939 having different commentators for each half, the first for northern listeners only, the second taking over for 'national' commentary. After the Second World War, from 1946, only the code's heartlands received commentary via the new North (of England) Home Service and that was still the case in 1957 prior to television becoming the dominant outlet for providing contact with events at Wembley.

THE RADIO TIMES

To accompany its first radio broadcast in 1927, the *Radio Times* included a plan of the playing area split into eight zones ('1' to '8'), enabling listeners to be advised where play was, a graphic repeated regularly over the next decade. The magazine also featured two rugby league articles during the pre-war period coinciding with Wembley; in 1935 Lance Todd wrote about the international aspect of the game and his thoughts on commentating, and in 1939 Fred A. Marsh ('Forward' of the *Sporting Chronicle*) focussed on the 1895 breakaway.

EARLY BBC RADIO CHALLENGE CUP FINAL LIVE COMMENTARY TEAMS

(Prior to 1958 when regular television coverage commenced)
- 1927: Ernest G. Blackwell
- 1928: no broadcast
- 1929: Revd Frank H. Chambers
- 1930: Ivor Halstead
- 1931: W.E. Dickman
- 1932: John Graham
- 1933–36: Lance B. Todd
- 1937: Lance B. Todd, Hubert Bateman
- 1938: Freddie Pemberton (first half), Hubert Bateman (second half)
- 1939: Alfred T. Grogen (first half), R.A. Colville (second half)
- 1941–45: no broadcast
- 1946: Harry Sunderland, Victor Smythe
- 1947: Harry Sunderland, Freddie Pemberton (Victor Smythe)
- 1948–49: Harry Sunderland, Freddie Pemberton
- 1950: Alan Clarke, Eric Mitchell, David Nicholls
- 1951: Harry Sunderland, Alan Dixon
- 1952: Alan Clarke, Harry Sunderland (George Duckworth)
- 1953–54: Alan Clarke, Alan Dixon (Harry Sunderland, Eddie Waring)
- 1954 replay (2nd half coverage only): Alan Clarke, Alan Dixon (Harry Sunderland, Eddie Waring)
- 1955: no broadcast
- 1956: Harry Sunderland, Keith Macklin (Eddie Waring)
- 1957: Alan Clarke, Harry Sunderland, Alan Dixon (Eddie Waring)

(Note: Above information taken from the *Radio Times*. Names in brackets are summarisers. Broadcast to North region only in 1927, 1932–33, 1946–57)

1927 RUGBY LEAGUE CHALLENGE CUP FINAL
Oldham v Swinton

Oldham gained revenge over Swinton in 1927, reversing the outcome of their previous year's Challenge Cup Final meeting with an emphatic 26–7 victory, the first occasion the same clubs had faced off in consecutive finals. Unlike their earlier encounter, Wigan's Central Park—staging its first final in the competition—was bathed in glorious hot sunshine. Oldham were forced into a late change, Freddie Ashworth replacing influenza victim Ambrose Baker amongst the forwards, whilst Swinton's Harry Entwistle—reportedly injured in the previous weekend's Championship Final—was bypassed in favour of Dick Cracknell in the pack, their full back Jack Pearson being absent since mid-season with a knee problem.

Swinton began with a flourish and but for poor finishing could have scored a couple of times, Chris Brockbank and Frank Evans both failing to collect vital last passes. Their reward was not far away, however, some excellent attacking play getting Brockbank over in the corner, Bert Morris missing the goal kick. Chances followed at both ends, Oldham's Sid Rix being thwarted by a great tackle from Frank Evans, and Swinton's Billo Rees being derailed through Abe Johnson's intervention. It was Johnson that pulled two points back after 24 minutes, Fred Beswick being penalised for a 'deliberate' knock-on. It was a score that lifted Oldham, although the next points were claimed by their opposition, Morris' brilliant penalty strike from halfway presenting the Lions with a 5–2 advantage after an obstruction by Albert Brough.

Action from the first final to be held at Wigan's Central Park, Swinton about to play the ball

WINNING CAPTAIN

Bob Sloman (Oldham 1927)

Bob Sloman was a 1921 recruit from the Plymouth Albion rugby union club, described as a tall second-row forward noted for his long striding runs through the opposition. He made a big impression on the international selectors, being picked for two tours (1924, 1928), making five Test appearances and playing five times for England. He played in four consecutive Rugby League Challenge Cup Finals with Oldham (1924 to 1927), winning twice (1925, 1927), to which he added the Lancashire Cup (1924) and Lancashire League (1921/22). He played the last of 268 matches for Oldham in 1929.

Oldham, though, claimed the lead just before half-time. Johnson hit the upright with a penalty effort but, shortly after, George Hesketh scooted away from a scrum before passing to Alf Higgs. The ball came loose but colleague Tom Holliday retrieved it to score in the corner, Johnson adding an excellent goal. The score was debated, some claiming Higgs knocked-on in the build up, others arguing a Swinton player knocked it away before Holliday picked up. Either way, Oldham led 7–5, Brough almost adding another touchdown in the closing seconds of the half, losing the ball over

Swinton's try-line after Hesketh sent him through.

Any thoughts of an equally close second half were soon dispelled. Johnson made an ambitious penalty attempt from inside his own half and there were early try-scoring opportunities for both teams before, 10 minutes after the restart, Oldham began their domination with the first of five further tries. The scorer was Rix who ran over the whitewash after a tremendous dummy and break by Hesketh. Brough added the goal, extending the lead to 12–5. The four remaining touchdowns came from Brough (following up his own kick-through after a Holliday play-the-ball), Bob Sloman (under the posts after receiving from Johnson following a brilliant passing move), Holliday (beating three opponents in a thrilling run from his own half) and Holliday again (racing in behind the posts from 25 yards out). Johnson, Brough (from in front of the posts) and Hesketh, in turn, missed the first three conversion attempts, Brough succeeding with the latter. Swinton—who could claim extenuating circumstances for their collapse losing two

A cigarette card caricature by 'Mac' featuring Oldham's Tom Holliday, scorer of three tries

Oldham pose in front of the club pavilion with the Challenge Cup. Back row: Marsden (trainer), Brough, Rix, Comm, Foote. Middle row: Higgs, Marlor, Scaife, Read, Baker, Ashworth, Holliday. Seated: Jeremiah, Jones, Sloman, Hesketh, Johnson

STATS

Oldham 26 Swinton 7

Saturday 7 May at Central Park, Wigan (3.30 pm)

Oldham (red and white hoops): Comm, Johnson, Rix, Higgs, Holliday, Hesketh, Jones, Read, Scaife, Marlor, Sloman (captain), Ashworth, Brough. Trainer: C.R. Marsden

Swinton (navy blue): Leigh, F. Evans, Halsall (captain), J. Evans, Brockbank, Rees, B. Evans, Strong, Blewer, Morris, Cracknell, Halliwell, Beswick. Trainer: W. Kearns

Referee: R. Robinson   Touch-judges: T. Johnson, J. Atkinson

Half-time: 7–5   Attendance: 33,448   Receipts: £3,170

Weather: sunny and hot

Cup presentation: Mrs E. Osborne, wife of Rugby League chairman

Progressive score:

Oldham	score (min)	Swinton
	0–3 (7)	Brockbank try
Johnson penalty	2–3 (24)	
	2–5 (37)	Morris penalty
Holliday try, Johnson goal	7–5 (39)	
Rix try, Brough goal	12–5 (50)	
Brough try	15–5 (55)	
Sloman try	18–5 (58)	
Holliday try	21–5 (-)	
Holliday try, Brough goal	26–5 (-)	
	26–7 (75)	Morris penalty

Route to the final:

First round: Oldham 8 Salford 0, Swinton 11 Huddersfield 2

Second round: Hunslet 3 Oldham 15, Swinton 10 York 8

Third round: Leeds 5 Oldham 11, Swinton 19 Hull 2

Semi-finals:
Oldham 7 Wakefield Trinity 3 (Central Park, Wigan, 18,000)

Swinton 10 Dewsbury 0 (Fartown, Huddersfield, 24,227)

Head-to-head form guide:

Oldham 0 Swinton 5 (League)

Swinton 8 Oldham 8 (League)

players midway through the second half in Beswick (succumbing to a first half shoulder injury) and Hector Halsall (carried off with a knee problem)—had the last word when Morris landed one of his two late penalty attempts.

In what was the first rugby league match broadcast on the radio, Oldham set records with four consecutive Challenge Cup Final appearances and seven overall. Meanwhile, Holliday—who went off injured after 30 minutes play and returned shortly after—equalled the three-try haul of Bob Wilson (Broughton Rangers, 1902) and Stanley Moorhouse (Huddersfield, 1913).

1928 RUGBY LEAGUE CHALLENGE CUP FINAL
Swinton v Warrington

The 1928 Swinton-Warrington Challenge Cup Final was settled in dramatic fashion by a drop-goal from Lions' centre Jack Evans. With the score tied at 3–3 the opportunity was controversially set up after Warrington full back Arthur Frowen was judged to have touched the ball as it sailed over his head towards the dead-ball line, Jack Evans having got a boot to it when Wires' skipper Tommy Flynn fumbled. A five-yard scrum was awarded despite Warrington protesting otherwise, the tension increasing as the Wilderspool outfit twice won the heel, the referee ordering a re-scrum on both occasions. On the third attempt Swinton secured possession, scrum half Albert Atkinson responding to Evans' signal—he clapped his hands—by quickly transferring the ball, the latter calmly slotting it between the uprights to set up a winning 5–3 score-line.

During a first half of 'strenuous struggle' Swinton unexpectedly won the scrum contest against Warrington's powerful pack, but their star-studded back division was unable to put the possession to good use through tight marking. Another factor was the disruption to the Lions' attacking machine by the loss of play-making scrum half Bryn Evans—taken ill on the morning of the match—Atkinson being a late replacement, whilst injury in the previous weekend's Good Friday encounter with Oldham meant full back Jack Pearson missed out for a second year. Try-scoring

chances were limited whilst penalty attempts by Warrington's Billy Rhodes (with two) and Jesse Meredith, and Swinton's Bert Morris were all off the mark.

The match developed into what the *Salford City Reporter* correspondent described as 'kick and rush style typical cup-tie football' although Swinton went down to 12 men following the temporary loss of Jack

---

WINNING CAPTAIN

Hector Halsall (Swinton 1928)

Plucked from Wigan reserves in 1920, centre Hector Halsall became one of the stars in Swinton's magnificent 1920s outfit. A quick-witted, inspirational player, he quickly established himself, becoming club captain in 1922/23, a role he retained until his farewell in 1930. With the Lions, he won the Rugby League Challenge Cup (1928—missing out in 1926 through injury after playing in the earlier rounds), Championship (1926/27, 1927/28), Lancashire Cup (1925, 1927) and Lancashire League (1924/25, 1927/28, 1928/29). He appeared in one Test (against Australia at Swinton, 1929), represented Lancashire (twice) and a Northern Rugby League XIII (versus the 1929 Australian tourists at Newcastle). After retiring he became Leigh coach, taking a similar role at Barrow in 1932 that he retained until 1950.

STATS

Swinton 5 Warrington 3

Saturday 14 April at Central Park, Wigan (3.30 pm)

Swinton (navy blue): Young, F. Evans, Halsall (captain), J. Evans, Brockbank, W. Rees, Atkinson, Strong, Blewer, Morris, Hodgson, Cracknell, Beswick. Trainer: W. Kearns

Warrington (primrose and blue hoops): Frowen, Rhodes, Meredith, Perkins, Davies, Flynn (captain), Kirk, Cunliffe, Peacock, Miller, Williams, Tranter, Seeling. Trainer: J. Fish

Referee: H. Horsfall   Touch-judges: J. Thomas, J. Houghton

Half-time: 3–0   Attendance: 33,909   Receipts: £3,158

Weather: fine with strong breeze

Cup presentation:
Mrs C. Preston, wife of Rugby League chairman

Progressive score:

Swinton	score (min)	Warrington
Brockbank try	3–0 (30)	
	3–3 (55)	Seeling try
J. Evans drop-goal	5–3 (-)	

Route to the final:

First round: Whitehaven Recreation 0 Swinton 44, Warrington 43 Kinsley (Wakefield) 2 (Kinsley gave up home advantage)

Second round:
Halifax 2 Swinton 3, Hull Kingston Rovers 0 Warrington 5

Third round:
Swinton 3 Castleford 0, Warrington 10 Huddersfield 3

Semi-finals:
Swinton 5 Hull 3 (Fartown, Huddersfield, 12,000),

Warrington 9 Leeds 2 (The Athletic Grounds, Rochdale, 22,000)

Head-to-head form guide:

Swinton 24 Warrington 4 (League)

Warrington 5 Swinton 8 (League)

Swinton 1927/28—the only Lancashire team to win the famed 'All Four Cups' in one season. Players only (in playing kit) are, fourth row (second row from back): Pardon, Buckingham, Fairhurst, Strong, Pearson, Leigh, Sulway. Third row: Beswick, H. Entwistle, Halliwell, Butters, Hodgson, Cracknell, Grimshaw, Morris, Young. Second row (seated): H. Evans, Brockbank, J. Evans, Halsall, B. Evans, F. Evans, On ground: Atkinson, Rees. Trainer Kearns is on the third row, extreme left

Evans, injured making a tackle on Les Perkins. His reappearance after 15 minutes' absence led to the opening score two minutes later when, in a move instigated by Atkinson, he shrugged off two defenders before transferring the ball to Hector Halsall who handed on to Frank Evans. The wingman looked like being tackled but colleague Chris Brockbank shot across from the other flank to create the extra man and score in the corner. Morris' goal effort was driven off course by the strong wind, the interval score being 3–0 despite two subsequent drop-goal attempts from Frowen.

Tragedy hit Warrington when halfback Billy Kirk—who required immediate on-field attention from a doctor—departed on a stretcher early in the second half with concussion and a damaged jaw. The Wires moved Dai Davies to halfback (his natural position) to cover the loss, loose forward Charlie Seeling—whose famous father of the same name appeared in the 1911 and 1920 Challenge Cup Finals with Wigan—

Swinton winger Chris Brockbank scored the opening try in the corner

relocating to the wing. Swinton, with the benefit of the wind and an extra man, were expected to press home their advantage, but it was Seeling that was on hand for the equalising try after clever play by Perkins, Rhodes missing the goal. The match, though, continued to be 'uninteresting' and 'all kick and rush' until Jack Evans' timely two-pointer surprised everyone, further Swinton goal attempts from Morris and Billy Young (both penalties) and Halsall (a long-range drop which hit the crossbar) being to no avail.

The 33,909 attendance—a Central Park record—witnessed what Swinton's local paper *The Journal* summed up as a 'disappointing game' although there were mitigating circumstances, Swinton playing their fourth game in nine days and Warrington their fifth over the same period. Whilst Swinton headed the League table, 17th placed Warrington were unexpected finalists, courtesy of a shock semi-final win over fancied Leeds.

EMPIRE STADIUM

Wembley Stadium was originally built as part of the British Empire Exhibition and officially opened by King George V on the occasion of its first FA Cup Final (Bolton Wanderers versus West Ham United) on 28 April 1923. Costing £750,000 its most iconic feature was the 126 feet (38 metres) tall twin towers. The original capacity was claimed to be 126,500 including 25,000 seated under cover but, at the aforementioned match, chaotic scenes ensued. Attracting an official attendance of 126,047, it was estimated 200,000 got inside, many having scaled the perimeter walls. As a result, the 1924 final became all-ticket with a revised capacity of just below 92,000, eventually raised to 100,000 for the 1950 FA Cup Final.

The British Empire Exhibition, incorporating exhibition halls that surrounded the stadium, opened on 23 April 1924 and closed during October 1925. Having been built through public subscription, there was the possibility of the site being demolished afterwards, having incurred huge debts, but it was rescued when the newly formed Wembley Stadium and Greyhound Racecourse Company Limited, led by Arthur J. Elvin, took over. Greyhound racing and, later, speedway racing became popular and regular features and, in 1934, the adjoining Empire Pool—which eventually became the Wembley Arena—was added, swimming and ice hockey being two of the main sports

A wide angled view of the Empire Stadium during the 1938 Challenge Cup Final

held. In 1948, the joint facility became the focal point of the London Olympic Games.

Floodlights costing £22,000 were added to the stadium in 1955 and, in 1963, new owners Associated-Rediffusion Limited—who took control in 1960—spent a further £500,000 converting it into an all-covered stadium, its 100,000 capacity now including 44,803 seats. A further £53,000 was invested in 1973 providing a more powerful floodlighting system. Wembley became an all-seated stadium from 1990, including 4,000 in the Olympic Gallery (a structure that was suspended from the roof), thereby trimming its capacity to 81,500.

Known as the Empire Stadium until 1972, and Wembley Stadium thereafter, it closed its doors for the last time in 2000 ahead of its major redevelopment.

MATCHES IN LONDON BEFORE 1929

Prior to the first Wembley Challenge Cup Final, the following rugby league matches took place in the capital:

- 8 Feb 1908: Northern Union 6 New Zealand 18 (attendance 14,000) at Stamford Bridge (Chelsea AFC)

- 12 Dec 1908: Northern Union 22 Australia 22 (2,014) at Park Royal (Queens Park Rangers AFC)

- 18 Oct 1911: England 6 Australia 11 (6,000) at Craven Cottage (Fulham AFC)

- 10 Oct 1921: England 5 Australia 4 (12,000) Highbury Stadium (Arsenal AFC)

- 11 Dec 1922: England 12 Wales 7 (3,000) Herne Hill Stadium (athletic/cycling venue)

PRESS REACTION TO THE FIRST WEMBLEY FINAL

Manchester Guardian: 'The most astounding revelations which the game gave to Southerner's were the terrific speed of which it was fought out and the goal kicking of Sullivan.'

The Times: 'The bringing of the Cup Final to London has been greeted as a dark conspiracy against amateurism.'

Daily Express: 'Most Rugby Union footballers said it was rotten. This was sheer prejudice. The play in the first half was the fastest seen this season.'

1929 RUGBY LEAGUE CHALLENGE CUP FINAL
Wigan v Dewsbury

The inaugural Wembley final, whilst hardly a classic, provided a memorable occasion for those present on what was, undoubtedly, one of the sport's most historic days. The clubs sharing centre stage could barely have been more contrasting; glamorous, skilful Wigan overflowing with international stars, mid-table Dewsbury—whose shock third round win at Warrington opened the door to Wembley—with one Welshman in an otherwise all-Yorkshire side, relying on grit and determination to achieve success. 'Dewsbury will probably place much reliance on their forwards,' said the *Dewsbury Reporter*, adding they 'must defend in the early stages and hold the Wigan stars.'

Although southerners in the 41,500 crowd would be curious to see the alien 13-a-side code at first hand,

Wigan stride out on to the Wembley pitch led by captain Jim Sullivan. It was not until the following year that both finalists emerged together

---

WINNING CAPTAIN

Jim Sullivan (Wigan 1929)

Jim Sullivan was 17 years old when enticed to Wigan from hometown Cardiff rugby union club in 1921, becoming British rugby league's dominant full back throughout the 1920s and 1930s. His capability as tactician, leader and defender was second to none and his incredible appetite for scoring goals set records still intact today. At Wigan, he retains club career records for goals (2,317), points (4,883) and appearances (774), whilst, in all matches, he holds the Rugby League record for goals (2,867) and appearances (928). His 22 goals against amateurs Flimby and Fothergill United in the 1925 Challenge Cup also remains a record for a match. His honours with Wigan, where he became captain in 1925, include the Rugby League Challenge Cup (1924, 1929), Championship (1921/22, 1925/26, 1933/34), Lancashire Cup (1922, 1928, 1938), and Lancashire League (1922/23, 1923/24, 1925/26). He made three tours (1924, 1928, 1932—the latter as captain), rejecting a fourth (1936) through personal reasons. He represented Great Britain (25 Tests—15 as captain) Wales (26 times—a record, 18 as captain), England (3), Other Nationalities (6), Glamorgan and Monmouthshire (12) and Glamorgan (1). Wigan player-coach from 1932, he finished playing in 1946, continuing as coach until 1952, before taking over at St Helens (1952–59) and Rochdale Hornets (1959–61). Returning to Wigan as coach in 1961, poor health prevented him commencing his duties, and he retired. During the Second World War he made guest appearances for Dewsbury (27), Keighley (3) and Bradford Northern (1). He was an inductee to the Rugby League Hall of Fame in 1988.

---

many were attracted by the Cherry and Whites' infusion of former rugby union talent. Their five Welsh 'converts' included legendary full back Jim Sullivan and former union internationals Johnny Ring and Wilf Hodder, whilst Scotland provided another ex-union 'cap' in centre Roy Kinnear, father of the similarly named late comedic actor. Dewsbury captain and loose forward, Joe Lyman, a veteran at 34, was undaunted stating: 'Our forwards are as mighty a lot as I have known and I think they will upset the calculations of the Wigan backs.'

Worryingly, many parts of the vast stadium looked empty 30 minutes before kick-off but then the crowds 'came in quickly', the assembled throng surrounding what the *Wigan Examiner* described as 'a huge bowling green'. The atmosphere built as the pre-match 'community singing', to the accompaniment of the Band of His Majesty's Welsh Guards, concluded with 'Abide With Me', giving birth to a great and moving Wembley tradition.

Lyman won the coin toss electing to take advantage of the strong wind, allowing Wigan's Syd Abram the honour of kicking off Wembley's first final. The ball went straight to Dewsbury's William Rhodes who transferred it to Cliff Smith, the centre kicking to touch in the Lancastrians' half. Sullivan then gave the audience an early demonstration of his kicking prowess when he 'gained considerable distance with a fine touch penalty kick' before, in the third minute, he registered the first points in front of the Twin Towers. This was from a 30-yard penalty goal after Dewsbury's Percy Brown caught the ball in an offside position from a kick by his full back Jack Davies.

Dewsbury fought back, attacking strongly to place the Wigan line 'under heavy pressure' with several 'furious' bursts from their forwards. Wigan's Len Mason was penalised for playing the ball incorrectly, Lyman missing a chance to level, his 'easy' penalty achieving neither height nor direction. Abram made history in the 14th minute scoring a spectacular

opening 40-yard try against the run of play. Arthur Binks had gathered a Harry Bland clearance kick, sending Abram haring towards the flank where he attempted to link with Lou Brown. With the winger covered, he continued his thrilling run, outpacing Davies to touch down in the corner, Smith vainly clinging on. Sullivan failed to convert from a difficult angle.

Seven minutes before the interval Davies eventually gave Dewsbury's reported 3,000 following something to cheer. Having fielded Sullivan's downfield kick, he landed an impressive, unexpected drop-goal that went high over the crossbar from just inside his own half, aided by a strong wind at a time when the stadium was still exposed to the elements. There was no further score before half-time, Sullivan missing a penalty and Joe Malkin almost crossing at the other end after the ball went loose near Wigan's try-line.

Dewsbury mounted a strong assault after the resumption, the Lancastrians having John Sherrington to thank when he halted a 50-yard move, overhauling Lyman from behind after he broke clear following an initial burst from left-wing pair Herbert Hirst and Henry Coates. After that scare, Wigan began to dominate, their pack gaining the upper hand. Binks

The Wigan Rugby Football Team. Wembley. 1929

Wigan's 1929 Wembley squad photographed at their Central Park home. Standing: Fishwick (kit man), Oakley, Davidson, Sherrington, Jones, Stephens, Mason, Hodder, Bennett, Beetham, McCarty (trainer). Seated: Parker, Binks, Ring, Sullivan, Brown, Kinnear, Abram

Dewsbury get a feel of the Wembley turf via a practice session the day before the final

STATS

Wigan 13 Dewsbury 2

Saturday 4 May at Wembley Stadium, London (3.00 pm)

Wigan (cherry and white hoops): Sullivan (captain), Ring, Parker, Kinnear, L. Brown, Abram, Binks, Hodder, Bennett, Beetham, Stephens, Mason, Sherrington. Trainer: T. McCarty

Dewsbury (red, amber and black hoops): Davies, Bailey, Smith, Hirst, Coates, Woolmore, Rudd, Hobson, P. Brown, Rhodes, Bland, Malkin, Joe Lyman (captain). Trainer: W.J. Hobbs

Referee: R. Robinson   Touch-judges: F.R. Wilson, T. Kiley

Half-time: 5–2 Attendance: 41,500 Receipts: £5,614

Weather: cloudy, strong wind

Cup presentation: Lord Daresbury

Progressive score:

Wigan	score (min)	Dewsbury
Sullivan penalty	2–0 (3)	
Abram try	5–0 (14)	
	5–2 (33)	Davies drop-goal
L. Brown try	8–2 (60)	
Kinnear try, Sullivan goal	13–2 (70)	

Route to the final:

First round:
Wigan 25 Batley 0, Dewsbury 37 Cottingham (Hull) 0

Second round:
Wigan 16 Hunslet 0, Dewsbury 14 Swinton 7

Third round:
St Helens 2 Wigan 2, Warrington 4 Dewsbury 10

Third round replay: Wigan 25 St Helens 5

Semi-finals: Wigan 7 St Helens Recreation 7 (Station Road, Swinton, 31,000),

Dewsbury 9 Castleford 3 (Fartown, Huddersfield, 25,000)

Semi-final replay: Wigan 13 St Helens Recreation 12 (Mather Lane, Leigh, 21,940)

Head-to-head form guide:

No previous meetings during season

was winning the scrum half battle against Jim Rudd, and almost scored after a 'dribble' by his forwards, whilst Kinnear also threatened with a strong burst covering half the field.

Wigan got the decisive score on the hour after the ball emerged from a scrum, Binks supplying Abrams. As John Woolmore moved in to tackle, the stand-off passed to Kinnear who evaded Smith and Tommy Bailey and, despite being detained by Davies, offloaded to Lou Brown who dived over in the corner amidst claims of a forward pass. Sullivan struck the crossbar with his goal attempt, and then hit the outside of a post moments later with a penalty but, at 8–2, Wigan looked comfortable at two scores ahead. Dewsbury suffered a blow 15 minutes from the end, Hirst quitting with a fractured rib. Five minutes later Binks scooted around Coates and Woolmore to retrieve his short kick, sending Kinnear in for a simple try beneath the posts. Sullivan's goal ended the scoring at 13–2.

A jubilant Sullivan told the *Wigan Examiner*: 'I thought we had the measure of our opponents when Abram scored his try,' adding 'our players had the advantage of being used to playing before a large crowd. I never felt nervous at any stage.'

It is part of rugby league folklore that the Yorkshire side suffered through being prevailed upon to sacrifice their usual style of forward dominated play, the *Dewsbury Reporter* commenting: 'I have wondered if they (Dewsbury) were trying to oblige the authorities by playing pretty football. There was none of their cup fighting qualities.' There is no contemporary evidence to support that suggestion, although Rugby League Chairman Fred Kennedy, reportedly, visited both dressing rooms prior to kick-off and implored the teams to play 'clean and sportsmanlike' as they were performing on a 'national stage'.

1930 RUGBY LEAGUE CHALLENGE CUP FINAL
Widnes v St Helens

Widnes line-up for a publicity shot taken at Wembley ahead of the final. From the left, Douglas (captain), Topping, Owen, Laughton, Dennett, Ratcliffe, W. Bradley, Fraser, J. Higgins, Stevens, Millington, Silcock, Hoey, A. Higgins, Kelsall, van Rooyen

Wembley's first 'giant killing' upset occurred at the 1930 Challenge Cup Final when Widnes, who finished 15th in the League, beat keen derby rivals and table toppers St Helens by 10–3. The Chemics were boosted by a massive turnout at Widnes railway station, crowds gathering one and a half hours before their departure. The *Widnes Weekly News* reported the station had 'never been so busy on platform tickets' noting that veteran South African prop George van Rooyen, the only non-Widnesian in the team, 'used his weight to push through the crowds'. Typical of Wembley 'send-offs' during that era, the team departed behind a black steam engine decorated in white with 'Play Up Widnes' emblazoned across the front.

Unlike the previous year, when they emerged separately, the teams marched into the arena side-by-side for the first time, accompanied by 'an ear splitting roar', one excited, agile Widnes youth climbing a goal post and placing his black and white hat at the top!

St Helens' star winger Alf Ellaby initiated the opening score after three minutes when, on receiving the ball from Billy Mercer, he drew out defenders before cutting smartly inside, kicking towards the goal. Although Ellaby was shoved into touch, forwards Lou Houghton and Trevor Hall followed up, the former taking advantage of a nervy-looking fumble by 20-year-old Peter Topping to touch down just shy of the dead-ball line. George Lewis missed the kick.

Widnes, though, looked the more motivated outfit

WINNING CAPTAIN

Paddy Douglas (Widnes 1930)

Halfback Patrick 'Paddy' Douglas made his debut for Widnes in 1923 having signed from his local junior club, Widnes Rovers. Small in stature at 5 feet 5 inches and weighing 10½ stone, he was regarded as a 'box of tricks' and extremely difficult to get hold of. Taking over as captain, he led Widnes to their first Rugby League Challenge Cup success in 1930, having been a Lancashire Cup runner-up in 1928. His last match for the club was in 1932 after 240 appearances. The 1979 tour captain, Doug Laughton, was his great grandson.

STATS

Widnes 10 St Helens 3

Saturday 3 May at Wembley Stadium, London (3.00 pm)

Widnes (black and white hoops): Fraser, Dennett, Ratcliffe, Topping, Owen, Douglas (captain), Laughton, Kelsall, Stevens, Silcock, van Rooyen, Millington, Hoey. Trainer: P. Lyons

St Helens (blue): Crooks, Ellaby, Mercer, Lewis (captain), Hardgrave, Fairclough, Groves, Hutt, Clarey, Houghton, Hall, Halfpenny, Harrison. Trainer: E. Forber

Referee: F. Peel   Touch-judges: L. Greenwood, T. Danson

Half-time: 10–3   Attendance: 36,544   Receipts: £3,102

Weather: sunny, very warm

Cup presentation: Lord Lonsdale

Progressive score:

Widnes	score (min)	St Helens
	0–3 (3)	Houghton try
Ratcliffe penalty-try, Hoey goal	5–3 (10)	
Dennett try	8–3 (33)	
Ratcliffe penalty	10–3 (39)	

Route to the final:

First round: Widnes 20 Bradford Northern 0, St Helens 9 St Helens Recreation 7

Second round: Swinton 7 Widnes 7, Leeds 5 St Helens 18

Second round replay: Widnes 6 Swinton 5

Third round: Widnes 19 Hull 5, St Helens 22 Hunslet 7

Semi-finals:

Widnes 10 Barrow 3 (Wilderspool, Warrington, 25,500),

St Helens 5 Wigan 5 (Station Road, Swinton, 37,169)

Semi-final replay:

St Helens 22 Wigan 10 (Mather Lane, Leigh, 24,000)

Head-to-head form guide:

St Helens 0 Widnes 3 (League)

Widnes 8 St Helens 21 (League)

Widnes skipper Paddy Douglas is grabbed from behind by St Helens wingman Alf Ellaby

and took their chance when it came. Albert Ratcliffe recovered a loose ball and kicked towards Saints' full back Charlie Crooks who misfielded. Ratcliffe got a boot to the ball, sending it under the posts and, although Crooks impeded him, referee Frank Peel awarded a penalty-try. Jimmy Hoey's goal edged the Chemics 5–3 ahead. Lewis had chances to bring his side back on terms, missing two penalty efforts, both for offside. Topping almost atoned for his earlier mistake when he 'brought the house down' with a tremendous run before Hall managed to terminate his progress.

On 33 minutes the Widnes fans went 'mad with delight' after Ratcliffe, having drawn Ellaby in from the touchline, kicked into the left corner, Jack Dennett

taking the ball to score Widnes' second try. Harry Owen was well off-target with the goal effort, Widnes leading 8–3. With pressure mounting on the Saints' defence, Lewis was forced to double up as an extra full back. Just before the break, Ratcliffe scored the last points of the afternoon, landing a penalty, awarded after Lewis failed to play the ball correctly.

Widnes fans were clearly enjoying their day out and threw berets into the air when their team reappeared for the second half, although their heroes proved less effective over the last 40 minutes, making several handling errors. St Helens got on top midway through the half, their forwards making several strong dribbling rushes, the ball being moved about more freely resulting in Les Fairclough, Roy Hardgrave and Ellaby all going close. A break in play due to an injury to Hardgrave gave Widnes a breather and they steadied their ship afterwards, holding on for a famous victory.

The *Manchester Guardian* said Widnes won due to their forwards 'commanding the scrummage as expected' adding they 'mastered in the loose also', a factor that gave halfbacks Paddy Douglas and Jerry Laughton plenty of freedom to dictate play. The result concluded a miserable week for St Helens, having also lost at home to Leeds in the Championship play-off. Ellaby, in a 1982 interview, claimed St Helens were tired following an exhaustive tour of the Houses of Parliament on the morning of the final, arranged by their local MP. It was a scenario not unfamiliar during an era when less thought was given to players' match preparation.

1931 RUGBY LEAGUE CHALLENGE CUP FINAL
Halifax v York

Having hosted an all-Lancashire contest the previous year, Wembley's turnstiles were opened in 1931 for its first White Rose decider, Halifax defeating York 22–8 in the stadium's most entertaining Challenge Cup Final so far. Pre-match drama occurred in Halifax's camp through the omission of winger Lou Brown who was in Wigan's line-up two years earlier. Having played in all previous rounds, he was sensationally suspended by the club after failing to report for the preceding weekend's game, his place going to Fred Adams. The York side, meanwhile, looked as though they would be without skipper Billie Thomas, but he passed a fitness test on his troublesome knee the day before, having seen a London specialist.

York got off to the stronger start and led after three minute's play when prop Dan Pascoe notched a 35-yard penalty following a play-the-ball infringement. A minute later Laurie Higgins missed a similar opportunity for a Halifax side that found it difficult to settle as York began to penetrate, particularly with their three-quarters. Pascoe was wide with his second penalty and then, midway through the half, the pressure told; Harold Thomas claimed the opening try for York, evading Ivor Davies to fly into the corner, having received the ball from Mel Rosser following a scrum. Pascoe missed the tricky conversion but York deservedly led 5–0. Halifax, in a rare visit to York's half of the field, failed with a penalty attempt from Adams

The Halifax Courier & Guardian produced this special postcard to celebrate their local side's first Wembley visit

as the Minster Men continued to entertain the crowd. Then, against the run of play, Halifax drew level when skipper Dai Rees opened up York's defence from inside his own 25-yard area, sending Herbert Haigh on a lengthy run down the right channel. Just yards from the try-line he transferred the ball to Adams out on the touchline, the winger returning it inside for Harold Bland to score. Adams added an excellent goal. The thrills continued when, four minutes later and on the stroke of half-time, Rosser put Harold Thomas in at the corner, restoring York's advantage at 8–5, Pascoe missing the conversion.

The second period saw a complete turnaround in

fortunes, Halifax dominating almost from the restart with some enterprising rugby. Despite having an Ivor Davies touchdown disallowed when he failed to ground properly, they took the lead through two goals; a penalty by Adams and a drop from Dick Davies. Within a minute of the latter, Halifax stretched their advantage when Ivor Davies was awarded a penalty-try after being obstructed in a race for the try-line. Adams added the extras and the Thrum Hallers were 14–8 to the good. York had a further setback when scrum half Arthur Lloyd retired for a brief period to receive treatment to an injury. Pascoe missed a penalty chance that would have brought York within one score but, instead, Halifax rubbed salt into the wounds of their withering opponents with two late tries, both from Higgins. Haigh provided the scoring pass for the first after an Ivor Davies break, Higgins squeezing over the try-line for the second despite an attempted Harold Thomas tackle. Adams converted the former, Dick Davies missing with the second attempt.

The elated Halifax team celebrated at the Great Central Hotel in Marylebone during the evening when the first song was 'Thompson at the Football Match' which, apparently 'brought the house down!' Back in Halifax, success tasted even better when Sir Harold Mackintosh, of the well-known Mackintosh's Sweets company provided a tin of toffee for each player, containing a note inviting them to accept 'sweets for victory!'

The two captains, Halifax's Dai Rees (left) and York's Billie Thomas join hands with referee Jack Eddon before kick-off

STATS

Halifax 22 York 8

Saturday 2 May at Wembley Stadium, London (3.00 pm)

Halifax (blue and white hoops): R. 'Dick' Davies, Adams, Higgs, Haigh, Higgins, I. Davies, Hanson, Bland, Rawnsley, Renton, Rees (captain), Sutcliffe, Atkinson. Trainer: D. Jenkins

York (amber and black narrow hoops): Owen, H Thomas, Rosser, W.J. 'Jack' Davies, W.J. 'Billy' Davies, Billie Thomas (captain), Lloyd, Davis, Myers, Pascoe, H. Davies, Layhe, Johnson. Trainer: G. Rees

Referee: J. Eddon

Touch-judges: H.W. Bateman, G. Ireland

Half-time: 5–8   Attendance: 40,368   Receipts: £3,908

Weather: sunny, very hot

Cup presentation: Lord Derby, Rugby League president

Progressive score:

Halifax	score (min)	York
	0–2 (3)	Pascoe penalty
	0–5 (20)	H. Thomas try
Bland try, Adams goal	5–5 (36)	
	5–8 (40)	H. Thomas try
Adams penalty	7–8 (57)	
R. Davies drop-goal	9–8 (65)	
I. Davies penalty-try, Adams goal	14–8 (66)	
Higgins try, Adams goal	19–8 (77)	
Higgins try	22–8 (79)	

Route to the final:

First round:
Dewsbury 2 Halifax 3, Bradford Northern 0 York 11

Second round: Swinton 0 Halifax 2, York 13 Huddersfield 2

Third round: Halifax 2 Oldham 2, York 12 Salford 2

Third round replay: Oldham 2 Halifax 2

Third round second replay:
Halifax 5 Oldham 2 (Fartown, Huddersfield)

Semi-finals:
Halifax 11 St Helens 2 (The Athletic Grounds, Rochdale, 21,674),

York 15 Warrington 5 (Headingley, Leeds, 32,419)

Head-to-head form guide:

York 3 Halifax 0 (Yorkshire Cup)

1932 RUGBY LEAGUE CHALLENGE CUP FINAL
Leeds v Swinton

The speed and skill of Leeds' Eric Harris provided the key moment of the 1932 Challenge Cup Final, the legendary wingman scoring what was, effectively, the winning try 13 minutes into the second half. Leeds were ahead 8–4 against a Swinton side seeking a record-making fourth success in the competition, when a scrum was formed on the halfway line. The Lions won the heel but when Billo Rees, having received the ball from halfback partner Bryn Evans, transferred to Harold Evans, it bounced off the latter's shoulder. Leeds' Jeff Moores scooped the ball up before passing to co-centre Frank O'Rourke who quickly transferred it to Harris. With space having opened up on the outside, Harris sprinted down the right touchline evading Jack Kenny on the way and, as he approached full back Bob Scott, found the extra gear to accelerate past him before diving over the whitewash in the corner. The *Leeds Mercury* correspondent, Herbert Campbell, said: 'It was an epic effort in such a game, and could have been scored only by a player of Harris' abnormal speed.' It was the only try scored against Swinton in that year's competition

but it was three points that made all the difference, being conjured up during a second half that mostly belonged to the Lancashire side.

Whilst described by the *Yorkshire Post* as 'a fast and gruelling game' the final did not produce the open play generally anticipated. The expert view was that Swinton's pack—considered the better of the two—would have to master the Leeds six to give their backs the chance of outplaying what was perceived as the Yorkshire outfit's superior back division. Joe Thompson won the coin toss allowing his Leeds side to begin with the advantage of a strong wind, his team subsequently building an 8–2 interval lead, all the points resulting from penalties. Thompson hit four for Leeds (three for illegal scrum feeding by Bryn Evans, another when Joe Wright played the ball incorrectly), Martin Hodgson replying with a superb touchline penalty into the teeth of the wind after Leslie Adams strayed offside at a scrum.

Swinton began asking questions of the Leeds defence after the break, reducing the deficit to four points through another excellent touchline penalty

A smiling Leeds captain Joe Thompson leads his team from the pitch—his four early penalty goals played a vital part in the success

from Hodgson. But the Headingley-based team produced the 'sucker punch' through Harris' try, a score that impacted on the assurance of Swinton's play for the following 10 minutes or so before the Lions roared back strongly in the closing period. But, despite intense pressure, their only reward in a thrilling finish was two further Hodgson penalties as Leeds held on to win 11–8.

Although not fulfilling predictions of surpassing the 39,003 attendance record for Wigan's Central Park (set

STATS

Leeds 11 Swinton 8

Saturday 9 April at Central Park, Wigan (3.30 pm)

Leeds (amber with blue bands): Brough, E. Harris, Moores, O'Rourke, Goulthorpe, Williams, Adams, Thompson (captain), Lowe, Smith, Cox, Douglas, Glossop. Trainer: B. Heyhirst

Swinton (navy blue): Scott, Buckingham, Green, H. Evans, Kenny, Rees, B. Evans (captain), Strong, Armitt, Wright, Hodgson, Beswick, Butters. Trainer: W. Kearns

Referee: F. Peel   Touch-judges: T. Baines, W. Ainscough

Half-time: 8–2   Attendance: 29,000   Receipts: £2,479

Weather: sunny, strong wind

Cup presentation: Mr E. Brown, Rugby League chairman

Progressive score:

Leeds	score (min)	Swinton
Thompson penalty	2–0 (8)	
Thompson penalty	4–0 (12)	
Thompson penalty	6–0 (15)	
Thompson penalty	8–0 (19)	
	8–2 (29)	Hodgson penalty
	8–4 (44)	Hodgson penalty
E. Harris try	11–4 (53)	
	11–6 (62)	Hodgson penalty
	11–8 (73)	Hodgson penalty

Route to the final:

First round: Hull 2 Leeds 5, Widnes 2 Swinton 25

Second round: Leeds 36 Keighley 2, Swinton 11 Batley 0

Third round: Leeds 21 Leigh 2, Castleford 2 Swinton 10

Semi-finals:

Leeds 2 Halifax 2 (Fartown, Huddersfield, 31,818),

Swinton 7 Wakefield Trinity 4 (The Athletic Grounds, Rochdale, 21,273)

Semi-final replay:

Leeds 9 Halifax 2 (Belle Vue, Wakefield, 21,000)

Head-to-head form guide:

Leeds 2 Swinton 4 (League)

Swinton 8 Leeds 11 (League)

WINNING CAPTAIN

Joe Thompson (Leeds 1932)

Although born in Hambrook, near Bristol, Joe Thompson was signed from Welsh rugby union in 1923 for a reported £300. Previously with the Abercarn and Cross Keys clubs, he represented Wales against England at Twickenham (January 1923). The powerful prop or back-row forward proved himself a colossus in the Leeds pack over the next 10 years during which he made 390 appearances (860 goals, 1,883 points) for the club. With Leeds he won the Rugby League Challenge Cup (1923, 1932), Yorkshire Cup (1928, 1930, 1932) and Yorkshire League (1927/28, 1930/31). He was a tourist three times (1924, 1928, 1932), played in 12 Tests, and made appearances for Wales (8), Other Nationalities (5) and Glamorgan & Monmouthshire (7). After retiring he had a brief spell as Leeds trainer during 1934/35.

Swinton's Bryn Evans (left) looks for an opening as a scrum breaks up

in 1930 at a Wigan-Warrington Challenge Cup tie), the occasion still captured the atmosphere associated with a cup final despite its temporary absence from Wembley. The Horwich RMI Band played a 'selection' during the build-up and at the interval and supported Arthur Craiger as he led the community singing (a role he fulfilled at Wembley's first Challenge Cup Final in 1929) as the crowd 'enthusiastically joined in'.

Leeds were without star winger Stanley Smith (pulled thigh muscle), Harry Goulthorpe replacing him, whilst for Swinton, Dick Green, who made his senior debut the previous week, replaced centre George Whittaker (shoulder injury), and forward Miller Strong took part after receiving a 'sending off sufficient' verdict following his recent dismissal. Leeds, like Swinton, displayed a mean defence throughout the tournament, winning the trophy without conceding a try in any round.

1933 RUGBY LEAGUE CHALLENGE CUP FINAL
Huddersfield v Warrington

The 1933 finale was hailed a 'thriller' and judged today as the best of Wembley's pre-war deciders, Huddersfield clinging on for a nerve-tingling 21–17 victory over Warrington. The telling factor between victory and defeat was the boot of Huddersfield skipper Len Bowkett whose 'sensational' kicking brought him a, then, Wembley record six goals from six attempts 'from all parts of the field' in a strong wind. The first attended by Royalty—The Prince of Wales presented the trophy—it attracted a Challenge Cup Final attendance of 41,874 with receipts of £6,465, both new highs.

Warrington's pack, led by Sam Hardman and Nat Bentham, dominated the opening, allowing scrum half Dai Davies to open out play, Tommy Thompson almost scoring in the corner after picking up a loose ball. Huddersfield withstood the pressure, a scrum infringement by Davies leading to them claiming the first points through a Bowkett penalty. He added a second five minutes later, Arthur Evans failing to play the ball correctly, placing the Fartowners 4–0 ahead. During this opening period Warrington full back Billy Holding, who was otherwise outstanding, missed with three penalty attempts. Bowkett was giving his team confidence and the pace quickened, Holding just managing to get across to snuff out an Ernie Mills threat after the Huddersfield winger intercepted a pass.

Eventually Leslie Adams broke through the middle

for Huddersfield, Fred Brindle being on hand to accept his perfectly timed pass for the first try. Bowkett converted for his third goal in nine minutes to build a 9–0 lead. In a thrilling conclusion to the first half, Warrington's supporters went almost delirious as their team produced a magnificent fight back. Bill Shankland knocked-on with the line open but, from the resultant scrum, Jack Oster's sharp pass sent Billy Dingsdale charging between Stanley Brogden and Tom Scourfield to score by the posts. Then Davies, having received a quick heel from the scrum, set off on

Huddersfield captain and six-goal hero Len Bowkett is chaired around the Wembley pitch by his delighted colleagues

a wonderful solo run to cross the try-line unopposed. Holding landed both goals, and Warrington returned to the changing rooms 10–9 ahead.

Almost inevitably, Bowkett restored the Yorkshire side's lead after the interval, succeeding with a long-distance penalty after Davies illegally 'fed' a scrum. The excitement continued as Warrington's pack spent the next 20 minutes trying to break Huddersfield's resistance but they would not yield. Then, as the Wires ran out of steam, the ever-threatening Adams broke through again, sending Mills flying in at the corner, Bowkett adding a great touchline goal. A penalty from Holding following a 'loose ensemble' in front of goal put Warrington back into striking distance at 16–12 but, when Huddersfield's Gwyn Richards charged down an Oster clearance kick, a favourable bounce brought him a try despite an attempted tackle. Bowkett added his sixth goal. With time evaporating, Warrington showed character as Davies scored another great individual try, eluding Richards and Bowkett before going around Scourfield. Holding's goal brought Warrington within four points but it proved the closing score.

Warrington, led by their pack, generally held the edge until midway through the second half, Bowkett saying afterwards: 'We won because our backs took all their chances, even the thinnest. Our forwards were beaten but their second half rally came at the right time for us.' Huddersfield—for whom winger Stephen Ray, scorer of 33 tries during the campaign, missed out with a sceptic thigh—looked an unlikely candidate for Wembley success earlier in the season. Their 'average' side was transformed during January through signing Australian winger Ray Markham (a 'passenger' for much of the final after an early shoulder injury), Leeds scrum half Adams and Hull Kingston Rovers loose forward Brindle.

His Royal Highness The Prince of Wales—the future King Edward VIII—is presented to the Warrington team by their (partially obscured) captain Bill Shankland. Players on view (from the left) are: Dai Davies, Billy Dingsdale, Nat Bentham, Arthur Evans (shaking hands), Sam Hardman and Bob Smith. This was the first occasion that a member of the Royal Family attended a Challenge Cup Final

---

STATS

Huddersfield 21 Warrington 17

Saturday 6 May at Wembley Stadium, London (3.00 pm)

Huddersfield (claret with gold chevron): Scourfield, Mills, Brogden, Bowkett (captain), Markham, Richards, Adams, Sherwood, Halliday, Banks, Tiffany, Talbot, Brindle. Trainer: C. Brockbank

Warrington (royal blue with primrose chevron): Holding, Blinkhorn, Shankland (captain), Dingsdale, Thompson, Oster, Davies, Miller, Bentham, Hardman, Evans, Smith, Seeling. Trainer: W. Bennett

Referee: F. Fairhurst   Touch-judges: F.C. Smythe, J.A. Hudson

Half-time: 9–10   Attendance: 41,874   Receipts: £6,465

Weather: sunny, strong wind

Cup presentation: H.R.H. The Prince of Wales

Progressive score:

Huddersfield	score (min)	Warrington
Bowkett penalty	2–0 (20)	
Bowkett penalty	4–0 (25)	
Brindle try, Bowkett goal	9–0 (28)	
	9–5 (30)	Dingsdale try, Holding goal
	9–10 (38)	Davies try, Holding goal
Bowkett penalty	11–10 (44)	
Mills try, Bowkett goal	16–10 (65)	
	16–12 (69)	Holding penalty
Richards try, Bowkett goal	21–12 (74)	
	21–17 (76)	Davies try, Holding goal

Route to the final:

First round:
Huddersfield 19 Dewsbury 7, Warrington 34 Leigh 3

Second round:
Barrow 0 Huddersfield 0, Batley 10 Warrington 20

Second round replay: Huddersfield 2 Barrow 0

Third round:
Swinton 5 Huddersfield 12, Wigan 7 Warrington 9

Semi-finals:
Huddersfield 30 Leeds 8 (Belle Vue, Wakefield, 36,359),
Warrington 11 St Helens 5 (Station Road, Swinton, 30,373)

Head-to-head form guide:

No previous meetings during season

1934 RUGBY LEAGUE CHALLENGE CUP FINAL
Hunslet v Widnes

Hunslet celebrated their only Wembley victory in 1934, defeating Widnes 11–5 although reduced to 12 players just before the interval. The *Widnes Weekly News* correspondent confessed he backed his team at half time, being only two points down after facing a strong wind and bright sunshine. But he added that 'when we fancied there was no doubt as to the result going well in our favour, and with only twelve Hunslet men on the field, we cracked up unexpectedly, left wide gaps in defence, and let the Yorkshire boys beat us soundly.' Widnes paraded the only team to ever appear at Wembley with 100% home grown talent, a fact confirmed when goal-kicking centre Joe Robinson, from Thatto Heath (four miles away), failed to recover from a bad injury incurred in the semi-final.

Hunslet did not get off to the best start when, having won a fifth-minute scrum near their own line, Chemics' forward Hughie McDowell peeled away, charging down a Billy Thornton clearance, the ball ricocheted into the air. Hunslet full back Jack Walkington was unable to recover it, McDowell following up to grab the ball a yard from the try-line, diving over in 'spectacular fashion' too far out for Albert

WINNING CAPTAIN

Jack Walkington (Hunslet 1934)

Leeds-born Jack Walkington was a product of local Burley rugby union club, signing with Hunslet for £300 in 1927. Beginning at centre, he soon established himself as a cool, resolute full back, capable of fielding the most difficult of kicks and clearing his line with consummate ease. He gained winners' medals for the Rugby League Challenge Cup (1934) and Championship (1937/38)—both as captain—and Yorkshire League (1931/32), his lengthy Parkside career ending in 1948, following a club record 572 matches. During the Second World War he appeared as a guest for Batley, Bramley, Dewsbury and Leeds. He represented England (3 times—including one wartime international) and Yorkshire (15). In 1950, he was appointed Hunslet team manager.

Ratcliffe's goal attempt. Fragmented play followed, free kicks regularly being awarded, Widnes' full back Walter Bradley struggling against the twin elements of sunshine and wind as Hunslet peppered him with high kicks. The Parksiders eventually reduced their arrears to one point when Mark Tolson's penalty succeeded from a difficult angle following a scrum offence.

Hunslet with the Challenge Cup, standing: Crowther, Dawson, Tolson, Beverley, Smith, Whitehead, White. Seated: J. Lewthwaite (chairman), Dennis, Morrell, Walkington, Winter, Broughton, Hannah (trainer). On ground: Todd, Thornton

The opening period was mostly 'uninspiring' with tackling dominant, although the last score of the half —on 26 minutes—was the afternoon's highlight. Walkington moved up as extra man following a scrum, taking the ball on the burst and veering right before passing to Ernest Winter who sent co-centre Cyril Morrell racing away on a spectacular run. Using winger George Dennis as a foil, Morrell outmanoeuvred Peter Topping to score with two defenders clinging on. Tolson missed the kick, Hunslet leading 5–3. It was bittersweet for Morrell, fracturing his collarbone in the act. After attention he returned, but withdrew permanently when it became apparent how severe his injury was.

STATS

Hunslet 11 Widnes 5

Saturday 5 May at Wembley Stadium, London (3.00 pm)

Hunslet (myrtle with flame and white bands): Walkington (captain), Dennis, Morrell, Winter, Broughton, Todd, Thornton, Tolson, White, Smith, Crowther, Dawson, Beverley. Trainer: W. Hannah

Widnes: (black and white hoops): Bradley, Owen, Topping, Jacks, Gallimore, Shannon, McCue, Silcock (captain), Jones, A. Higgins, McDowell, Ratcliffe, Millington. Trainer: P. Lyons

Referee: A. Holbrook Touch-judges: J. McEwan, H.C. Norrey

Half-time: 5–3   Attendance: 41,280   Receipts: £6,686

Weather: sunny, windy

Cup presentation: Lord Derby, Rugby League president

Progressive score:

Hunslet	score (min)	Widnes
	0–3 (5)	McDowell try
Tolson penalty	2–3 (16)	
Morrell try	5–3 (26)	
	5–5 (42)	Ratcliffe penalty
Beverley try	8–5 (50)	
Smith try	11–5 (76)	

Route to the final:

First round: Leigh 6 Hunslet 8, Widnes 12 Leeds 3

Second round:
Castleford 4 Hunslet 4, Hull Kingston Rovers 0 Widnes 10

Second round replay: Hunslet 23 Castleford 0

Third round: Hunslet 2 York 0, Halifax 3 Widnes 5

Semi-finals:
Hunslet 12 Huddersfield 7 (Belle Vue, Wakefield, 27,450),

Widnes 7 Oldham 4 (Station Road, Swinton)

Head-to-head form guide:

No previous meetings during season

Two minutes into the second half Widnes drew level, Ratcliffe kicking a penalty for obstruction. Widnes began to press, Ratcliffe missing a penalty and Topping almost engineering a try after evading four defenders on a sizzling run. Kicking ahead, he regained possession but when he passed inside, the move broke down and an opportunity was lost. Hunslet relieved the pressure with a hefty free kick and was soon on the assault. From a scrum Thornton kidded Widnes' defence with a pass to Frank Dawson who nipped around the blind side 12 yards out before transferring to Harry Beverley (relocated to centre in place of Morrell) who scored unopposed. Tolson was unable to convert.

Despite their one-man advantage, Widnes tired as Hunslet took control, second-row men Hector Crowther and Dawson leading the bombardment. Tolson missed two penalties and Ratcliffe one before Hunslet sealed their win four minutes from time with a move that covered half the field. George Todd sent Dawson down the middle and he headed left where, of all people, prop Len Smith was up in support to take the pass and crash over in the corner, Tolson missing the goal. Widnes tried in vain to rally, Ratcliffe missing another penalty and Percy Jacks attempting a last ditch 'up and under', Hunslet's defence recovering before the Widnes forwards arrived on the scene.

The *Yorkshire Post* commented it was 'not a good game for those who enjoy passing and running but there were thrills with some of the finest forward play seen at Wembley.' Both visited White City Stadium the previous evening to witness London Highfield beat Bramley 59–11.

Hunslet prop Len Smith scores the match-clinching try to the obvious delight of team-mate George Broughton. Widnes' Peter Topping is the player on the right

1935 RUGBY LEAGUE CHALLENGE CUP FINAL
Castleford v Huddersfield

Castleford captain Arthur Atkinson is all smiles as he carries the trophy down the steps from the Royal Box

Castleford provided Wembley's first 'Fairy Tale' result in 1935, the so-called 'Babes' lifting the Challenge Cup nine years after admittance to the Rugby Football League. Their 11–8 victory over Huddersfield was considered a triumph for an enthusiastic hard working side that displayed few nerves. It was a day their travelling fans were determined to enjoy whatever the result, bringing Wembley to life before kick-off by singing their own 'terrace' songs like 'We're Out to Win the Cup this Year' (to the tune of 'On Ilkley Moor

Baht'at') and 'Roll Along, Castleford Forwards, Roll Along'. Whilst Castleford reported fit, Huddersfield competed without Australian wingman Ernie Mills, his previous month's knee ligament injury failing to heal.

Castleford soon pushed deep into Huddersfield territory, scrum half Leslie Adams finding touch just three yards from their try-line. From the resulting scrum, Huddersfield were penalised, Castleford's George Lewis missing the penalty attempt after just three minutes' play. Castleford, though, began opening up play in brilliant fashion with some excellent wide passing, skipper Arthur Atkinson agonisingly dropping the ball in the fifth minute with the line at his mercy. Another penalty was awarded to Castleford, this time Atkinson missing through hitting the wall of Huddersfield defenders lined up in front of him. The Fartown outfit then took a surprise lead when Dai Davies duped Adams with a dummy pass, setting up a move that resulted in Idris Towill introducing another 'dummy' to beat Atkinson and score. Herbert Sherwood missed the goal.

Castleford kept their composure and continued to dictate, Atkinson again knocking-on in front of an open line, his bad luck continuing when his 23rd minute

WINNING CAPTAIN

Arthur Atkinson (Castleford 1935)

Arthur Atkinson was one of the first stars at Castleford, the strong running centre making his debut in 1926, a few weeks into their first season as members of the Rugby Football League. His last match for them was not until 1942, after 431 appearances, 157 tries and 230 goals (including a 75-yard effort at St Helens in 1929). He took over as captain in 1928/29, leading his team to success in the Rugby League Challenge Cup (1935) and Yorkshire League (1932/33, 1938/39). He was a tourist twice (1932, 1936), played in 11 Tests and was selected by England (7 times) and Yorkshire (14). In 1940 he made one wartime guest appearance with Batley.

penalty hit an upright. When Huddersfield's Ray Markham was judged offside under his own posts Castleford spurned the easy two points. Instead, Adams took a quick 'tap' but referee Albert Harding ruled out his touchdown attempt. Moments later, Atkinson landed a morale-boosting long-range penalty effort off the touchline. Almost from the restart stand-off Billy Davies burst through for Castleford and, when challenged, passed to the supporting Jim Croston who raced clear before sending Tommy Askin over for a try. Atkinson missed the conversion, leading his troops in at half-time 5–3 ahead.

Huddersfield's pack showed greater resolve in the opening period of the second half but unyielding Castleford soaked up the pressure and were soon back on top, grabbing two crucial tries in four minutes. The first was when Huddersfield's Tom Scourfield attempted to clear the ball after Castleford kicked it towards his line, the missile going astray as Ted Sadler moved quickly on to him, Adams picking up to go over. The next came after Askin broke away, starting a move that saw the ball travel to the opposite flank for Bernard Cunniffe to cross in the corner, resisting Markham in the process. Atkinson was off-target with both conversions but at 11–3 their supporters were already celebrating as 'Castleford hats were thrown in the air'. The pace slowed although Castleford retained their grip until the last 10 minutes. It was then that Huddersfield posed a threat after their free kick found touch in Castleford's half. A spectacular last-ditch tackle by Atkinson stopped Henry Tiffany in the act of touching down before, a minute later, Sherwood reduced the deficit with a penalty. The atmosphere was 'electric' as Huddersfield attempted to close the

six-point margin, a kick-through by skipper Alex Fiddes forcing Lewis into his first mistake, losing the ball to present the Scot with a simple try. With the full-time whistle moments away, Sherwood missed the difficult kick.

Whilst Castleford were left to celebrate—particularly Adams with his third Challenge Cup winning medal from four finals with three different clubs—the *Huddersfield Examiner* conceded that 'at no stage did Huddersfield look confident'.

STATS

Castleford 11 Huddersfield 8

Saturday 4 May at Wembley Stadium, London (3.00 pm)

Castleford (white with amber and black chevron): Lewis, Cunniffe, Atkinson (captain), Croston, Askin, Davies, Adams, McManus, Haley, Taylor, Crossley, Smith, Sadler. Trainer: W. Rhodes

Huddersfield (claret with narrow gold hoops): Scourfield, Mountain, Towill, Fiddes (captain), Markham, Richards, Davies, Roberts, Watson, Sherwood, Tiffany, Fuller, Talbot. Trainer: C. Brockbank

Referee: A.E. Harding

Touch-judges: F.W. Wright, I.J. Fowler

Half-time: 5–3   Attendance: 39,000   Receipts: £5,533

Weather: sunny and windy

Cup presentation: Lord Cozens Hardy

Progressive score:

Castleford	score (min)	Huddersfield
	0–3 (18)	Towill try
Atkinson penalty	2–3 (27)	
Askin try	5–3 (29)	
Adams try	8–3 (45)	
Cunniffe try	11–3 (49)	
	11–5 (72)	Sherwood penalty
	11–8 (78)	Fiddes try

Route to the final:

First round: Castleford 33 Astley and Tyldesley Collieries 4, Leeds 3 Huddersfield 4

Second round: Liverpool Stanley 2 Castleford 8, Huddersfield 6 Oldham 0

Third round: Castleford 10 Hunslet 3, Huddersfield 4 Widnes 0

Semi-finals:
Castleford 11 Barrow 5 (Station Road, Swinton, 24,469), Huddersfield 21 Hull 5 (Headingley, Leeds, 37,111)

Head-to-head form guide:

Huddersfield 6 Castleford 6 (Yorkshire Cup)

Castleford 3 Huddersfield 2 (Yorkshire Cup replay)

Castleford 12 Huddersfield 9 (League)

Huddersfield 5 Castleford 3 (League)

Castleford's team in 1935, standing: Haley, Atkinson, Knowles, Lewis, Croston, McManus, Taylor, Sadler, Smith. Stooping: Cunniffe. Kneeling: Askin, Adams, Davies. Crossley was absent on this occasion

1936 RUGBY LEAGUE CHALLENGE CUP FINAL
Leeds v Warrington

Leeds equalled Huddersfield's record of four Challenge Cup successes by comfortably disposing of Warrington 18–2 in the 1936 final in what was Wembley's biggest winning margin to date. There was little doubt over Leeds' superiority, their four tries including two of the best so far seen at the stadium. However, their first try of the afternoon courted controversy. It began in the Leeds half during the eighth minute after the ball found its way to their Australian wing Eric Harris on the right flank. He roared down the touchline, catching the defence unawares with his cross-field kick towards the posts. Team-mate Iorwerth Isaac took it in his stride to score near the uprights as the Wires defence 'looked on in amazement' having barely moved, believing the Welsh loose forward would be given offside. Their protests went unheeded and Evan Williams converted to put Leeds 5–0 up.

The early stages of the match was the only time Warrington looked capable of matching their opponents, missing a couple of excellent chances to get back on terms as Jack Garrett and Ben Hawker both lost the ball during a two minute spell with the line open each time, the latter after a wonderful Griff Jenkins break. Warrington's pack, though, ran out of steam, the Leeds forwards, ably led by Aubrey Casewell, tackling vigorously whilst Jim Brough was causing all sorts of problems with his lengthy clearance kicks. The Wires did get some reward, though, when Bill Shankland landed a long-range penalty in the 29th minute,

following foul play by Eric Harris. Four minutes later Fred Harris scored what many rated the try of the match. The Leeds centre took possession after some smart passing along the line and immediately headed for the sideline where he looked set to work his familiar 'scissors' movement with wing partner Eric Harris. As the latter turned inside, Fred Harris dummied his pass

The victorious Leeds outfit, at back: Hall, Isaac, Jubb, Brogden. Middle row: Eaton, Smith, Dyer, Casewell, E. Harris, Satterthwaite, Whitehead. Seated: Parker, F. Harris, Brough, Ralph, Williams

STATS

Leeds 18 Warrington 2

Saturday 18 April at Wembley Stadium, London (3.00 pm)

Leeds (blue with amber collar and cuffs): Brough (captain), E. Harris, F. Harris, Parker, Brogden, Ralph, Williams, Satterthwaite, Hall, Dyer, Jubb, Casewell, Isaac. Trainer: W. Smith

Warrington (primrose with blue collar and cuffs): Shankland (captain), Garrett, Hawker, Dingsdale, Jenkins, Newcombe, Goodall, Hardman, Cotton, Miller, Flannery, Arkwright, Chadwick. Trainer: W. Bennett

Referee: A.S. Dobson   Touch-judges: W. Lynch, W. Wood

Half-time: 10–2 Attendance: 51,250 Receipts: £7,070

Weather: sunny, very warm

Cup presentation: Lord Derby, Rugby League president

Progressive score:

Leeds	score (min)	Warrington
Isaac try, Williams goal	5–0 (8)	
	5–2 (29)	Shankland penalty
F. Harris try	8–2 (33)	
Williams penalty	10–2 (39)	
E. Harris try, Williams goal	15–2 (66)	
Parker try	18–2 (75)	

Route to the final:

First round: Leeds 18 Dewsbury 7, Barrow 8 Warrington 17

Second round:
Streatham and Mitcham 3 Leeds 13, Halifax 2 Warrington 2

Second round replay: Warrington 18 Halifax 15

Third round: Hull 4 Leeds 5, Warrington 5 Wigan 2

Semi-finals:
Leeds 10 Huddersfield 5 (BelleVue, Wakefield, 37,906),
Warrington 7 Salford 2 (Central Park, Wigan, 41,538)

Head-to-head form guide:

Warrington 5 Leeds 3 (League)

Leeds 29 Warrington 6 (League)

Leeds (in the dark shorts) attempt to dribble the ball through the Warrington defence, a mode of play extinct in the modern game

and sped down the wing, kicking the ball over Shankland, and following up for a sensational touchdown. Williams missed the goal but made amends with a penalty just before half-time for a 10–2 lead.

WINNING CAPTAIN

Jim Brough (Leeds 1936)

Legendary Cumbrian full back Jim Brough signed for Leeds in 1925 from hometown Silloth rugby union club for a reported £600, having represented England twice (New Zealand and Wales, both 1925) and won the county title with Cumberland (1923/24). A 'complete' defender, who could tackle resolutely and kick with assurance, he was also a powerful runner with the ball in hand, an attribute enabling him to play many of his rugby league representative games in the centre. He toured twice (1928, 1936—the latter as captain), made five Test appearances and played for England (11 times) and Cumberland (24). With Leeds he won the Rugby League Challenge Cup (1932, 1936, 1942), Yorkshire Cup (1928, 1930, 1932, 1934, 1935) and Yorkshire League (1927/28, 1930/31, 1933/34, 1934/35, 1936/37, 1937/38). He retired in 1938 to take up a job in South Africa, but was back in Leeds' colours the following year after the Second World War broke out. During the war he made spasmodic appearances for the club until his 442nd and last in 1944. He later had spells as coach of Leeds, Whitehaven, Workington Town and Batley, accompanying the 1958 tourists in that role.

The second half belonged to Leeds. Eric Harris knocked-on within a yard of the try-line but, soon after, Fred Harris sent him on his way for another wonderful Leeds score. In a barn-storming run he evaded three assailants and kicked ahead outpacing two more defenders before regaining the ball to go over near the posts. Williams added the goal. In the closing minutes Brough linked up with his three-quarter line to make the extra man before Gwyn Parker shrugged off several Warrington players to score, Williams being unable to append the extra points.

The foundation for victory was laid by the Leeds forwards who, despite losing the scrums by an incredible 46–18, subdued Warrington's much vaunted pack in the loose. It allowed their 'classy' backs—whose strength could be judged by the fact that winger Stanley Smith, due to join the upcoming tour 'Down Under', was not selected—the freedom of the park. The match, though, was dubbed one of 'the poorest' and 'most disappointing' of the seven finals played at the stadium so far. The scrums were generally untidy, the referee having to speak to both sets of forwards several times, the *Yorkshire Post* referring to 'displays of temper not seen before at Wembley'. The occasion attracted the highest attendance and receipts for a match in Britain.

1937 RUGBY LEAGUE CHALLENGE CUP FINAL
Widnes v Keighley

The romance and unpredictably associated with the Challenge Cup was fully illustrated in 1937 when Widnes and Keighley took to the field at Wembley having finished 20th and 18th in the League, respectively. The

---

WINNING CAPTAIN

Nat Silcock (Widnes 1937)

Prop forward Nat Silcock was one of the 'stand out' players of the Widnes side during the inter-war years, taking part in two tours (1932, 1936), making 12 Test appearances, and representing England (8 times) and Lancashire (14). Surprisingly quick in loose play and noted for his 'dummy' passes, he proved an ideal leader, being the first player to twice captain a team at Wembley (1934, 1937). Widnes-born and a product of the town's St Patrick's Juniors team, his career with the Chemics covered 438 matches from 1923, twice winning the Rugby League Challenge Cup (1930, 1937). His last appearance was in November 1938 when, reportedly, illness and injury prevented him from continuing. His son, also Nat, was a tourist in 1954.

STATS

Widnes 18 Keighley 5

Saturday 8 May at Wembley Stadium, London (3.00 pm)

Widnes (black and white hoops): Bradley, Whyte, Topping, Barber, Evans, Shannon, McCue, Silcock (captain), J. Jones, A. Higgins, McDowell, Roberts, Millington. Trainer: P. Lyons

Keighley (red with white collar and cuffs): Herbert, Sherburn, Towill, Parker, Lloyd, Bevan, Davies (captain), Traill, Halliday, H. Jones, Dixon, Talbot, Gill. Trainer: H. Slater

Referee: P. Cowell Touch-judges: R. Rawlinson, T. Tucker

Half-time: 8–0   Attendance: 47,699   Receipts: £6,704

Weather: sunny, very hot

Cup presentation: Lord Cozens Hardy

Progressive score:

Widnes	score (min)	Keighley
Shannon try, Topping goal	5–0 (7)	
McCue try	8–0 (28)	
	8–2 (42)	Sherburn penalty
Barber try, Topping goal	13–2 (58)	
Silcock try	16–2 (63)	
Topping penalty	18–2 (67)	
	18–5 (76)	Lloyd try

Route to the final:

First round:
Widnes 39 Higginshaw (Oldham) 2, Hunslet 2 Keighley 5

Second round: Widnes 12 Dewsbury 7 (original meeting abandoned at half-time due to bad weather Widnes leading 8–0, Keighley 11 Broughton Rangers 5

Third round:
Widnes 7 Swinton 2, Liverpool Stanley 2 Keighley 7

Semi-finals:
Widnes 13 Wigan 9 (Wilderspool, Warrington, 29,260), Keighley 0 Wakefield Trinity 0 (Headingley, Leeds, 39,998)

Semi-final replay:
Keighley 5 Wakefield Trinity 3 (Fartown, Huddersfield, 14,000)

Head-to-head form guide:

No previous meetings during season

---

occasion, though, still attracted a healthy looking attendance exceeding 47,000 who witnessed a game that, whilst not reaching great heights, was fought out in a sporting, clean manner. Keighley, making their only appearance in the final to date, made a late decision to include Iorweth Herbert at full back over experienced Len Bowkett, Huddersfield's 1933 hero.

The Lawkholme Lane side almost scored in the opening minutes after stand-off Llew Bevan—one of eight Welsh players in their team—kicked the ball over Alan Evans' head. The Widnes winger tried to claim possession but failed to hold the ball and Keighley's Joe Sherburn kicked it on, colleague Reg Lloyd giving chase before the Chemics' Walter Bradley just managed to clear the danger. Keighley posed only a spasmodic threat thereafter, Widnes' dominating pack allowing scrum half Tommy McCue to enjoy an outstanding match.

Peter Topping missed a 6th minute Widnes penalty before, a minute later, McCue—taking the ball from a scrum—found an opening near Keighley's posts. Outwitting their halfbacks he spurted towards the try-line before passing to the supporting Tommy Shannon who, after juggling the ball, went over near the posts. Topping's goal made it 5–0. Keighley's chance to trouble the scoreboard came and went with two missed penalties from Sherburn—one of which looked fairly simple—whilst Gwyn Parker and Idris Towill both came close to the Widnes try-line to no avail. They were made to pay on 28 minutes after Widnes' Harry Millington gained possession from a Keighley play-the-ball (at that time the defending player could challenge for the ball) inside the opposition 25-yard area, feeding McCue who took it on the burst to go beneath the posts. The *Widnes Weekly News* claimed he 'baffled the defence so much they did not know which way he was going'. Topping surprisingly hit the upright with his goal attempt, Widnes going in at half-time 8–0 up.

Two minutes after the break, Keighley gave their fans some hope when Sherburn kicked a difficult angled goal, Widnes having incurred a penalty when the Yorkshire side's forwards broke on a dribbling rush. The score lifted them and, for the next quarter-hour they looked more potent; McCue saving the day when he thwarted a Parker and Lloyd move down the left wing after Bradley was beaten, and Fred Talbot crossing Widnes' try-line before being recalled for an infringement. But disaster struck Keighley midway through the half when Bevan, inside his own 25-yard area, attempted a pass to Towill that fell short. Widnes' Ken Barber seized the opportunity, picking it up and, despite a slight stumble, raced under the posts. Topping's goal made it 13–2. Five minutes later Millington recovered another loose ball, beating off three would-be tacklers before passing to McCue who gave a dummy pass before transferring to skipper Nat

The players that made history as part of Keighley's only team, to date, to reach a Challenge Cup Final. Standing: Towill, Halliday, Talbot, Traill, Dixon, Jones, Sherburn, Gill. Kneeling: Parker, Lloyd, Davies, Bevan, Herbert

Silcock who then produced his own dummy towards colleagues on his left before going through the resultant gap to score. Topping missed the conversion but added a penalty, given for obstruction, a few minutes later. At 16 points clear, Widnes was well in control, but Keighley had the last say. In the closing minutes, Lloyd—then the youngest Wembley finalist at 17 years, 249 days old—scored a try, evading Bradley's flying tackle after Bevan had created an opening for Parker, the latter supplying the scoring pass. Sherburn missed the goal.

The *Keighley News* correspondent admitted that the 'Widnes triumph was much too emphatic to satisfy Keighley folk that any sort of challenge had been given.'

The teams walk across the Wembley pitch led by their ball-carrying captains; Widnes' Nat Silcock (in hoops) and Keighley's Dai Davies. Despite an attendance exceeding 47,000, Wembley's vast open terraces look devoid of spectators

1938 RUGBY LEAGUE CHALLENGE CUP FINAL
Salford v Barrow

Salford won the 1938 Challenge Cup—their only success in the competition to date—by defeating first-time finalists Barrow 7–4 after a dramatic finish to a dull, dour struggle that could only be described as a battle of attrition. Their hero of the hour was Albert Gear, scorer of the game's solitary try in the dying minutes when the teams were locked at 4–4. Salford's Harold Osbaldestin had caught a Barrow clearance

with less than two minutes to go and booted it straight back towards the opposition's line. Gear later recalled: 'It landed in front of their forwards but the bounce was a bit tricky. (Barrow's Alec) Troup was fumbling to get at the ball and eventually took it. To my surprise he threw out a wild pass. I ran up and kicked it with my left foot, but not too far, and managed to catch it on the bounce.' Gear dived over the try-line between Fred French and Jim Thornburrow 10 yards to the right of the posts, sending Salford fans hoarse. Skipper Gus Risman was wide with the conversion but the final whistle blew immediately afterwards. Troup's unfortunate error was due, in part, to a bad knee injury that saw him retire for several minutes during the first half, and later interfered with his mobility, whilst Gear was still feeling dazed after colliding earlier with colleague Osbaldestin.

Barrow placed their reliance on a powerful pack and, with Salford taking them on upfront, the match developed into a down-the-middle stalemate, the backs having few chances. Risman and French each missed early penalty opportunities before the latter succeeded in the 8th minute after Risman was caught offside. Risman then had two further chances, the second levelling the scores. French missed another penalty and then, at the opposite end two minutes later, he kicked out 'on the full' from in front of his own posts, a scrum being awarded at the point of contact. Salford won the heel, Billy Watkins passing to Risman whose drop-goal gave the Red Devils a 4–2 lead, the latter subsequently missing with another penalty seconds before the interval.

After the break, there were few highlights prior to Gear's winner; French missed a penalty, team-mate Billy Little later succeeding with a 66th minute drop-

Salford captain Gus Risman holds the trophy aloft supported by team-mates Barney Hudson (left) and Billy Watkins

STATS

Salford 7 Barrow 4

Saturday 7 May at Wembley Stadium, London (3.30 pm)

Salford (red): Osbaldestin, Hudson, Gear, Brown, Edwards, Risman (captain), Watkins, Williams, Day, Davies, Dalton, Thomas, Feetham. Team manager: L.B. Todd

Barrow (royal blue): French, Cumberbatch, Higgins, McDonnell, Thornburrow, Lloyd, Little, Rawlings, McKeating, Skelly, Troup (captain), Ayres, Marklew. Trainer: H. Halsall

Referee: F. Peel   Touch-judges: J. Probert, T. Moran

Half-time: 4–2   Attendance: 51,243   Receipts: £7,174

Weather: sunny, very warm

Cup presentation:
Donald Bradman, Australian cricket captain

Progressive score:

Salford	score (min)	Barrow
	0–2 (8)	French penalty
Risman penalty	2–2 (23)	
Risman drop-goal	4–2 (31)	
	4–4 (66)	Little drop-goal
Gear try	7–4 (79)	

Route to the final:

First round: Salford 38 Hull 2, Barrow 83 Maryport 3

Second round:
Liverpool Stanley 3 Salford 11, Barrow 26 Bramley 4

Third round: Salford 19 St Helens Recreation 0, Barrow 7 Leeds 5

Semi-finals: Salford 6 Swinton 0 (Belle Vue Stadium, Manchester, 31,664),

Barrow 4 Halifax 2 (Fartown, Huddersfield, 31,384)

Head-to-head form guide:

Salford 5 Barrow 10 (League)

Barrow 31 Salford 0 (League)

The moment that determined the outcome! Albert Gear plunges over the try-line despite the tackle of Barrow winger Jim Thornburrow (number 5) as a Salford colleague leans over to offer congratulations

WINNING CAPTAIN

Gus Risman (Salford 1938, Workington Town 1952)

Augustus John 'Gus' Risman was one of rugby league's greatest performers, the gifted Welsh back being inducted into Rugby League's Hall of Fame in 1988. Born in Cardiff, he signed for Salford aged 17 in 1929, having played rugby union for Dinas Powis and Cardiff Scottish. With Salford, where he became captain in 1935, he won the Rugby League Challenge Cup (1938), Championship (1932/33, 1936/37, 1938/39), Lancashire Cup (1931, 1934, 1935, 1936) and Lancashire League (1932/33, 1933/34, 1934/35, 1936/37, 1938/39). He set club records that stood until the 1970s for goals (796) and points (2,021) in a career, and goals (116) and points (277) in a season (both 1933/34), twice landing 13 goals in a match (1933, 1940), a feat not exceeded until 2003. Risman toured three times (1932, 1936, 1946), the latter as captain. He made 17 Test appearances (9 as captain) and represented Wales (18 times), England (1) and Glamorgan & Monmouthshire (3). During the Second World War, he was a guest for several clubs, winning the Rugby League Challenge Cup (Leeds 1942), Championship (Bradford Northern 1940/41, Dewsbury 1941/42) and Yorkshire Cup (Bradford Northern 1941). In 1946, he transferred to Workington Town for £750 as player-coach, leading them to success in the Rugby League Challenge Cup (1952) and Championship (1950/51). Again, he established club records for goals (716) and points (1,531) in a career, and goals (138) and points (294) in a season (both 1953/54), unchallenged until the late 1970s. He left Town in 1954, playing nine matches for Batley that year before retiring. He later coached Oldham, Bradford Northern and Salford.

goal to level the scores at 4–4. Little tried to edge his team ahead with a repeat four minutes later but was off-target setting the scene for Salford's late winner. The *North-Western Daily Mail* said: 'After-match scenes (of celebration) were themselves more memorable than the actual play,' Gear recalling that 'the forwards and halfbacks cancelled each other out. I don't think I had a pass all through the match. Both teams were frightened of opening up and making mistakes.'

Salford's success climaxed what many believe was the finest decade in the club's history, the Challenge Cup being the one honour that had eluded them, team manager, Lance Todd later commenting: 'It was the culmination of hard work, and the realisation of the dream of everybody connected with the club.'

1939 RUGBY LEAGUE CHALLENGE CUP FINAL
Halifax v Salford

Halifax won a one-sided, although entertaining decider against Salford in 1939, the Red Devils being the first to reach successive Wembley finals. Supporters making up the record 55,453 Challenge Cup Final attendance were determined not to let anything ruin their big day, the *Halifax Courier* firmly stating 'Budget taxes and international affairs take second place today'. The latter was a reference to Adolph Hitler's Germany casting a dark cloud over peace in Europe with the 1939 final destined to be the last before the Second World War. The Salford camp was ravaged by influenza in the days before the match, resulting in centre Albert Gear having to remain at home and listen to the radio broadcast in bed!

Halifax were well on top in a whirlwind opening, winning the first four scrums, skipper and loose forward Harry Beverley, together with centres Charlie Smith and Jack Treen giving outstanding performances. Salford were placed under severe pressure, receiving a let-off when Jim Bevan lost the ball as he looked like scoring, and then Beverley and Harry Field both being forced back from their try-line. Beverley was a real thorn in Salford's side, his repeated breaks paying off in the 16th minute when he transferred to the supporting George Todd who sent

The two teams march out together; Salford (nearest camera) led by Charles Riley (chairman), Lance Todd (secretary-manager) and Gus Risman (captain), Halifax headed by E.O. Bower (chairman), Arthur Archbell (secretary-manager) and Harry Beverley (captain)

Halifax captain Harry Beverley receives the Challenge Cup from the Earl de la Warr watched by defeated Salford skipper Gus Risman who contemplates what might have been! At the time it was usual for both team captains to attend the cup presentation together

WINNING CAPTAIN

Harry Beverley (Halifax 1939)

Harry Beverley signed for his local club Hunslet in 1926, going on to make 327 appearances for the Parkside outfit including their 1934 Rugby League Challenge Cup victory and Yorkshire League title in 1931/32. Beginning as a centre he quickly developed into a clever ball-playing loose forward, Halifax paying out £850 in 1937, then a record for a forward. Made captain, he led the Thrum Hallers to their 1939 Challenge Cup success, playing what turned out to be his last—and 112th—match for the club in the 1941 Challenge Cup Final. Essential wartime work saw him based near York and he played on loan for York from 1941 until 1945 before retiring. He also assisted Batley four times during 1942/43. He was a tourist in 1936, made six Test appearances and represented England (5 times) and Yorkshire (7). He later coached Halifax, Doncaster and Bramley, becoming a director of the latter.

Jack Treen dives over to score Halifax's vital second try

STATS

Halifax 20 Salford 3

Saturday 6 May at Wembley Stadium, London (3.30 pm)

Halifax (blue and white hoops): Lockwood, Bevan, Smith, Treen, Bassett, Todd, Goodall, Baynham, Field, Irving, Cox, Chadwick, Beverley (captain). Trainer: W. Bennett

Salford (red): Osbaldestin, Hudson, Miller, Risman (captain), Edwards, Kenny, Watkins, Bradbury, Day, Davies, Dalton, Thomas, Feetham. Team manager: L.B. Todd

Referee: G.S. Phillips

Touch-judges: E.J. Tilvington, W. Woolam

Half-time: 10–0   Attendance: 55,453   Receipts: £7,681

Weather: sunny, very warm

Cup presentation: Earl de la Warr

Progressive score:

Halifax	score (min)	Salford
Smith try, Lockwood goal	5–0 (16)	
Treen try, Lockwood goal	10–0 (31)	
	10–3 (44)	Risman try
Todd try, Lockwood goal	15–3 (53)	
Bevan try, Lockwood goal	20–3 (77)	

Route to the final:

First round: Halifax 8 Barrow 3, Salford 11 St Helens 0

Second round:
Halifax 6 Hull Kingston Rovers 2, Salford 18 Hunslet 2

Third round:
Wakefield Trinity 5 Halifax 5, Salford 20 Bramley 0

Third round replay: Halifax 15 Wakefield Trinity 12

Semi-finals:
Halifax 10 Leeds 4 (Odsal Stadium, Bradford, 64,453),
Salford 11 Wigan 2 (The Athletic Grounds, Rochdale, 40,000)

Head-to-head form guide:

Halifax 11 Salford 10 (League)

Salford 31 Halifax 13 (League)

Smith over for the touchdown, putting the 'Halifax crowd in raptures of delight'. The assault continued; Jack Cox having a try written off for a forward pass, Bevan beaten to a touchdown by Salford's Harold Thomas. With a half-hour gone Smith broke after a scrum, Treen accepting his pass before crashing over the Salford line. With Hubert Lockwood converting both first half efforts, Halifax led 10–0 at the break.

Salford looked sharper after the resumption and this time it was Halifax's turn to defend. A scrum on the Thrum Hallers' line saw Billy Watkins retrieve the ball and, when held up on the try-line, he got his pass to Gus Risman who scored, although the Salford captain missed the conversion. Tragedy struck Salford in the 50th minute and, more specifically, their full back Harold Osbaldestin who, on catching the ball, sank to the ground with no one near him. He was carried off with an Achilles tendon injury and never played again. Centre Sammy Miller moved to full back, loose forward Jack Feetham joining the three-quarters. Whilst Osbaldestin was being taken down the tunnel, Treen made a brilliant break, using wing partner Arthur Bassett as a foil before passing to Todd who beat a flimsy looking defence to score beneath the posts. In the closing minutes Salford's Alan Edwards, who had made several telling runs, was beaten to a high ball by Bevan who stepped inside for another great try. Lockwood was again on the mark for both second half tries, completing a comprehensive 20–3 victory.

A delighted Beverley said afterwards: 'So well have the whole team responded that the plan of campaign worked out at our Harrow headquarters was followed to the letter.' An indication of the growing popularity of the Wembley experience was the British record attendance of 64,453 for the Halifax-Leeds semi-final, played at Odsal Stadium.

SECOND WORLD WAR

Great Britain and France declared war on Germany on 3 September 1939 following the latter's invasion of Poland, the rugby league season just a few weeks old with the New Zealanders having commenced their tour the previous day. The Rugby League Council decided to shelve existing League fixtures, replacing them with separate Lancashire and Yorkshire Emergency Leagues to ease travel, an Emergency Committee appointed to oversee matters for the duration. It was subsequently agreed that players with travelling difficulties could play for other more accessible clubs as a guest, provided their parent club agreed. Fearing enemy bombing, government restrictions meant a crowd limit of 8,000 was imposed, although grounds holding over 60,000 (such as Bradford's Odsal Stadium) were allowed 15,000. These upper levels were raised as the war progressed.

The Challenge Cup competition was not played during the 1939/40 season but, on 18 December 1940 at an Emergency Committee Meeting at the Grosvenor Hotel, Manchester, the minutes recorded that 'it was decided to consider the question of playing The Challenge Cup at the January meeting.' That subsequent meeting took place on 15 January at the Griffin Hotel, Leeds, the decision being taken to revive the competition at the end of the 1940/41

The Rugby League Challenge Cup was not contested in 1940

season with war savings certificates given to players instead of medals, four to the winners, three to the losers. It was agreed that, for the opening two rounds and due to their extreme locations, Hull would not meet a Lancashire club nor would Barrow meet a Yorkshire one, although it transpired that the latter did not participate until 1943. Also—mindful of the use of guest players—it was decided a player could only appear for one club during the competition. It was agreed that should a match be level after the 80 minutes play and 20 minutes extra time, the tie would continue until someone scored, Castleford consequently defeating Featherstone Rovers 8–5 in the 1941 first round after 118 minutes play.

The Challenge Cup competition continued throughout the remainder of the war period. A two-leg home-and-away system was used for the 1941 semi-finals and, in 1942, extended to every round prior to the final. Thereafter, all rounds including the final were decided on that basis. Not all clubs continued to operate during the war period and amateur clubs did not take part in the Challenge Cup. Thus, instead of the usual 32 teams in the competition proper, 1941 featured just 21 (14 Yorkshire, 7 Lancashire) and, for the remaining four wartime contests, only four Lancashire clubs participated each time, the lowest overall entry being 15 in 1943.

With peace returning in 1945 the Rugby Football League agreed an initial five-year deal to resume at Wembley, the venue taking 20% of the receipts after the deduction of entertainment tax. Interestingly, a two-leg system continued, the first round decided on that basis from 1946 until 1954, Bradford Northern winning at Wembley in 1947 and 1949 after losing their opening leg.

Former Wigan player and Salford manager Lance Todd, who was a captain in the Salford Battalion Home Guard during the Second World War, leads his men during a parade. Killed in a road accident in 1942, the New Zealander subsequently had the Challenge Cup Final man of the match award named after him when it returned to Wembley

1941 RUGBY LEAGUE CHALLENGE CUP FINAL
Leeds v Halifax

The Challenge Cup was back on the agenda in 1941 after a one-year gap due to the Second World War, holders Halifax being well beaten by a Leeds team that scored all five tries in winning 19–2. It was not a good final, being full of over-exuberance, the protagonists 'too keen' and time wasting being the order of the day with players often 'scrambling on the ground after the ball was played.'

STATS

Leeds 19 Halifax 2

Saturday 17 May at Odsal Stadium, Bradford (3.30 pm)

Leeds (white): Eaton, Batten (Hunslet), Evans, Hey (captain), Lawrenson (Wigan), Morris, Jenkins, Prosser, Murphy, Bennett (Hunslet), Satterthwaite, Pearson (Bramley), Tattersfield. Trainer: W. Smith

Halifax (blue and white hoops): Bassett, Bevan, Smith, Rule, Doyle, Todd, McCue (Widnes), Osborne (Salford), Meek, Irving, Millington (Widnes), Brereton, Beverley (captain). Trainer: W. Bennett

Referee: P. Cowell Touch-judges: E. Willis, C. Snowden

Half-time: 5–2 Attendance: 28,500 Receipts: £1,703

Weather: unknown

Cup presentation:
Mr Alfred Townend, Rugby League chairman

Progressive score:

Leeds	score (min)	Halifax
Eaton penalty	2–0 (-)	
	2–2 (-)	Meek penalty
Jenkins try	5–2 (-)	

Note: Second half progressive score not available due to limited wartime sports reporting. Leeds added four tries, the sequence being Hey (55 min), Hey (57 min), Lawrenson, Lawrenson, with Eaton converting one of them.

Route to the final:

First round: Leeds (bye), Halifax 24 Broughton Rangers 12

Second round: Dewsbury 5 Leeds 6, York 6 Halifax 13

Third round: Hunslet 10 Leeds 17, Halifax 10 Huddersfield 5

Semi-finals (2 legs): Leeds 22 Bradford Northern 12

Halifax 16 Wakefield Trinity 12

Head-to-head form guide:

Halifax 17 Leeds 15 (League)

Leeds 28 Halifax 7 (League)

The Headingley side led by only three points at the interval, an unconverted try from Dai Jenkins after colleague Oliver Morris swooped on a loose ball, and a penalty goal apiece from Charlie Eaton (Leeds) and Mel Meek (Halifax) providing the scores. Leeds took a firmer grip on proceedings in the second half, Vic Hey scoring touchdowns in the 55th and 57th minutes, the first—after taking advantage of a 'slip' by Halifax's Arthur Bassett—proving the turning point of the match. Their superiority on the day was confirmed with two late tries from Johnny Lawrenson.

Favourites Leeds—whose semi-final win over Bradford Northern had been unexpected—were clear and deserving winners, looking faster all round. Halifax did have some excuses to offer through second half injuries to Harry Beverley (rib) and Harry Millington (shoulder), the former quitting some 15

WINNING CAPTAIN

Vic Hey (Leeds 1941, 1942)

Australian Vic Hey was a headline-making £1,400 capture for Leeds in 1937, the stand-off having impressed in Test matches against Britain (during the 1933/34 Kangaroos tour and the 1936 Lions visit 'Down Under'). Born in Liverpool, New South Wales, and described as 'a powerfully built pocket battleship of a player' his stay with Leeds encompassed the Second World War, winning the Rugby League Challenge Cup (1941, 1942), Yorkshire Cup (1937) and Yorkshire League (1937/38). He transferred to Dewsbury as player-coach in 1944, helping them win the Yorkshire League (1946/47—being Championship runners-up the same season). His planned return home in 1947 was delayed whilst he awaited a passage and he played nine times for Hunslet on a short-term contract at the end of that year before departing. Prior to Leeds, his Australian career saw him play for Western Suburbs in Sydney (1933 to 1935, winning the 1934 Premiership), and Queensland clubs Toowoomba (1936) and Ipswich (1937). On returning he joined Parramatta as player-coach in 1948, playing his last match in 1949 but continuing as coach until 1953. He subsequently coached Canterbury (1955–56), Western Suburbs (1958–59) and Australia (1950–55—including the 1954 World Cup in France). He made six Test appearances with Australia and represented New South Wales (11 times) and Queensland (3). During the Second World War he made guest appearances with Dewsbury (1941/42 to 1943/44) prior to his permanent move, and Batley (1942/43).

CROWD RELATED PROBLEMS

Several earlier Challenge Cup Finals experienced unfortunate incidents outside the field of play. Here is a selection:

- 1901 (Headingley): After five minutes' play, barricades on the terrace gave way through congestion, spectators spilling onto the pitch. One journalist blamed poor crowd distribution as, apparently, there was ample space in other areas. Some spectators took to sitting on the pavilion and stand roofs. No one was reported injured.

- 1903 (Headingley): Shortly after kick-off, play was stopped when a barrier gave way in the pavilion corner. Police escorted spectators to the side of the pitch where they sat out the match on the grass. No one was reported injured.

- 1909 (Headingley): Thirty minutes before kick-off, a surging crowd forced its way towards the turnstiles at the 'best entrance', and, unable to get inside 'quick enough', forced the gate down, estimates of 1,000 to 2,000 entering without paying.

- 1921 (The Cliff, Broughton): Two outer gates were broken open before kick-off, 'hundreds' entering without paying. Crush barriers and perimeter boarding was also broken down. No one was reported injured.

- 1922 (Headingley): Minutes before the players emerged for kick-off, barricades collapsed at one end, the crowd surging onto the field. Police escorted people to the side of the touchline where they sat out the remainder of the match, one journalist commenting it was 'a privilege which hundreds were quick to avail themselves of.' As the second half was about to start more barriers gave way and there was a 'fresh inrush of spectators onto the field', mounted police keeping the touchline clear. One report said that the closed outer gates had been reopened on police advice to allow delayed supporters to enter, but it created congestion inside. Another scribe suggested entry had been forced. During the second half, Rochdale Hornets' Dicky Padden 'forcibly removed' a spectator from the touchline so he could attempt a conversion!

- 1924 (Athletic Grounds, Rochdale): The biggest pre-Wembley Challenge Cup Final crowd spilled over the barriers and across the track that surrounded the pitch, encroaching the playing area throughout the match, resulting in many incidents of players 'colliding' with spectators. At one point the referee—the Reverend Frank Chambers—held up the game whilst spectators were asked to retreat. He also dispensed with a half-time break in case they surged further forward.

minutes from the end. They also suffered a pre-match blow when full back Hubert Lockwood had to withdraw, winger Bassett covering for him but found wanting with his defensive positioning.

The Leeds halfback partnership of Jenkins and Morris were credited as the architects of victory, their speed and dexterity proving too much for the Halifax defence to cope with. The attendance of 28,500—testing Odsal Stadium's, then, wartime limit of 30,000—was the largest so far during the war.

Johnny Lawrenson—the on-loan Wigan three-quarter grabbed two late tries for Leeds

1942 RUGBY LEAGUE CHALLENGE CUP FINAL
Leeds v Halifax

Leeds retained the Challenge Cup in 1942, repeating their previous year's success over Halifax, this time by 15–10. Although the scores were much closer, Leeds again claimed all the tries, registering three, whilst Halifax—appearing in their third consecutive final—relied on Hubert Lockwood's marksmanship.

All Leeds' tries came about during the first half, Alan Edwards getting the first in the opening minutes through following up a cross-field kick with dazzling pace to dive over in the corner, Jim Bevan unable to stop him. Oliver Morris got the second, benefiting from a neat kick by Dai Jenkins over the top of a scrum after the ball had emerged. Edwards then grabbed his second and Leeds' third, attributed to poor defence on the part of Halifax. With Risman succeeding with one conversion attempt and Lockwood contributing three penalties for Halifax, the half-time score stood at 11–6.

The only points after the interval came through further penalty goals—two each from Risman and Lockwood—although Morris almost got his second try after a great run, only for Albert Doyle to race across the field and detain him. Leeds were handicapped through a pulled leg muscle incurred by centre and captain Vic Hey in the early stages of the match, spending the remainder as a bystander on the wing.

Despite that handicap, the Leeds backs looked sharper than Halifax's, the Thrum Hall side being left to rue several missed second half chances through lack of support.

Leeds made it six Challenge Cup triumphs from six finals, the June date being the latest staging yet for the decider. They were well served by full back and former tour captain Jim Brough who, having played his last match for them in 1939, had recently returned to action at the age of 38.

STATS

Leeds 15 Halifax 10

Saturday 6 June at Odsal Stadium, Bradford (3.30 pm)

Leeds: Brough, Edwards (Salford), Risman (Salford), Hey (captain), Evans, Morris, Jenkins, Prosser, Murphy, Satterthwaite, Gregory (Warrington), Brown (Batley), Tattersfield. Trainer: W. Smith

Halifax: Lockwood (captain), Bevan, Smith, Rule, Doyle, Todd, McCue (Widnes), Brereton, Jones (Broughton R), Irving, Millington (Widnes), Meek, Dixon. Trainer: W. Bennett

Referee: P. Cowell Touch-judges: W.P. Thompson, C. Ramsden

Half-time: 11–6 Attendance: 15,250 Receipts: £1,276

Weather: unknown

Cup presentation: unconfirmed (Dr Herbert Vere Evatt, Special Envoy of Australian Government, was invited by RFL)

Progressive score:

Note: Progressive score not available due to limited wartime sports reporting. In the first half Leeds scored three tries, the sequence being Edwards, Morris, Edwards, with Risman converting one of them. Halifax scored three penalties through Lockwood. In the second half Risman and Lockwood scored two penalties each.

Route to the final:

First round (2 legs): Leeds (bye), Halifax (bye)

Second round (2 legs):
Leeds 8 Wakefield Trinity 3, Halifax 24 Huddersfield 15

Third round (2 legs):
Leeds 29 Hull 20, Halifax 31 Bradford Northern 27

Semi-finals (2 legs): Leeds 17 Oldham 5, Halifax 26 Wigan 16

Head-to-head form guide:

No previous meetings during season

1943 RUGBY LEAGUE CHALLENGE CUP FINAL
Dewsbury v Leeds

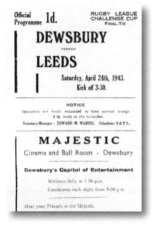

The Dewsbury programme for the first leg played at Crown Flatt. Note the name of 'Edward M. Waring' who later gained fame on BBC television as their rugby league commentator and, from 1967 until 1979, as co-presenter of the popular It's a Knockout game show

The Second World War was into its fourth year when Dewsbury met Leeds in 1943 to settle the first ever two-legged Challenge Cup Final. It produced an enthralling contest, Dewsbury eventually scraping through 16–15 despite registering four tries to their opponents' one, both teams winning at home. Although Leeds had forwards capable of taking on anybody, it was in their backs—for so long one of their strengths—where they struggled to match Dewsbury. Under entrepreneurial manager and future BBC television commentator Eddie Waring, the Crown Flatt outfit had utilised the occupants of nearby Caulms

Wood army camp to boost their squad. They employed nine on-loan players in their line-up against Leeds, including Salford's former Test stars Barney Hudson and Alan Edwards.

Dewsbury hosted the first leg and set off like an express train, the *Yorkshire Post* commenting they 'started as though they would sweep Leeds out of the ground'. They should have scored in the opening minutes after an excellent passing move but, with the Leeds defence opened up, Jimmy Robinson's final delivery to Reg Lloyd was poor. But their first try was not far off and, from a scrum, Harry Royal transferred the ball to Charlie Seeling who 'strolled through an opening wide enough for a tank', the *Yorkshire Post* using an analogy relevant to the times. Next to cross the whitewash was Tom Kenny who scurried over after combining with halfback partner, Royal. With Seeling converting both tries, Dewsbury led 10–0. Leeds were struggling to prise an opening, eventually succeeding when Charlie Eaton followed up a kick and, aided by George Bunter's handling error, scored a try that he also augmented. An unconverted try from Robinson closed the first half scoring giving Dewsbury a satisfactory 13–5 lead.

Dewsbury claimed their second Challenge Cup win in 1942. Standing: Robinson, Seeling, Smith, Curran, Hammond, Gardner, Kershaw. Seated: Walsh (in uniform), Bunter, Edwards, Hudson, Waring (manager), Francis, Royal, Kenny, Morrell (in suit)

WINNING CAPTAIN

Barney Hudson (Dewsbury 1943)

Bernard 'Barney' Hudson was already a seasoned performer before becoming a Dewsbury 'guest' during the Second World War. A no nonsense right winger with a direct running style, he was a native of Horden, County Durham, joining Salford in 1928 from Hartlepool Rovers rugby union club. At Salford, he won the Rugby League Challenge Cup (1938), Championship (1932/33, 1936/37, 1938/39), Lancashire Cup (1931, 1934, 1935, 1936, missing the latter final through injury), and Lancashire League (1932/33, 1933/34, 1934/35, 1936/37, 1938/39). He played in eight Tests and represented England six times, being a tourist in 1932 and 1936. Well into his mid-30s when appearing in Dewsbury colours, he helped them win the Challenge Cup (1943), Championship (1941/42) and Yorkshire Cup (1942). He was captain for the former and their 1942/43 'Championship', although Dewsbury were subsequently stripped of their title. His final match with Salford was in 1946 having registered a club record 282 tries that stood until 1983.

Some of the second half play was described as 'too keen', the first points going to Leeds via an Eaton drop-goal. Dewsbury then scored what the *Manchester Guardian* considered 'the best try of the match', Edwards taking advantage after Leeds' Sid Rookes spilt a ball kicked in his direction following a length-of-field Dewsbury move. An Eaton penalty goal ended the scoring to put Leeds just seven points in arrears at 16–9 with their home leg due two days later on Easter Monday.

Rookes, having injured his hand, stood down for Leeds in the concluding tie, but they welcomed back previously unavailable Eric Batten. The rematch saw the Headingley side's forwards in control for long periods, keeping the game tight and showing reluctance to involve a set of backs lacking penetration, excepting Dai Jenkins. With a strong first half wind aiding territorial advantage, Leeds banged over three goals through Eaton (penalty), Jack Walkington (long-range drop-goal) and Jenkins (drop-goal after the Loiner's won a scrum in front of the posts). Although it brought them within one point, it was anticipated that Dewsbury—having the elements in their favour—would romp away after the interval. However, in a fiercely contested and gripping 40 minutes, the Leeds forwards outplayed Dewsbury's sextet but, whilst preventing them from increasing their score, proved equally impotent, losing by the odd point in 31.

Dewsbury's second Challenge Cup win, after a 31-year gap, was their third success of the season having won the Championship and Yorkshire Cup, although they were later stripped of the former through fielding an ineligible player in the play-offs.

STATS

Dewsbury 16 Leeds 9 (1st leg)

Saturday 24 April at Crown Flatt, Dewsbury (3.30 pm)

Dewsbury: Bunter (Broughton R), Hudson (captain, Salford), Edwards (Salford), Robinson (Castleford), Lloyd (Castleford), Kenny (Salford), Royal, Hammond, Curran (Salford), Gardner (Salford), Kershaw, Smith (Wakefield T), Seeling. Team manager: E. Waring

Leeds: Walkington (captain, Hunslet), Eaton, Rookes (Hunslet), Warrior, Callaghan, Evans, Jenkins, Prosser, Murphy, Satterthwaite, Jubb, Gregory (Warrington), Tattersfield. Trainer: W. Smith

Referee: G.S. Phillips
Touch-judges: W. Woodruff, W. Marsden
Half-time: 13–5 Attendance: 10,470 Receipts: £823
Weather: dry, windy

Progressive score:

Dewsbury	score (min)	Leeds
Seeling try, Seeling goal	5–0 (-)	
Kenny try, Seeling goal	10–0 (-)	
	10–5 (-)	Eaton try, Eaton goal
Robinson try	13–5 (-)	
	13–7 (-)	Eaton drop-goal
Edwards try	16–7 (-)	
	16–9 (-)	Eaton penalty

Leeds 6 Dewsbury 0 (2nd leg)

Monday 26 April at Headingley, Leeds (3.30 pm)

Leeds: unchanged except three-quarters were Batten (Hunslet), Warrior, Eaton, Callaghan

Dewsbury: unchanged

Referee: G.S. Phillips Touch-judges: W.H. Hargreave, A. Ball
Half-time: 6–0 Attendance: 16,000 Receipts: £1,521
Weather: dry, strong wind
Cup presentation: Robert F. Anderton, Rugby League chairman

Progressive score:

Leeds	score (min)	Dewsbury
Eaton penalty	2–0 (-)	
Walkington drop-goal	4–0 (-)	
Jenkins drop-goal	6–0 (-)	

Route to the final:

First round (2 legs): Dewsbury 42 Hull 12, Leeds 32 York 7
Second round (2 legs): Dewsbury 25 Huddersfield 18, Leeds 18 Wakefield Trinity 13
Semi-finals (2 legs): Dewsbury 68 Oldham 8, Leeds 30 Keighley 5

Head-to-head form guide:

Leeds 15 Dewsbury 7 (Yorkshire Cup)
Dewsbury 18 Leeds 5 (Yorkshire Cup)
Leeds 8 Dewsbury 22 (League)
Dewsbury 5 Leeds 5 (League)

1944 RUGBY LEAGUE CHALLENGE CUP FINAL
Bradford Northern v Wigan

Bradford Northern and Wigan fought out a titanic two-match duel to settle the 1944 Challenge Cup contest, the Yorkshire side claiming their first triumph since being reborn from the ashes of the old Bradford club in 1907. Neither tie contained flowing rugby with both defences on top, Northern's heavier pack dominating possession each time, gaining a two-third share of the aggregate 140 scrums (a total not unusual at that time).

For the opening leg at Wigan's Central Park, Bradford travelled without skipper Trevor Foster who

Three key players in Bradford Northern's success; Eric Batten, Ernest Ward and Trevor Foster, the latter pair sharing the captaincy over the two legs

was obliged to take part in the Northern Command (rugby union) Sevens at Headingley the same day, three-quarters Jack Kitching and Emlyn Walters plus forward Herbert Smith also being unavailable. Wigan missed injured scrum half Tommy Bradshaw (shoulder) whilst on-loan Warrington winger Albert Johnson was on service duty. Full back Joe Jones also withdrew with an injury, 40-year-old veteran Jim Sullivan being included for his third match of the season.

Aided by their overwhelming possession, Bradford camped in Wigan's 25-yard area in the early stages but, despite a few threatening bursts from their backs, failed to penetrate. Wigan held firm, their scrum half, Hector Gee, scooping up a loose ball before despatching it to Ernie Ashcroft on the flank. The winger, with little room, managed to get around Bradford's defensive line before transferring to Jack Blan who sent Jim Featherstone over. Sullivan missed the goal, later failing with a penalty.

Bradford were on top most of the second half, Eric Batten just being beaten for a touchdown and missing a drop-goal, whilst Ernest Ward was off-target with two penalties. In the later stages, Northern almost drew level when Batten leapt over Ashcroft (a style perfected by his father, Billy, and since outlawed) but, with a try looking certain, Sullivan pulled off a tremendous tackle that belied his years, Wigan surviving for a 3–0 win.

The return leg at Odsal attracted a new wartime record 30,000 crowd. Bradford stand-off Willie Davies was unable to obtain RAF leave, although Foster, Kitching and Walters returned. For Wigan, Jones was fit again, reclaiming his place from Sullivan. Bradford were expected to overcome their three-point deficit and, after Billy Belshaw missed a couple of penalties for Wigan, Batten brought them level overall at 3–3 when, in the 11th minute, having received possession from Ernest Ward following a scrum, he managed to dive over the try-line after initially juggling the ball. Ernest Ward failed to augment. Belshaw attempted to

100

resurrect the Cherry and Whites' lead, twice missing penalty attempts, the latter effort being charged down.

Wigan tried valiantly after the break, Belshaw missing another penalty and Jones being wide with a drop-goal, but Bradford regained command. The turning point of a no-quarter-asked encounter occurred

BRADFORD, SATURDAY, 15 APRIL, 1944

RUGBY LEAGUE CUP FINAL
ODSAL STADIUM, APRIL 22nd, 1944
RESERVED SEATS:
Centre Stand 6/-, End Stand 4/6, New Stand—seat g'td 3/6.
Tickets available on Monday at Odsal Stadium; Messrs. Knutton's, Town Hall Sq.: Pickersgill's, Broadway; and Carter's Bridge St. All applications by post must include stamped addressed envelope and remittance.

The Bradford Telegraph & Argus promoted the second leg at the head of its front page

six minutes from the end, George Carmichael striking a penalty after Ernest Ward (who himself had missed three further penalty attempts) took a blow to the face. In the last minute, Northern's heavyweight prop Frank Whitcombe barged over, Carmichael failing to augment as Bradford claimed victory 8–3.

Bradford refused to change colours for the second leg (the rule then being the home team wore alternate strip if there was a clash) and Wigan, who had changed for the first leg, swapped into blue jerseys. Bradford were subsequently fined 10 guineas (£10.50) for breaching the rules, team manager Dai Rees being censored for his 'attitude' towards the Rugby Football League chairman and vice-chairman before the game!

STATS

Wigan 3 Bradford Northern 0 (1st leg)

Saturday 15 April at Central Park, Wigan (3.30 pm)

Wigan (blue): Sullivan, Lawrenson, Belshaw (Warrington), Maloney (Liverpool Stanley), Ashcroft, Ryan, H. Gee, K. Gee, Egan (captain), J. Blan, Featherstone, Watkins, Bowen. Trainer: E. Parkes

Bradford Northern (white with red, amber and black band): Carmichael, Batten, Bennett, E. Ward (captain), Best, Davies, D. Ward, Whitcombe, Darlison, Higson, Roberts, Hutchinson, Marklew (Barrow). Team manager: D. Rees

Referee: S. Adams Touch-judges: unknown

Half-time: 3–0 Attendance: 22,000 Receipts: £1,640

Weather: unknown

Progressive score:

Wigan	score (min)	Bradford Northern
Featherstone try	3–0 (23)	

Bradford Northern 8 Wigan 0 (2nd leg)

Saturday 22 April at Odsal Stadium, Bradford (3.30 pm)

Bradford Northern (white with red, amber and black band): Carmichael, Batten, Kitching, E. Ward, Walters, Bennett, D. Ward, Whitcombe, Darlison, Higson, Foster (captain), Roberts, Hutchinson

Wigan (blue): unchanged except Jones for Sullivan

Referee: P. Cowell Touch-judges: unknown

Half-time: 3–0 Attendance: 30,000 Receipts: £2,200

Weather: unknown

Cup presentation:
Mrs R.F. Anderton, wife of Rugby League chairman

Progressive score:

Bradford Northern	score (min)	Wigan
Batten try	3–0 (11)	
Carmichael penalty	5–0 (74)	
Whitcombe try	8–0 (80)	

Route to the final:

First round (2 legs): Bradford Northern 20 Wakefield Trinity 9, Wigan 33 Oldham 8

Second round (2 legs): Bradford Northern 35 Keighley 14, Wigan 25 Dewsbury 5

Semi-finals (2 legs):
Bradford Northern 9 Halifax 5, Wigan 16 Leeds 14

Head-to-head form guide:

Wigan 15 Bradford Northern 11 (League)

WINNING CAPTAIN

Trevor Foster (Bradford Northern 1944—2nd leg)

Back-row forward Trevor Foster is one of the most fondly remembered players in Bradford's history. Born in Newport, South Wales, he played rugby union for his local Pill Harriers club before joining Newport. Bradford Northern signed him in October 1938, his early rugby league career being disrupted through the Second World War. He made the last of 432 appearances for Bradford in 1955, having enjoyed success in the Rugby League Challenge Cup (1944, 1947, 1949), Championship (1939/40, 1940/41, 1944/45—missing the final of the latter through military duties), Yorkshire Cup (1941—April, 1941—December, 1943, 1948, 1949, 1953) and Yorkshire League (1939/40, 1940/41, 1947/48). Possessing strength, allied to pace, he was a tourist in 1946, made three Test appearances and represented Wales (16 times—including four appearances during wartime and seven as captain). He later coached Bradford Northern (1960) and Leeds (1961–63), retaining links with the Bradford club throughout his life.

1945 RUGBY LEAGUE CHALLENGE CUP FINAL
Huddersfield v Bradford Northern

The third and last two-legged wartime Challenge Cup Final was another close affair, Huddersfield defeating holders Bradford Northern 13–9 over the 160 minutes play. Bradford were delighted when skipper Ernest Ward received a late release from an inter-services rugby union match for the opening tie, providing a timely replacement for full back George Carmichael who had cried off with injury, stand-off Willie Davies also being unavailable.

Huddersfield scored first after Bill Leake's precision kick found touch near the corner. The Fartowners won the scrum and Randall Lewis burst through Northern's defence, but the ball went loose after a failed interception of his pass to Ossie Peake. Tommy Grahame recovered it before sending Peake over for the try, the wingman stepping inside a defender. Jeff Bawden added the goal. With wet weather creating handling problems and difficult under-foot conditions, play became scrappy. Bawden was wide with a long-range penalty, Ernest Ward having better success for Bradford from 25 yards after Albert Pepperell was guilty of illegal scrum-feeding. Most of the pressure was on Bradford's line; Jack

WINNING CAPTAIN

Alex Fiddes (Huddersfield 1945)

Alex Fiddes signed for Huddersfield from hometown Hawick rugby union club in 1933, quickly building a reputation as a forceful, skilful centre. He played 467 times for the club, winning the Rugby League Challenge Cup (1945) and Yorkshire Cup (1938). He made wartime guest appearances with Bradford Northern and Keighley (once each in 1943) and Castleford (twice, 1944/45). His last Huddersfield match was in 1947, after which he coached Huddersfield and Batley. Included in an 'England Rugby League' party for a brief visit to France in 1938, he was considered a near-certainty to tour in 1940 until war intervened. Born in Scotland, he is—excepting Australasian and Welsh players—the only non-Englishman to captain a Challenge Cup winning team.

Miller failing with a drop-goal, Peake almost scoring in the corner. Bawden then landed a goal from the first of his two penalty strikes before half-time, placing Huddersfield 7–2 up. A second half stalemate saw Bradford have more of the game, Ernest Ward kicking another penalty, Alex Fiddes being off-target with a later attempt for Huddersfield, the final score standing at 7–4.

Huddersfield's Joe Bradbury missed the Odsal leg having sustained a shoulder injury, Australian Grahame retaining his place courtesy of extra navy leave, Bradford welcoming Davies back. In another tight match, poor conditions again made handling hazardous. On a muddy, treacherous pitch, Bradford fought hard to close the three-point gap. Ernest Ward was short with a penalty but Huddersfield, despite a poor first half display, held on.

Bradford appeared to have turned things around after the interval when

Huddersfield were the last wartime Challenge Cup winners. Players only (in playing kit) are, standing: Aspinall, Baxter, Mallinson, Leake, Brook, Givvons. Seated: McGurk, Bawden, Fiddes, Grahame, Pepperell. Kneeling: Burrow (left), Miller (right). Trainer Spencer is standing extreme right (next to Givvons)

Huddersfield's Les Baxter lost the ball, Davies picking up to put Eric Batten over, Ernest Ward's conversion making it 9–7 for Northern overall. But, instead of lifting Bradford, it triggered greater resolve from Huddersfield. Miller drove Bradford back with a great kick to touch near their try-line and, from a succeeding scrum, the ball moved swiftly to Bawden who evaded the cover to dive in at the corner. He failed to augment but Huddersfield held an aggregate one-point advantage and began bombarding their opposition as the match opened out. Bradford had their moments, Batten twice intercepting but without an end product. For Huddersfield, Lewis almost got over and Fiddes had a score disallowed through an earlier knock-on. Eventually, Bawden claimed his second try after dribbling the ball into the in-goal after a Bradford move broke down. He again missed the goal, but Huddersfield scented victory, the *Yorkshire Post* commenting 'in the end their mastery was complete, and in the last quarter they swarmed confident and aggressive in the Bradford half.'

With the war in Europe drawing to a close (Adolph Hitler's death was announced during the week) there was a relaxed feeling at Odsal, the military band being accompanied by 'a great deal of ringing of bells' on the terraces before the match. A patriotic touch was the use of Union Jacks and the Stars and Stripes as corner flags. Maurice Blein, secretary of the revived French Rugby League, was a special guest and Sir Edwin Morris of Northern Command presented the trophy.

STATS

Huddersfield 7 Bradford Northern 4 (1st leg)

Saturday 28 April at Fartown, Huddersfield (3.30 pm)

Huddersfield (claret with narrow gold hoops): Leake, Peake (Warrington), Fiddes (captain), Lewis (Swinton), Bawden, Grahame, Pepperell, Bradbury (Salford), Whitehead, Miller (Warrington), Mallinson, Baxter, Givvons. Trainer: S. Spencer

Bradford Northern (white with red, amber and black band): E. Ward (captain), Batten, Edwards (Salford), Kitching, Best, Bennett, D. Ward, Whitcombe, Darlison, Higson, Roberts, Marklew, Hutchinson. Team manager: D. Rees

Referee: F. Fairhurst Touch-judges: unknown

Half-time: 7–2 Attendance: 9,041 Receipts: £1,184

Weather: rain, slippery conditions

Progressive score:

Huddersfield	score (min)	Bradford Northern
Peake try, Bawden goal	5–0 (12)	
	5–2 (33)	E. Ward penalty
Bawden penalty	7–2 (-)	
	7–4 (-)	E. Ward penalty

Bradford Northern 5 Huddersfield 6 (2nd leg)

Saturday 5 May at Odsal Stadium, Bradford (3.30 pm)

Bradford Northern (white with red, amber and black band): unchanged except Davies for Bennett, Smith for Marklew

Huddersfield (claret with narrow gold hoops): unchanged except forwards were: Mallinson, Whitehead, Miller, Givvons, Aspinall, Baxter

Referee: G.S. Phillips Touch-judges: unknown

Half-time: 0–0 Attendance: 17,500 Receipts: £2,050

Weather: rain, slippery conditions

Cup presentation: Sir Edwin Morris, General Officer Commanding, Northern Command

Progressive score:

Bradford Northern	score (min)	Huddersfield
Batten try, E. Ward goal	5–0 (-)	
	5–3 (-)	Bawden try
	5–6 (-)	Bawden try

Route to the final:

First round (2 legs): Huddersfield 38 Leeds 8, Bradford Northern 49 St Helens 21

Second round (2 legs): Huddersfield 22 Barrow 9, Bradford N 21 Wakefield T 18

Semi-finals (2 legs): Huddersfield 10 Halifax 9, Bradford Northern 35 Keighley 8

Head-to-head form guide:

Huddersfield 11 Bradford Northern 6 (League)

Bradford Northern 22 Huddersfield 8 (League)

1946 RUGBY LEAGUE CHALLENGE CUP FINAL
Wakefield Trinity v Wigan

When the Challenge Cup Final returned to Wembley in 1946 following a seven-year absence, Rugby League's officials could hardly have dreamt of such a dramatic, nerve-tingling conclusion. With just over a minute left, Wakefield Trinity trailed Wigan 12–11 when the Cherry and Whites were penalised; a planned move having broken down just inside their own 25-yard area, causing Eddie Watkins and Jack Blan to collide, obstructing a Wakefield player. Just 10 yards in from the touchline, Wakefield captain Billy Stott, taking his time, stepped up to the ball. The tension was captured perfectly in the words of the *Wakefield Express* writer: 'If he missed would there be another chance to retrieve the position within one minute? The eyes of those on the main stand shifted uneasily between Stott and the clock, the minute hand of which moved slowly, aye, mockingly it seemed, forward. The critical moment arrived and with deliberation and coolness Stott's left swung behind the ball.' It produced a sensational winning goal as 'a roar went up from all sides of the huge bowl' placing Wakefield ahead for the first time in the match, 13–12. It capped a man of the match performance for Stott, earning himself the inaugural Lance Todd Trophy.

Wakefield should have opened the scoring, Stott missing an early penalty, Wigan going ahead in the seventh minute through a Jack Blan try, following a dribbling rush by their pack towards Trinity's try-line. Aided by some excellent touch finding from Tommy Bradshaw's boot, Wigan got on top of a nervous Wakefield and winger Brian Nordgren added a second touchdown, sidestepping Denis Baddeley as he sprinted half the length of the field off a Gordon Ratcliffe pass before placing the ball in the corner. It pushed Wigan six points ahead with a quarter of the match gone, Nordgren having missed both conversions plus a penalty in between. Trinity, after their uncertain start, became more organised, the experienced Stott proving a calming influence. Having almost scored

The car park fills up outside the Empire Stadium in 1946 as the crowd builds ahead of the first peacetime final in seven years

Billy Stott, the Wakefield Trinity captain and first winner of the Lance Todd Trophy, is carried triumphantly around the Wembley pitch, Billy Teall (left) and Mick Exley grabbing a leg each

himself following an interception and then failing with a long distance penalty attempt, Stott sent Ron Rylance clear, the winger returning the ball inside to him. The Trinity skipper then brushed off two challengers on what was described as 'a death or glory charge' for the line, diving over Jack Cunliffe to score,

FOR THOSE NOT CONVERSANT

The move south to Wembley set the expectation of attracting an audience that would include spectators more familiar with rugby union rules. It prompted the Rugby League authorities to include a section in the 1929 Challenge Cup Final programme headed 'Important Points' and began: 'For those who are not conversant with some of the more important rules of the Rugby League game.' In essence it sought to explain the key differences between the two rugby codes. Although not reiterated in the 1930 edition, a similar feature appeared in all Wembley programmes from 1931 until 1950. Apart from 1972 (under the heading 'To Help The Newcomers') further education was not deemed necessary until the last final held at the old Wembley in 1999 ('Watching Rugby League'), no doubt to assist those enticed through the presence of London Broncos. With the Challenge Cup Finals being held in rugby union 'territory' at Murrayfield, Twickenham and Cardiff's Millennium Stadium from 2000 until 2006, it was logical to repeat the exercise during that period (2001 at Twickenham being an exception).

the *Wakefield Express* noting: 'The memory of his try will never fade.' Minutes later Watkins' drop-goal attempt for Wigan fell just beneath the crossbar. Stott, who had been unable to convert his try, then notched a penalty for offside shortly before half-time.

Trailing 6–5, Wakefield threatened first in the second half, Jim Croston almost scoring. Stott blotted his copybook by missing a Mick Exley pass, Wigan's Stan Jolley retrieving it before sprinting 70 yards for a try in the corner, beating Croston and Billy Teall on the way. Nordgren missed the difficult kick, and was also off the mark with a penalty. Stott made up for his error, crossing the try-line unopposed seven minutes later off a wide Herbert Goodfellow pass, although missing the goal that would have put Trinity ahead. Wigan regained the momentum, Cunliffe beating three defenders before putting Nordgren in, the latter again failing to augment as Wigan led 12–8. It seemed all over for Trinity when Nordgren shot down the wing, handing off Baddeley and going round Teall, but he stepped into touch. In a topsy-turvy finish Croston forced his way through a narrow gap for a try nine minutes from the end. Stott, though, missed the goal leaving Wakefield one point in arrears. As the minutes ticked away Wigan hung on—until that fateful last few minutes.

A post-script to Stott's match-winner came in the dying seconds after Wigan were awarded a penalty for offside five yards inside their own half. The kick, though, was too much for Nordgren, falling short as the final whistle blew, his seventh miss from seven attempts. The New Zealander, who otherwise had an outstanding game, bemoaned later that 'I am the unhappiest man in London.'

Post-match analysis suggested that Wigan, having played the more attractive rugby, should have won, the *Sunday Express* comment that 'Wigan will count themselves the unluckiest team to lose at Wembley' was a typical reaction. Wakefield, though, deserved full credit for a gutsy, never-say-die effort, in which their forwards always had the measure of Wigan's pack. For the first time, the Lions tour to Australasia clashed with the final, Wigan having four players (forwards Joe Egan and Ken Gee, backs Martin Ryan and Ted Ward) and Wakefield one (second-rower Harry Murphy) aboard the aircraft carrier HMS Indomitable. Wigan stand-off Jack Fleming was also out of the reckoning through breaking his collarbone a month earlier, whilst their prop Frank Barton, home on Army leave from Austria, played his first game since November.

Pressure for Wakefield Trinity as their loose forward Len Bratley is tackled near his own line by Wigan's George Banks

WINNING CAPTAIN

Billy Stott (Wakefield Trinity 1946)

Billy Stott began his career at stand-off with local team Featherstone Rovers in 1930, eventually moving into the centre. He transferred to Broughton Rangers for a 'substantial fee' in 1933, playing once for England and seven times for Yorkshire during his time there. His next move was to Oldham for £800 in 1939, Wakefield Trinity picking him up for just £95 in 1944. At five feet seven inches and 13 stone, he was by then a stocky looking player who, whilst lacking the pace of earlier years, provided experience and leadership to Wakefield in the early post-war years. He won the Rugby League Challenge Cup (1946), Yorkshire Cup (1947) and Yorkshire League (1945/46) with Trinity. Retiring in 1948, he became club coach.

STATS

Wakefield Trinity 13 Wigan 12

Saturday 4 May at Wembley Stadium, London (3.30 pm)

Wakefield Trinity (blue with red band): Teale, Rylance, Stott (captain), Croston, Baddeley, Jones, Goodfellow, Wilkinson, Marson, Higgins, Exley, Howes, Bratley. Player/team manager: J. Croston

Wigan (cherry and white hoops): Cunliffe, Nordgren, Ratcliffe, Ashcroft, Jolley, Lowrey, Bradshaw, Banks, J. Blan, Barton, Watkins (captain), Atkinson W. Blan. Coach: J. Sullivan

Referee: A. Hill Touch-judges: R. Kendal, S. Duncan

Half-time: 5–6 Attendance: 54,730 Receipts: £12,013

Weather: sunny and hot

Lance Todd Trophy: Stott (Wakefield Trinity)

Cup presentation:
The Rt Hon. Clement Attlee, Prime Minister

Progressive score:

Wakefield Trinity	score (min)	Wigan
	0–3 (7)	J. Blan try
	0–6 (19)	Nordgren try
Stott try	3–6 (25)	
Stott penalty	5–6 (35)	
	5–9 (50)	Jolley try
Stott try	8–9 (57)	
	8–12 (65)	Nordgren try
Croston try	11–12 (71)	
Stott penalty	13–12 (79)	

Route to the final:

First round (2 legs): Wakefield Trinity 19 Huddersfield 5, Wigan 18 Swinton 7

Second round: Wakefield Trinity 10 Halifax 0, Wigan 37 Keighley 0

Third round: Wakefield Trinity 14 Workington Town 4, Barrow 3 Wigan 13

Semi-finals:
Wakefield Trinity 7 Hunslet 3 (Headingley, Leeds, 33,000), Wigan 12 Widnes 5 (Station Road, Swinton, 36,976)

Head-to-head form guide:

No previous meetings during season

1947 RUGBY LEAGUE CHALLENGE CUP FINAL
Bradford Northern v Leeds

Bradford Northern made a triumphant Wembley debut in 1947, defeating favourites Leeds 8–4 in front of a world record attendance of 77,605 (surpassing the 70,204 for the 1932 First Test in Australia). Although most forms of entertainment in early post-war Britain were supported enthusiastically and in great numbers, it illustrated how attractive the Rugby League's 'Wembley weekend' had become in the sporting calendar, the *Yorkshire Post* commenting that over half the crowd was not from the north. For the first time since 1933, the occasion had a Royal presence, The Duke of Gloucester presenting the trophy.

Unfortunately, and probably due to nerves, the game itself did not match the expectation of it being a 'classic' through a succession of endless and untidy scrums, both sides being guilty of not observing the play-the-ball rules correctly, the *Yorkshire Post* noting that 'the game was not a spectacle' referring to it as a 'tedious series of interruptions'. The only first half score, following a lot of Leeds pressure by their forwards came in the 27th minute when the Headingley side's New Zealand full back, Bert Cook, landed a tricky angled penalty goal.

The second period saw Bradford—who played without winger Alan Edwards due to a shoulder

THE CHALLENGE CUP

The original Northern Union Challenge Cup was made by Lloyd, Payne and Amiel, of Thomas Street, Manchester, at a cost of 60 guineas, a case for its 'safe keeping' adding a further £5. It stood 36 inches tall and rested on a black ebony base eight inches deep. Fattorini and Sons of Bradford—who designed the Challenge Cup—provided medals for the winners and losers. The trophy retained its inscription 'The Northern Rugby Football Union Challenge Cup' despite being competed for as the Rugby League Challenge Cup from 1923 (reflecting the decision of the Northern Rugby Football Union to rename itself as The Rugby Football League in 1922). Because the lid frequently fell off, particularly during post-match celebrations, it was decided to remove the lower 'neck' section of its ornate top for greater stability, the new look appearing for the 1969 final. However, as the trophy became more battered and worn over time, it was replaced with an exact copy produced by Jack Spencer Ltd of Sheffield, which made its debut in 2001—complete with a new neck!

injury—gain the ascendancy in the forward battle, stand-off Willie Davies making in-roads with several dangerous breaks as a result, enabling their backs to move the ball about more. Nine minutes after the

Bradford Northern enjoy their first Wembley success as skipper Ernest Ward shows off the coveted trophy, Vic Darlison (to the left) and George Carmichael taking the strain!

interval, in what was considered the 'highlight' of the match, Northern's Jack Kitching provided a defence-splitting pass to his co-centre and captain, Ernest Ward, who sent Emlyn Walters in for a great try in the corner. Incredibly they were the first points conceded by Leeds in all rounds of that year's competition. Ernest Ward missed the goal but Bradford led for the first time, 3–2. It was short lived, however, Cook—facing the 'breeze'—regaining the lead moments later with a magnificent second penalty from halfway that just crept over the crossbar. With the outcome poised to go either way, tension mounted, Ernest Ward missing with a penalty attempt. He quickly made amends with an unexpected 56th minute drop-goal after retrieving possession when

Trevor Foster's late try for Bradford Northern seals victory

Kitching lost the ball in a tackle. Consequently Northern were ahead 5–4, the lead having changed hands three times since half-time. The remaining 20 minutes were played out almost exclusively in Leeds' 25-yard area as their forwards struggled to contain Bradford's. With just minutes left, Northern's Trevor Foster grabbed a loose ball misfielded by Cook to run in a second try, Ernest Ward missing the goal. In the final analysis, Leeds lost because their powerful pack, considered the stronger of the two, failed to master Bradford's on the day. As a result, Leeds' backs never really got into the game. The *Yorkshire Post* writer Alf Drewry had no doubt as to who the match-winner was, writing: 'It was Davies' pace over the first five yards, his excellent passing and his unerring judgement in kicking that accounted more than anything for Northern's clear cut superiority behind the scrum.'

STATS

Bradford Northern 8 Leeds 4

Saturday 3 May at Wembley Stadium, London (3.30 pm)

Bradford Northern (white with red, amber and black band): Carmichael, Batten, Kitching, E. Ward (captain), Walters, Davies, D. Ward, Whitcombe, Darlison, Smith, Tyler, Foster, Evans. Team manager: D. Rees

Leeds (amber): Cook, Cornelius, Price, L. Williams, Whitehead, R. Williams, Jenkins, Brereton, Murphy, Prosser, Watson, Clues, Owens (captain). Coach: F. Dawson

Referee: P. Cowell Touch-judges: N.T. Railton, T. Watkinson

Half-time: 0–2 Attendance: 77,605 Receipts: £17,434

Weather: sunny and windy

Lance Todd Trophy: Davies (Bradford Northern)

Cup presentation: H.R.H. The Duke of Gloucester

Progressive score:

Bradford Northern	score (min)	Leeds
	0–2 (27)	Cook penalty
Walters try	3–2 (49)	
	3–4 (51)	Cook penalty
E. Ward drop-goal	5–4 (56)	
Foster try	8–4 (79)	

Route to the final:

First round (2 legs):
Bradford Northern 12 Salford 5, Leeds 18 Barrow 0

Second round:
Huddersfield 0 Bradford Northern 8, Leeds 5 Hunslet 0

Third round:
Bradford Northern 10 Workington Town 3, Wigan 0 Leeds 5

Semi-finals: Bradford Northern 11 Warrington 7 (Station Road, Swinton, 33,474),

Leeds 21 Wakefield Trinity 0 (Fartown, Huddersfield, 35,136)

Head-to-head form guide:

Bradford Northern 25 Leeds 5 (League)

WINNING CAPTAIN

Ernest Ward (Bradford Northern 1944—1st leg, 1947, 1949)

Ernest Ward signed for Bradford Northern from Dewsbury Boys' Club in 1936, aged 16. A skilful centre, master tactician, and reliable goal-kicker, he won the Rugby League Challenge Cup (1944, 1947, 1949), Championship (1940/41, 1944/45), Yorkshire Cup (1941—April, 1941—December, 1943, 1945, 1948, 1949) and Yorkshire League (1939/40, 1940/41, 1947/48) with Northern. He represented Great Britain (21 times—10 as captain), England (20), Yorkshire (11), and was a tourist in 1946 and 1950, being captain for the latter. In 1953, after 391 Bradford appearances (538 goals, 117 tries), he joined Castleford as player-coach, concluding his playing career with Batley in 1956. His father, also Ernest, appeared for Dewsbury in the 1912 Challenge Cup Final.

Graham Morris

1948 RUGBY LEAGUE CHALLENGE CUP FINAL
Wigan v Bradford Northern

Wigan took on holders Bradford Northern in 1948 with the knowledge that their opponents had won 15–3 at Central Park seven days earlier in a Championship play-off. The re-match caught the imagination, the Challenge Cup Final attracting over 90,000 for the first time. It was also the first witnessed by a reigning monarch, King George VI presenting the trophy to Joe Egan after Wigan's triumph. An otherwise perfect occasion was spoilt by the un-Wembley-like weather of heavy rain and driving wind, which made playing conditions difficult. There was disappointment for Northern's veteran full back George Carmichael, his place going to Bill Leake, despite playing in all the previous ties, whilst centre Jack Kitching had been out injured for three months.

Wigan had the first try-scoring opportunity when Tommy Bradshaw, Cec Mountford and Ted Ward combined to set up Gordon Ratcliffe on a 50-yard burst. Having kicked ahead, Ratcliffe looked likely to score beneath the posts but he 'turned' awkwardly and the opportunity vanished. The Cherry and Whites registered the first score, however, when Bradford winger Eric Batten, having lost the ball, kicked it away, only for Jack Hilton to charge it down and dribble past him before diving in at the corner for the touchdown. Ted Ward,

having fallen short with two earlier penalty attempts, kicked an excellent goal from near the touchline, Wigan leading by five points with a quarter of the match played. Northern, though, struck back within four minutes, Alan Edwards pouncing on to Ken Traill's cross-kick into the left corner just ahead of Ratcliffe to claim the try. Ernest Ward made a disappointing attempt at goal. Batten had a chance to make up for his earlier mistake but was unable to latch on to a wide pass in the slippery conditions with the line open. As the half drew to a close Ernest Ward had an opportunity to tie the scores, missing a penalty.

With just two points separating the teams, the second-half became a very tight affair, Wigan being generally on top, Bradford defending well. Ted Ward and Ernest Ward each missed two penalties (including a long-range effort by the former that dropped just short), whilst Wigan's Bill Hudson (just failing after he kicked into the corner) and Bradford's Trevor Foster (held short by Martin Ryan after being put through by Ernest Ward) came closest to increasing the try count. But, the only second half score came in the final minutes after Bradford had dropped the ball out from under their posts. Wigan's second-row pairing of Les White and Billy Blan dribbled

The teams walk out led by their captains; Ernest Ward of Bradford Northern, left, and Wigan's Joe Egan. Wembley's once empty end terraces of pre-war finals are now a memory, the match eclipsing the previous rugby league world record crowd attracting 91,465

Wigan loose forward Bill Hudson gets the ball wide to winger Gordon Ratcliffe following a scrum

it back and over the try-line, prop Frank Barton dropping on it to claim the touchdown. Hindered by the difficult conditions underfoot, Ted Ward hit the near upright with a simple kick, leaving Wigan victorious by 8–3.

Hudson proved to be one of Wigan's unsung heroes through keeping close tabs on Traill, Bradford's loose forward having been a major factor in the Yorkshire side's previous win over the Cherry and Whites. Disappointed Bradford skipper Ernest Ward said afterwards: 'The slippery surface of the new ball and the ground conditions spoiled the game. Wigan took their chances while we allowed ours to go astray.' The final was the first shown live on BBC television, albeit in the London region only.

WINNING CAPTAIN

Joe Egan (Wigan 1948)

Hooker Joe Egan had more to his game than winning scrum possession, being wonderfully adroit in setting up attacks for supporting pack colleagues, his long-term front-row partnership with prop Ken Gee being particularly fruitful. He began as a full back playing for local clubs Wigan St Patrick's and Highfield Old Boys, signing with Wigan in 1937 aged 17. He quickly established himself, taking over as skipper in 1942. With Wigan, he won the Rugby League Challenge Cup (1948), Championship (1943/44, 1945/46—missing the final through touring, 1946/47, 1949/50—again missing the final through touring), Lancashire Cup (1938, 1946, 1947, 1948, 1949), and Lancashire League (1940/41, 1945/46, 1946/47, 1949/50). A tourist twice (1946, 1950), he appeared in 14 Tests for Great Britain, representing England (19 times) and Lancashire (10). In 1950 he joined Leigh as captain-coach for a Rugby League record £5,000, leading them to Lancashire Cup success in 1952. His last Leigh match was in 1955, continuing as coach before reuniting with Wigan in a similar capacity (1956–61). He later coached Widnes, Warrington and Blackpool Borough and was in charge of Great Britain for the 1954 World Cup. During the Second World War, he made a guest appearance for Oldham (1943).

STATS

Wigan 8 Bradford Northern 3

Saturday 1 May at Wembley Stadium, London (3.00 pm)

Wigan (cherry and white hoops): Ryan, Ratcliffe, E. 'Ted' Ward, Ashcroft, Hilton, Mountford, Bradshaw, Gee, Egan (captain), Barton, White, W. Blan, Hudson. Coach: J. Sullivan

Bradford Northern (white with amber, red and black chevron): Leake, Batten, Case, Ernest Ward (captain), Edwards, Davies, D. Ward, Whitcombe, Darlison, Smith, Tyler, Foster, Traill. Team manager: D. Rees

Referee: G.S. Phillips Touch-judges: T.E. Rees, H. Squires

Half-time: 5–3   Attendance: 91,465   Receipts: £21,121

Weather: heavy rain and wind

Lance Todd Trophy: Whitcombe (Bradford Northern)

Cup presentation: H.M. King George VI

Progressive score:

Wigan	score (min)	Bradford Northern
Hilton try, Ted Ward goal	5–0 (20)	
	5–3 (24)	Edwards try
Barton try	8–3 (79)	

Route to the final:

First round (2 legs): Wigan 46 Castleford 7, Bradford Northern 17 Huddersfield 8

Second round: Wigan 17 Leeds 3, Wakefield Trinity 3 Bradford Northern 3

Second round replay: Bradford Northern 9 Wakefield Trinity 2

Third round: Warrington 10 Wigan 13, Bradford Northern 30 Oldham 0

Semi-finals: Wigan 11 Rochdale Hornets 0 (Station Road, Swinton, 26,004), Bradford Northern 14 Hunslet 7 (Headingley, Leeds, 38,125)

Head-to-head form guide:

Bradford Northern 5 Wigan 16 (League)

Wigan 14 Bradford Northern 7 (League)

Wigan 3 Bradford Northern 15 (Championship semi-final)

1949 RUGBY LEAGUE CHALLENGE CUP FINAL
Bradford Northern v Halifax

Bradford Northern became the first club to reach three consecutive Wembley finals when they took on Yorkshire rivals, Halifax, in the 1949 decider. In all three visits they played in front of Royalty, the cup being presented this time by The Duke of Edinburgh. The occasion produced another world record crowd, the 'all ticket' match attracting 95,050. Bradford were clear favourites, their team containing only one player, Ron Greaves, who had not already sampled the Wembley experience. The *Bradford Telegraph & Argus* reported that the two captains would toss a coin on the pitch before kick-off, whereas previously at Wembley it had taken place in the changing rooms.

Bradford got off to a confident start, their forwards charging into Halifax from the beginning, ably led by veteran prop, Frank Whitcombe. It looked ominous for the Thrum Hall side when Northern skipper Ernest Ward sent a neat kick through their defence for

Scrum half Stan Kielty transfers the ball to John Rothwell as Halifax try to mount an attack

STATS
Bradford Northern 12 Halifax 0

Saturday 7 May at Wembley Stadium, London (3.00 pm)

Bradford Northern (white with red, amber and black band): Leake, Batten, Kitching, E. Ward (captain), Edwards, Davies, D. Ward, Whitcombe, Darlison, Greaves, Tyler, Foster, Traill. Team manager: D. Rees

Halifax (blue and white hoops): Chalkey, Daniels, Reid, Price (captain), MacDonald, Kenny, Kielty, Condon, Ackerley, Rothwell, Healy, Pansegrouw, Mawson. Coach: A. Atkinson

Referee: G.S. Phillips Touch-judges: J. Holmes, A. Bolton

Half-time: 5–0 Attendance: 95,050 Receipts: £21,930

Weather: sunny and warm

Lance Todd Trophy: E. Ward (Bradford Northern)

Cup presentation: H.R.H. The Duke of Edinburgh

Progressive score:

Bradford Northern	score (min)	Halifax
Batten try, E. Ward goal	5–0 (10)	
E. Ward penalty	7–0 (60)	
Foster try, E. Ward goal	12–0 (72)	

Route to the final:

First round (2 legs):
Bradford Northern 8 St Helens 4, Halifax 10 Hull 4

Second round:
Bradford Northern 11 Castleford 5, Halifax 5 Swinton 0

Third round:
Bradford Northern 8 Belle Vue Rangers 7, Oldham 2 Halifax 7

Semi-finals: Bradford Northern 10 Barrow 0 (Station Road, Swinton, 26,900),

Halifax 11 Huddersfield 10 (Odsal Stadium, Bradford, 64,250)

Head-to-head form guide:

No previous meetings during season

Eric Batten to score by the corner flag after just 10 minutes, to which the former added an excellent conversion. Batten had, in fact, fractured his shoulder in the opening minutes of the match but bravely played for the full 80. Northern's pack, winning most of the scrums, continued to dominate the opening half but Halifax defended well, no further score being registered before the break.

It was a similar story in the second period; Bradford

Bradford Northern's Ken Traill delivers the ball to Willie Davies as Halifax defender Jack Pansegrouw (left) prepares to take defensive action

dictating play as their backs gradually opened out more, Halifax sticking manfully to their task. Midway through the half Ernest Ward kicked an excellent penalty—another touchline effort. But, despite leading 7–0, it was only eight minutes from the end that Bradford could consider the trophy as theirs; a clever move from Donald Ward (Ernest's brother) and Ken

Ernest Ward—Bradford Northern skipper and Lance Todd Trophy winner—addresses the crowd after the match

Traill put Trevor Foster in beneath the posts, Ernest Ward adding the goal to complete a 12–0 score-line.

The recent reintroduction of the virtually retired Whitcombe to the front row by Bradford team manager Dai Rees was hailed 'a master stroke', his weight, at 18½ stone, being considered to have had a major influence on the outcome. Although Halifax gained the unwanted distinction of being the first side unable to score at Wembley, they deserved huge credit for reaching the final, having finished 25th in the League, the lowest placing of any finalist. Bradford set down a milestone of their own as the first Wembley runners-up to return the following year as victors.

Ernest Ward, in a message relayed from London to their supporters via the *Bradford Telegraph and Argus*, said: 'We have set up an outstanding record for the city, and we think it is appropriate that on the third successive appearance we should win the cup. We are eagerly awaiting our return to Bradford. It has been a great weekend which will live long in our memories!'

UNUSUAL FAVOURS!

In the earlier years of the Challenge Cup competition supporters celebrated a trip to the final in ways that would appear eccentric to today's followers. Below are a few examples:

- 1897: An enterprising printer produced 'funeral' cards to sell to St Helens fans at the final, anticipating the demise of opponents Batley. When Batley won, the seller scratched out 'Yorkshire' and inserted 'St Helens'. The *Batley News* remarked 'it is not often we hear of Lancashire Tykes', the revised wording being: 'In memory of the St Helens Tykes who succumbed whilst struggling for the Cup.'

- 1901: A train transporting Warrington supporters to Leeds for the final included saloons that had been reserved for the 'better off', one having a piano installed for the occasion so fans could entertain themselves by singing.

- 1904: The *Warrington Guardian* reported that most Wires followers wore club 'favours' of primrose and blue but, because their star player was Jack Fish, 'others exposed various kinds of fish—the raw kind—and needless to add they were given a wide berth, for they left a strong aroma in their train which was not of a savoury nature.' That theme also occurred in 1901 when Warrington youths tied haddock around their hats!

- 1909: Wakefield Trinity supporters took their 'favourite whippets' covered in red and blue coats with bells attached. Other Wakefield fans took a young goat, bought in Manchester after the semi-final win over Wigan, which was 'bedecked with the Trinity colours and proved quite an attraction.'

1950 RUGBY LEAGUE CHALLENGE CUP FINAL
Warrington v Widnes

Warrington earned their first Challenge Cup success since 1907 by convincingly defeating local rivals Widnes 19–0 in the 1950 showdown. It was 'third time lucky' for Warrington having lost twice at Wembley in the 1930s whilst, for Widnes, the match represented a record fourth appearance at the stadium. Amazingly, only five players from outside the town represented the club in those four visits, three of them in their 1950 line-up. For the second, and last time the Lions' latest tour to the Southern Hemisphere diluted the occasion through the absence of four leading players—all forwards—who had already set sail; Warrington's Jim Featherstone and Bob Ryan, and Widnes' Fred Higgins and Danny Naughton. Whilst both sides still

Warrington's Gerald Lowe (left) and Albert Johnson get to grips with Widnes winger John Parkes

Harry Bath holds up the Challenge Cup whilst being carried around the Wembley pitch by his Warrington team. Lance Todd Trophy winner Gerry Helme takes care of the plinth

boasted strong packs, Warrington had, on paper, the better back division.

It was Widnes that applied the early pressure, a chance being lost when Tommy Sale mishandled. However, the length-of-field touch-finding accuracy of Warrington scrum half Gerry Helme began pushing them back downfield, Wires' legendary Australian wing, Brian Bevan almost getting a try but for a forward pass. With a quarter-hour gone, Helme played the ball back to Harold Palin—who had missed with a 10th minute penalty—the loose forward calmly slotting a left-footed 15-yard drop-goal to open the scoring. Three minutes later he was on target again with a wonderful 35-yard penalty, 10 yards from the touchline, following a scrum infringement. Widnes failed with a penalty opportunity from Colin Hutton but, overall, they were looking rattled as indecision gifted free kicks to their opponents. The opening try went to Warrington after their second-row Gerald Lowe was tackled near the Widnes line. From the play-the-ball, acting-halfback Palin sent captain Harry Bath through, the Australian knocking two defenders out of the way with two more clinging on as he scored. Palin kicked a magnificent goal from a difficult angle for a 9–0 lead after 22 minutes.

With Helme continuing to despatch long kicks into touch, Widnes could not settle into a rhythm. From a

STATS

Warrington 19 Widnes 0

Saturday 6 May at Wembley Stadium, London (3.00 pm)

Warrington (white with primrose and blue bands): Jones, Bevan, Ryder, A. Naughton, Johnson, Knowelden, Helme, Derbyshire, Fishwick, Fisher, Bath (captain), Lowe, Palin. Team manager: C. Brockbank

Widnes (black and white hoops): Bradley, Parkes, Hutton, Sale (captain), Malone, Fleming, Anderson, Rowbottom, Band, Wilcox, Leigh, J. Naughton, Reynolds. Coach: T. Shannon

Referee: A.S. Dobson

Touch-judges: J.P. Hebblethwaite, J.B. McWalters

Half-time: 14–0 Attendance: 94,249 Receipts: £24,782

Weather: sunny and cloudy

Lance Todd Trophy: Helme (Warrington)

Cup presentation:
The Rt Hon. Clement Attlee, Prime Minister

Progressive score:

Warrington	score (min)	Widnes
Palin drop-goal	2–0 (15)	
Palin penalty	4–0 (18)	
Bath try, Palin goal	9–0 (22)	
Ryder try	12–0 (33)	
Palin penalty	14–0 (38)	
Palin penalty	16–0 (58)	
Knowelden try	19–0 (67)	

Route to the final:

First round (2 legs): Warrington 36 Hull KR 6, Widnes 42 Rochdale Hornets 2

Second round: Warrington 17 Swinton 2, Batley 4 Widnes 12

Third round: Warrington 21 Hunslet 7, Widnes 12 Barrow 7

Semi-finals:
Warrington 16 Leeds 4 (Odsal Stadium, Bradford, 70,198),
Widnes 8 Bradford Northern 0 (Central Park, Wigan, 24,783)

Head-to-head form guide:

Warrington 12 Widnes 7 (League)

Widnes 8 Warrington 17 (League)

WINNING CAPTAIN

Harry Bath (Warrington 1950)

Australian second-row or prop Harry Bath enjoyed tremendous success at club level in England and his homeland. A product of Brisbane Souths, he began his senior career at Sydney club Balmain, playing there in 1946 and 1947, winning the Grand Final both seasons. He relocated to England after signing with Barrow for 1947/48, but unable to settle, transferred to Warrington in March 1948, five months after his Barrow debut. His 10 League appearances helped the Wires claim the 1947/48 Championship, although unable to participate in the play-offs through registering after the deadline. His imposing presence and skilful ball-distribution helped Warrington achieve further success, winning the Rugby League Challenge Cup (1950, 1954), Championship (1954, 1955) and Lancashire League (1947/48, 1948/49, 1950/51, 1953/54, 1954/55, 1955/56). His last Warrington appearance was in 1957 after 346 matches (90 tries, 812 goals, 1,894 points), and he still holds the club record of 363 points in a season (1952/53). Back in Sydney, he spent three seasons with St George, winning the Grand Final each time (1957, 1958, 1959). In Australia he represented Queensland (twice) and New South Wales (3 times), his time in England effectively denying him selection for Australia. He did, however, make 12 appearances for Other Nationalities whilst with Warrington. He later coached Australia (1962, 1968–72), Balmain (1961–66), Newtown (1969–71) and St George (1977–81).

scrum, Wires' stand-off Bryn Knowelden burst through a gap, Helme continuing the move to send Ron Ryder on a race towards the corner where he dived over the try-line to score. This time Palin missed the goal but—after Hutton had failed with another attempt for Widnes—made amends five minutes later with a penalty goal, given for offside, placing Warrington comfortably ahead 14–0 at the interval.

The Wire eased up a little in the second half and Gus Malone almost got over the whitewash for a Widnes try but that was the nearest they came to troubling the scoreboard. Palin added a further penalty when Harry Anderson was ruled offside, Knowelden claiming the final try, beating off Charlie Reynolds and Frank Bradley after receiving a reverse pass from Helme as he came away from a scrum on the 'blind' side. Palin missed the goal.

Bath—the first overseas captain to lift the Challenge Cup at Wembley—said to the cheering fans outside Warrington Town Hall on the following Monday: 'It's a great day for Warrington and it's a great day for our club, directors, manager and staff. We feel very proud to be able to come back to you and say: "Here is the Challenge Cup as a reward for your support during the season."'

Graham Morris

1951 RUGBY LEAGUE CHALLENGE CUP FINAL
Wigan v Barrow

Wigan celebrate as Cec Mountford raises the cup for the press photographers

Wigan were always favourites to beat Barrow in the 1951 Challenge Cup Final, the Cherry and Whites being a major force in the game since the conclusion of the Second World War. Barrow—placed 20th in the League—had produced a major surprise by defeating Leeds in a semi-final replay but, nonetheless, created

Barrow winger Frank Castle attempts to thwart a Wigan attack

tremendous enthusiasm in the shipbuilding town ahead of the match. It was reported that the British Railways Carriage and Wagon Department were fulfilling their biggest ever maintenance and cleaning operation to ensure 20 engines and 360 carriages were available to transport the bulk of Barrow's 12,000 fans making the long journey south. Their team, meanwhile, had trained on the local golf links, believing its surface came closest to replicating Wembley's famous lush turf.

Wigan—followed by an estimated 15,000 supporters—looked the better team throughout a final where the miserable and wet ball-handling conditions were instrumental in creating a match that, according to the *North Western Evening Mail*, was 'almost completely lacking in spectacle'. It developed into a hard fought forward battle, the backs having very few opportunities. Despite winning 10–0, Wigan's performance was described as 'mediocre', although Barrow earned plaudits for a great defensive effort throughout. The only score in the opening half came in the sixth minute, Ken Gee kicking a goal after Barrow's ex-Wigan scrum half Ted Toohey was penalised for illegal scrum feeding. A subsequent penalty attempt by Willie Horne for Barrow

Ken Gee's try 10 minutes from the end secured the cup for Wigan

STATS

Wigan 10 Barrow 0

Saturday 5 May at Wembley Stadium, London (3.00 pm)

Wigan (cherry and white hoops): Cunliffe, Hilton, Broome, Roughley, Nordgren, Mountford (captain), Bradshaw, Gee, Curran, Barton, Silcock, Slevin, W. Blan. Coach: J. Sullivan

Barrow (blue and white hoops): Stretch, Lewthwaite, Jackson, Goodwin, Castle, Horne (captain), Toohey, Longman, McKinnell, Hartley, Grundy, Atkinson, McGregor. Trainer: M. Hughes

Referee: M. Coates Touch-judges: R. Stead, C.M. Moseley

Half-time: 2–0 Attendance: 94,262 Receipts: £24,797

Weather: heavy rain at times, ground very wet

Lance Todd Trophy: Mountford (Wigan)

Cup presentation: H.R.H. The Duke of Gloucester

Progressive score:

Wigan	score (min)	Barrow
Gee penalty	2–0 (6)	
Hilton try	5–0 (59)	
Gee try, Mountford goal	10–0 (70)	

Route to the final:

First round (2 legs):
Wigan 50 Rochdale Hornets 5, Barrow 62 Llanelli 14

Second round:
Wigan 16 Batley 8, Barrow 12 Workington Town 5

Third round:
Wigan 2 Huddersfield 0, Barrow 5 Bradford Northern 4

Semi-finals:
Wigan 3 Warrington 2 (Station Road, Swinton, 44,621),
Barrow 14 Leeds 14 (Odsal Stadium, Bradford, 57,729)

Semi-final replay:
Barrow 28 Leeds 13 (Fartown, Huddersfield, 31,078)

Head-to-head form guide:

Barrow 14 Wigan 23 (League)

Wigan 32 Barrow 10 (League)

plus two more from Gee all failed to find their target.

After the interval, Wigan came the closest to notching further points; Brian Nordgren almost getting over after a great effort down the left saw him halted 'inches short', Gee missing another penalty, and Billy Blan crossing the try-line but being unable to ground the ball. Almost an hour had been played before the first try came about, Wigan's Tommy Bradshaw making a sudden switch of direction in attack that caused Barrow loose forward Hugh McGregor to slip on the sodden grass. It afforded space for the scrum half to transfer the ball to Cec Mountford who opened up Barrow's defence for Jack Broome to send wing partner Jack Hilton away, sidestepping Frank Castle and fending off Harry Stretch to score in the corner. Gee missed the goal attempt. Ten minutes from the end, Wigan's George Roughley was tackled inside the Barrow 25-yard area, the ball squirting loose. Gee snapped it up and, using a neat sidestep and dummy pass, crashed over the line with Stretch and Frank Longman trying to restrain him. Mountford took over the goal-kicking task, his conversion notching the final score.

Wigan took part without three-quarters Gordon Ratcliffe (a pulled groin muscle from previous week) and Ernie Ashcroft (omitted despite appearing in every round), whilst New Zealander Mountford, who had been a doubtful starter due to a bruised hip, caught the eye at Wembley with his 'weaving' runs to become the first overseas recipient of the Lance Todd Trophy.

WINNING CAPTAIN

Cec Mountford (Wigan 1951)

New Zealand stand-off Cec Mountford signed for Wigan in 1946, becoming one of the most dazzling halfbacks in British rugby league. Born in Blackball, his fleet-footedness earned him the name 'The Blackball Bullet'. With Wigan, he won the Rugby League Challenge Cup (1948, 1951), Championship (1946/47, 1949/50), Lancashire Cup (1946, 1948, 1949, 1950), and Lancashire League (1946/47, 1949/50). He took over as Wigan captain at the conclusion of 1949/50 through Joe Egan's absence with the tourists, a role made permanent after the latter transferred to Leigh on his return. Having represented West Coast province and South Island in New Zealand, he appeared four times for Other Nationalities whilst at Wigan. He became Warrington coach in 1951, although it was the next year before Wigan agreed to his transfer as a player. His final Warrington match was in 1953 although he remained as coach until 1961 before returning to New Zealand. Excepting a spell as Blackpool Borough coach (1972–73), he continued coaching in New Zealand, including the national side (1979–82). In 1987 he received the MBE for services to New Zealand rugby league, becoming an inaugural member of New Zealand's Sports Hall of Fame in 1990.

1952 RUGBY LEAGUE CHALLENGE CUP FINAL
Workington Town v Featherstone Rovers

Featherstone Rovers' Eric Batten (on ground in white jersey—arm raised) had this try claim ruled out shortly before half-time, the touch judge raising his flag as he stumbles over Workington Town's George Wilson. Other Workington players are: Gus Risman (number 1), Tony Paskins (on ground), and Jim Wareing (extreme right)

The 1952 Challenge Cup Final was the stuff dreams are made of, Workington Town and Featherstone Rovers each gracing Wembley with their presence for the first time. In both cases there was romanticism attached; shock finalists Featherstone—admitted to the professional ranks in 1921—represented a small Yorkshire mining community and lay 22nd in the League, whilst Workington—founded in 1945—were in only their seventh season and the first Cumberland club to reach Wembley. The pair produced one of the most enjoyable and entertaining of Wembley occasions, the *Pontefract & Castleford Express* describing it as 'a thrilling spectacular game'.

Workington got off to a quick start when player-coach Gus Risman—at 41 the oldest to play at Wembley—kicked a 30-yard penalty in the opening minute after Rovers' prop John Daly was caught offside. It was Featherstone second-row Laurie Gant—doubtful the previous day through influenza—that made the first telling break but he lacked support and, in the ninth minute, their full back Freddie Miller

hit the post with a penalty. Seven minutes later, Town's Johnny Lawrenson, receiving the ball from Billy Ivison after a play-the-ball, raced clear and, as Don Metcalfe challenged, kicked ahead, the pair giving chase. Lawrenson regained possession and, tackled by Metcalfe, played it quickly forward (as allowed at the time), diving on it to score. However, he injured his ribs in the process, later requiring attention during the interval. Risman's goal made it 7–0.

Both teams were showing signs of the famous 'Wembley nerves' as Miller opened Featherstone's account with two excellent penalties, from 50 and 45 yards. The Rovers sensed a comeback and began warming to their task, being on top during the last 15 minutes before the break as Workington began looking vulnerable. Rovers' scrum half, Ray Evans, put through a dangerous kick but Tony Paskins saved the situation, and Miller failed with a drop-goal attempt. Stand-off Ray Cording went on a brilliant run for Featherstone, sidestepping several defenders before being held on the line. Then, when player-coach Eric Batten dived in at the corner, the score was, crucially, ruled out, the touch-judge raising his flag after the winger struck the corner-flag. Town survived and could have increased their 7–4 lead but Risman missed a penalty.

Featherstone fans went wild with delight three minutes into the second half after Metcalfe sent Batten jinking past three defenders to score in the

The Rugby League Challenge Cup goes to Cumberland for the first time! Workington Town captain Gus Risman holds the cup up whilst Lance Todd Trophy winner Billy Ivison (on ground—extreme right) looks after its plinth

corner, their forwards Will Bradshaw and Cliff Lambert making the early running. Miller missed the goal, the scores being level at 7–7. Featherstone, sniffing glory, pounded their opponents for the next 10 minutes but without making the breakthrough. It was then that Ivison—whose performance throughout made him the most convincing Lance Todd Trophy winner to date—created a brilliant try that determined the final course of the match, the *Sporting Chronicle* saying 'he shook off tackles to race from his own 25 to halfway. The opening and try scoring pass to (Johnny) Mudge was perfect.' Risman missed the conversion but the pendulum had swung in Town's favour. A minute later, disaster struck Featherstone when Daly's attempted pass to Norman Mitchell was intercepted by Lawrenson, who sprinted 85 yards for a try near the posts, chased all the way by Mitchell. This time Risman was on target and the Cumbrians led 15–7.

Workington were playing exhilarating rugby, whilst Rovers were also prepared to show the ball plenty of air. From a scrum, Town moved the ball out left, stand-off Jack Thomas making the break for Paskins. The latter returned the ball to Thomas who sent winger George Wilson over despite the efforts of Miller and Metcalfe, Risman missing the goal. Rovers eventually got a reward; Evans grabbed a late consolation try after receiving the ball on his own 25-yard line from a play-the-ball and sidestepping his way through Workington defenders to go 75 yards for what was claimed as 'the greatest individual effort seen at Wembley'. Miller missed the goal.

Described by the *Sporting Chronicle* as 'the best post war final for thrills' it was the first Challenge Cup Final broadcast into northern homes by BBC television.

STATS

Workington Town 18 Featherstone Rovers 10

Saturday 19 April at Wembley Stadium, London (3.00 pm)

Workington Town (royal blue): Risman (captain), Lawrenson, Paskins, Gibson, G. Wilson, Thomas, Pepperell, Hayton, McKeating, Wareing, Mudge, B. Wilson, Ivison. Player-manager: A.J. Risman

Featherstone Rovers (white): Miller, Batten (captain), Metcalfe, Tennant, Mitchell, Cording, Evans, Welburn, Bradshaw, Daly, Hulme, Gant, Lambert. Player-coach: E. Batten

Referee: C.F. Appleton

Touch-judges: W.H. Skerrett, W.H. Hargrave

Half-time: 7–4   Attendance: 72,093   Receipts: £22,374

Weather: sunny, slight breeze

Lance Todd Trophy: Ivison (Workington Town)

Cup presentation: The Rt Hon. Anthony Eden, Secretary of State for Foreign Affairs

Progressive score:

Workington Town	score (min)	Featherstone Rovers
Risman penalty	2–0 (1)	
Lawrenson try, Risman goal	7–0 (16)	
	7–2 (19)	Miller penalty
	7–4 (25)	Miller penalty
	7–7 (43)	Batten try
Mudge try	10–7 (57)	
Lawrenson try, Risman goal	15–7 (58)	
G. Wilson try	18–7 (66)	
	18–10 (76)	Evans try

Route to the final:

First round (2 legs): Workington T 60 York 12, Featherstone R 25 Rochdale H 9

Second round: Workington Town 15 St Helens 4, Batley 4 Featherstone Rovers 11

Third round: Workington Town 14 Warrington 0, Featherstone Rovers 14 Wigan 11

Semi-finals:
Workington Town 5 Barrow 2 (Central Park, Wigan, 31,200),
    Featherstone Rovers 6 Leigh 2 (Headingley, Leeds, 33,962)

Head-to-head form guide:

1953 RUGBY LEAGUE CHALLENGE CUP FINAL
Huddersfield v St Helens

The Huddersfield-St Helens Challenge Cup Final of 1953 served up an exciting contest that produced an unlikely hero in Huddersfield stand-off Peter Ramsden. On what was his 19th birthday, he scored two crucial tries to become the youngest ever Lance Todd Trophy recipient. But it was a match marred by controversy, the Saints—on the verge of becoming one of the great sides under former Wigan coach Jim Sullivan—suffering most of the post-match flack following a 63rd minute flashpoint. Huddersfield's Lionel Cooper was heading down the middle when he dummied a pass to team-mate John Hunter. Although Hunter did not have possession, Saints winger Stewart Llewellyn, connected with his right arm and the Australian was 'out for the count'. As the jeers rang out he was removed on a stretcher, but returned later.

On a beautiful sunny afternoon, Ramsden struck his first blow in the 29th minute when he burst through St Helens' defence. Although he had two players in support, he sped for the line, crossing for the touchdown with Saints prop Alan Prescott in attendance, amidst protests he grounded short. Pat Devery converted. Within minutes of the interval, St

Russell Pepperell (Huddersfield 1953)

Russell Pepperell signed for Huddersfield in late 1938 from hometown Seaton (Cumberland) amateur club. His debut was in 1939 and, despite missing two complete seasons due to the Second World War, he still made 352 appearances for the Fartown club, his last being 1956. He also made one wartime 'guest' appearance with Bradford Northern during 1943. A gifted, evasive back, he was equally adept at full back, centre or stand-off, representing England (4 times) and Cumberland (16—many as captain). With Huddersfield, he won the Rugby League Challenge Cup (1953), Championship (1948/49), Yorkshire Cup (1950, 1952) and Yorkshire League (1948/49, 1949/50, 1951/52). Having held a player-coach role with Huddersfield, he later coached Keighley before moving to Australia where he took charge at Manly-Warringah (1964–65). He was one of three talented brothers who all joined Huddersfield and gained international and county honours, Stanley being the eldest, Albert—the youngest—eventually transferring to Workington Town.

Helens got themselves back on level terms. George Langfield landed a penalty after Jimmy Honey was fouled and, from the restart, full back Glyn Moses

Huddersfield hero Peter Ramsden scores his first try despite the efforts of St Helens' Alan Prescott. There were protests that Ramsden grounded short of the try-line although he appears to have got the ball over it in this picture

119

Destination Wembley

St Helens' Steve Llewellyn (left) looks on as a colleague stops Huddersfield centre Pat Devery in his tracks

fielded the kick and spurted forward, linking with Stan McCormick who cut to the right to feed Duggie Greenall. The St Helens skipper handed on to Llewellyn who raced 50 yards for the try-line, beating Hunter en route for a fabulous try. Langfield was unable to append the extras.

St Helens began the second half where they left off, McCormick being on hand from a scrum to take the ball forward. Greenall continued the move by sending Llewellyn away, the former accepting the return pass before re-supplying the Welsh flyer who was just stopped short of the try-line. Getting quickly to his feet, his play-the-ball enabled Greenall to send Langfield over before Huddersfield's defence could organise. Langfield missed the simple conversion and, five minutes later, the Hunter-Llewellyn incident occurred. Down to 12 men, Huddersfield heeled a scrum two yards from the Saints try-line, Billy Banks racing over before anyone could react, Cooper's goal giving the Fartowners a 10–8 lead.

With confidence flowing, Huddersfield were entertaining the crowd with some exciting rugby, Banks almost going over again. Saints recovered, McCormick being stalled after a great break down the centre, although managing to off-load to Langfield who coolly dropped a goal, dramatically squaring the match 10–10. Hunter returned seven minutes from time, Ramsden confirming his man of the match status two minutes later with the winning try after Dave Valentine and Jim Bowden had beaten off some poor tackling in a move started on halfway. Cooper added the goal, concluding the scoring at 15–10.

As Ramsden and skipper Valentine were 'chaired' around the field by jubilant colleagues, the St Helens players were booed off by some sections of the crowd. In the aftermath, opinions in the local press were polarised, the *Huddersfield Examiner* claiming the final had 'more fouls and dirty play than ever seen at

Wembley'. The *St Helens Newspaper & Advertiser*, whilst agreeing 'Saints were guilty of high tackling and on occasions flying fists', felt the incidents had been overplayed, claiming 'it happens two or three times as much in any League game'. Greenall said in a 1967 interview: 'I think it was the unfair booing which made us lay it on Huddersfield when we met them in the League semi-final the following Saturday,' referring to an overwhelming 46–0 victory.

STATS

Huddersfield 15 St Helens 10

Saturday 25 April at Wembley Stadium, London (3.00 pm)

Huddersfield (claret with narrow gold hoops): Hunter, Henderson, Pepperell (captain), Devery, Cooper, Ramsden, Banks, Slevin, Curran, Bowden, Brown, Large, Valentine. Player-coach: R. Pepperell

St Helens (white with red band): Moses, Llewellyn, Greenall (captain), Gullick, McCormick, Honey, Langfield, Prescott, Blakemore, Parr, Parsons, Bretherton, Cale. Coach: J. Sullivan

Referee: G.S. Phillips
Touch-judges: A.E. Durkin, R.L. Thomas
Half-time: 5–5 Attendance: 89,588 Receipts: £30,865
Weather: sunny
Lance Todd Trophy: Ramsden (Huddersfield)
Cup presentation: His Grace The Duke of Norfolk

Progressive score:

Huddersfield	score (min)	St Helens
Ramsden try, Devery goal	5–0 (29)	
	5–2 (39)	Langfield penalty
	5–5 (40)	Llewellyn try
	5–8 (58)	Langfield try
Banks try, Cooper goal	10–8 (65)	
	10–10 (72)	Langfield drop-goal
Ramsden try, Cooper goal	15–10 (75)	

Route to the final:

First round (2 legs): Huddersfield 42 Castleford 16, St Helens 25 Oldham 9

Second round: Huddersfield 21 Barrow 7, St Helens 28 Belle Vue Rangers 0

Third round: Bradford Northern 7 Huddersfield 17, Leigh 3 St Helens 12

Semi-finals:
Huddersfield 7 Wigan 0 (Odsal Stadium, Bradford, 58,722),
St Helens 9 Warrington 3 (Station Road, Swinton, 38,059)

Head-to-head form guide:

St Helens 14 Huddersfield 17 (League)
Huddersfield 10 St Helens 10 (League)

1954 RUGBY LEAGUE CHALLENGE CUP FINAL
Warrington v Halifax

The 1954 Challenge Cup Final between Warrington and Halifax is remembered not for their Wembley meeting—one of the poorest games seen at the stadium—but the famous, drama-filled replay at Odsal Stadium, Bradford, 11 days later, a match that attracted a world record crowd for the sport. Officially recorded as 102,569, thousands more were known to have climbed in, estimates of 120,000 being freely quoted later. It was a Wednesday evening that unravelled itself like no other in the annals of British rugby league. Officials had anticipated the attendance could exceed the 81,841 that went to Wembley, the *Warrington Guardian* commenting before the initial match in London that 'there was ample accommodation for 90,000 in case of a replay at Odsal'. Spectators were still being admitted at half-time, this despite hundreds being moved inside the perimeter fence during the first half to ease congestion. Many of

Warrington's Brian Bevan makes a break down the wing at Wembley as his Halifax namesake Dai Bevan (right) prepares to move in. The Halifax player (number 3) tangled up with a Warrington opponent is Tommy Lynch

CHANGING FORMATS

- 1897: Draw for the first Challenge Cup competition (which was drawn all the way through to the final) actually made during September 1896. Opening round took place 20 March, the contest continuing on consecutive weekends culminating in the final five weeks later. Total of 52 teams participated.

- 1901: Rounds became integrated with closing League fixtures.

- 1903: Draw made after each round for first time, 'adding to interest and excitement.'

- 1904: First round proper reduced to 32 teams (leading clubs seeded directly into it), and preceded by an 'Intermediate Round'. (Note: Up to 1903 the first round proper had included approximately 60 teams, around half being 'junior' clubs, resulting in many high scores in the opening rounds.)

- 1908: Intermediate round scrapped and competition proper commenced with a first round of 32 teams with fewer junior clubs. Opening round brought forward from March to February, introducing a pattern of fortnightly rounds that would continue until 1928.

- 1929: Due to the final moving to Wembley, a slight adjustment was made whereby the gap between semi-finals and final was extended from two to several weeks, allowing

clubs and supporters time to prepare. Also decided that, unlike previously, no senior matches should be played on Cup Final day, with junior clubs allowed to postpone fixtures by one week.

- 1982: With total professional clubs now exceeding 32 it was necessary to add a 'Preliminary Round' involving several clubs, drawn at random prior to first round proper.

- 1994: Competition proper dramatically expanded to include six rounds prior to semi-final stage rather than the previous three. The first round consisted of amateur clubs, professional clubs outside the First Division entering at the third round, and First Division (later Super League) clubs entering at the fourth round. Preliminary round dispensed with.

- 1996: Although the Rugby League transferred to a summer season in this year, the Challenge Cup continued during the same months, effectively becoming an early-season rather than end-of-season tournament.

- 2005: The final is given a new, later slot towards the end of August, instead of April/May. Earlier rounds played at the rate of approximately one per month during season, according to television schedules.

those present in the vast bowl saw little of the match, although they could be counted amongst the lucky ones because thousands never even reached the stadium. So badly clogged up were the roads carrying supporters over the Pennines, it was described as 'one huge traffic jam'. Halifax's team coach required a police escort down the 'wrong' side of the road to get them there, with traffic, reportedly, still arriving back in Warrington at 5.00 am the following day!

The replay, though, was a far better game than its predecessor, Halifax skipper Alvin Ackerley repeating his Wembley feat of dominating the scrums, this time by 31–16. But Halifax still failed to discover their best form although having three try-scoring claims rejected by referee Ron Gelder; Tommy Lynch and Stan Kielty in the first half and Arthur Daniels near the final whistle. The Thrum Hall side looked uncertain at the start, Warrington forward Gerald Lowe breaking through in the ninth minute and, when held, passing over his assailant's head to the supporting Jim Challinor who raced through an opening for the first try, Halifax complaining a forward pass had been ignored. Harry Bath was just wide with the conversion. Halifax's Tyssull Griffiths failed with two drop-goal attempts, Bath missing three penalties, the

latter from his own half. Just before half-time, Griffiths fared better with a penalty in front of the posts, given for offside, Warrington leading 3–2.

After the break Stan McCormick (Warrington) and Kielty missed further drop-goal efforts before Bath's 57th minute penalty (offside at a play-the-ball) found the target. Griffiths responded in kind from a difficult 28-yard angle four minutes later (McCormick obstructing Daniels). At 5–4 to Warrington and with 12 minutes remaining, the stage was set for a moment of genius from Warrington scrum half Gerry Helme. The first player to receive the Lance Todd Trophy for a second time, he deceived the Halifax defence by appearing to look for support, before accelerating through a gap aided by a dummy pass to beat Griffiths and Daniels. He slid over for the try despite stumbling on turf that had been placed in the corners to cover the surrounding speedway track. Bath missed the goal and Warrington led 8–4. The Wires were down to 12 men when Ray Price was carried off injured but

The winning try! A beaming Gerry Helme (with ball) appears to be saying 'the cup is ours' as he looks across to Warrington colleague Ron Ryder. The other Warrington player about to assist Helme to his feet is Jim Challinor, the Halifax players being Ken Dean (6) and Derrick Schofield (extreme right)

STATS

Warrington 4 Halifax 4

Saturday 24 April at Wembley Stadium, London (3.00 pm)

Warrington (white with primrose and blue bands): Frodsham (captain), B. Bevan, Challinor, Stevens, McCormick, Price, Helme, D. Naughton, Wright, Lowe, Bath, Heathwood, Ryan. Coach: C. Mountford

Halifax (blue and white hoops): Griffiths, Daniels, Lynch, Todd, D.R. Bevan, Dean, Kielty, Thorley, Ackerley (captain), Wilkinson, Fearnley, Schofield, Clarkson. Coach: F. Dawson

Referee: R. Gelder

Touch-judges: K.W. Bland, W.L. Desmond

Half-time: 0–4 Attendance: 81,841 Receipts: £29,706

Weather: dry and warm

Progressive score:

Warrington	score (min)	Halifax
	0–2 (16)	Griffiths penalty
	0–4 (25)	Griffiths penalty
Bath penalty	2–4 (51)	
Bath penalty	4–4 (66)	

Replay: Warrington 8 Halifax 4

Wednesday 5 May at Odsal Stadium, Bradford (7.00 pm)

Warrington (white with primrose and blue bands): unchanged except Ryder for Stevens

Halifax (blue and white hoops): unchanged except Mather for Todd

Referee: R. Gelder

Touch-judges: K.W. Bland, W.L. Desmond

Half-time: 3–2 Attendance: 102,569 Receipts: £18,623

Weather: overcast and dull, light rain

Lance Todd Trophy: Helme (Warrington)

Cup presentation: C.W. Robinson, Rugby League chairman

Progressive score:

Warrington	score (min)	Halifax
Challinor try	3–0 (9)	
	3–2 (39)	Griffiths penalty
Bath penalty	5–2 (57)	
	5–4 (61)	Griffiths penalty
Helme try	8–4 (68)	

Route to the final:

First round (2 legs): Warrington 47 Bramley 5, Halifax 34 Dewsbury 9

Second round: Oldham 4 Warrington 7, Halifax 24 Keighley 5

Third round: Warrington 26 York 5, Wigan 0 Halifax 2

Semi-finals:

Warrington 8 Leeds 4 (Station Road, Swinton, 37,249),

Halifax 18 Hunslet 3 (Odsal Stadium, Bradford, 46,961)

Head-to-head form guide:

No previous meetings during season

he shortly returned. With time running out drama struck when Daniels was denied the try that could have swung the outcome, recovering a ball kicked through by Kielty. Tackled short, he rolled over to place the ball down, the referee ruling it was not properly grounded as Halifax protested vehemently.

Their earlier Wembley date was described as lacking skill and attacking ideas, a fact endorsed by slow handclapping in the crowd during the second half. Even Warrington's replay hero Helme and halfback partner Price had been below par, whilst Halifax with a 14–4 scrum advantage after the interval, kept play tight. In the only Wembley final without a try all the points came via penalties; two from eight attempts by Bath (a play-the-ball offence and illegal scrum-feeding by Kielty) and two out of five by Griffiths (both offside by Lowe), his last miss being a heart-stopping moment two minutes from time, shaving the outside of the post.

Warrington competed in both games without captain and centre Ally Naughton (calf injury) and forwards Ted White (leg) and Sid Phillips (collar bone) whilst, for the replay, Ron Ryder was preferred to Arnold Stevens and Halifax replaced the injured Peter Todd with Billy Mather.

Action at Wembley as Halifax's Derrick Schofield passes the ball inside to Peter Todd

1955 RUGBY LEAGUE CHALLENGE CUP FINAL
Barrow v Workington Town

A unique confrontation between two of rugby league's North West coastal outposts awaited spectators at the 1955 Challenge Cup Final, north Lancashire's Barrow taking on Cumberland's Workington Town. Both were making their second Wembley appearance of the 1950s, the return proving happiest for Barrow who made it 'third time lucky' after losing there in 1938 and 1951. Their 21–12 victory followed an engrossing second half that featured a 14-minute burst when all five of the afternoon's tries were scored, a sharp contrast to a 'featureless' opening 40 minutes. Workington only finalised their line-up one hour before kick-off, Ken Faulder—normally a halfback—taking Bill Ivill's wing slot, with 18-year-old Brian Edgar figuring in the pack for Norman Herbert, the two unfortunates failing late fitness checks.

Workington took five minutes to register the opening points, Australian centre Tony Paskins kicking a difficult angled 45-yard penalty following a scrum indiscretion. Eleven minutes later, Barrow captain-coach Willie Horne, having missed an earlier attempt, equalised following another scrum offence, the ball rebounding off the far post. Paskins and Horne both failed with further penalties, the teams being tied 2–2 at half-time. General opinion was Workington had had the better of a dull opening half, Barrow being cited as

A wonderful day for Barrow as Willie Horne lifts the trophy. The other player being chaired by his colleagues (holding plinth, left) is Lance Todd Trophy winner Jack Grundy

WINNING CAPTAIN

Willie Horne (Barrow 1955)

Willie Horne's name is the most revered in Barrow's history, his career with them covering 462 appearances (112 tries, 741 goals, 1,818 points) from 1943 until 1959. Born in Barrow he was signed from the Risedale Old Boys club, having previously attracted Oldham's interest, playing two first team trials during December 1942. A brilliant, attacking stand-off, renowned for his precision passes, he was an accomplished marksman and one of the first to use the 'round the corner' kicking style. With Horne at the helm—he was appointed captain in 1950 and player-coach from 1953—Barrow enjoyed their finest period during the 1950s, winning the Rugby League Challenge Cup (1955—runners-up 1951 and 1957) and Lancashire Cup (1954). A tourist twice (1946, 1950), he represented Great Britain (9 times—including 8 Tests), England (14) and Lancashire (14). After retiring as a player he continued as Barrow coach until 1960.

performing well below their best with 'bunching' and losing possession their biggest crimes.

The second half gave the crowd far more to enthuse over. Barrow led for the first time six minutes after the restart, Horne kicking his second penalty after Johnny Mudge committed a foul at a play-the-ball, adding a drop-goal two minutes later to extend the advantage to 6–2. Workington, though, had other matters to concentrate on for, whilst Horne dropped his goal,

Town's 18-year-old scrum half, Sol Roper, lay on the ground having injured his shoulder and had to leave on a stretcher. Winger Ike Southward took up his position, replaced in turn by Edgar, reducing them to a five-man pack. Unsurprisingly this lifted Barrow, whose forwards, led by Jack Grundy, threw everything at their opponents. Vince McKeating claimed their first try when Workington lost possession on halfway, Grundy breaking through the defence after recovering the ball to send the hooker on his way. There were vigorous protests that Grundy's pass was forward but it stood, Horne appending the two points. Roper, meanwhile, reappeared but went on the wing.

The last quarter really brought the crowd to life with some of the most entertaining rugby seen at the stadium. Confident Barrow were in full flow, Phil Jackson finding an opening to go roaring downfield before despatching 15-stone co-centre Dennis Goodwin who brushed off defenders before scoring a great try. Horne added the goal and, with 14 minutes left and leading 16–2, victory looked a formality. Workington, though, had not given up, Eppie Gibson charging through a gap to send Faulder haring down the left touchline. Faulder, having returned the ball inside to Gibson, then cut infield to accept the return pass and score. Paskins converted, reducing the deficit to nine points. The thrills continued as Barrow scored again, the fourth try in 11 minutes going to Frank Castle, who, following a break by Bill Healey and

continued by Grundy, shot down the left flank beating Roper and Joe Vickers on his way to the try-line. Horne's sixth goal—equalling Bowkett's 1933 Wembley record—made it 21–7. Workington had the last word, Gibson spotting an opening to roar away, dummying his pass to Faulder before going over for a magnificent try, Paskins adding the goal.

Barrow's Dennis Goodwin (left, with ball) appears to be weighing up his options

---

STATS

Barrow 21 Workington Town 12

Saturday 30 April at Wembley Stadium, London (3.00 pm)

Barrow (blue with white chevron): Best, Lewthwaite, Jackson, Goodwin, Castle, Horne (captain), Toohey, Belshaw, McKeating, Barton, Grundy, Parker, Healey. Player-coach: W. Horne

Workington Town (white): Vickers, Southward, Paskins, Gibson, Faulder, Wookey, Roper, Hayton, Lymer, Key, Edgar, Mudge, Ivison (captain). Team manager: J. Brough

Referee: R. Gelder Touch-judges: W. Ainscough, M. Mullery

Half-time: 2–2 Attendance: 66,513 Receipts: £27,453

Weather: sunny with slight breeze

Lance Todd Trophy: Grundy (Barrow)

Cup presentation: H.R.H. The Duke of Edinburgh

Progressive score:

Barrow	score (min)	Workington Town
	0–2 (5)	Paskins penalty
Horne penalty	2–2 (16)	
Horne penalty	4–2 (46)	
Horne drop-goal	6–2 (48)	
McKeating try, Horne goal	11–2 (60)	
Goodwin try, Horne goal	16–2 (66)	
	16–7 (68)	Faulder try, Paskins goal
Castle try, Horne goal	21–7 (71)	
	21–12 (74)	Gibson try, Paskins goal

Route to the final:

First round: Dewsbury 8 Barrow 11, Workington Town 43 Dewsbury Celtic 0

Second round: Salford 0 Barrow 13, Workington Town 13 Leeds 7

Third round: Rochdale Hornets 2 Barrow 15, Workington Town 14 St Helens 4

Semi-finals:
Barrow 9 Hunslet 6 (Central Park, Wigan, 25,493),
Workington Town 13 Featherstone Rovers 2 (Headingley, Leeds, 36,077)

Head-to-head form guide:

Barrow 5 Workington Town 3 (League)

Workington 11 Barrow 19 (League)

1956 RUGBY LEAGUE CHALLENGE CUP FINAL
St Helens v Halifax

St Helens finally got their hands on the Challenge Cup in 1956 having been runners-up four times, twice at Wembley. Maybe Saints' fans had an inkling something big was on the horizon, the *St Helens Newspaper* saying 'interest was higher, the fever pitch much greater' around the town than for their last appearance in 1953, despite opponents Halifax being favourites. Enthusiasm was fuelled by a thrilling 10–5 extra-time semi-final replay win over holders Barrow. Played at Wigan in front of a, then, record Central Park attendance of 44,731, victory was triggered by a sensational 80-yard try that 'came right out of the blue' from winger Stewart Llewellyn, breaking a scoreless deadlock in the 86th minute.

Tommy Lynch of Halifax tries to overcome some determined tackling from the St Helens duo of Frank Carlton (on ground) and Brian Howard

St Helens went into the final without stand-off John 'Todder' Dickinson, considered by the *St Helens Reporter* as 'the king-pin of Saints attacking machinery', having injured his leg in the previous weekend's Championship semi-final defeat, also against Halifax, Bill Finnan taking his place. Another casualty from that match was 21-year-old prop Abe Terry with an ankle injury. St Helens skipper Alan Prescott was unperturbed saying 'we lost at Thrum Hall but this is Wembley and Wembley is different', his confidence being borne out as they defeated Halifax 13–2. All the points came in the last quarter-hour when St Helens played enthralling rugby against a tiring opposition, following 'a stirring forward battle' in which both defences had been unwilling to yield an inch. The only real scoring chances beforehand had been through missed penalties; four by St Helens' Austin Rhodes (two each half), two from Halifax's Tyssul Griffiths (one each half, the first after three minutes).

Prescott demonstrated that Halifax's defensive wall was beginning to crack when he made a tremendous break midway through the second half taking him into their 25-yard area. According to 'Wanderer' of the *St Helens Reporter* 'it was like a Clarion call' and, true enough, in the 66th minute, Saints' winger Frank Carlton got the first points with a brilliant try, racing down the touchline and beating Griffiths, his centre Brian Howard having drawn opposition winger Arthur Daniels to create the overlap. Rhodes landed the goal and it was 5–0.

With the drawbridge prised open at last, the Knowsley Road side scored their second four minutes later, Llewellyn making a glorious break down the right flank to score in the corner. Rhodes was successful with the difficult conversion for what looked a winning 10–0 lead with 10 minutes remaining. A penalty from Griffiths after St Helens offended at a play-the-ball provided the Yorkshire side with a glimmer of hope but it was little more than that. Saints' forward George Parsons made a futile attempt at a drop-goal before Prescott added a third touchdown in the final minute, Rhodes hitting an upright with his goal attempt.

126

STATS

St Helens 13 Halifax 2

Saturday 28 April at Wembley Stadium, London (3.00 pm)

St Helens (white with red band): Moses, Llewellyn, Greenall, Howard, Carlton, Finnan, Rhodes, Prescott (captain), McIntyre, Silcock, Parsons, Robinson, Karalius. Coach: J. Sullivan

Halifax (blue and white hoops): Griffiths, Daniels, Lynch, Palmer, Freeman, Dean, Kielty, Wilkinson, Ackerley (captain), Henderson, Fearnley, Pearce, Traill. Coach: F. Dawson

Referee: R. Gelder

Touch-judges: G.L.T. Smithson, S.J. Heesom

Half-time: 0–0 Attendance: 79,341 Receipts: £29,424

Weather: sunny Lance Todd Trophy: Prescott (St Helens)

Cup presentation: The Earl Alexander of Tunis

Progressive score:

St Helens	score (min)	Halifax
Carlton try, Rhodes goal	5–0 (66)	
Llewellyn try, Rhodes goal	10–0 (70)	
	10–2 (73)	Griffiths penalty
Prescott try	13–2 (80)	

Route to the final:

First round: St Helens 15 Warrington 6, Widnes 10 Halifax 22

Second round: St Helens 48 Castleford 5, Halifax 10 Workington Town 3

Third round: St Helens 53 Bradford Northern 6, Leeds 9 Halifax 14

Semi-finals: St Helens 5 Barrow 5 (Station Road, Swinton, 38,897), Halifax 11 Wigan 10 (Odsal Stadium, Bradford, 52,273)

Semi-final replay: St Helens 10 Barrow 5 (Central Park, Wigan, 44,731)

Head-to-head form guide:

St Helens 13 Halifax 8 (League)

Halifax 12 St Helens 0 (League)

Halifax 23 St Helens 8 (Championship semi-final)

The bravery of rugby league players was demonstrated through St Helens' Vince Karalius competing with a badly torn ear, a legacy from that earlier meeting with Halifax. Halifax, too, had problems. Johnnie Freeman came out for the second half with one 'good' leg, having been helped off close to half-time following a missed flying tackle on Llewellyn that saw him hurtle onto the surrounding track, whilst Griffiths went through the pain-barrier with a broken cheekbone. Inflicted in an earlier match, the seriousness was not realised at the time of the Challenge Cup Final, but cost him his place in the subsequent Championship Final clash with Hull.

St Helens captain Alan Prescott smiles for the cameras!

WINNING CAPTAIN

Alan Prescott (St Helens 1956)

Widnes-born Alan Prescott signed for Halifax as a winger in 1943 from his local club, St Marie's. As he matured, putting on weight, he relocated to loose forward with some success, St Helens snapping him up for £2,275 in 1948. Saints soon moved him to prop where his ability to provide precision passes to supporting colleagues came to the fore. His qualities of leadership led to the captaincy of St Helens in 1955 and, eventually, Great Britain. He gained several winners' medals with St Helens; Rugby League Challenge Cup (1956), Championship (1952/53, 1958/59), Lancashire Cup (1953) and Lancashire League (1952/53, 1959/60). He represented Great Britain in 31 Test and international fixtures (18 as captain), England (10 times) and Lancashire (15). He was a tourist twice (1954, 1958—the latter as captain when he famously led his side to victory in the second Test against Australia despite a broken right arm), and captain of Britain's 1957 World Cup squad. His 405th and last match for St Helens was in 1960, later coaching St Helens, Leigh and Workington Town. He made two wartime guest appearances with Huddersfield during 1943/44.

1957 RUGBY LEAGUE CHALLENGE CUP FINAL
Leeds v Barrow

Leeds earned their first post-Second World War Challenge Cup success in a final that embraced one of Wembley's most exciting finishes, a spirited late fight back from Barrow almost wresting the trophy from their grip. Although not a classic, spoilt in part by numerous handling errors, particularly from Barrow, it contained several memorable moments, the *Yorkshire Post* saying both teams 'showed enterprise and gave the feeling something could always happen'. Whilst Leeds had no difficulty naming their side, Barrow only decided their line-up on the eve of the final, their reticence due to injury concerns; Joe Ball, Jim Lewthwaite and Frank Castle only being confirmed the evening before the match, whilst knee ligament problems—aggravated in the previous weekend's match—ruled out second-rower Dennis Goodwin. The Shipbuilders also sprung a surprise, preferring Reg Parker at prop ahead of Frank Barton for what would have been a record fifth Wembley appearance. The ex-Wigan player was so dejected he never played again.

The opening half belonged to Leeds, who provided most of the attacking moves against an uncertain Barrow. Nonetheless, the Lancastrians defended doggedly, Leeds captain Keith McLellan being held short by Parker midway through the half before Pat Quinn eventually touched down for the Headingley side shortly afterwards. The only first half score, it came when the full back moved into the line at a play-the-ball to accept Bernard Prior's pass before 'dummying' towards Lewis Jones and pushing his way over at the corner. Jones missed the goal attempt. Ball failed with a 40-yard penalty for Barrow before Leeds almost scored again, George Broughton being forced into the corner flag by Lewthwaite.

A minute after the interval, Leeds increased their lead, Jeff Stevenson taking the ball from a scrum to work a pre-planned move that saw both centres—Jones and McLellan—run in opposite directions behind the scrum to confuse the defence. Instead of the ball going to stand-off Jack Lendill, it found its way to Jones who fed Delmos Hodgkinson. Taking the pass at speed the latter raced down the right wing, cutting inside Ball for a breathtaking try. Jones, who also

Don Robinson scores Leeds' third try squeezing in between Barrow's John Rea (on his back) and Jim Lewthwaite

WINNING CAPTAIN

Keith McLellan (Leeds 1957)

Unlike most Australian signings, Keith McLellan came to England from rugby union, the Easts (Sydney) centre being recommended to Leeds by their former 1930s player Frank O'Rourke. A robust, strong tackling, powerful running player, he joined Leeds in February 1952, reportedly on a seven-year £4,000 contract, making 215 appearances before returning home in December 1958, playing his last match during September that year. With Leeds he won the Rugby League Challenge Cup (1957) and Yorkshire League (1954/55, 1956/57), his sole representative honour being for a Northern Rugby League XIII against France at Headingley in 1958.

missed a first half penalty, was again off-target with the conversion. Ball too, was unsuccessful with a second penalty attempt, Willie Horne taking over and succeeding with the third, reducing the arrears to 6–2.

Leeds' Don Robinson (grounded short) and Barrow's Don Wilson (failed to ground) had tries disallowed—both protesting—before a calamitous moment hit Barrow; their second-row Jack Grundy delivered a wayward pass 10 yards from his own try-line but, instead of finding a colleague, the ball was accepted by Robinson who picked up and scored virtually unopposed. Grundy said later: 'I heard someone call and thought it was one of our lads.' Jones failed to land the conversion but Leeds led 9–2.

Unexpectedly, Barrow dominated the remainder of the match, creating a thrilling finale. Lewthwaite was stopped on Leeds' try-line by McLellan, then, with 16 minutes left, a spellbinding move involving Wilson, Bill Healey, Grundy and Castle sent Phil Jackson racing away, eluding Broughton's tackle to touch down at the corner. Horne struck a tremendous goal,

Leeds full back Pat Quinn (number 1, on ground) gets the first try despite the appeal from Barrow's Jim Lewthwaite (arms raised high)

reducing the margin to two points. Wembley was buzzing as Barrow tore into Leeds but dropped passes continued to stifle their moves although Castle almost got over the whitewash, being tackled by Quinn as he tried to cut inside after beating two defenders. In the final minute Robinson appeared to make it safe for Leeds as he reached over the Barrow try-line but was penalised for a double movement. From the resultant tap-penalty Horne sent John Rea on a tremendous run into the Leeds half, the 20-year-old electing to kick when he appeared to have ample support, Broughton, who had raced across, gratefully gathering the ball.

1958 RUGBY LEAGUE CHALLENGE CUP FINAL
Wigan v Workington Town

One of the most memorable and vital tackles seen at Wembley occurred in the 1958 Challenge Cup Final as Wigan clung on to their 13–9 lead over Workington Town. Awarded a penalty 13 minutes from full time, the Cumbrians elected to run the ball, Harry Archer and John O'Neill sending Ike Southward on a sizzling touchline run. It looked a certain try and possible match-winner until Wigan second-row forward Norman Cherrington somehow got across in time to make a desperate diving tackle that caused the wingman to lose the ball as he crossed in the corner. It was Workington's last throw of the dice, Cherrington becoming the unexpected hero of a star-studded Wigan side.

In what was considered an exciting final, Wigan threatened early, Eric Ashton almost breaking through from the kick-off and then Billy Boston being held by John McAvoy after one of the Welshman's block-busting runs. Another chance was lost when full back Jack Cunliffe missed a 45-yard penalty. It was Workington, though, that took the lead in the 11th minute, Southward outpacing Mick Sullivan in a 35-yard dash to register a thrilling try after Brian Edgar, having made the break, offloaded to him as Cunliffe

tackled. Southward, who converted, almost scored again, but failed to hold on after an interception. Town received a setback when stand-off Harry Archer had to be helped off after a high tackle from Sullivan. Wigan, meanwhile began to step up the pressure, Terry O'Grady taking possession on the right flank before cutting inside to supply Boston who sent Sullivan over near the corner. Cunliffe's goal levelled the score at 5–5.

The Cherry and Whites almost claimed the lead when Rees Thomas touched down, but it was wiped out due to a forward pass. Workington were back to 13 men when Archer—looking dazed—returned after 10 minutes' absence, but it did not prevent Wigan obtaining a second try; O'Grady and Cunliffe sent Thomas on a brilliant run past three defenders, the scrum half transferring to prop John Barton who charged through two assailants to score. Cunliffe added the extras. Southward pulled two points back to make it 10–7, succeeding with the second of his two penalty attempts following an obstruction by Brian McTigue.

After the interval, Workington suffered early disruption when forwards Edgar (concussed) and Andy Key (ankle) were injured, the former leaving the

Mick Sullivan races over for Wigan's first try having received the ball from Billy Boston (number 4, on ground) who was playing in an unaccustomed role of centre

field for four minutes. Wigan grabbed a third try after McTigue got the ball 10 yards from the right touchline and close to Town's try-line, dummying and sidestepping before diving in at the corner. Cunliffe missed the kick. When Southward, after failing with one attempt, notched a 61st minute penalty for 'loose arm' in the scrum, the score closing to 13–9, Workington looked a different proposition. McAvoy and Archer both made powerful breaks but lacked support, Town's best chance being snuffed out when Cherrington produced his decisive tackle.

Wigan's veteran centre Ernie Ashcroft missed the occasion, breaking a rib one month earlier, wing sensation Boston relocating inside to cover his position, whilst loose forward Roy Evans was a late withdrawal due to a heavy cold, Bernard McGurrin deputising. The occasion was broadcast live on BBC television for the first time since 1952 (when Workington were also involved), the Rugby Football League having rejected offers in the interim. It has been screened every year since after initial concerns about its detrimental effect on the attendance.

STATS

Wigan 13 Workington Town 9

Saturday 10 May at Wembley Stadium, London (3.00 pm)

Wigan (cherry and white hoops): Cunliffe, O'Grady, Ashton (captain), Boston, Sullivan, Bolton, Thomas, Barton, Sayer, McTigue, Cherrington, Collier, McGurrin. Coach: J. Egan

Workington Town (white with royal blue band): McAvoy, Southward, O'Neill, Leatherbarrow, Wookey, Archer, Roper (captain), Herbert, Eden, Key, Edgar, Thompson, Eve. Team manager: J. Brough

Referee: R. Gelder Touch-judges: A.S. Young, E. Bleasdale

Half-time: 10–7 Attendance: 66,109 Receipts: £33,175

Weather: sunny with strong breeze

Lance Todd Trophy: Thomas (Wigan)

Cup presentation:
The Rt. Hon. John Hay Whitney, United States Ambassador

Progressive score:

Wigan	score (min)	Workington Town
	0–5 (11)	Southward try, Southward goal
Sullivan try, Cunliffe goal	5–5 (17)	
Barton try, Cunliffe goal	10–5 (28)	
	10–7 (35)	Southward penalty
McTigue try	13–7 (50)	
	13–9 (61)	Southward penalty

Route to the final:

First round:
Wigan 39 Whitehaven 10, Workington Town 3 Leigh 0

Second round:
Wakefield Trinity 5 Wigan 11, Widnes 5 Workington Town 8

Third round:
Oldham 0 Wigan 8, Workington Town 11 Warrington 0

Semi-finals:
Wigan 5 Rochdale Hornets 3 (Station Road, Swinton, 28,597),

Workington Town 8 Featherstone Rovers 2 (Odsal Stadium, Bradford, 31,715)

Head-to-head form guide:

Wigan 35 Workington Town 11 (League)

Workington Town 8 Wigan 3 (League)

Wigan loose forward Bernard McGurrin searches for a way past Workington Town's John O'Neill (left) and Ike Southward, scorer of all the Cumbrian team's points

WINNING CAPTAIN

Eric Ashton (Wigan 1958, 1959, 1965)

Eric Ashton was one of rugby league's greatest ever centres, a classy player and magnificent captain and ambassador for club and country. After playing rugby league at school, he took up rugby union during National Service with the Army, being selected for inter-services matches. Wigan were alerted, giving him a trial following his release in 1955. Signed immediately, he became club captain two years later, his right wing partnership with Billy Boston becoming legendary. At Wigan, he won the Rugby League Challenge Cup (1958, 1959, 1965), Championship (1959/60), Lancashire Cup (1966), Lancashire League (1958/59, 1961/62), and BBC 2 Floodlit Trophy (1968). Included in Great Britain's World Cup squad (1957 and 1960—captain/coach of the latter), and tour party (1958 and 1962—captain of the latter), he represented Britain in 26 internationals (captain 15 times), England (once) and Lancashire (10 times). Wigan player-coach from 1963, he remained in charge until 1973, retiring as a player in 1969 following 497 appearances. He later coached Leeds (1973–74), St Helens (1974–80), Great Britain (1979 tour), and England (1978–80). He received the MBE in 1966 and was elected to the Rugby League Hall of Fame in 2005.

1959 RUGBY LEAGUE CHALLENGE CUP FINAL
Wigan v Hull

Wigan convincingly defeated Hull 30–13 in the 1959 Challenge Cup decider in a disappointing first Wembley appearance for the Boulevard side. Hull's awesome pack, on which much of their success was built, produced a below average performance, allowing Wigan to control the crucial upfront battle. Despite the one-sided nature of the match, the *Sunday Observer*'s Garrett Colter declared it the 'most entertaining Wembley final in recent years'. Both were

The giant Wembley scoreboard in the background indicates Wigan lead 10–2 as Billy Boston attempts to make progress down the right flank. The legendary wingman went on to notch two tries

at full strength; Wigan skipper Eric Ashton required a pre-match pain-killing injection on an injured leg, Hull preferring 20-year-old Arthur Keegan at full back ahead of the more experienced Peter Bateson, the goal-kicking duo having shared the role throughout the season.

As anticipated Hull's pack began with fire but

Wigan repelled them and, after eight minutes, Ashton cracked their defence, transferring to co-centre Keith Holden who sidestepped Brian Cooper and Keegan to go beneath the posts, Fred Griffiths converting. Undeterred, Hull's forwards continued to pound Wigan's defences, Keegan cutting the lead through a long-range penalty, following a scrum infringement. But the Airlie Birds had an unsettled look and careless passing near the opposition's try-line led to a second Wigan try after David Bolton recovered a loose ball. The stand-off beat two defenders before passing to Mick Sullivan who got the crowd on their toes as he raced 75 yards to score in the corner. The Lancashire side were now playing brilliantly and another long-distance thriller followed when Bolton sprinted 60 yards after a break by Brian McTigue, to place the ball beneath the posts. Griffiths added both goals, the first ricocheting off a post, placing Wigan comfortably ahead 15–2 after 30 minutes.

Keegan notched his second penalty, awarded for an illegal scrum feed by Wigan's Rees Thomas, but the Cherry and Whites still had one more ace to play before half-time. It was another breathtaking score, brought about once more by the tremendous pace of Bolton who, after good work from Ashton and Roy Evans, sprinted away and, when tackled, sent a long pass into the waiting arms of Billy Boston whose arcing 20-yard run took him over at the corner. Griffiths added an excellent goal and Wigan looked well in control with a 20–4 half-time lead.

After the break Hull made in-roads into Wigan territory but Tom Finn, following a tap-penalty, lost the ball near their try-line. It resulted in Wigan prop John Barton charging up the field and, enterprisingly, kicking the ball towards the Hull line before regaining it to touch down under the posts. But, as Wigan fans responded with a slow handclap, referee Charlie Appleton disallowed the effort for obstruction. Stan Cowan looked a candidate for claiming Hull's first try but passed inside when he seemed to have a chance of going for the try-line himself. Keegan kicked a penalty from in front of the posts before Wigan had another try ruled out, this time by Holden following a McTigue break. Keegan's fourth penalty (for ball 'stealing') kept Hull in contention, reducing the deficit to 12 points at 20–8. But, with an hour played, it provided a wake-up call for Wigan, who registered two further tries; McTigue (diving over the line after the defence had been prised open) and Boston (following up after Bolton made another quicksilver break before grubber-kicking ahead). Griffiths converted the former, placing the match well beyond Hull's grasp. With eight minutes remaining, Finn scored a consolation, sidestepping his way over the try-line off a Jim Drake pass, Keegan adding his fifth goal. Griffiths—with his sixth success to equal the Wembley record—supplied a long-range penalty to complete the scoring.

The (Manchester based) *News Chronicle* writer Tom Longworth said: 'Wigan played almost to perfection turning defence into attack in amazing fashion, and leaving Hull with no counter.' Wigan set several Wembley records; most appearances (6), most wins (5), highest score (30), and the first to win successive finals at the stadium.

Wigan register their fifth try as Brian McTigue crowns his man-of-the-match performance

---

STATS

Wigan 30 Hull 13

Saturday 9 May at Wembley Stadium, London (3.00 pm)

Wigan (cherry and white hoops): Griffiths, Boston, Ashton (captain), Holden, Sullivan, Bolton, Thomas, Bretherton, Sayer, Barton, McTigue, Cherrington, Evans. Coach: J. Egan

Hull (white with black chevron): Keegan, Cowan, Cooper, Saville, Watts, Matthews, Finn, Scott, Harris, J. Drake, Sykes, W. Drake, Whiteley (captain). Coach: R. Francis

Referee: C.F. Appleton Touch-judges: H. Shaw, H. Hudson

Half-time: 20–4 Attendance: 79,811 Receipts: £35,718

Weather: sunny and cloudy, slight breeze

Lance Todd Trophy: McTigue (Wigan)

Cup presentation: H.R.H. The Princess Royal

Progressive score:

Wigan	score (min)	Hull
Holden try, Griffiths goal	5–0 (8)	
	5–2 (12)	Keegan penalty
Sullivan try, Griffiths goal	10–2 (22)	
Bolton try, Griffiths goal	15–2 (30)	
	15–4 (32)	Keegan penalty
Boston try, Griffiths goal	20–4 (35)	
	20–6 (49)	Keegan penalty
	20–8 (58)	Keegan penalty
McTigue try, Griffiths goal	25–8 (60)	
Boston try	28–8 (70)	
	28–13 (72)	Finn try, Keegan goal
Griffiths penalty	30–13 (78)	

Route to the final:

First round: Wigan 12 Leeds 5, Hull 11 Blackpool Borough 2

Second round: Wigan 22 Hunslet 4, Hull 4 Wakefield Trinity 4

Second round replay: Wakefield Trinity 10 Hull 16

Third round: Halifax 0 Wigan 26, Hull 23 Hull Kingston Rovers 9

Semi-finals: Wigan 5 Leigh 0 (Station Road, Swinton, 27,900), Hull 15 Featherstone Rovers 5 (Odsal Stadium, Bradford, 52,500)

Head-to-head form guide:

Hull 34 Wigan 15 (League)

Wigan 31 Hull 7 (League)

1960 RUGBY LEAGUE CHALLENGE CUP FINAL
Wakefield Trinity v Hull

When Wakefield Trinity triumphed at Wembley in 1960, few at the club dared imagine they were embarking on an unprecedented period of success under the famed Twin Towers. Chairman Stuart Hadfield, told the *Wakefield Express*: 'It has been a long ambition of mine to be chairman of Trinity when they won the cup', little realising that he would live that dream of leading his players onto the Wembley turf three times in four seasons, each resulting in victory! Wakefield entered the 1960 confrontation with Hull minus two regulars; stand-off Harold Poynton had strained his shoulder ligaments in the previous weekend's Championship play-off—also versus Hull—whilst forward Malcolm Sampson had damaged a wrist in an earlier motoring accident, having able deputies in Ken Rollin and Len Chamberlain, respectively.

Trinity's injury problems, though, paled against Hull's, which was without parallel in Challenge Cup Final history. Just five of the previous year's Wembley team played, their predicament gauged by the fact they named a 20-man squad the preceding Tuesday,

altering the list as the week progressed! Even the *Hull Daily Mail* was caught out, their Wembley Special, profiling 17 players, missing four that eventually played! Amongst the backs, goal-kicking full back Peter Bateson (severe concussion) and winger Terry Devonshire (shoulder) were ruled out, whilst three others played out of position. But it was the forwards that suffered most, half their famed pack being unavailable; Jim Drake (sprained ankle), twin Bill Drake (groin strain) and Cyril Sykes (shoulder). With potential replacements also injured, Mike Smith became the first player to make his senior debut at Wembley.

Watched by Her Majesty Queen Elizabeth II—attending the Challenge Cup Final for the first time—Wakefield produced a sizzling display, vanquishing Hull 38–5. Given the Airlie Birds' pre-match problems, the outcome was predictable, although they performed creditably in the opening half, being only two points down at the turnaround. Neil Fox kicked a second minute penalty for Trinity, for obstruction,

Hull centre Nan Halafihi (with ball) looks for support on the inside

Wakefield Trinity's Keith Holliday concludes a spectacular break from midfield by scoring Wembley's 100th Challenge Cup Final try in the 59th minute

STATS

Wakefield Trinity 38 Hull 5

Saturday 14 May at Wembley Stadium, London (3.00 pm)

Wakefield Trinity (white with red and blue band): Round, Smith, Skene, Fox, Etty, Rollin, Holliday, Wilkinson, Oakes, Vines, Firth, Chamberlain, Turner (captain). Coach: K. Traill

Hull (black and white irregular hoop): Kershaw, Harrison, Cowan, Halifihi, Johnson, Broadhurst, Finn, Scott, Harris, Evans, Sutton, Smith, Whiteley (captain). Coach: R Francis

Referee: E. Clay Touch-judges: J.W. Jowett, W. Rigby

Half-time: 7–5 Attendance: 79,773 Receipts: £35,754

Weather: sunny and warm   Lance Todd Trophy: Harris (Hull)

Cup presentation: H.M. Queen Elizabeth II

Progressive score:

Wakefield Trinity	score (min)	Hull
Fox penalty	2–0 (2)	
Rollin try	5–0 (3)	
	5–5 (12)	Cowan try, Evans goal
Fox penalty	7–5 (15)	
Fox try	10–5 (45)	
Skene try	13–5 (49)	
Holliday try, Fox goal	18–5 (59)	
Skene try, Fox goal	23–5 (63)	
Fox try, Fox goal	28–5 (71)	
Smith try, Fox goal	33–5 (77)	
Holliday try, Fox goal	38–5 (80)	

Route to the final:

First round: St Helens 10 Wakefield Trinity 15, York 0 Hull 2

Second round: Widnes 2 Wakefield Trinity 5, Keighley 2 Hull 32

Third round: Whitehaven 10 Wakefield Trinity 21, Hull 12 Wigan 8

Semi-finals: Wakefield T 11 Featherstone R 2 (Odsal Stadium, Bradford, 55,800), Hull 12 Oldham 9 (Station Road, Swinton, 27,592)

Head-to-head form guide:

Wakefield Trinity 34 Hull 9 (League)

Hull 11 Wakefield Trinity 5 (League)

Wakefield Trinity 24 Hull 4 (Championship semi-final)

followed quickly by a sensational Rollin try. Put through a gap by Derek Turner, he raced downfield and kicked over Jack Kershaw's head, reclaiming the ball before going over the line between two defenders, Fox missing the goal. Hull's reorganised pack dug in, defending well for the remainder of the half, Kershaw, who had received pain-killing injections and deputised as goal-kicker, missing two penalty chances, the second of which—from 40 yards—did not lift sufficient to reach the posts. Hull gave their fans some joy when Stan Cowan dodged over for a try under the posts, sent on his way by Frank Broadhurst after winning a scrum on Trinity's 25-yard line (it was later realised Cowan fractured a rib in scoring). Sam Evans added the goal to level the score. Fox regained Wakefield's lead at 7–5 with a penalty for offside at a play-the-ball, Evans failing to respond in kind with an attempt the following minute and another just before the interval.

The second half was all Wakefield's, their 31 points without reply building a record Wembley score. The half began with a great 60-yard run from Hull skipper Johnny Whiteley that lacked support, the ball being lost, before Wakefield slipped into top gear. They ran in seven excellent tries; two from Fox (the first following a Rollin break, the second a 50-yard race after a Gerry Round pass), two by Alan Skene (a thrilling 75-yard run after collecting a poorly kicked ball from Hull, the next a sprint down the left touchline after Turner broke three tackles), two through Keith Holliday (a 70-yard dash off a Turner pass, plus a wonderful late solo effort), and one by

Fred Smith (put through a gap by John Etty). Fox—who missed a 68th minute penalty—converted five for a personal Wembley record goal (7) and points (20) tally.

For Hull, Lance Todd Trophy winner, Tommy Harris earned huge praise for a courageous display in defeat; concussed 10 minutes before the interval, returning several minutes later, and finally quitting 15 minutes from the end, when he was taken to hospital.

1961 RUGBY LEAGUE CHALLENGE CUP FINAL
St Helens v Wigan

Not this time! The threat of St Helens' Tom van Vollenhoven was averted on this occasion, the flying winger having stepped on the touchline

Known as 'the shirt-sleeved final' due to the baking heat, the abiding memory of the 1961 Challenge Cup decider between St Helens and Wigan was Tom van Vollenhoven's spectacular try for Saints 17 minutes from full time. With his team clinging precariously to a 5–4 lead, colleague Dick Huddart recovered a loose ball 10 yards from his own line and transferred it to Ken Large. The centre sent his wing partner van Vollenhoven on his way, the South African flyer accelerating past Frank Carlton and drawing Wigan full back Fred Griffiths before returning the ball inside to Large. Eric Ashton and Billy Boston raced across from the other flank to cover the cracks in defence, but, as Large took Ashton's tackle, he off-loaded to van Vollenhoven who sprinted for the corner before turning to go behind the posts. It was one of Wembley's most sensational scores, described by Alwyn Thomas in the *St Helens Newspaper* as 'the try Saints supporters had travelled 200 miles to see'.

Wigan had taken first blood, Griffiths kicking an angled 40-yard penalty when Alex Murphy was given offside. Boston almost scored but was halted near the try-line, Griffiths then missing a penalty awarded in front of the St Helens posts. Saints began to apply

WINNING CAPTAIN

Vince Karalius (St Helens 1961, Widnes 1964)

Loose forward Vince Karalius signed for St Helens in 1951 from Widnes amateurs West Bank for a reported £200 signing on fee, making his senior debut in 1952. With St Helens, where he became captain in 1960, he won the Rugby League Challenge Cup (1956, 1961), Championship (1952/53—although not selected for the final, 1958/59), Lancashire Cup (1953, 1960, 1961) and Lancashire League (1952/53, 1959/60). After 252 St Helens appearances he transferred to hometown Widnes in 1962 for £4,500, leading them to victory in the 1964 Rugby League Challenge Cup. His 132nd and last Widnes match was in 1966, later coaching Widnes (1972–75, 1983–84) and Wigan (1976–79). A tourist in 1958, his determination and deadly tackling prompting the Australian's to nickname him 'The Wild Bull of the Pampas'. He represented Great Britain (12 times—including three in the 1960 World Cup) and Lancashire (10). Elected into the Rugby League Hall of Fame in 2000, he had several rugby league-playing brothers, most notably Tony, a hooker who also played for Great Britain.

pressure, creating some anxious moments for Wigan; van Vollenhoven knocked-on after intercepting Brian McTigue's pass, Vince Karalius broke from the base of a scrum but lacked support. It developed into a fierce opening half; Murphy appeared to be laid out off the ball, whilst Boston and Mick Sullivan had an altercation when the former 'crash tackled' the latter after he raced back into his own in-goal area to recover the ball. Saints went ahead when Karalius' short pass

Vince Karalius enjoys his moment of glory with the Challenge Cup

found Huddart who burst through two defenders before sending Murphy roaring over the try-line with Boston in vain pursuit. Austin Rhodes missed the goal, but then tacked on a penalty from halfway after Geoff Lyons obstructed Don Vines making it 5–2 to St Helens. There were further near-misses as half-time drew closer, van Vollenhoven being resisted twice whilst, for Wigan, a great chance was lost when Terry Entwistle turned inside having created a 3-to-1 overlap.

After the break Ashton put Carlton in under the posts, but the pass was declared forward. Griffiths landed a goal—Wilf Smith being penalised for illegal scrum-feeding in front of his own posts—and could have put his side ahead, but hit the upright with another penalty chance. Boston lit up Wembley with a great run to the corner, three defenders forcing him into the flag. It signalled a 'wake up' call that swung the momentum towards St Helens, setting the stage for van Vollenhoven's wonderful try, Rhodes converting. At 10–4 for St Helens, close calls followed at each end, van Vollenhoven (twice) and Bolton both threatening to score. The only remaining points, though, came from late penalties by Rhodes (Frank Collier obstructing Murphy) and Griffiths (for offside), St Helens winning after a titanic struggle 12–6.

The post-match feeling was that Wigan had looked short of pace against St Helens, whose captain, Karalius, had been proved spot on in his pre-game analysis when he said 'I think we have the edge on Wigan, good side as they are. Saints have more match winners and because we are the younger side, I think we shall last the game better.'

STATS

St Helens 12 Wigan 6

Saturday 13 May at Wembley Stadium, London (3.00 pm)

St Helens (white with red chevron): Rhodes, van Vollenhoven, Large, McGinn, Sullivan, Murphy, Smith, Terry, Dagnall, Watson, Vines, Huddart, Karalius (captain). Coach: A. Prescott

Wigan (red): Griffiths, Boston, Ashton (captain), Bootle, Carlton, Bolton, Entwistle, Barton, Sayer, McTigue, Lyon, Collier, Evans. Coach: J. Egan

Referee: T.W. Watkinson
Touch-judges: E.R. Jones, C.B. Watson
Half-time: 5–2 Attendance: 94,672 Receipts: £38,479
Weather: sunny and hot
Lance Todd Trophy: Huddart (St Helens)
Cup presentation: Lord Derby, Rugby League president

Progressive score:

St Helens	score (min)	Wigan
	0–2 (4)	Griffiths penalty
Murphy try	3–2 (32)	
Rhodes penalty	5–2 (35)	
	5–4 (45)	Griffiths penalty
van Vollenhoven try, Rhodes goal	10–4 (63)	
Rhodes penalty	12–4 (71)	
	12–6 (79)	Griffiths penalty

Route to the final:

First round: St Helens 5 Widnes 5, Leeds 5 Wigan 5

First round replays:
Widnes 10 St Helens 29, Wigan 32 Leeds 7

Second round:
Castleford 10 St Helens 18, Wakefield Trinity 0 Wigan 2

Third round: St Helens 17 Swinton 9, Wigan 22 Salford 5

Semi-finals:
St Helens 26 Hull 9 (Odsal Stadium, Bradford, 42,074),
Wigan 19 Halifax 10 (Station Road, Swinton, 35,398)

Head-to-head form guide:

St Helens 7 Wigan 4 (Lancashire Cup)
St Helens 11 Wigan 6 (League)
Wigan 12 St Helens 2 (League)

1962 RUGBY LEAGUE CHALLENGE CUP FINAL
Wakefield Trinity v Huddersfield

Huddersfield's 1962 Wembley date with Wakefield Trinity was a surprise even for their own followers, the *Huddersfield Examiner* saying: 'I doubt if the most fervent supporters in their hearts could consider them Trophy material. They are a team of triers ready to snap up chances.' A couple of days before the final, two of Wakefield's players failed fitness tests; second-row Don Vines (thigh muscle), who was due to make a third consecutive Wembley appearance, and hooker Milan Kosanovic (ankle). On the left wing, Trinity selected 21-year-old Ken Hirst ahead of former South African rugby union internationals, Jan Prinsloo and Colin Greenwood, all three having featured during the campaign. Huddersfield omitted Welsh stand-off Gwyn Davies—their outstanding back in the earlier rounds—even though he had recovered from wrist and hip injuries, the club unwilling to disrupt a line-up that produced a shock in winning their Championship semi-final at Wigan the previous week.

Favourites Wakefield won 12–6 but as a contest it was as dull as the weather, remembered mostly for

Neil Fox's Challenge Cup Final record of three drop-goals that proved decisive to the outcome. All came directly from play-the-ball situations, being supplied, in turn, by acting-halfbacks Geoff Oakes, Brian Briggs and Derek Turner. His first opened the scoring in the 18th minute, to which he added a try two minutes later when, having sent Hirst on a run, he was on hand to accept the return inside pass and charge into the corner. During this spell, concussed skipper Turner left the field for 10 minutes, being less influential afterwards. Huddersfield worked hard to get points on the board, Frank Dyson missing with a 24th minute

Wakefield Trinity players enjoy a victory parade as they show off the Challenge Cup. From the left; skipper Derek Turner (arm raised in salute), Ken Hirst (in background, slightly obscured), Albert Firth, Gerry Round, Geoff Oakes, Keith Holliday and Denis Williamson, both holding the cup, and Brian Briggs

---

WINNING CAPTAIN

Derek Turner (Wakefield Trinity 1960, 1962, 1963)

Loose forward Derek 'Rocky' Turner enjoyed a magnificent career covering over 530 first class matches, encompassing three senior clubs; Hull Kingston Rovers (1951–55), Oldham (1955–59) and Wakefield Trinity (1959–66). Originated from Wakefield, he played for both Ossett and Shaw Cross Boys' Club (Dewsbury) before joining Rovers (playing his first few matches as a centre), transferring to Oldham (for £2,750), then Trinity (£8,000—a record at the time for a forward and becoming captain in the 1959/60 season). Regarded as a fearless and fearsome forward, he won the Championship (1956/57), Lancashire Cup (1956, 1957, 1958) and Lancashire League (1956/57, 1957/58) whilst with Oldham, and the Rugby League Challenge Cup (1960, 1962, 1963), Yorkshire Cup (1960, 1961) and Yorkshire League (1958/59, 1959/60, 1961/62, 1965/66) with Wakefield. He represented Great Britain in 24 international matches (including the 1957 and 1960 World Cups and 1962 tour—he withdrew in 1958 through injury) and Yorkshire 10 times. He initially retired in 1964 but returned to Trinity in 1965 to support the development of their younger players. He later coached Castleford (1968–69), Leeds (1969–73) and Wakefield (1983/84).

45-yard penalty before, six minutes later, his captain Tommy Smales scored a try in the left corner after sustained pressure. Dyson missed the goal as colleague Ray Haywood limped off having suffered a badly sprained ankle in the build-up to the score. Although he returned, the centre subsequently missed the following weekend's Championship Final. Five minutes from half-time, Dyson was wide with another penalty attempt.

After the break, Huddersfield, down 5–3, continued to defend well, frustrating any attempt from Trinity to open the game out for their speedier back division. Fox's second drop-goal in the 62nd minute was—like the first—quickly followed by a Trinity try, Hirst again being involved. Taking a pass from Briggs he commenced a dazzling run from inside his own 25-yard area, sprinting past two opponents before arcing round full back Dyson and outpacing the pursuing Smales to touch down at the corner. The score remained at 10–3 for Wakefield—Dyson and Fox both missed penalties, the latter hitting the upright—until three minutes from the end when Peter Ramsden (a

Ken Hirst—scorer of Wakefield Trinity's second try—attempts to keep the ball alive despite the efforts of Huddersfield's Aiden Breen

STATS

Wakefield Trinity 12 Huddersfield 6

Saturday 12 May at Wembley Stadium, London (3.00 pm)

Wakefield Trinity (white with red and blue band): Round, Smith, Skene, Fox, Hirst, Poynton, Holliday, Wilkinson, Oakes, Firth, Briggs, Williamson, Turner (captain). Coach: K. Traill

Huddersfield (claret with narrow gold hoops): Dyson, Breen, Booth, Haywood, Wicks, Deighton, Smales (captain), Slevin, Close, Noble, Clark, Bowman, Ramsden. Coach: D. Valentine

Referee: D.T.H. Davies

Touch-judges: H. Holland, G.W. Wilkinson

Half-time: 5–3 Attendance: 81,263 Receipts: £33,390

Weather: overcast and dull

Lance Todd Trophy: Fox (Wakefield Trinity)

Cup presentation: The Earl Alexander of Tunis

Progressive score:

Wakefield Trinity	score (min)	Huddersfield
Fox drop-goal	2–0 (18)	
Fox try	5–0 (20)	
	5–3 (30)	Smales try
Fox drop-goal	7–3 (62)	
Hirst try	10–3 (64)	
	10–6 (77)	Ramsden try
Fox drop-goal	12–6 (80)	

Route to the final:

First round:
Wakefield Trinity 40 Warrington 18, York 7 Huddersfield 8

Second round: Blackpool Borough 4 Wakefield T 16, St Helens 2 Huddersfield 13

Third round:
Wakefield Trinity 5 Wigan 4, Castleford 4 Huddersfield 4

Third round replay: Huddersfield 10 Castleford 4

Semi-finals: Wakefield T 9 Featherstone Rovers 0 (Odsal Stadium, Bradford, 43,627), Huddersfield 6 Hull Kingston Rovers 0 (Odsal Stadium, Bradford, 31,153)

Head-to-head form guide:

No previous meetings during season

survivor from their 1953 Wembley win) bamboozled the defence to such a degree he crossed for a try with two unmarked colleagues by his side. Although there were only four points in it, it was too late, Fox confirming victory with his final drop-goal in the dying seconds.

To date it is the only Wembley final without place-goals being scored, Fox and Dyson missing two conversions each. Trinity admitted Fox's drop-goals had been pre-planned to counter the limited running chances anticipated against Huddersfield's suffocating defence. The Fartown men turned the tables seven days later, beating Trinity 14–5 in the Championship Final, thereby denying them the kudos of joining the elite list of clubs to complete an 'All Four Cups' season.

1963 RUGBY LEAGUE CHALLENGE CUP FINAL
Wakefield Trinity v Wigan

Frank Pitchford sends out a pass for Wigan watched by colleague Roy Evans and Wakefield Trinity's Keith Holliday (right)

Two of the era's Wembley giants met to settle the 1963 Challenge Cup Final; Wakefield Trinity making their third visit of the 1960s, Wigan appearing a fourth time since 1958. On paper, Trinity looked weaker than in those earlier two finals, but confounded the pundits with a comprehensive 25–10 victory.

Wigan could have placed the match beyond reach before half-time, Wakefield—reportedly with several players not 100% fit—appearing nervous for much of the opening period. Billy Boston created panic in their ranks after four minutes, charging towards the corner off Alan Davies' pass. Overhauled near the corner, he released the ball to David Bolton but it was dropped. Stan McLeod was next up to set Trinity's alarm bells ringing, being tackled from behind with only Ian Brooke barring his route, whilst Eric Ashton—having beaten Gerry Round—crossed the whitewash, but was penalised for a double movement. There were also three missed penalties from Ashton during the opening quarter (including an ambitious halfway effort that just fell below the crossbar). These were followed, during the second quarter, by three unsuccessful penalty attempts by Wakefield's Neil Fox (one from halfway fell well short, another being an

uncharacteristic failure from in front of the posts).

Although 35 points were scored during the afternoon, the first came just two minutes before the interval and went Wakefield's way. Derek Turner found a gap, making a 40-yard break before passing to Roger Pearman. The loose forward—playing only his 7th senior match—off-loaded out of a two-man tackle to Keith Holliday, the latter sending Malcolm Sampson over beneath the posts from 15 yards out, Fox adding the elusive goal. Wigan tried to hit back quickly but, when Geoff Lyon got within five yards of Trinity's try-line, Bolton was heavily concussed attempting to take his pass. Half-time arrived with ambulance men still in attendance and he was removed on a stretcher.

Wigan resumed with 12 men, Bolton not recovering; McLeod taking his full back role, Lyon moving to stand-off. Despite their handicap, Wigan scored two minutes into the half, Davies and Frank Carlton finding an opening for Frank Pitchford who wrong-footed Round to go over in the left corner. Ashton's kick, though, hardly rose above the ground. Fox was short with another penalty four minutes later before, in the 50th minute, Trinity got their second touchdown, Harold Poynton and Pearman benefiting when Wigan's John Barton spilt the ball to send Gert Coetzer on a searing touchline run past two defenders to go in at the corner. Fox kicked a great goal, stretching the lead to 10–3. Although advised against it, Bolton returned in the 58th minute, but looked hazy. Three penalty goals quickly forward, two from Ashton (both for scrum offences) being dissected by

Wigan's Frank Carlton (in hoops) competes for possession with Wakefield's Ian Brooke (left) and Colin Greenwood

STATS

Wakefield Trinity 25 Wigan 10

Saturday 11 May at Wembley Stadium, London (3.00 pm)

Wakefield Trinity (white with red and blue chevron): Round, Greenwood, Brooke, Fox, Coetzer, Poynton, Holliday, Wilkinson, Kosanovic, Sampson, Vines, Turner (captain), Pearman. Coach: K. Traill

Wigan (cherry and white hoops): Bolton, Boston, Ashton (captain), Davies, Carlton, McLeod, Pitchford, Barton, Sayer, McTigue, Collier, Lyon, Evans. Coach: G. Jenkins

Referee: D.T.H. Davies

Touch-judges: G. Battersby, F.G. Smart

Half-time: 5–0 Attendance: 84,492 Receipts: £44,521

Weather: sunny and warm

Lance Todd Trophy: Poynton (Wakefield Trinity)

Cup presentation: Field-Marshall The Rt Hon. Viscount Montgomery of Alamein

Progressive score:

Wakefield Trinity	score (min)	Wigan
Sampson try, Fox goal	5–0 (38)	
	5–3 (42)	Pitchford try
Coetzer try, Fox goal	10–3 (50)	
	10–5 (59)	Ashton penalty
Fox penalty	12–5 (63)	
	12–7 (64)	Ashton penalty
Poynton try, Fox goal	17–7 (69)	
	17–10 (73)	Carlton try
Coetzer try	20–10 (78)	
Brooke try, Fox goal	25–10 (80)	

Route to the final:

First round: Wakefield Trinity 15 Bradford Northern 3, Hull 0 Wigan 7

Second round: Wakefield Trinity 14 Liverpool City 12, Wigan 20 Leeds 11

Third round: York 9 Wakefield Trinity 9, Oldham 0 Wigan 18

Third round replay: Wakefield Trinity 25 York 11

Semi-finals: Wakefield Trinity 5 Warrington 2 (Station Road, Swinton, 15,566),

Wigan 18 Hull Kingston Rovers 4 (Headingley, Leeds, 21,479)

Head-to-head form guide:

No previous meetings during the season

one from Fox (high tackle by Brian McTigue on Sampson), the score standing at 12–7.

The match turned emphatically in Wakefield's favour in the 69th minute when Bolton, having broken down the right channel with Boston to his right and Ashton on his left, had his inside pass to the latter intercepted by Poynton—the only player barring their progress—who raced in unopposed to score near the corner. Fox added an excellent goal. A Boston charge almost produced a McLeod try in the right corner before play swung quickly to the left flank for Davies to send Carlton over. Ashton was well wide with the conversion, Wigan trailing by seven. But Wakefield were in no mood to let go and, playing excellent rugby, added two late tries through Coetzer (outmanoeuvring Roy Evans following Pearman's pass after the latter extricated himself from Boston) and Brooke (breaking Bolton's tackle after Poynton and Holliday worked the opening). Fox—well off-target with the first shot—converted Brooke's effort to end the scoring.

It was four Wembley wins from four visits for Wakefield in the stadium's first rematch following their 1946 meeting. Their prop Jack Wilkinson, celebrated a record fifth Wembley appearance (two with Halifax, three for Trinity), whilst Turner became the first captain to receive the trophy three times at the famous venue.

141

1964 RUGBY LEAGUE CHALLENGE CUP FINAL
Widnes v Hull Kingston Rovers

The 1964 Challenge Cup Final climaxed a unique year with 10 replays required in the competition proper to determine the two Wembley finalists. Eventual winners Widnes were involved in five of them, two being second replays, whilst Wembley opponents Hull Kingston Rovers needed three matches to overcome Oldham in the semi-final. History was made through both semi-final match-ups finishing all square, the Rovers versus Oldham clash requiring a third meeting after the first replay, at Swinton on a Wednesday evening, was abandoned. At a time when most grounds, including Swinton's Station Road, had no floodlights, referee Dennis Davies curtailed proceedings due to fading light with Oldham leading 17–14 12 minutes into extra time. Rovers won the rematch to earn a Wembley debut whilst, to date, Oldham are still awaiting theirs.

Widnes prop Edgar Bate, who had appeared in seven of their nine ties, suffered disappointment when the pace of Arthur Hughes was preferred for Wembley's open spaces, whilst a thigh injury for Rhodesian wingman John Gaydon meant he lost out to

Bill Thompson. For Rovers, 21-year-old Brian Mennell, with only three first team games under his belt, replaced suspended prop John Taylor, sent off the previous weekend against Huddersfield. After Taylor's suspension was confirmed, Mennell—who was outstanding in a reserves match on the Tuesday—was added to the squad when it was realised the pulled thigh muscle of standby ex-Hull prop Jim Drake was not responding to treatment.

Widnes enjoyed most of the first half play due to hooker George Kemel mopping up the scrums, allowing his pack-mates, ably led by the experienced Vince Karalius and Frank Collier, to dictate. Full backs Cyril Kellett (Rovers) and Bob Randall (Widnes) both missed early penalties, but the only score before half-time was Randall's 35th minute long-range penalty.

Having gained ascendancy upfront, Widnes' back division began to show their mettle after the break with two tries in four minutes. The first was credited to Alan Briers, who—having received a well-timed Karalius pass—evaded three defenders down the flank before veering inside for the touchdown, the second going to Frank Myler who raced untouched to go under the posts, an opening having been created by forwards Wally Hurstfield and Hughes.

Frank Collier puts the finishing touch on his player of the match performance by claiming the concluding Widnes try just minutes from the end

Randall succeeded with the second of his two conversions to open up a 10–0 lead and, with the Rovers having been slight favourites, the Widnes following 'erupted' at the prospect of an upset, the *Widnes Weekly News* noting: 'The whole atmosphere of the game changed. Instead of being strained and taut, something had snapped and the whole stadium took on a cavalier feeling.'

The Rovers only points came after they won a scrum, Arthur Bunting sending halfback partner Alan Burwell racing towards the left hand corner and out of Randall's reach for a well executed long-range try, Cyril Kellett appending a magnificent goal. The score motivated the Yorkshire side and they stormed back at their opponents, winger Graham Paul twice going close. Widnes held firm and began searching for a 'killer' try, Hughes crossing the try-line but being denied through a forward pass. With two minutes remaining Lance Todd Trophy winner Collier charged over for the final score to make it 13–5, Kemel creating the gap with a dummy pass. Randall, who missed the conversion, said afterwards: 'I can't remember taking the goal kick after Frank Collier's try. I knew we had won and I didn't know whether I was on my head or my heels!'

Widnes centre Alan Briers is about to place the ball down for the opening try as colleague Bob Chisnall (number 2) begins the celebration!

STATS

Widnes 13 Hull Kingston Rovers 5

Saturday 9 May at Wembley Stadium, London (3.00 pm)

Widnes (black and white hoops): Randall, Chisnall, Briers, Myler, Thompson, Lowe, Owen, Hurstfield, Kemel, Collier, Measures, Hughes, Karalius (captain). Coach: J. Egan

Hull Kingston Rovers (red): Kellett, Paul, Major, Elliott, Blackmore, Burwell, Bunting, Tyson, Flanagan, Mennell, Palmer, Clark, Poole (captain). Coach: C. Hutton

Referee: R.L. Thomas

Touch-judges: R. Syers, T.G. Fellows

Half-time: 2–0 Attendance: 84,488 Receipts: £44,840

Weather: sunny

Lance Todd Trophy: Collier (Widnes)

Cup presentation: Lord Derby, Rugby League president

Progressive score:

Widnes	score (min)	Hull Kingston Rovers
Randall penalty	2–0 (35)	
Briers try	5–0 (52)	
Myler try, Randall goal	10–0 (56)	
	10–5 (63)	Burwell try, Kellett goal
Collier try	13–5 (78)	

Route to the final:

First round:
Leigh 2 Widnes 2,
Hull Kingston Rovers 12 Rochdale Hornets 12

First round replays:
Widnes 11 Leigh 11,
Rochdale Hornets 7 Hull Kingston R 22

First round second replay:
Widnes 14 Leigh 2 (Knowsley Road, St Helens)

Second round:
Widnes 16 Liverpool City 6,
York 7 Hull Kingston Rovers 23

Third round:
Widnes 5 Swinton 5,
Hull Kingston Rovers 38 Barrow 4

Third round replay: Swinton 0 Widnes 0

Third round second replay:
Widnes 15 Swinton 3 (Central Park, Wigan)

Semi-finals:
Widnes 7 Castleford 7 (Station Road, Swinton, 25,602),
Hull Kingston Rovers 5 Oldham 5 (Headingley, Leeds, 28,556)

Semi-final replays:
Widnes 7 Castleford 5 (Belle Vue, Wakefield, 28,732),
Hull Kingston Rovers 14 Oldham 17 (Station Road, Swinton, 27,209—abandoned during extra time due to fading light)

Semi-final second replay:
Hull KR 12 Oldham 2 (Fartown, Huddersfield, 32,757)

Head-to-head form guide:

No previous meetings during season

1965 RUGBY LEAGUE CHALLENGE CUP FINAL
Wigan v Hunslet

In 1965 Wembley hosted what was then hailed as the best Challenge Cup Final seen at the stadium, underdogs Hunslet playing the game of their lives against Wigan to twice fight back before succumbing 20–16. It was not only the fluctuating scoreboard that kept the crowd in a state of excitement, but the pace and quality of the match. Maybe the 'outsider' tag gave the south Leeds team a 'devil may care' attitude as they surprised many through their willingness to take on Wigan in the open. Amazingly, the Cherry and Whites paraded eight players making Wembley debuts despite the club appearing in four of the previous seven finals. Only Eric Ashton, Billy Boston, Roy Evans, Keith Holden and Brian McTigue, amongst their starting 13, had sampled its atmosphere, John Barton missing the occasion after breaking his right arm the previous month.

The game began sensationally, Wigan's Laurie Gilfedder landing Wembley's quickest goal, the ball sailing over the crossbar from his centre-spot penalty kick just 54 seconds after Hunslet's Alan Marchant propelled it directly out of play from kick-off. The Parksiders levelled through Billy Langton's 45-yard penalty (Evans obstructing Bernard Prior) and almost took a 13th minute lead when John Griffiths dived over Wigan's try-line in the right corner after Fred Ward's dummy created space, the Welsh winger being visibly aggrieved that the touch-judge ruled he was pushed out of play by Trevor Lake.

Three minutes later Langton failed to find touch after Wigan were penalised and the Central Park side capitalised, Gilfedder and Ray Ashby finding room down the right, Holden bursting through on the inside for a fabulous try. Gilfedder missed the goal. Langton responded with a penalty (Colin Clarke 'loose arm' in a scrum), missing another, more ambitious attempt four minutes later. Gilfedder found the target with another penalty strike (Hunslet offside) making it 7–4 to Wigan. The match was being played at a terrific, flowing pace, Wigan looking increasingly threatening as full back Ashby linked up on attack. It looked likely they might run away with it when Lake rounded the defence to score 15 yards left of the uprights, having been put through by Holden, Gilfedder's goal bringing the score to 12–4. Hunslet refused to capitulate and, two minutes before the interval, Brian Gabbitas sent Geoff Shelton racing under the posts, sidestepping four defenders for

One of Wembley's most memorable tries was this 59th minute effort of Wigan's speedy wingman Trevor Lake seen here diving in at the left corner despite a desperate tackle from Hunslet's John Griffiths

Hunslet's Alan Preece is grounded by Wigan pairing Laurie Gilfedder (left) and Tony Stephens

a try that had the stadium buzzing. Langton's goal left Hunslet three points adrift at half-time.

Four minutes after the restart, Hunslet spilt the ball whilst mounting a strong attack, allowing McTigue and Evans to send Gilfedder on a 45-yard race for Hunslet's try-line, evading Shelton and Langton before scoring in the corner. Ashton, deputising for a gasping Gilfedder, notched an excellent touchline goal. Holden then had a try disallowed under the posts for a double movement whilst, for Hunslet, Langton missed a 30-yard penalty shot. Undaunted, the Parksiders pummelled Wigan's line, three try-scoring chances, in almost as many minutes, going begging through poor passes at the vital moment. In the latter instance they were soon made to suffer as Ashby, from just inside the Wigan 25-yard area, burst through three defenders to race 30 yards towards the left, transferring to the speedy Lake on halfway. An exhilarating chase to the corner ended as the winger avoided Griffiths' desperate tackle to dive over for one of Wembley's most spectacular touchdowns. Gilfedder's kick was poor, hardly rising above the ground and he was also well wide with a straightforward penalty attempt shortly afterwards although, at 20–9 and under 20 minutes left, Wigan looked safe.

Hunslet, though, had other ideas. Led by second-rowers Geoff Gunney and Bill Ramsey, their forwards gained control, Griffiths haring past four defenders to go between the posts. Langton's conversion, plus a penalty (offside at a scrum) brought them to within

four points with as many minutes remaining. Hunslet were on fire but Wigan held on for an unforgettable win. The *Wigan Observer* said 'Wigan were matched step for step by Hunslet, who not only rose to the occasion but soared high above it.' For the first time the teams had substitutes on the bench; two each, allowed until half-time and for injury only.

STATS

Wigan 20 Hunslet 16

Saturday 8 May at Wembley Stadium, London (3.00 pm)

Wigan (cherry and white hoops): Ashby, Boston, Ashton (captain), Holden, Lake, C. Hill, Parr, Gardiner, Clarke, McTigue, A. Stephens, Evans, Gilfedder. Substitutes: Kevin O'Loughlin (dnp), Lyon (dnp). Player-coach: E. Ashton

Hunslet (white with chocolate chevron): Langton, Griffiths, Shelton, Preece, Lee, Gabbitas, Marchant, Hartley, Prior, Eyre, Ramsey, Gunney, Ward (captain). Substitutes: Render (dnp), Baldwinson (dnp). Player-coach: F. Ward

Referee: J. Manley Touch-judges: A. Bagnall, R. Oliver

Half-time: 12–9 Attendance: 89,016 Receipts: £48,080

Weather: sunny and warm

Lance Todd Trophy (joint winners): Ashby (Wigan), Gabbitas (Hunslet)

Cup presentation: H.R.H. The Princess Alexandra

Progressive score:

Wigan	score (min)	Hunslet
Gilfedder penalty	2–0 (1)	
	2–2 (4)	Langton penalty
Holden try	5–2 (16)	
	5–4 (25)	Langton penalty
Gilfedder penalty	7–4 (30)	
Lake try, Gilfedder goal	12–4 (33)	
	12–9 (38)	Shelton try, Langton goal
Gilfedder try, Ashton goal	17–9 (44)	
Lake try	20–9 (59)	
	20–14 (65)	Griffiths try, Langton goal
	20–16 (76)	Langton penalty

Route to the final:

First round: Wigan 16 Barrow 0, Hunslet 12 Oldham 4

Second round: Wigan 7 St Helens 2, Hunslet 24 Batley 4

Third round: Workington Town 4 Wigan 10, Hunslet 7 Leeds 5

Semi-finals:

Wigan 25 Swinton 10 (Knowsley Road, St Helens, 26,658), Hunslet 8 Wakefield Trinity 0 (Headingley, Leeds, 21,262)

Head-to-head form guide:

No previous meetings during season

1966 RUGBY LEAGUE CHALLENGE CUP FINAL
St Helens v Wigan

A new Wembley rugby league record 98,536 crowd saw St Helens defeat Wigan in a surprisingly one-sided 1966 Challenge Cup Final. The 21–2 score-line owed much to the audacity of Alex Murphy, who took advantage of Wigan hooker Colin Clarke (father of Sky TV pundit Phil Clarke) being suspended, stand-in Tom Woosey not being a specialist rake. Murphy's tactic—emulated by Saints colleague Tommy Bishop—was to stray offside whenever the opposition threatened their territory, thereby conceding a penalty. Although Wigan gained yardage by finding touch, Murphy knew his hooker Bill

An overjoyed Alex Murphy lifts the trophy after St Helens' unexpectedly one-sided victory over Wigan. The player examining his winners' medal (extreme right) is future BBC television rugby league commentator Ray French whilst Len Killeen (left of the two players kneeling, looking straight at the camera) enjoyed a personal triumph by winning the Lance Todd Trophy

Sayer was likely to win possession from the resultant scrum (a tap restart to the non-offending side not being in the rule book at that time). Jeering came from the stands, referee Harry Hunt warning Murphy several times about his ploy, but no firmer action resulted.

St Helens scored three sparkling tries and Len

Killeen's goal kicking was amongst the finest seen at Wembley. He opened the scoring with two penalties, the first, a straight-forward 30-yard effort (for offside), eclipsed five minutes later by a fantastic 65-yard strike from inside his own half, 8 yards from touch (future BBC television commentator Ray French having been struck by Harry Major at a play-the-ball). Ron Barker wrote in *The Rugby Leaguer*: 'Many fine goals have been scored at Wembley in the 37 years the Challenge Cup Final has been staged at the stadium but the Killeen effort will surely go down on record as the best yet.' Between Killeen's two efforts, there were close calls at each end; Billy Boston's rip-roaring charge for Wigan requiring three opponents to keep him out and a tremendous break by Murphy being nullified by Eric Ashton.

Wigan looked insecure and slower than St Helens, Saints' John Mantle shrugging off two defenders in the 17th minute to cross the try-line on the right after Peter Harvey's reverse pass had sent Tom van Vollenhoven on his way, the winger transferring to Mantle as Ray Ashby moved in to tackle. Killeen's goal made it 9–0. St Helens almost had another when Bishop went over behind Wigan's goal but Murphy's pass was ruled forward. In the latter stages of the first half, Laurie Gilfedder attempted four penalty goals for Wigan, succeeding with a difficult 45 yard effort from near the left touchline after Murphy was lectured by Hunt for his persistent offside. The goal lifted Wigan for the remaining 10 minutes of the half, Trevor Lake flying past two defenders on a great touchline run, Frank Barrow's desperate tackle bringing him down,

St Helens loose forward John Mantle dives over for the opening try of the match with colleague Tom van Vollenhoven in close support. The dismayed Wigan players are captain Eric Ashton (left) and Trevor Lake (on ground)

STATS

St Helens 21 Wigan 2

Saturday 21 May at Wembley Stadium, London (3.00 pm)

St Helens (white with red chevron): F. Barrow, van Vollenhoven, Murphy (captain), Benyon, Killeen, Harvey, Bishop, Halsall, Sayer, Watson, French, Warlow, Mantle. Substitutes: A. Barrow (dnp), Hitchen (dnp). Coach: J. Coan

Wigan (red with white chevron): Ashby, Boston, D. Stephens, Ashton (captain), Lake, C. Hill, Parr, Gardiner, Woosey, McTigue, A. Stephens, Gilfedder, Major. Substitutes: Hesketh (dnp), Lyon (dnp). Player-coach: E. Ashton

Referee: H.G. Hunt Touch-judges: D.T. James, L. Wingfield

Half-time: 9–2 Attendance: 98,536 Receipts: £50,409

Weather: dry and sultry

Lance Todd Trophy: Killeen (St Helens)

Cup presentation:
The Rt Hon. Harold Wilson, Prime Minister

Progressive score:

St Helens	score (min)	Wigan
Killeen penalty	2–0 (4)	
Killeen penalty	4–0 (9)	
Mantle try, Killeen goal	9–0 (17)	
	9–2 (30)	Gilfedder penalty
Killeen penalty	11–2 (44)	
Killeen try	14–2 (54)	
Bishop try, Killeen goal	19–2 (71)	
Murphy drop-goal	21–2 (78)	

Route to the final:

First round:
Wakefield Trinity 0 St Helens 10, Wigan 8 Halifax 4

Second round:
St Helens 16 Swinton 4, Wigan 40 Whitehaven 6

Third round: St Helens 12 Hull Kingston Rovers 10, Bradford Northern 6 Wigan 15

Semi-finals:
St Helens 12 Dewsbury 5 (Station Road, Swinton, 13,046),
Wigan 7 Leeds 2 (Fartown, Huddersfield, 22,758)

Head-to-head form guide:

Wigan 17 St Helens 8 (League)

St Helens 17 Wigan 10 (League)

Two minutes into the second half Murphy was 'flattened' but recovered after attention, Killeen kicking a penalty shortly after when Billy Benyon—having kicked the ball—went down to a high Danny Gardiner tackle. Lake made another threatening run, reaching Saints' 25-yard line with only van Vollenhoven to beat but, so powerful was the latter's tackle, Lake was later thought to have cracked a rib. Killeen missed an ambitious 70-yard penalty before scoring the try of the match; a perfectly weighted grubber-kick towards the left corner flag from Benyon, after Bishop's earlier break, enabled him to take the ball at speed in one perfect movement for the touchdown. He missed the difficult conversion plus another penalty three minutes later, the scoreboard showing 14–2.

Wigan looked weary, van Vollenhoven having a score disallowed following a flowing passing move, the right corner flag being dislodged as he crossed the try-line. Bishop claimed the third try, recovering his own kick to dive between the posts despite Ashby's attention, Killeen adding the extras. Bishop almost scored again and then, with four minutes left, Major was knocked out attempting to tackle Saints' Albert Halsall. Taken off on a stretcher, he was unable to collect his medal from Prime Minister, Harold Wilson.

The scoring concluded with Murphy's drop-goal, the last significant action seeing Ashby hauled down near St Helens' try-line in the final minute.

St Helens were without halfback Bob Prosser (facial injury) and loose forward Kel Coslett (rib), both hurt the previous weekend. Wigan's Ashton, Boston and Brian McTigue shared a record sixth Wembley final appearance.

ROYALTY AT THE CHALLENGE CUP FINAL

Members of the Royal Family have been Guest of Honour at the Rugby League Challenge Cup Final on 16 occasions, all at the former Wembley Stadium. His Majesty King George V, patron of the Rugby Football League since he acceded to the, then, Northern Union's request to accept that position in 1911, was invited to the inaugural 1929 Wembley final. Unable to attend, he sent the following message via his equerry: 'I am commanded to convey to the Rugby Football League the expression of the King's best thanks for the loyal message and greeting to its patron on the occasion of the first cup final in London, and to wish all present at the match an enjoyable afternoon.'

There was also no Royal presence in 1930, the *St Helens Reporter* saying: 'Everyone from Lancashire asked "What's wrong with the Prince of Wales not coming?" It's pure snobbishness by them Rugby Union chaps that stops Royalty from coming.' The King did accept an invitation in 1933 'giving a tremendous boost to the pro-Wembley brigade only four years after moving the final south' but subsequently, the *Warrington Guardian* reported: 'It is learned it is unlikely the King will attend. Although His Majesty has now thrown off the affects of a slight cold from which he has been suffering it is thought advisable he should not go in case of bad weather. The Prince of Wales will represent his father at the match.' The attendance of The Prince of Wales (the future King Edward VIII) was historic, as the first Royal guest at the Challenge Cup Final. He apparently told Huddersfield captain Len Bowkett, whilst presenting him with the cup, that he had 'enjoyed the game tremendously'.

King George V was due to attend in 1934 but before the match Lord Derby (who subsequently presented the cup) announced to the assembled crowd by microphone: 'I have just left His Majesty who has commissioned me on his behalf and on behalf of Her Majesty to say how deeply they regret they are unable to be with us at this match. They had looked forward to doing so, especially after the disappointment of last year, but they found the weather was so unpropitious that it would be inadvisable that His Majesty should come.'

It was in 1948 that King George VI became the first reigning monarch to attend, presenting the trophy to

Her Majesty Queen Elizabeth II presents the Challenge Cup to Wakefield Trinity captain Derek Turner in 1960

Wigan's Joe Egan. It occurred during a three-final sequence (1947 to 1949) when Royalty appeared, Bradford Northern being in all of them. During the 1950s and 1960s, the presence of Royalty became more frequent, although, over the past 22 finals, only The Duke of Edinburgh, in 1995, has attended.

ROYAL PRESENTATIONS

Members of the Royal Family have presented the cup on the following occasions:
- 1933: H.R.H. The Prince of Wales
- 1947: H.R.H. The Duke of Gloucester
- 1948: H.M. King George VI
- 1949: H.R.H. The Duke of Edinburgh
- 1951: H.R.H. The Duke of Gloucester
- 1955: H.R.H. The Duke of Edinburgh
- 1959: H.R.H. The Princess Royal
- 1960: H.M. Queen Elizabeth II
- 1965: H.R.H. Princess Alexandra
- 1967: H.M. Queen Elizabeth II
- 1968: H.R.H. The Duke of Kent
- 1975: H.R.H. Princess Alexandra
- 1980: H.M. Queen Elizabeth, The Queen Mother
- 1986: H.R.H. Princess Alexandra
- 1987: H.R.H. The Duke of Edinburgh
- 1995: H.R.H. The Duke of Edinburgh

(Note: The Earl Mountbatten of Burma presented the cup in 1973. Although not a member of the Royal Family, he was the uncle of The Duke of Edinburgh.)

1967 RUGBY LEAGUE CHALLENGE CUP FINAL
Featherstone Rovers v Barrow

Featherstone Rovers were shock winners of the 1967 Challenge Cup competition. Placed 20th in the League table, they fully merited their first Challenge Cup success having eliminated four of Yorkshire's finest—all 'top eight' teams that season—in Bradford Northern, Wakefield Trinity, Castleford and Leeds. Opponents Barrow were also a surprise package, having finished 15th in the League and reaching Wembley by avoiding the 'big guns', although their third round win at Hull was rated an outstanding achievement.

Confusion arose over the prospective jerseys, both clubs having a predominantly blue kit. Featherstone, reportedly, were instructed by the Rugby Football League to wear blue and white hoops of equal width rather than their traditional blue with narrow white hoops. But, when a publicity photograph of the two Wembley strips, worn by female models, appeared in the *North-Western Evening Mail* eight days before the final, nothing had changed, Featherstone claiming they received no instructions. Barrow, who usually wore blue with a white chevron, quickly ordered an extra kit of white with a blue chevron, subsequently transferring the club badge. The Rugby Football League, possibly influenced by Barrow's initiative, sanctioned the

change on the Wednesday before the match.

Featherstone made a late decision to omit centre John Newlove, favouring winger Vaughan Thomas, possibly to counter the pace of Barrow's Mike Murray, Gary Jordan relocating from wing to centre. The first final under the new limited tackles rule (then set at four and amended to six in 1972), neither team had played for almost a month due to their lack of

Barrow's Mike Sanderson (with ball) succumbs to the tackle of Featherstone Rovers' Jim Thompson (on ground)

involvement in the Championship play-off.

On a perfect sunny day, Tommy Smales began the scoring for Featherstone with a 45-yard 2nd minute penalty, awarded for illegal scrum-feeding by Ged Smith. Barrow had the better of the early exchanges, winning the scrums and preventing Rovers' powerful forwards from dominating play. Their international winger Bill Burgess made an exciting 50-yard run before being tackled, Henry Delooze succeeding with the third of his four penalty shots during this spell, given for obstruction on Tom Brophy. It was Brophy that put the Shipbuilders ahead 7–2, racing around Brian Wrigglesworth, Delooze—who also converted—having made a tremendous break before providing the pass.

The setback triggered an alarm bell for Rovers, and their forwards began pounding Barrow's defence, Ken Greatorex being forced into touch at the left corner. Jim Thompson made a great run and, though tackled, played the ball quickly, acting-halfback Graham Harris

BBC television's David Coleman conducts a post-match interview with Featherstone's Lance Todd Trophy winner Carl Dooler whilst the Rovers' three try scorers—Tom Smales (left), Arnie Morgan (behind Coleman), and Vaughan Thomas—wait their turn

sending heavyweight prop Arnie Morgan charging between the posts. Smales—having just missed a penalty—augmented to tie the scores. Carl Dooler's spectacular 40-yard drop-goal two minutes later inched Featherstone 9–7 ahead, Delooze missing another penalty six minutes from half-time.

Featherstone's pack continued to wear down their opposition after the interval, although Barrow missed a golden opportunity in the 41st minute when Wrigglesworth lost the ball. Ged Smith retrieved it for Barrow in his own half, running 40 yards with an unmarked Murray in support but he seemed unaware of his winger and was overpowered. Smales made a poor drop-goal attempt but, a minute later, Ged Smith—on being tackled by Keith Cotton—made a desperation pass to Murray that went astray, being snapped up by Thomas who raced 30 yards unopposed to go under the posts. Smales added the goal and it was

STATS

Featherstone Rovers 17 Barrow 12

Saturday 13 May at Wembley Stadium, London (3.00 pm)

Featherstone Rovers (blue with narrow white hoops): Wrigglesworth, Thomas, Cotton, Jordan, Greatorex, M. Smith, Dooler, Tonks, Harris, Dixon (captain), Morgan, Thompson, Smales. Substitutes: Hartley (dnp), Kosanovic (dnp). Coach: L. Gant

Barrow (white with royal blue chevron): Tees, Burgess, Challinor (captain), Hughes, Murray, Brophy, G. Smith, Kelland, Redhead, Hopwood, Sanderson, Delooze, Watson. Substitutes: Wear (dnp), Kirchin (dnp). Player-coach: J. Challinor

Referee: E. Clay Touch-judges: J. Senin, R. Welsby

Half-time: 9–7 Attendance: 76,290 Receipts: £53,465

Weather: sunny and warm

Lance Todd Trophy: Dooler (Featherstone Rovers)

Cup presentation: H.M. Queen Elizabeth II

Progressive score:

Featherstone Rovers	score (min)	Barrow
Smales penalty	2–0 (2)	
	2–2 (11)	Delooze penalty
	2–7 (16)	Brophy try, Delooze goal
Morgan try, Smales goal	7–7 (29)	
Dooler drop-goal	9–7 (31)	
Thomas try, Smales goal	14–7 (47)	
Smales try	17–7 (64)	
	17–12 (79)	Watson try, Tees goal

Route to the final:

First round: Bradford Northern 8 Featherstone Rovers 15, Whitehaven 2 Barrow 8

Second round: Featherstone R 11 Wakefield Trinity 7, Barrow 8 Liverpool City 4

Third round: Featherstone Rovers 8 Castleford 7, Hull 5 Barrow 6

Semi-finals: Featherstone Rovers 16 Leeds 8 (Fartown, Huddersfield, 20,052),

Barrow 14 Dewsbury 9 (Station Road, Swinton, 13,744)

Head-to-head form guide:

No previous meetings during season

14–7. It was all Featherstone, Malcolm Dixon (twice) and Dooler failing with drop-goal attempts before, in the 64th minute, the latter broke from a play-the-ball, passing inside for Smales who scored a try he was unable to convert. Late pressure brought Barrow a consolation try, Mike Watson diving over as he was tackled, Eddie Tees tagging on the goal as the match ended, the final score being 17–12.

Graham Morris

1968 RUGBY LEAGUE CHALLENGE CUP FINAL
Leeds v Wakefield Trinity

Remembered as 'The Watersplash Final', the 1968 Challenge Cup decider between Leeds and Wakefield Trinity has become one of the most talked of in the history of the competition. Saturated from the previous day's heavy rain and virtually unplayable due to a torrential downpour one hour before the start, the playing area was completely flooded. Had it not been such an important occasion it would unquestionably have been postponed but, instead, it produced a surreal, although memorable match. One of those memories occurred in the fateful last seconds when Wakefield's

Leeds won 11–10, scoring one try to Wakefield's two, all resulting from the ball being hacked over the try-line. Although the sun broke through just before kick-off, the deluge began again five minutes before half time, the pounding rain being accompanied by thunder, lightning and even hailstone, handling becoming difficult as players slid all over the pitch. Wakefield built up a 7–4 interval lead, claiming the only first half try when Ken Hirst dribbled the ball across the Leeds try-line for the touchdown after the Loiner's winger John Atkinson unwittingly kept the ball infield as he slid out of play attempting to cover Fox's kick

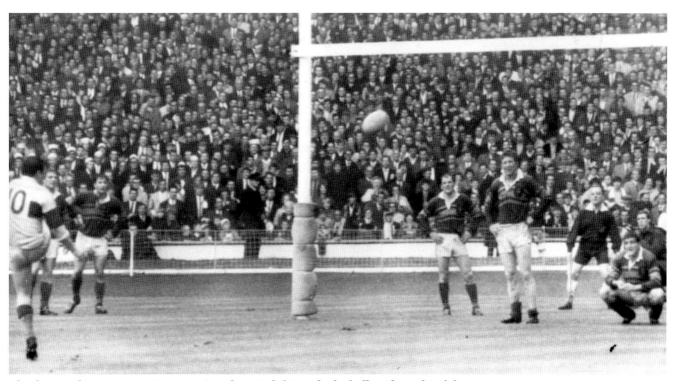

The decisive last minute as Don Fox (number 10, left) sends the ball to the right of the posts

Don Fox missed what would have been the winning conversion from in front of the posts. In one of the most poignant moments in Wembley history, Fox slipped on the treacherous surface, the ball skidding off the mound of mud he had created as a 'tee' to skew wide of the right post. As the Leeds players lined up behind the goal jumped into the air with unexpected jubilation, Fox sank to his knees. It was a tragic situation for a great player whose outstanding performance had already earned him the Lance Todd Trophy.

to the right corner. Fox, deputising as marksman for his brother Neil (the centre being absent due to a groin injury), added a magnificent conversion, 10 yards from the touchline. The other first half scores resulted from three penalties; two by Bev Risman for Leeds (illegal scrum-feeding and obstruction), one from Fox (obstruction). Risman also missed an 11th minute penalty, whilst early drop-goal attempts for Leeds from Barry Seabourne and Atkinson hardly rose above the sodden turf.

No more points accrued until the dramatic last 11

minutes, Leeds turning the game their way to lead 11–7 through a penalty-try for Atkinson awarded after he kicked the ball over the try-line, Gert Coetzer impeding him (a decision Wakefield disputed) in the desperate scramble to make the first touch. Risman converted, subsequently adding a 40-yard penalty with one minute remaining after a high tackle by Harold Poynton on Seabourne. Wakefield's Ray Owen placed the ball on the centre-spot for the restart and was about to kick to his forwards gathered on the left when Fox impulsively ran up and grubber kicked to the more spacious right. Hirst realised what was happening and was first to reach the ball, twice kicking towards the Leeds posts as desperate defenders slid around. The ball settled behind the goal,

Leeds prop Ken Eyre almost disappears from view amidst the spray closely watched by the Wakefield Trinity trio (in lighter jerseys) of Ray Owen (left), Gary Cooper and Gert Coetzer (number 4)

WINNING CAPTAIN

Mick Clark (Leeds 1968)

Michael 'Mick' Clark had a 'stop-start' career before fulfilling his early promise after joining Leeds from Salford for £2,000 in 1963. During his time at Headingley the former back-row forward blossomed into a purposeful pack-leading prop, capable of off-loading the ball to devastating effect in the tackle. Raised in Middleton, south Leeds, he played rugby league at school and soccer during Army National Service in Malaya. On demob, his brother Jack—a Dewsbury winger—suggested he went to Crown Flatt for a trial, subsequently signing and making his debut in the three-quarters in 1958 before graduating to the pack. In 1961, he transferred to Huddersfield, appearing in their 1962 Challenge Cup Final side beaten at Wembley, but losing his place for the following week's unexpected Championship Final win over Wakefield Trinity. After 19 months at Fartown he joined Salford in October 1962, remaining there for 11 months. With Leeds, he won the Rugby League Challenge Cup (1968), Championship (1968/69), Yorkshire Cup (1968) and Yorkshire League (1966/67, 1967/68, 1968/69). His rise to prominence brought him selection for Great Britain (5 times—including the 1968 World Cup in Australia and New Zealand) and Yorkshire (3). He went to Keighley as player-coach in 1969, making his last appearance in 1972.

Hirst diving on it, Wakefield, trailing by one point, requiring that late conversion to win.

The match was a landmark for both clubs; Wakefield effectively drawing the curtain on one of their most glorious periods, Leeds embarking on an unprecedented trophy-laden era.

STATS

Leeds 11 Wakefield Trinity 10

Saturday 11 May at Wembley Stadium, London (3.00 pm)

Leeds (blue with amber bands): Risman, Smith, Hynes, Watson, Atkinson, Shoebottom, Seabourne, Clark (captain), Crosby, K. Eyre, Ramsey, A. Eyre, Batten. Substitutes: Langley (dnp), Hick (dnp). Coach: R. Francis

Wakefield Trinity (white with red and blue band): Cooper, Hirst, Brooke, Coetzer, Batty, Poynton (captain), Owen, Jeanes, Shepherd, D. Fox, Haigh, McLeod, Hawley. Substitutes: Paley (dnp), Round (dnp). Coach: K. Traill

Referee: J.P. Hebblethwaite

Touch-judges: A. Fairbotham, F.J. Howker

Half-time: 4–7   Attendance: 87,100   Receipts: £56,171

Weather: torrential rain and thunderstorms

Lance Todd Trophy: D. Fox (Wakefield Trinity)

Cup presentation: H.R.H. The Duke of Kent

Progressive score:

Leeds	score (min)	Wakefield Trinity
Risman penalty	2–0 (3)	
	2–2 (6)	D. Fox penalty
Risman penalty	4–2 (13)	
	4–7 (15)	Hirst try, D. Fox goal
Atkinson penalty-try, Risman goal	9–7 (69)	
Risman penalty	11–7 (79)	
	11–10 (80)	Hirst try

Route to the final:

First round:
Leeds 23 Liverpool City 12, Barrow 4 Wakefield Trinity 8

Second round:
Leeds 29 Bramley 0, Salford 4 Wakefield Trinity 8

Third round:
Oldham 0 Leeds 13, Wakefield Trinity 18 Castleford 5

Semi-finals:
Leeds 25 Wigan 4 (Station Road, Swinton, 30,058),

Wakefield Trinity 0 Huddersfield 0 (Odsal Stadium, Huddersfield, 21,569)

Semi-final replay: Wakefield Trinity 15 Huddersfield 10 (Headingley, Leeds, 20,983)

Head-to-head form guide:

Leeds 21 Wakefield Trinity 4 (League)

Wakefield Trinity 10 Leeds 5 (League)

Graham Morris

1969 RUGBY LEAGUE CHALLENGE CUP FINAL
Castleford v Salford

It was a long time between drinks for Castleford and Salford, who both graced Wembley in 1969 following an absence of 34 and 30 years, respectively. The composition of the two teams was quite marked; Castleford comprised mostly home-grown talent, halfbacks Alan Hardisty and Keith Hepworth and prop Johnny Ward having played together for the local Ashton Road School, whilst Salford, under entrepreneurial chairman Brian Snape, relied on big money buys, most notably ex-Wales rugby union fly-half David Watkins. But, whilst Salford's new-look line-up was still in the process of gelling, Castleford had already developed into a formidable workmanlike side that feared nobody.

Although both clubs were noted for flair—Castleford being known as 'Classy Cas'—the Challenge Cup Final was a disappointment, the

Salford winger Bill Burgess breaks down the right flank

STATS

Castleford 11 Salford 6

Saturday 17 May at Wembley Stadium, London (3.00 pm)

Castleford (white with black and amber chevron): Edwards, Briggs, Howe, Thomas, Lowndes, Hardisty (captain), Hepworth, Hartley, Dickinson, Ward, Redfearn, Lockwood, Reilly. Substitutes: Harris (dnp), Fox (dnp). Coach: D. Turner

Salford (red): Gwilliam, Burgess, Whitehead, Hesketh, Jackson, Watkins (captain), Brennan, Ogden, Dickens, Bott, Coulman, Dixon, Hill. Substitutes: Prosser (dnp), Smethurst (dnp). Coach: G. Jenkins

Referee: D.S. Brown Touch-judges: T.A. Rynn, J. Shackleton

Half-time: 3–4 Attendance: 97,939 Receipts: £58,848

Weather: sunny with showers

Lance Todd Trophy: Reilly (Castleford)

Cup presentation:
Sir Denis Blundell, High Commissioner for New Zealand

Progressive score:

Castleford	score (min)	Salford
	0–2 (3)	Hill penalty
Howe try	3–2 (32)	
	3–4 (35)	Hill penalty
Hardisty try, Redfearn goal	8–4 (53)	
	8–6 (59)	Hill penalty
Hepworth try	11–6 (76)	

Route to the final:

First round: Hunslet 9 Castleford 19, Salford 17 Batley 2

Second round:
Castleford 12 Wigan 8, Salford 12 Workington Town 5

Third round: Castleford 9 Leeds 5, Salford 20 Widnes 7

Semi-finals:
Castleford 16 Wakefield Trinity 10 (Headingley, Leeds, 21,497), Salford 15 Warrington 8 (Central Park, Wigan, 20,600)

Head-to-head form guide:

No previous meetings during season

153

Yorkshire side justifying their tag of favourites by deservedly winning a forward-dominated encounter 11–6. But it was also an ill tempered affair, particularly in the first half when 15 penalties were awarded, Eddie Waring, who commentated on the match for BBC television, saying in the next day's *Sunday Mirror* that 'had the match been played in the north I feel some players could have got their marching orders.' The first incident occurred in the opening seconds, Salford winger Bill Burgess being floored in an off-the-ball incident whilst the ball sailed through the air from kick-off, although resuming after treatment.

Salford scored first when Ron Hill—signed from Castleford a few months earlier—kicking a 3rd minute penalty awarded for 'stealing' in the tackle, the ball scraping the inside of the post as it went over. Several altercations took place in the early stages and Castleford's Johnny Ward and Salford's Terry Ogden had to be separated by a touch-judge. Hill missed a second penalty in the seventh minute, Salford fluffing a great chance when Stuart Whitehead succumbed to a broken Castleford defence with Burgess and Jackie Brennan unmarked on either side. Further scuffles followed, Mick Redfearn being wide with a 15th minute penalty after a foul by Hill. The misdemeanours continued, a touch-judge running on again when Redfearn fouled Hill, a further stoppage ensuing whilst Brian Lockwood received the 'magic sponge'.

Hill missed a 21st-minute long-range penalty before, 11 minutes later, Hepworth—suffering with double vision from an earlier knock—took possession from a scrum in Salford's 25-yard area, loose forward Malcolm Reilly peeling away from the pack as extra man to take the ball. It travelled to the arms of Hardisty who sent Keith Howe over for a try, breaking free of Chris Hesketh's tackle in the process. Redfearn's kick fell short, Salford retaking the lead moments later through another Hill penalty for 'loose arm' in the scrum. Three minutes before the interval, Hesketh broke through Castleford's defence on the left channel, beating five defenders in a bewildering run before going over the try-line, referee Deryk Brown penalising his effort—on a touch-judge's advice—for a 'double movement'.

At 4–3 to Salford, the closeness of the score kept the atmosphere tense during a less tempestuous second half during which Castleford began to get on top. It was 21-year-old Reilly that altered the course of the match 13 minutes after the break, evading a defender before shrugging off Brennan—almost

throwing him over his shoulder in the process—to go through a gap and resist three more tackles before delivering the scoring pass to Hardisty, who shot under the posts. Redfearn added the goal, Hill reducing Salford's deficit to two points with a penalty, again for 'loose arm' in a scrum. With 12 minutes remaining, Redfearn was wide with a penalty, but the Wheldon Road side were not going to let go and exerted tremendous pressure during the closing stages. Three times they came close to crossing Salford's try-line, Hardisty also failing with a drop-goal attempt before Ward conjured up the killer try, beating three men before sending Hepworth over, Redfearn missing the goal. In the final seconds Salford were awarded a penalty for a scrum offence near the right touchline but Brennan's up-and-under from 30 yards out bounced harmlessly over the dead-ball line, leaving Castleford to claim a well-merited victory, having scored three tries whilst conceding none.

Keith Hepworth scores Castleford's third try with two minutes remaining, Salford's David Watkins being unable to get back in time

1970 RUGBY LEAGUE CHALLENGE CUP FINAL
Castleford v Wigan

Graham Morris

Castleford loose forward Malcolm Reilly (with ball) prepares to resist the challenge of Wigan's Bill Ashurst

Castleford made a quick return to Wembley, retaining the Challenge Cup in 1970 after a low scoring but intriguing forward battle with Wigan. The victors were restricted to one try but kept their own line intact for a second successive year. The *Pontefract & Castleford Express* writer G.F. Potts noted it was 'a better final than last year's but with one incident, alas, which out-blotted last year's rancour', a reference to the 17th minute injury of Wigan full back Colin Tyrer. Whether his resultant absence affected the outcome is impossible to say, post-match opinion being divided, but there is little doubt that the Wigan points-machine—he had scored 17 tries that season and notched his 167th goal in the second minute of the final—was sorely missed by his colleagues.

Tyrer's goal was the result of a penalty that was awarded 40 yards out by referee Fred Lindop, Castleford hooker Clive Dickinson being judged to have fouled Peter Rowe. Alan Hardisty tried to respond for Castleford, but his drop-goal was poor. Moments later, his halfback partner Keith Hepworth charged down a Wigan clearance kick, but was hauled down by Doug Laughton as he chased after the ball

inside Wigan's 25-yard area, Mick Redfearn's subsequent penalty levelling the scores. It looked as though a high-scoring final was unfolding when Alan Lowndes claimed an 11th minute try after Dickinson

WINNING CAPTAIN

Alan Hardisty (Castleford 1969, 1970)

Alan Hardisty—one of the classiest stand-offs of his era—seemed to glide past defenders with ease, scoring a club record 206 tries in 401 Castleford appearances. A product of the local Ashton Road School, his Castleford career spanned 1958 until 1971 during which he notably led them to Rugby League Challenge Cup glory in 1969 and 1970. Other successes included the BBC2 Floodlit Trophy (1965/66, 1966/67, 1967/68) and Yorkshire League (1964/65). His move to Leeds in 1971—where he was joined by former Castleford halfback partner Keith Hepworth—brought a new lease of life, winning the Championship (1971/72), League Leaders' Trophy (1971/72), Players' No.6 Trophy (1972/73) and Yorkshire Cup (1972, 1973). In 1974, he went to Australia as player-coach at Rockhampton in the Queensland League, returning to Britain as coach to Dewsbury (1974–75), York (1980–82) and Halifax (1989). He made 12 Test appearances, represented Yorkshire five times and was a tourist in 1966 and 1970.

155

attempt—added a wondrous 60-yard touchline effort in the closing seconds of the half (Bill Ramsey being ruled offside at a play-the-ball), placing Leigh 13–0 up at the break.

Leeds' John Holmes missed a long-range penalty seven minutes into the second half but was on target two minutes later after Murphy 'stole' the ball from Ramsey during a tackle in front of the posts. Murphy replied with a 40-yard drop-goal, Ferguson's penalty four minutes later (illegal scrum-feeding by Seabourne) extending Leigh's advantage to 17–2, Hynes' exit following four minutes afterwards through the intervention of touch-judge T. Clayton. Substitute Les Chisnall consequently replaced Murphy, who went off on a stretcher. Meanwhile Leigh increased their lead through an awesome 45-yard drop-goal from David Eckersley. Leeds almost got their first try in the 73rd minute, David Hick being bundled into touch at the right corner flag. A minute later—to thunderous Leigh cheering—Murphy emerged from the tunnel, although taking no further part and going to the bench. He was in time to see Eckersley race under the posts for a try after spotting a gap whilst about to attempt another drop, Ferguson converting. Tony Wainwright grabbed a last minute penalty-try for Leeds, Ferguson

having blatantly grabbed him by the shoulders after he had kicked the ball towards the try-line, Holmes adding the extra points to complete the scoring at 24–7.

STATS

Leigh 24 Leeds 7

Saturday 15 May at Wembley Stadium, London (3.00 pm)

Leigh (red and white hoops): Eckersley, Ferguson, Dorrington, Collins, Walsh, Barrow, Murphy (captain), Watts, Ashcroft, Fiddler, Grimes, Clarkson, Smethurst. Substitutes: L. Chisnall, Lester (dnp). Player-coach: A. Murphy

Leeds (blue with amber bands): Holmes, Langley, Hynes (captain), Cowan, Atkinson, Wainwright, Seabourne, Burke, Fisher, Barnard, Hick, Haigh, Ramsey. Substitutes: Dyl, Cookson (dnp). Coach: D. Turner

Referee: W.H. Thompson
Touch-judges: T. Clayton, J. Meadows

Half-time: 13–0 Attendance: 85,514 Receipts: £84,452

Weather: sunny, some cloud

Lance Todd Trophy: A Murphy (Leigh)

Cup presentation:
The Rt Hon. Reginald Maudling MP, Home Secretary

Progressive score:

Leigh	score (min)	Leeds
Fiddler drop-goal	2–0 (5)	
Ferguson penalty	4–0 (11)	
Dorrington try, Ferguson goal	9–0 (26)	
Murphy drop-goal	11–0 (34)	
Ferguson penalty	13–0 (40)	
	13–2 (49)	Holmes penalty
Murphy drop-goal	15–2 (57)	
Ferguson penalty	17–2 (61)	
Eckersley drop-goal	19–2 (69)	
Eckersley try, Ferguson goal	24–2 (76)	
	24–7 (80)	Wainwright penalty-try, Holmes goal

Route to the final:

First round:
Leigh 9 Bradford Northern 2, Leeds 49 Oldham 2

Second round: Widnes 11 Leigh 14, Leeds 4 St Helens 0

Third round: Leigh 8 Hull 4, Bramley 0 Leeds 14

Semi-finals:
Leigh 10 Huddersfield 4 (Central Park, Wigan, 14,875),

Leeds 19 Castleford 8 (Odsal Stadium, Bradford, 24,464)

Head-to-head form guide:

Leigh 36 Leeds 8 (League)

Leeds 28 Leigh 10 (League)

Stan Dorrington scores the opening try off a pass by Alex Murphy (number 7) with Leeds' Ron Cowan (nearest camera) and Bill Ramsey unable to intervene

Graham Morris

1972 RUGBY LEAGUE CHALLENGE CUP FINAL
St Helens v Leeds

For the second consecutive year Leeds entered the Challenge Cup Final as favourites but again suffered the frustration of defeat, St Helens' 16–13 victory being determined through the marksmanship of the opposing kickers. Injury problems also influenced the outcome with Leeds including full back John Holmes despite carrying an ankle injury. It was a calculated risk that backfired after just 26 seconds when St Helens' Graham Rees registered Wembley's quickest score. With Holmes unable to execute the clearance kicks on the completion of what was, then, a four-tackle rule, it was decided Phil Cookson and Terry Clawson would deputise. Leeds had first possession but, after three tackles, both players called to acting-halfback Tony Fisher for the ball. In the confusion, it went loose, Keith Hepworth's hastily taken kick being charged down by Rees who collected the ball and scampered over for a try.

It's mine! St Helens captain and winner of the Lance Todd Trophy Kel Coslett holds the Challenge Cup

STATS

St Helens 16 Leeds 13

Saturday 13 May at Wembley Stadium, London (3.00 pm)

St Helens (white with red chevron): Pimblett, Jones, Benyon, Walsh, Wilson, Kelly, Heaton, Rees, Greenall, Stephens, Mantle, E. Chisnall, Coslett (captain). Substitutes: Whittle (dnp), Earl (dnp). Coach: J. Challinor

Leeds (blue with amber bands): Holmes, A. Smith, Hynes, Dyl, Atkinson, Hardisty (captain), Hepworth, Clawson, Fisher, Ramsey, Cookson, Haigh, Batten. Substitutes: Langley, Ward (dnp). Coach: D. Turner

Referee: E. Lawrinson Touch-judges: L. Hardy, J. Heap

Half-time: 12–6 Attendance: 89,495 Receipts: £86,414

Weather: light drizzle, overcast

Lance Todd Trophy: Coslett (St Helens)

Cup presentation:
The Rt Hon. Walter Annenberg, United States Ambassador

Progressive score:

St Helens	score (min)	Leeds
Rees try, Coslett goal	5–0 (1)	
	5–2 (11)	Clawson penalty
Jones try	8–2 (16)	
Coslett penalty	10–2 (22)	
	10–4 (25)	Clawson penalty
Coslett penalty	12–4 (28)	
	12–6 (40)	Clawson penalty
	12–9 (42)	Cookson try
Coslett penalty	14–9 (47)	
Coslett drop-goal	16–9 (61)	
	16–11 (62)	Clawson penalty
	16–13 (66)	Clawson penalty

Route to the final:

First round: Oldham 6 St Helens 8, Leeds 17 Widnes 8

Second round: St Helens 32 Huddersfield 9, Hull 5 Leeds 16

Third round: York 5 St Helens 32, Leeds 11 Wakefield Trinity 5

Semi-finals:
St Helens 10 Warrington 10 (Central Park, Wigan, 19,300), Leeds 16 Halifax 3 (Odsal Stadium, Bradford, 17,008)

Semi-final replay:
St Helens 10 Warrington 6 (Central Park, Wigan, 32,180)

Head-to-head form guide:

Leeds 20 St Helens 13 (League)

Leeds 0 St Helens 17 (BBC2 Floodlit Trophy)

St Helens 15 Leeds 15 (League)

WINNING CAPTAIN

Kel Coslett (St Helens 1972, 1976)

Kel Coslett joined St Helens as a full back from Aberavon rugby union club in 1962, having represented Wales three times that year. Born in Bynea, South Wales, he proved an accomplished goal-kicker, creating club records for St Helens of 214 goals and 452 points in a season (1971/72) and 1,639 goals and 3,413 points in a career. His last match for Saints was in 1976 after establishing another club record with 531 appearances. In 1967, his career reached new heights when moved to loose forward, being ideally built at six feet tall and over 14 stone. In the pack his timing of a pass was put to good use, his ability to read a game leading to him taking over as captain in 1971. At St Helens he won the Rugby League Challenge Cup (1972, 1976), Championship (1965/66—missing the final through injury, 1969/70, 1970/71, 1974/75), Premiership Trophy (1976), League Leaders' Trophy (1964/65, 1965/66), Western Division Championship (1963/64), Lancashire Cup (1962, 1963, 1967, 1968), Lancashire League (1964/65, 1965/66, 1966/67, 1968/69) and BBC2 Floodlit Trophy ((1971, 1975). In rugby league, he played for Wales (12 times, including the 1975 World Cup) and Other Nationalities (once—at county level). He became Rochdale Hornets player-coach (1976–79), later coaching Wigan (1979–80), St Helens (1980–82) and Wales (1977–82).

St Helens, who themselves were missing hooker Tony Karalius (knee injury) and second-rower Eric Prescott (shoulder)—casualties of the previous week's Championship semi-final win at Bradford Northern—added a second touchdown in the 16th minute when Jeff Heaton's break enabled John Mantle and Eric Chisnall to put Les Jones in at the corner, the score building towards a 12–6 interval lead. Just 70 seconds into the second half, Leeds scored their only try, Fisher sending Ray Batten clear, the latter's short pass despatching Cookson under the posts. Crucially, Clawson's conversion attempt never rose above ground, one of four goal chances he missed during the match (three in front of the posts). Nonetheless, he kept Leeds in contention by landing five of his eight penalty attempts. His first three successes (awarded, respectively, for Kel Coslett drop-kicking the ball out on the full from a 25-yard restart, Les Greenall having 'feet up' in a scrum, and offside at a play-the-ball) provided Leeds' only first half points, whilst the latter two (both for interference at the play-the-ball) pulled Leeds to within three points at 16–13, ensuring a tense finale when a try could have settled the issue either way.

Coslett, meanwhile, notched four from six place goal attempts (he missed a conversion and 71st minute penalty), including three penalties (given, in sequence, for a foul on Rees during a tackle inside St Helens' half, a Hepworth foul on Ken Kelly, and an illegal scrum-feed). He also hit the target with a 'towering' 35-yard drop-goal, two other 'drop' efforts during the match—from Leeds' Alan Hardisty (46th minute) and Billy Benyon (74th—which struck the back of a Leeds player)—failing.

St Helens coach Jim Challinor later admitted: 'It was a vital moment when Clawson missed the conversion. With one point in it the pressure would have been on.' Clawson, obviously distraught, said: 'They won't say it, but I'm responsible for us losing.' But in rugby league, like any other sport, you are as good as your last match, and his moment of triumph came the following week when his immaculate kicking in the Championship Final win over St Helens earned him the Harry Sunderland Trophy.

The corner flag has been dislodged but not before Les Jones had gained St Helens' second touchdown at the expense of Leeds winger John Atkinson

Graham Morris

1973 RUGBY LEAGUE CHALLENGE CUP FINAL
Featherstone Rovers v Bradford Northern

Featherstone Rovers centre Mick Smith escapes the Bradford Northern defenders

Bradford Northern appeared at Wembley for the first time since their historic trio of late-1940s finals, but 1973 was not a happy return, Featherstone Rovers hitting them with a 17-point blitz in the opening 20 minutes. It paved the way to a comprehensive 33–14

WINNING CAPTAIN

John Newlove (Featherstone Rovers 1973)

John Newlove originated from Pontefract, joining Featherstone Rovers from the Ackworth amateur club in 1966. A quick, skilful centre, he later switched to stand-off where his tactical awareness came to the fore. With Featherstone he won the Rugby League Challenge Cup (1973) and Championship (1976/77—missing the latter half of the season through injury). After 381 appearances (147 tries) he transferred to Hull in 1978, winning the Second Division Championship (1978/79) and BBC2 Floodlit Trophy (1979/80), his last match being in 1981. A Yorkshire representative (3 times), he had three rugby league-playing sons, most notably Paul, who made 20 Test appearances.

victory, the early damage being inflicted by Rovers' forwards, Bradford's pack being completely overwhelmed in that opening quarter.

Cyril Kellett opened the scoring for Featherstone on two minutes with a penalty (for incorrect play-the-ball), Eddie Tees missing one at the opposite end in the sixth minute before Featherstone ran in three tries in just over 10 minutes. They fell to skipper John Newlove (racing over untouched after Alan Rhodes turned the ball inside following a powerful forward charge), Vince Farrar (roaring past three defenders after Les Tonks provided the pass having busted two tackles following a Rhodes break) and Newlove again (sent under the posts by hooker Keith Bridges). With Cyril Kellett augmenting all three it was the quickest opening 17 points in Wembley history. Bradford decided a change was necessary, prop Kel Earl being superseded by Arnie Long. The swap appeared to steady Northern's rocking boat, three penalty goals from Tees (for an 'infringement' on Bradford's Barry Seabourne, followed by two for scrum offences) clocking up a more respectable 17–6 score by half-time.

Bradford produced a grittier performance in the

Vince Farrar claims Featherstone Rovers' second touchdown

STATS

Featherstone Rovers 33 Bradford Northern 14

Saturday 12 May at Wembley Stadium, London (3.00 pm)

Featherstone Rovers (blue with narrow white hoops): C. Kellett, Coventry, Smith, Newlove (captain), K. Kellett, Mason, Nash, Tonks, Bridges, Farrar, Rhodes, Thompson, Stone. Substitutes: Hartley, Hollis. Coach: P. Fox

Bradford Northern (white with red, amber and black band): Tees (captain), Lamb, Stockwell, Watson, Redfearn, Blacker, Seasbourne, Hogan, Dunn, Earl, Joyce, Pattinson, Fearnley. Substitutes: Treasure, Long. Coach: I. Brooke

Referee: M.J. Naughton Touch-judges: B. Baker, K. Ashall

Half-time: 17–6 Attendance: 72,395 Receipts: £125,826

Weather: sunny and warm

Lance Todd Trophy: Nash (Featherstone Rovers)

Cup presentation: The Earl Mountbatten of Burma

Progressive score:

Featherstone Rovers	score (min)	Bradford Northern
C. Kellett penalty	2–0 (2)	
Newlove try, C. Kellett goal	7–0 (9)	
Farrar try, C. Kellett goal	12–0 (13)	
Newlove try, C. Kellett goal	17–0 (20)	
	17–2 (28)	Tees penalty
	17–4 (31)	Tees penalty
	17–6 (39)	Tees penalty
C. Kellett penalty	19–6 (49)	
	19–9 (58)	Redfearn try
Smith try, C. Kellett goal	24–9 (63)	
	24–14 (67)	Fearnley try, Tees goal
Nash drop-goal	26–14 (70)	
Hartley try, C. Kellett goal	31–14 (78)	
C. Kellett penalty	33–14 (79)	

Route to the final:

First round: Featherstone Rovers 18 Salford 11, Bradford Northern 17 Whitehaven 4

Second round: Featherstone R 30 Rochdale Hornets 19, Bradford N 13 Hull KR 8

Third round: Warrington 14 Featherstone Rovers 18, Bradford Northern 11 Wigan 7

Semi-finals: Featherstone Rovers 17 Castleford 3 (Headingley, Leeds, 15,369),

Bradford Northern 23 Dewsbury 7 (Headingley, Leeds, 14,028)

Head-to-head form guide:

Featherstone Rovers 20 Bradford Northern 15 (League)

Bradford Northern 14 Featherstone Rovers 26 (League)

second spell and, after Cyril Kellett bagged another penalty (following a punch by a Northern forward in a scrum), they managed their first try when David Redfearn finished off an excellent bout of passing to cross in the corner. Tees—who had failed with a 47th minute penalty—missed the difficult conversion, Featherstone leading 19–9. Five minutes later the Rovers conjured up the game's best try, Rhodes creating the opening for stand-off Mel Mason to send Mick Smith on a dazzling sidestepping run to finish beneath the posts, Cyril Kellett adding the goal. But Bradford were handling the pressure better and, when their centre Bernard Watson was held up over the Rovers try-line, he managed to slip the ball out to Stan Fearnley who dived over. Tees' goal brought up a 24–14 score-line. The remaining points, though, went Featherstone's way as they underlined their superiority, scrum half Steve Nash landing a neat drop-goal, David Hartley claiming their fifth try when, tackled short, he quickly played the ball forward to himself before diving over. Cyril Kellett converted, adding a 40-yard penalty (Barry Hollis being fouled in a tackle) to conclude the scoring. The 34-year-old veteran's eight goals from eight attempts created a new Challenge Cup Final record, surpassing the seven of Frank Young (1910) and Neil Fox (1960).

1974 RUGBY LEAGUE CHALLENGE CUP FINAL
Warrington v Featherstone Rovers

Warrington returned to Wembley in triumph in 1974 after a 20-year absence, defeating holders Featherstone Rovers 24–9 in a match that, whilst lacking entertaining rugby, was packed with incident. In the opening minutes, Warrington's Alex Murphy was penalised for a high tackle on David Hartley, Harold Box kicking the resultant goal, an episode that set the tone for the first half as penalties dominated proceedings. Warrington built an 8–4 lead—via four Derek Whitehead penalty goals (Box fouling Murphy, Billy Harris foul tackle on David Wright, Steve Nash offside, and Jim Thompson interference at a play-the-ball) to Box's two (his second being for Barry Philbin's foul in a tackle)—before the first try was awarded six

minutes from the interval. It went to Featherstone, executed from a set move following a tap-penalty, Nash passing the ball to Thompson who sent John Newlove racing through three defenders to cross the try-line near the posts. Box converted making it 9–8 for the Rovers. It rewarded a spell of pressure from Featherstone after Warrington had dominated the opening 30 minutes, the power shift occurring, in part, through the influential Murphy's absence, having departed with a rib injury after twice receiving on-field attention from the trainer.

After the break, Warrington responded with 16 unanswered points despite emerging from the changing rooms minus scrum half Parry Gordon, who had a hip injury. Murphy, having had several pain-killing injections, re-entered the arena in his place. He made an impact within three minutes, his incisive 20-yard break catapulting Derek Noonan downfield, the centre sending Kevin Ashcroft diving over for a try. Whitehead appended the goal before contributing two

WINNING CAPTAIN

Alex Murphy (St Helens 1966, Leigh 1971, Warrington 1974)

Generally regarded as Britain's greatest post-Second World War scrum half, Alex Murphy was a typical cocky halfback, but one that possessed every quality; quick acceleration, superbly timed passes, and a brilliant kicking game. Born at Thatto Heath and a product of St Austin's School, he signed with St Helens aged 16 in 1955. With Saints he won the Rugby League Challenge Cup (1961, 1966), Championship (1958/59, 1965/66), League Leaders' Trophy (1964/65, 1965/66), Western Division Championship (1963/64), Lancashire Cup (1960, 1961, 1963, 1964, missing their 1962 win through injury) and Lancashire League (1959/60, 1964/65, 1965/66). A Great Britain tourist (1958, 1962) and World Cup squad member (1960), he represented Britain in 27 Tests, England (twice) and Lancashire (14 times). Taking over as Leigh coach in 1966, it was 1967 before St Helens agreed his £5,500 transfer as a player. He led Leigh to victory in the Rugby League Challenge Cup (1971), BBC2 Floodlit Trophy (1969) and Lancashire Cup (1970). He moved to Warrington in 1971 as player-coach, winning the League Leaders' Trophy (1972/73), followed by four trophies in 1973/74; the Rugby League Challenge Cup, Club Championship, Players' No.6 Trophy, and Captain Morgan Trophy, although not appearing in the finals of the latter two. He stopped playing in 1975, continuing as Warrington coach until 1978, followed by further appointments at Salford (1978–80), Leigh (1980–82, 1985, 1990–91), Wigan (1982–84), St Helens (1985–90), and Huddersfield (1991–94). He also coached England (1975—including that year's World Cup) and Lancashire (1973–78, 1985–88). He was awarded the OBE in 1999, and inducted into the Rugby League Hall of Fame in 1988.

Warrington full back Derek Whitehead contributed eight goals in a man-of-the-match performance

All eyes are trained on referee Sam Shepherd (off camera) who subsequently confirmed John Newlove's try for Featherstone Rovers

further penalties (following a scrum altercation, and an offside at a play-the-ball) as the Wires jumped into a 17–9 lead. Warrington were unstoppable during the final quarter, Murphy adding two drop-goals (he attempted four during the half) and Mike Nicholas (whose subsequent knee injury cost him his upcoming Great Britain tour place) roaring past four defenders for another try after receiving the ball from acting-halfback Ashcroft. The second half contained further unsavoury moments, one flare-up, involving several players, leaving Featherstone's Keith Bridges prostrate on the ground. Helped off, he later returned but collapsed with concussion and had to be carried from the pitch.

One of the afternoon's highlights was Whitehead's immaculate kicking which produced seven goals (his third successful penalty being from the centre spot), missing three others (the conversion of Nicholas' try plus 7th and 50th minute penalties). The match was another personal achievement for Warrington player-coach Murphy—who joined the club within days of leading Leigh to their 1971 Wembley success—becoming the first to captain three different clubs to Wembley victory (St Helens, Leigh and Warrington).

Featherstone had sprung a selection surprise by starting with Alan Rhodes, the second-rower having just returned from injury, whilst halfback Mel Mason—expected to at least get a bench spot—was omitted from the 15.

STATS

Warrington 24 Featherstone Rovers 9

Saturday 11 May at Wembley Stadium, London (3.00 pm)

Warrington (white with primrose and blue chevrons): Whitehead, M. Philbin, Noonan, Whittle, Bevan, Murphy (captain), Gordon, Chisnall, Ashcroft, Brady, Wright, Nicholas, B. Philbin. Substitutes: Pickup, Wanbon. Player-coach: A. Murphy

Featherstone Rovers (blue with narrow white hoops): Box, Dyas, Smith, Hartley, Bray, Newlove (captain), Nash, Tonks, Bridges, Harris, Rhodes, Thompson, Bell. Substitutes: Busfield, Stone. Coach: P. Fox

Referee: S. Shepherd Touch-judges: E. Leach, G. Priestley

Half-time: 8–9 Attendance: 77,400 Receipts: £132,021

Weather: fine and windy

Lance Todd Trophy: Whitehead (Warrington)

Cup presentation:
Hon. John Armstrong, High Commissioner for Australia

Progressive score:

Warrington	score (min)	Featherstone Rovers
	0–2 (3)	Box penalty
Whitehead penalty	2–2 (10)	
Whitehead penalty	4–2 (13)	
	4–4 (15)	Box penalty
Whitehead penalty	6–4 (19)	
Whitehead penalty	8–4 (22)	
	8–9 (34)	Newlove try, Box goal
Ashcroft try, Whitehead goal	13–9 (43)	
Whitehead penalty	15–9 (47)	
Whitehead penalty	17–9 (56)	
Murphy drop-goal	19–9 (59)	
Murphy drop-goal	21–9 (72)	
Nicholas try	24–9 (74)	

Route to the final:

First round: Warrington 34 Huddersfield 4, Barrow 3 Featherstone Rovers 11

Second round: Warrington 21 Huyton 6, Hull Kingston Rovers 9 Featherstone R 12

Third round: Wigan 6 Warrington 10, Bradford Northern 0 Featherstone Rovers 5

Semi-finals:
Warrington 17 Dewsbury 7 (Central Park, Wigan, 11,789), Featherstone Rovers 21 Leigh 14 (Headingley, Leeds, 7,971)

Head-to-head form guide:

Featherstone Rovers 18 Warrington 8 (League)

Warrington 4 Featherstone Rovers 0 (Captain Morgan Trophy Final at The Willows, Salford)

Warrington 9 Featherstone Rovers 7 (League)

SCHOOLS CURTAIN RAISER

Schoolboy Under-11s

In 1975 the modern tradition of playing school age curtain raisers to the Challenge Cup Final began at Wembley, with school authorities asked to select schoolboy under-11s teams to represent their towns and communities. Joe Lydon and David Hulme took part in the inaugural match, for Wigan and Widnes, respectively, the first of many players who subsequently returned to appear in a Challenge Cup Final itself. From 1988 it was called The Steve Mullaney Memorial Match in memory of the youngster who scored a try for Wakefield in the 1986 game, but sadly died in a road accident in 1987. (The present day curtain raiser—the Champion Schools' Final for Year 7 boys—still bears his name.) In 1993 the occasion was referred to as a School, rather than Schoolboy curtain raiser, with Rochdale's Sophie Cox being the first girl to take part.

Schools Little League

From 1995 the Under-11s schools matches gave way to the 'Little League' Mod-League rules that required 11 players-a-side on a reduced sized playing area. As well as boys, this form of rugby encouraged the involvement of girls, several taking part. The Challenge Cup centenary was celebrated in 1997 through the Batley & Dewsbury team meeting St Helens, both wearing kits based on the colours worn by the Batley and St Helens clubs 100 years earlier. Unfortunately a bomb scare (a suspect package was discovered in the stadium at midday but later declared safe) put proceedings behind schedule, resulting in the match being reduced from 24 minutes to 14.

Champion Schools' Year 7 Final

The Champion Schools tournament for boys began in 2003, held at Year 7 (under–12s) to Year 11 (under–16s) level. From 2004 a similar series for girls was launched. All the finals take place over the Challenge Cup Final weekend at various venues with the boys Year 7 Final played as a curtain raiser to the Rugby League Challenge Cup Final.

EARLY CURTAIN RAISER

A junior 'appetizer' took place before the Challenge Cup Final at Headingley in 1906 with the final of the Leeds and District Intermediate Competition between Wellington Clarence and Burley Lawn Old Boys. In 1930 St Helens and Swinton schoolboys were due to meet in the Lancashire schools final and the Rugby Football League was asked to consider it as a Wembley curtain raiser. It was argued that it could encourage London schools to take up the sport, but the idea was not adopted.

RESULTS

Under-11s:
1975: Widnes 8 Wigan 0
1976: Hull 5 Leeds 5
1977: Old 10 Hull 5
1978: Leigh 10 York 5
1979: St Helens 15 Wakefield 5
1980: Hunslet 5 Warrington 5
1981: Castleford 13 Salford 0
1982: Wigan 30 Morley 5
1983: Widnes 13 Dewsbury & Batley 1
1984: Hull 5 Oldham 5
1985: Leigh 12 Huddersfield 0
1986: Wakefield 17 St Helens 0
1987: Leeds 10 Warrington 0
1988: West Cumbria 6 York 6
1989: Wigan 6 Castleford 0
1990: Widnes 36 Doncaster 0
1991: Halifax 22 Runcorn 0
1992: Oldham 22 Dewsbury & Batley 6
1993: Rochdale 12 Sheffield 6
1994: Leigh 26 Hunslet & Morley 0

Little League:
1995: Warrington 30 Bradford 6

1996: Leeds 18 West Cumbria 6
1997: Batley & Dewsbury 6 St Helens 6
1998: Hull 18 Salford 0
1999: Gateshead 28 Dublin 20
2000: Scarborough 32 Glasgow 0
2001: London 32 Thames Valley 20
2002: Edinburgh 28 Glasgow 4

Champion Schools Year 7 Final:
2003: St Augustines (St Helens) 20 St Peters (Wigan) 4
2004: Wade Deacon (Widnes) 32 Whitchurch High (Cardiff) 10
2005: Brynteg (Bridgend) 40 Castleford High 4
2006: Wade Deacon (Halton) 20 Abraham Guest (Wigan & Leigh) 4
2007: Normanton Freeston 12 Castleford High 10
2008: Standish High (Wigan) 58 Pickering High (Hull) 8
2009: Outwood Grange College (Wakefield) 22 Castleford High 12

1975 RUGBY LEAGUE CHALLENGE CUP FINAL
Widnes v Warrington

John Bevan scores for Warrington after just five minutes' play

Widnes took possession of the Challenge Cup in 1975 to begin a period of unprecedented success for the club during which they appeared at Wembley seven times in 10 seasons, earning the title 'Cup Kings'. They began their domination through defeating holders and derby rivals Warrington 14–7 in what was, due to boundary changes introduced in 1974, the first 'all-Cheshire' final. It was also the first time a player flew from Australia especially for the occasion, Widnes retrieving Canterbury-Bankstown winger Chris Anderson, scorer of 18 tries in 18 matches during a loan spell earlier that season. It began a trend whereby clubs sought permission of a player's Australian club—which they had usually rejoined around February—for their temporary re-release.

Warrington struck in the fifth minute, John Bevan—who registered a 'hat-trick' of tries in the semi-final win over Leeds—diving over between Keith Elwell and Mick George near the posts. The move began with a Kevin Ashcroft grubber-kick, the ball hitting Elwell on the shin, Warrington's David Chisnall getting a boot to it, causing it to bounce erratically before Bevan pounced. Derek Whitehead augmented. But, after Ray Dutton—having missed in the third and

WINNING CAPTAIN

Doug Laughton (Widnes 1975)

Widnes-born Doug Laughton—a skilful, ball-playing loose forward who possessed the ability to lead from the front—achieved a lot in rugby league. He began his professional career in 1962, signing for St Helens from the Lowerhouse (Widnes) amateur club and winning the Championship (1965/66), League Leaders' Trophy (1964/65, 1965/66), Western Division Championship (1963/64), Lancashire Cup (1964) and Lancashire League (1964/65, 1965/66). After transferring to Wigan for £6,000 in 1967, he added further medals for the League Leaders' Trophy (1970/71), Lancashire Cup (1971), Lancashire League (1969/70) and BBC2 Floodlit Trophy (1968). He returned to his roots in 1973, joining Widnes for another £6,000 transfer fee, enjoying further success through winning the Rugby League Challenge Cup (1975, 1979), Championship (1977/78), Lancashire Cup (1974, 1976 and 1978) and BBC2 Floodlit Trophy (1978). He became Widnes player-coach in 1978, continuing at the helm until 1983, although playing his last match in 1979. He had two more spells as Widnes coach (1986–91, 1995–97) and was in charge at Leeds (1991–1995). He was a tourist twice (1970, 1979—captain on the latter) and thought to be a potential captain of the 1974 tour before deciding to temporarily join Australian club Canterbury-Bankstown. He represented Great Britain (15 times—including the 1970 World Cup), England (2) and Lancashire (11).

Room to spare for Widnes prop Jim Mills as he places the ball for his team's only try

14th minutes—succeeded with his third penalty attempt (Alan Whittle offside), Widnes got on top, looking quicker and more enthusiastic. Eric Hughes almost scored, eluding three defenders in a brilliant touchline run before Whitehead got across to push him into the corner flag, referee Peter Geraghty consulting a touch-judge before ruling no try. Dutton added another penalty (Mick Adams, having kicked over Whitehead's head and catching it on the bounce, being tripped by the full back).

Widnes' Mal Aspey and John Foran were both held short of the try-line before, at the other end, Whitehead cross-kicked for Bevan to give chase, the winger just being beaten to the ball by George who ran 40 yards to cover the danger. The Chemics got the next touchdown after Aspey broke three tackles before being held by a desperate defence, the ball then shooting across to the right flank, Hughes penetrating a huge gap to allow prop Jim Mills to outflank a stretched defence and score. Dutton converted, adding an easy penalty at the end of the half (Parry Gordon penalised for illegal scrum-feeding), Widnes leaving the field 11–5 ahead.

Three minutes into the second-half Widnes' Reg Bowden was judged guilty of incorrectly feeding the scrum, his protest costing another 10 yards, Whitehead duly obliging with a 45-yard goal. Seven minutes later, Dutton landed a 30-yard drop-goal, Wembley's first under the new one-point value. Shortly afterwards he added a penalty from close range—his sixth goal of the match—on a touch-judge's intervention (for a Chisnall high tackle on Adams in front of the posts). Seven minutes later Bevan recovered the ball in his own half

when a Widnes move faltered, racing through a gap before being hauled down from behind near the Chemics' 25-yard area. In the 68th minute Dutton attempted another drop-goal but, under pressure, missed, there being no further score.

The final was the 'swan-song' for Widnes coach Vince Karalius who decided to step down after over three years in charge to concentrate on his business, his announcement being made a few hours after the match ended.

STATS

Widnes 14 Warrington 7

Saturday 10 May at Wembley-Stadium, London (3.00 pm)

Widnes (white): Dutton, Prescott, George, Aspey, Anderson, Hughes, Bowden, Mills, Elwell, Sheridan, Foran, Adams, Laughton (captain). Substitutes: J. O'Neill (dnp), Nelson (dnp). Coach: V. Karalius

Warrington (blue with primrose collar): Whitehead, M. Philbin, Noonan, Reynolds, Bevan, Whittle, Gordon, Chisnall (captain), Ashcroft, Wanbon, Conroy, Martyn, B. Philbin. Substitutes: Briggs, Nicholas. Coach: A. Murphy

Referee: P. Geraghty Touch-judges: R. Appleyard, E. Lea

Half-time: 11–5 Attendance: 85,098 Receipts: £140,684

Weather: sunny and cloudy

Lance Todd Trophy: Dutton (Widnes)

Cup presentation: H.R.H. The Princess Alexandra

Progressive score:

Widnes	score (min)	Warrington
	0–5 (5)	Bevan try, Whitehead goal
Dutton penalty	2–5 (17)	
Dutton penalty	4–5 (25)	
Mills try, Dutton goal	9–5 (31)	
Dutton penalty	11–5 (40)	
	11–7 (43)	Whitehead penalty
Dutton drop-goal	12–7 (50)	
Dutton penalty	14–7 (53)	

Route to the final:

First round: Swinton 4 Widnes 13, Warrington 32 Halifax 6

Second round: Hull 12 Widnes 13, Wigan 17 Warrington 24

Third round: Oldham 4 Widnes 10, New Hunslet 3 Warrington 23

Semi-finals:

Widnes 13 Wakefield Trinity 7 (Odsal Stadium, Bradford, 9,155),

Warrington 11 Leeds 4 (Central Park, Wigan, 13,168)

Head-to-head form guide:

Warrington 8 Widnes 8 (League)

Widnes 7 Warrington 11 (League)

1976 RUGBY LEAGUE CHALLENGE CUP FINAL
St Helens v Widnes

On a sweltering hot sunny day, St Helens upset the odds with a sensational late scoring burst to defeat favourites Widnes 20–5 in the 1976 Challenge Cup Final, claiming three tries in the last 13 minutes. It was an unexpected climax, given that St Helens—dubbed 'Dad's Army' after the popular television comedy series of the time—paraded six players over 30 years old (including a front-row with a combined age of 99) and were not expected to last the distance against their younger opposition in the extreme 100 degree heat inside the stadium.

With 15 minutes to go and clinging to a 6–5 lead, St Helens received a setback when Billy Benyon—who had shown outstanding form—had to retire with a bad cut to his head, to be replaced by Peter Glynn. But it was the Saints that seized the initiative; Kel Coslett

having a touchdown ruled out for not grounding properly, winger Roy Mathias being stopped in the corner. It was left to Geoff Pimblett to commence the scoring spree in the 67th minute with his second drop-goal of the match. From the restart, Pimblett was again to the fore, taking possession and racing downfield before being tackled by Ray Dutton. But his quick play-the-ball allowed Derek Noonan to draw the defence before transferring to Tony Karalius, whose masterful inside pass got Jeff Heaton over the try-line by the posts. Pimblett added the goal. Six minutes later Les Jones covered 80 yards in an exciting break down the right flank (being tackled by David Jenkins on the way but quickly playing the ball to himself before continuing his run) eventually being halted on the try-line by Dennis O'Neill. With Widnes' defence in

A shirt sleeved crowd look on as St Helens hooker Tony Karalius prepares to release the ball with Widnes' John Foran (number 12) barring his way

Jeff Heaton's try with 12 minutes to go opened the floodgates for St Helens

Mantle said afterwards: 'We are like marathon runners. We may be the wrong side of 30 but we kept going.' It was the third consecutive time that the previous year's Challenge Cup winners had failed to defend their trophy at Wembley, Widnes following the footsteps of Featherstone Rovers and Warrington. Widnes coach Frank Myler had delayed his selection until the last moment to allow Mal Aspey time to recover from a heel injury, but it was in vain, the centre having to pull out.

disarray, it set up the position for Pimblett and Karalius to get Glynn in for what was, in effect, the winning score, Pimblett's conversion placing Saints 17–5 ahead. Mathias then had a try in the corner disallowed for a forward pass before Glynn—who earned the title 'super-sub' for his late contribution—completed the scoring, kicking the ball over the defence and re-gathering to cross the whitewash despite O'Neill's tackle. Pimblett was unable to add the extra points.

St Helens had controlled the majority of the first half play and, after Dutton had missed a long-distance penalty for Widnes, struck the first blow when an excellent passing move sent Benyon racing through a gap. The stand-off provided a short pass for Eddie Cunningham who ran over for a try near the posts, Pimblett kicking the goal. Minutes later Dutton pulled off a try-saving tackle on Benyon, who had been put through by David Hull. Dutton then pulled two points back for Widnes, his penalty following a foul by St Helens prop John Mantle on Reg Bowden. Widnes tried desperately to get into Saints' in-goal area, Doug Laughton and Alan Prescott both getting close whilst, at the other end, Dutton was called upon to do another piece of last-ditch defending, this time on Mathias. Pimblett increased Saints lead to 6–2 with his first drop-goal in the 34th minute, Dutton adding a second goal just before half-time after Heaton was penalised for illegal scrum-feeding. Ten minutes into the second half, Keith Elwell's drop-goal reduced the St Helens lead to just 6–5, but the Saints confounded predictions that they were about to wilt in the afternoon sun.

STATS

St Helens 20 Widnes 5

Saturday 8 May at Wembley Stadium, London (3.00 pm)

St Helens (white with red chevron): Pimblett, Jones, Cunningham, Noonan, Mathias, Benyon, Heaton, Mantle, Karalius, Coslett (captain), Nicholls, E. Chisnall, Hull. Substitutes: Glynn, James. Coach: E. Ashton

Widnes (white with black stripes on sleeves): Dutton, Prescott, Hughes, George, Jenkins, Eckersley, Bowden (captain), Nelson, Elwell, Wood, Adams, Foran, Laughton. Substitutes: D. O'Neill, Sheridan. Coach: F. Myler

Referee: R. Moore Touch-judges: J. Brierley, R.J. Percival

Half-time: 6–4 Attendance: 89,982 Receipts: £190,129

Weather: sunny and hot

Lance Todd Trophy: Pimblett (St Helens)

Cup presentation: The Rt Hon. Mrs Margaret Thatcher MP

Progressive score:

St Helens	score (min)	Widnes
Cunningham try, Pimblett goal	5–0 (12)	
	5–2 (22)	Dutton penalty
Pimblett drop-goal	6–2 (34)	
	6–4 (40)	Dutton penalty
	6–5 (50)	Elwell drop-goal
Pimblett drop-goal	7–5 (67)	
Heaton try, Pimblett goal	12–5 (68)	
Glynn try, Pimblett goal	17–5 (74)	
Glynn try	20–5 (78)	

Route to the final:

First round: Hull 3 St Helens 5, Widnes 26 Batley 4

Second round: Salford 11 St Helens 17, Widnes 7 Wigan 5

Third round: St Helens 17 Oldham 9, Warrington 0 Widnes 6

Semi-finals:
St Helens 5 Keighley 4 (Fartown, Huddersfield, 9,829),
Widnes 15 Featherstone Rovers 9 (Station Road, Swinton, 13,019)

Head-to-head form guide:

St Helens 12 Widnes 4 (League)

Widnes 23 St Helens 7 (League)

1977 RUGBY LEAGUE CHALLENGE CUP FINAL
Leeds v Widnes

The Les Dyl try that put Leeds in front for the first time

Leeds captured the Rugby League Challenge Cup in 1977 after a nine-year wait, providing the perfect response to detractors who had written them off after sliding from their exalted position of the past decade. In the midst of a team-rebuilding programme, it was two of the Yorkshire side's emerging talents that stole the show in the 16–7 win over Widnes; 19-year-old scrum half Kevin Dick, and prop Steve Pitchford. Dick—appearing in his first ever Challenge Cup tie following the tragic death of Chris Sanderson during a match at Salford two weeks earlier—was a thorn in the side of Widnes, displaying an array of skills in scoring 10 of his team's points. Pitchford, meanwhile, appeared to take on Widnes' pack on his own during the second half, bulldozing his way through the opposition as he helped turn the match in Leeds' favour.

Having changed ends 7–5 behind, Leeds took control in the second period, aided by an unfortunate and accidental intervention from referee Vince Moss in the 53rd minute. After taking a tap restart on his own 25-yard line, Widnes scrum half and captain Reg Bowden hit the official—who was stood at his side—

with the ball when he attempted a pass. As per the rules, the referee awarded a scrum, Leeds winning the resultant possession, Les Dyl going over like a bullet to

WINNING CAPTAIN

David Ward (Leeds 1977, 1978)

David Ward was born in Morley, signing for Leeds from Shaw Cross Boys' Club of Dewsbury during 1971. He was a workman-like, skilful hooker, just 23 years old when he led Leeds to Wembley success in 1977, being the inaugural recipient of the prestigious Man of Steel Award the same year. His list of successes with the Headingley club include the Rugby League Challenge Cup (1977, 1978), Premiership Trophy (1975, 1979), Championship (1971/72), League Leaders' Trophy (1971/72), Players' No.6 Trophy (1973), John Player Trophy (1984) and Yorkshire Cup (1972, 1973, 1976, 1979 and 1980). He represented Great Britain in 12 Tests (he was in the 1977 World Cup squad and 1979 tour party), and appeared for England and Yorkshire six times each. Concluding his playing career in 1986, he coached Hunslet (1986–88), Leeds (1989–91), Batley (1991–94, 1997–2000, 2001) and Featherstone Rovers (1994–97). His son Danny (a prop) has played for several Super League clubs over the last decade.

put his side 8–7 up. From that moment, the Headingley outfit, inspired by Pitchford's irresistible surges, became masters of their own destiny. John Holmes was off-target with a 59th minute drop-goal (he subsequently made a poor drop attempt in the dying seconds of the match) before, a minute later, one of Pitchford's steamroller runs led to Dyl being tackled just short of the try-line. From the play-the-ball acting-halfback Dick cheekily dummied his way under the posts for Leeds' third and final touchdown, which he also converted for a 13–7 lead. Dick, having failed with the routine looking conversion to Dyl's try plus a 68th minute penalty and 73rd minute drop attempt, was clearly unfazed, claiming a late drop-goal and penalty, the latter after Widnes strayed offside at a play-the-ball.

Box-of-tricks Dick had slotted over a 35-yard penalty goal in only the third minute of the match, calmly regaining his feet after being fouled by Bill Ramsey. Shortly after, Widnes almost scored when Dennis O'Neill made a terrific run but was stopped by Holmes near the line, John Atkinson then having a Leeds try disallowed following a Pitchford break, due to a forward pass. Ray Dutton equalised for Widnes with a penalty awarded for offside and then appended the conversion after Mal Aspey beat off four defenders in a great run to score near the posts, scrum half Reg Bowden having switched the point of attack. Widnes led 7–2 but Leeds pulled three points back before the interval when Atkinson beat Stuart Wright to the ball, his momentum taking him over in the left corner following a Holmes cross-kick. Dick just missed the goal.

Leeds prop Steve Pitchford battles through the Widnes defence

STATS

Leeds 16 Widnes 7

Saturday 7 May at Wembley Stadium, London (3.00 pm)

Leeds (blue with amber bands): Murrell, A. Smith, Hague, Dyl, Atkinson, Holmes, Dick, Harrison, Ward (captain), Pitchford, Eccles, Cookson, Fearnley. Substitutes: D. Smith, Dickinson. Coach: S. Hynes

Widnes (white with black stripes on sleeves): Dutton, Wright, Aspey, Eckersley, D. O'Neill, Hughes, Bowden (captain), Ramsey, Elwell, Mills, Dearden, Adams, Laughton. Substitutes: George, Foran. Coach: F. Myler

Referee: V. Moss Touch-judges: E. Glazebrook, E.B. Kent

Half-time: 5–7 Attendance: 80,871 Receipts: 241,488

Weather: sunny and cloudy

Lance Todd Trophy: Pitchford (Leeds)

Cup presentation:
The Rt Hon. Denis Howell MP, Environment Minister

Progressive score:

Leeds	score (min)	Widnes
Dick penalty	2–0 (3)	
	2–2 (12)	Dutton penalty
	2–7 (19)	Aspey try, Dutton goal
Atkinson try	5–7 (27)	
Dyl try	8–7 (53)	
Dick try, Dick goal	13–7 (61)	
Dick drop-goal	14–7 (77)	
Dick penalty	16–7 (79)	

Route to the final:

First round: Leeds 40 Batley 6, Bramley 6 Widnes 11

Second round: Leeds 21 Barrow 11, Widnes 36 Swinton 5

Third round: Workington Town 2 Leeds 8, Widnes 19 Bradford Northern 5

Semi-finals:
Leeds 7 St Helens 2 (Central Park, Wigan, 12,974),
Widnes 14 Hull Kingston Rovers 5 (Headingley, Leeds, 17,053)

Head-to-head form guide:

Widnes 17 Leeds 20 (League)

Leeds 8 Widnes 24 (League)

The result justified the vote of confidence given to under-fire coach Syd Hynes just before the final. Hynes—two years into the job—told the *Yorkshire Post*: 'I have always said it would take three years to get the best out of the young players at Headingley. We are at Wembley after two years, but I believe the real improvement will come next year.' Widnes, meanwhile, had the slight consolation of equalling Bradford Northern's feat of reaching three consecutive Wembley finals.

1978 RUGBY LEAGUE CHALLENGE CUP FINAL
Leeds v St Helens

The Challenge Cup remained inside the Leeds trophy cabinet for another year following their thrilling 1978 encounter with St Helens, winning 14–12 after a match hailed by some critics at the time as the most entertaining at Wembley so far. It is a debateable claim, although few would argue against it being the most exciting since the 1965 Hunslet-Wigan encounter, Leeds staging what was then Wembley's best-ever comeback after being 10–0 down in the 13th minute.

John Atkinson—in his fifth Wembley final—inspired Leeds' recovery with a brilliant try in the 23rd minute after a 30-yard sprint that took him past Harry Pinner and Geoff Pimblett to score in the corner, a perfect Les Dyl pass having created the overlap following a cross-field passing move. Willie Oulton added a great goal. St Helens, though, discounted thoughts of a collapse, prop Mel James being held just short of the line five minutes later. Then, in the 35th minute, Pimblett knocked over a simple 20-yard penalty after Leeds' Graham Eccles obstructed David Chisnall as he chased his own kick towards the posts. In the dying minutes of the half, Oulton was wide with a 35-yard penalty, Saints leading 12–5 at the interval.

Leeds coach Syd Hynes instructed his troops to drive up the middle after the resumption and 'resist any temptation' to open out. The tactic seemed to work when, within a minute, a few powerful bursts set up the position for a successful David Ward drop-goal from in front of the posts. That one point lifted their spirits and they began controlling the forward battle, mounting one charge after another, David Smith scoring a 55th minute touchdown in the corner after Neil Hague's wide pass concluded an excellent passing move. Oulton's difficult touchline kick sailed across the face of the goal, leaving Leeds trailing by three points.

Pimblett tried to rejuvenate St Helens but hit the post with a 66th minute drop-goal attempt. Leeds, though, were unrelenting and, six minutes later, Phil Cookson crashed through three defenders to run 20 yards for a try off a brilliant John Holmes inside pass. Oulton was inches wide with the kick and, at 12–12 and with only eight minutes remaining, it developed into a nail-biting finish for the fans of both teams. The

---

STATS

Leeds 14 St Helens 12

Saturday 13 May at Wembley Stadium, London (3.00 pm)

Leeds (blue with amber bands): Oulton, D. Smith, Hague, Dyl, Atkinson, Holmes, Sanderson, Harrison, Ward (captain), Pitchford, Eccles, Cookson, Crane. Substitutes: Dick, Dickinson. Coach: S. Hynes

St Helens (white with red chevron): Pimblett (captain), Jones, Noonan, Glynn, Mathias, Francis, Gwilliam, D. Chisnall, Liptrot, James, Nicholls, Cunningham, Pinner. Substitutes: Ashton (dnp), Karalius (dnp). Coach: E. Ashton

Referee: W.H. Thompson

Touch-judges: K.L. Gaskell, H. Goodman

Half-time: 5–12 Attendance: 95,872 Receipts: £330,575

Weather: sunny and cloudy

Lance Todd Trophy: Nicholls (St Helens)

Cup presentation: Lord Derby, Rugby League president

Progressive score:

Leeds	score (min)	St Helens
	0–5 (5)	Liptrot try, Pimblett goal
	0–10 (13)	Francis try, Pimblett goal
Atkinson try, Oulton goal	5–10 (23)	
	5–12 (35)	Pimblett penalty
Ward drop-goal	6–12 (41)	
D. Smith try	9–12 (55)	
Cookson try	12–12 (72)	
Holmes drop-goal	13–12 (76)	
Ward drop-goal	14–12 (79)	

Route to the final:

First round: Leeds 25 Halifax 5, St Helens 36 Huyton 8

Second round: Wakefield Trinity 6 Leeds 28, Oldham 11 St Helens 26

Third round: Leeds 16 Bradford Northern 8, St Helens 31 Huddersfield 5

Semi-finals: Leeds 14 Featherstone Rovers 9 (Odsal Stadium, Bradford, 12,824), St Helens 12 Warrington 8 (Central Park, Wigan, 16,167)

Head-to-head form guide:

Leeds 6 St Helens 17 (League)

St Helens 19 Leeds 10 (League)

deadlock broke in the 76th minute when Holmes—with his weaker left foot—landed a drop-goal from just inside Saints' 25-yard area, slipping onto his back in the process. Three minutes later, Ward got another from in front of the posts, making it 14–12. The tension was almost unbearable as St Helens mounted one final assault, the ball being whipped out smartly to the right but Derek Noonan was unable to hold on to Peter Glynn's potential match-winning pass and Leeds supporters breathed a big sigh of relief. Noonan later told the *St Helens Newspaper*: 'The ball hit my arm and jumped up. I grabbed for it but it had gone.'

St Helens had slipped quickly into gear at the start of the match, Pimblett being wide with a 2nd minute drop-goal attempt. Graham Liptrot claimed their first try three minutes later, grabbing the ball to dive in at the corner after Oulton failed to deal with a Pinner 'up and under' that landed near the posts in the in-goal area, the ball ricocheting off Atkinson. Four minutes later, Oulton missed a fairly simple penalty as Saints continued to take the game to Leeds, Roy Matthias being held just shy of the posts after a thrilling 40-yard burst. But, in the following minute, Bill Francis sidestepped his way over for a try off a Ken Gwilliam

pass following a scrum five yards from the Leeds try-line. Pimblett converted both tries for a 10–0 lead and, although he was wide with an 18th minute drop-goal, it was beginning to look easy. Several post-match analysts pondered whether Saints had peaked too early.

George Nicholls—who gave an outstanding performance for St Helens in defeat—fends off Leeds' Kevin Dick

St Helens' Bill Francis (left) and Geoff Pimblett (number 1) are unable to prevent John Holmes' dramatic drop-goal that put Leeds ahead for the first time with just four minutes remaining

1979 RUGBY LEAGUE CHALLENGE CUP FINAL
Widnes v Wakefield Trinity

Widnes concluded the 1970s with their second Wembley success from four visits during the decade, overcoming surprise Challenge Cup finalists Wakefield Trinity 12–3. The Chemics had entered into the match as 6–4 favourites, Wakefield—who reached Wembley after stunning St Helens in the semi-final with a late Andrew Fletcher try—took to the field without loose forward, Paul McDermott, who broke an arm three weeks earlier.

Despite pre-match misgivings Trinity held their own in a scoreless, although forgettable, opening half and, if anything, had slightly the better of the exchanges, Mick Burke twice being called upon to detain Fletcher. Other incidents of note included Widnes' Keith Elwell losing the ball during a concerted attack on Wakefield's try-line in the 24th minute, and goal misses from Trinity's Alan McCurrie (36th minute drop) and Keith Smith (40th minute penalty).

The tempo picked up after the half-time break. Wakefield were moving the ball around smartly but, when they lost it, their second-row Bill Ashurst fouled Eric Hughes in a tackle, Mick Burke consequently kicking a 45-yard penalty to open the scoring. Nine minutes later, Ashurst sent David Topliss away on a great run, Mick Adams making a late try-saving tackle. Widnes, though, were gaining confidence and, when Smith kicked the ball into their half, Chemics full back David Eckersley took possession and transferred to

SPONSORS OF THE CHALLENGE CUP

In 1979 the Rugby League Challenge Cup took on a sponsor's name for the first time, being known as the State Express Challenge Cup. The famous trophy has been prefixed by a sponsor's name ever since, as per the following list.

- 1979 to 1980: State Express
- 1981: Three Fives
- 1982 to 1984: State Express
- 1985 to 2001: Silk Cut
- 2002: Kellogg's Nutri-Grain
- 2003 to 2006: Powergen
- 2007 to 2009: Carnegie

Action stations as Widnes' Keith Elwell gets the ball away despite close attention from the Wakefield Trinity defence

The two teams enter the arena, Widnes (nearest camera) being led out by their captain Reg Bowden

STATS

Widnes 12 Wakefield Trinity 3

Saturday 5 May at Wembley Stadium, London (3.00 pm)

Widnes (white with black stripes on sleeves): Eckersley, Wright, Aspey, George, M. Burke, Hughes, Bowden (captain), Mills, Elwell, Shaw, Adams, Dearden, Laughton. Substitutes: M. O'Neill, Hull. Player-coach: D. Laughton

Wakefield Trinity (blue with white with red band): Sheard, Fletcher, Smith, Diamond, Juliff, Topliss (captain), Lampkowski, J. Burke, McCurrie, Skerrett, Ashurst, Keith Rayne, Idle. Substitutes: Midgley (dnp), Kevin Rayne (dnp). Coach: W. Kirkbride

Referee: J.E. Jackson

Touch-judges: W.J. Fiddes, H. McGuire

Half-time: 0–0 Attendance: 94,218 Receipts: £383,157

Weather: sunny

Lance Todd Trophy: Topliss (Wakefield Trinity)

Cup presentation: Lord Daresbury

Progressive score:

Widnes	score (min)	Wakefield Trinity
M. Burke penalty	2–0 (50)	
Wright try, M. Burke goal	7–0 (59)	
Elwell drop-goal	8–0 (64)	
	8–3 (66)	Fletcher try
Eckersley drop-goal	9–3 (70)	
Hughes try	12–3 (76)	

Route to the final:

First round: Widnes 12 Workington Town 5, Wakefield T 10 Featherstone Rovers 7

Second round: Widnes 21 Wigan 5, Oldham 7 Wakefield Trinity 19

Third round: Huddersfield 0 Widnes 14, Wakefield Trinity 8 Barrow 5

Semi-finals:

Widnes 14 Bradford Northern 11 (Station Road, Swinton, 14,324),

Wakefield Trinity 9 St Helens 7 (Headingley, Leeds, 12,393)

Head-to-head form guide:

Wakefield Trinity 8 Widnes 0 (League)

Widnes 28 Wakefield Trinity 11 (League)

With the ball planted firmly onto the in-goal area in the background, Widnes' Eric Hughes (left) races away in triumph having clinched the match with four minutes remaining. Team-mates Mal Aspey (arms raised) and Mick Adams join the celebration

WINNING CAPTAIN

Reg Bowden (Widnes 1979)

Wily, competitive scrum half Reg Bowden was signed from Ditton Youth Club in 1968, making his Widnes debut in 1969. With Bowden—who took over as captain in 1975—dictating play in the middle, Widnes built a reputation as the 'Cup Kings' of the 1970s and he enjoyed success in the Rugby League Challenge Cup (1975, 1979), Premiership Trophy (1980), Championship (1977/78), Players' No.6 Trophy (1975/76), John Player Trophy (1978/79), BBC2 Floodlit Trophy (1978/79) and Lancashire Cup (1974, 1975, 1976, 1978, 1979). Having played 376 times for the Chemics he left in 1980 to take over as player-coach of the new London-based Fulham (now evolved into Harlequins RL club), capturing the Second Division Championship with them in 1982/83. After 120 appearances he returned north in 1984 as player-coach of Warrington, competing in 11 matches later that year and continuing as coach until 1986. He represented Lancashire 10 times.

Stuart Wright. The winger ran 10 yards before kicking towards the right corner flag, winning the race with Steve Diamond to toe the ball across the whitewash and score. Mick Burke added a morale-boosting touchline goal to put Widnes 7–0 in front.

Elwell extended the margin with a drop-goal, Trinity responding two minutes later with their only score. Attacking down the right flank, their back-row forward Keith Rayne kicked over Mick Burke's head, Fletcher racing past him to grab the ball and cross the line in the corner. Claims of a knock-on were dismissed, Smith missing the tricky conversion. At 8–3 Wakefield were within one score of tying the game but Eckersley's drop-goal 10 minutes from the end again shunted Widnes out of reach. In the 76th minute, it was all over when Adams passed to Hughes, who shaped to take a drop-goal but then, employing a dummy pass, shot 20 yards through a confused defence to score. Mick Burke missed the goal.

It was a relief for Widnes skipper Reg Bowden, having been captain for their Wembley losses in 1976 and 1977. Before the match he told the *Widnes Weekly News*: 'It took over a month to get over the last two Wembley defeats. It was a terrible feeling. I never felt so bad about anything in all my life.' Their victory completed the club's most successful campaign to date, having won the John Player Trophy, BBC2 Floodlit Trophy and Lancashire Cup.

1980 RUGBY LEAGUE CHALLENGE CUP FINAL
Hull Kingston Rovers v Hull

The City of Hull converged on Wembley Stadium in 1980 to settle their own domestic battle for supremacy, Hull Kingston Rovers and Hull going head-to-head for possession of the Rugby League's 'blue riband'. It was also a special day for two popular veterans, Rovers' Roger Millward (their captain-coach) and Clive Sullivan (who had spent most of his career with Hull) both appearing in their first Challenge Cup Final. Hull—with club skipper Vince Farrar on the substitutes' bench—decided to start with Steve Norton as on-field captain.

The match has entered the annals of rugby league history due to its uniqueness, although it was not an outstanding game. Both teams seemed inhibited by

Roger Millward embellished his distinguished career by lifting the Challenge Cup. Hull Kingston Rovers colleagues are Phil Hogan (supporting his captain), Steve Hartley (holding a leg!) and Lance Todd Trophy winner Brian Lockwood (right)

WINNING CAPTAIN

Roger Millward (Hull Kingston Rovers 1980)

Rugby league supporters were alerted to the sublime skills of stand-off Roger Millward during the 1963/64 season when representing Castleford Under-17s in a televised inter-town competition. Signing for Castleford in 1964, he was, at 5 feet 4 inches tall, a fearless defender, his devastating bursts earning him the nickname 'Roger the Dodger'. He was a BBC2 Floodlit Trophy winner in 1965/66, but unable to gain a regular place due to the impeccable Alan Hardisty/Keith Hepworth halfback pairing, transferred to Hull Kingston Rovers for £6,000 in 1966. He made 407 appearances (207 tries, 607 goals, 1,825 points) for the Rovers, winning the Rugby League Challenge Cup (1980), Championship (1978/79), BBC2 Floodlit Trophy (1977/78) and Yorkshire Cup (1966, 1967, 1971, 1974). He toured three times (1970, 1974, 1979), represented Great Britain (29 times, including the 1968 and 1977 World Cup, being captain 10 times), England (17, including the 1975 World Cup) and Yorkshire (12). Having broken his jaw in the 1980 Challenge Cup Final, he came back in the 'A' (reserve) team in October 1980 but broke it again, ending his playing career. He became player-coach in 1977, continuing as coach until 1991, later taking charge at Halifax (1991–92) and Ryedale-York (1994). During the 1976 close season he played for Australian club Cronulla-Sutherland. He received the MBE in 1983 and was voted into the Rugby League Hall of Fame in 2000.

the enormity of the occasion, their 'derby' clash creating an atmosphere inside the stadium rarely equalled. Rovers' back division was also handicapped following a 13th minute injury to chief playmaker Millward who fractured his jaw (for the third time that season) following a late challenge by Ron Wileman. Although in obvious pain, he remained on the field.

Rovers' only try came in the eighth minute, Millward having found touch 35 yards from Hull's line with a penalty kick. From the tap restart, the ball transferred through David Watkinson, Roy Holdstock and Allan Agar to prop Brian Lockwood who delivered one of Wembley's most famous passes, using a pre-planned move from his time in Australian club rugby. Looking as though he was about to supply the supporting Len Casey, thereby attracting Hull's defence towards the loose forward, he released the ball with superb timing to Steve Hubbard, the right winger having come off his flank to cut inside Lockwood.

Lockwood's delayed pass sent him through a huge gap and he sprinted diagonally for a sensational try near the left corner. Hubbard failed to augment his score but referee Fred Lindop awarded a follow-on penalty (from in front of the posts) because Paul Woods fouled him as he scored, making no mistake this time. Five minutes later, he added another penalty from 20 yards

Steve Hubbard scores Hull Kingston Rovers' only try, Hull tackler Graham Bray unable to prevent the score. Paul Woods, the other Hull player closing in, was penalised for his subsequent foul on Hubbard resulting in a penalty goal by the latter after his conversion attempt

STATS

Hull Kingston Rovers 10 Hull 5

Saturday 3 May at Wembley Stadium, London (3.00 pm)

Hull Kingston Rovers (white with red band): Hall, Hubbard, Smith, Hartley, Sullivan, Millward (captain), Agar, Holdstock, Watkinson, Lockwood, Lowe, Rose, Casey. Substitutes: Hogan, Millington. Player-coach: R. Millward

Hull (black and white irregular hoops): Woods, Bray, Walters, Wilby, Prendiville, Newlove, Pickerill, Tindall, Wileman, Stone, Birdsall, Lloyd, Norton (captain). Substitutes: Hancock, Farrar. Team manager: A. Bunting

Referee: G.F. Lindop

Touch-judges: J.S. Reagan, F.J. Tomlinson

Half-time: 8–3 Attendance: 95,000 Receipts: £448,202

Weather: sunny and windy

Lance Todd Trophy: Lockwood (Hull KR)

Cup presentation:
H.M. Queen Elizabeth, The Queen Mother

Progressive score:

Hull Kingston Rovers	score (min)	Hull
Hubbard try	3–0 (8)	
Hubbard penalty	5–0 (10)	
Hubbard penalty	7–0 (15)	
	7–3 (28)	Wilby try
Millward drop-goal	8–3 (40)	
	8–5 (51)	Lloyd penalty
Hubbard penalty	10–5 (75)	

Route to the final:

First round:
Wigan 13 Hull Kingston Rovers 18, Hull 33 Millom 10

Second round:
Hull Kingston Rovers 28 Castleford 3, Hull 18 York 8

Third round: Hull Kingston Rovers 23 Warrington 11, Bradford Northern 0 Hull 3

Semi-finals:
Hull Kingston Rovers 20 Halifax 7 (Headingley, Leeds, 17,910)

Hull 10 Widnes 5 (Station Road, Swinton, 18,347)

Head-to-head form guide:

Hull 20 Hull Kingston Rovers 20 (League)

Hull 13 Hull Kingston Rovers 3
(BBC2 Floodlit Trophy Final)

Hull Kingston Rovers 29 Hull 14 (League)

(Charlie Stone fouling Holdstock) for a 7–0 lead.

Hull supporters had something to enthuse over in the 28th minute after their forwards won a scrum near Rovers' try-line. Clive Pickerill collected the ball, passing with urgency to John Newlove who raced round the back of the scrum, drawing Rovers' Mike Smith before sending colleague Tim Wilby over for a try 10 yards from the corner flag. Sammy Lloyd—having tried four times to stand the ball up—missed the conversion. Millward made the interval score 8–3 with an excellent 30-yard drop-goal from acting-halfback at a play-the-ball.

Eleven minutes after the resumption Lloyd managed his only success from four penalty goal strikes (Allan Agar dissent towards the referee) reducing the margin to three points. The tension mounted during a half strewn with handling errors, both sides struggling to get over the whitewash. Five tries were ruled out; two by Rovers from Steve Hartley (forward pass) and Hubbard (lost ball), three by Hull from Wileman (not grounded), Keith Tindall (forward pass) and Graham Bray (obstruction). The only remaining score was Hubbard's 75th minute penalty (Lloyd obstructing Millward), completing a famous 10–5 victory for Rovers.

1981 RUGBY LEAGUE CHALLENGE CUP FINAL
Widnes v Hull Kingston Rovers

Widnes celebrated a 10th Wembley visit with an 18–9 victory over holders Hull Kingston Rovers, equalling Wigan's record of six wins at the stadium. Although it was their fifth Challenge Cup Final since 1975, the Chemics had several new faces, including a Hull Kingston Rovers hero of the previous year, Brian Lockwood, who emulated Alex Murphy's record of winning at Wembley with three different clubs. There was also a 19-year-old named Andy Gregory who had broken into the senior squad during mid-season and was destined to make the venue a second home.

Widnes full back Mick Burke stamped his influence on the match in the fourth minute after Rovers' winger Peter Muscroft was ruled offside. Widnes took a quick tap-penalty, Burke going wide to take Eric Hughes' pass on the opposition's 25-yard line before directing a short kick towards the in-goal area and racing past three defenders, the ball standing up perfectly for him to collect it and dive over. Three minutes later Steve Hubbard placed Rovers' first points on the scoreboard with a penalty following Eric Hughes' high tackle on Phil Lowe. Widnes, though, were taking command, the Rovers, who appeared shaken by the early try, making several unforced mistakes and coughing up possession.

Mick George (centre) celebrates his try for Widnes with Stuart Wright (left) and Eric Prescott

---

WINNING CAPTAIN

Mick Adams (Widnes 1981)

Mick Adams signed for hometown Widnes in 1971 from the club's 'B' team having previously played for the Blackbrook (St Helens) amateur club. Initially used as a reserve full back, he began establishing himself in the back-row of the pack in 1973. A shrewd passer, noted for his style of running with the ball held to his chest, he took over as loose forward in 1979 when Doug Laughton retired, replacing the departed Reg Bowden as team captain in 1980. At Widnes, he won the Rugby League Challenge Cup (1975, 1979, 1981, 1984), Premiership Trophy (1980, 1982, 1983), Championship (1977/78), Players' No.6 Trophy (1975/76), John Player Trophy (1978/79), BBC2 Floodlit Trophy (1978/79) and Lancashire Cup (1974, 1975, 1976, 1978, 1979). He was a tourist twice (1979, 1984), appeared in 13 Test matches, represented England (6 times—including the 1975 World Cup) and Lancashire (12). He retired in 1984 after 416 matches for Widnes. He spent the 1975 and 1976 close seasons in Australia—where he later emigrated—playing for Canterbury-Bankstown.

Burke—having failed to convert his try—was on song with a 22nd minute penalty, awarded in front of the posts after David Watkinson fouled Lockwood. Burke was again in evidence four minutes later, linking up from the back to take Lockwood's defence-splitting pass and send Mick George roaring past Roy Holdstock

for a second touchdown. Burke added the extra points, Hubbard reducing Rovers' arrears on the half-hour with a 40-yard penalty following a foul on Paul Harkin, which sailed between the uprights. Six minutes before the interval, Mick Adams completed a satisfactory opening half for Widnes with a 35-yard drop-goal pushing his team further ahead 11–4.

The second half had a sensational start when Gregory took a long pass from Adams to go through the heart of the Rovers defence, placing the ball behind the posts for an outstanding solo try that virtually guaranteed the trophy was headed for Naughton Park. Burke's goal, plus his penalty three minutes later after Gregory was on the end of a late Len Casey tackle, made the score 18–4. The Rovers tried to raise their performance, versatile full back David Hall being moved to loose forward where his ball distribution increased his side's potency. It paid off when Chris Burton strolled over from Casey's pass close in, Hubbard adding the goal. Although 25 minutes were left, it was to be the last score of the afternoon, Widnes owing much of their success to the spadework of forwards Les Gorley, Mike O'Neill and Eric Prescott.

Gregory, interviewed in *Open Rugby* magazine, said of his timely second half try: 'Doug Laughton and Mick Adams told me to "keep out of it in the first half". They said it was a big park and I wouldn't know where I was and to take my time. After the interval they said "go out and enjoy it".'

STATS

Widnes 18 Hull Kingston Rovers 9

Saturday 2 May at Wembley Stadium, London (3.00 pm)

Widnes (white with black stripes on sleeves): Burke, Wright, George, Cunningham, Bentley, Hughes, Gregory, M. O'Neill, Elwell, Lockwood, Gorley, Prescott, Adams (captain). Substitutes: J. Myler, Shaw. Coach: D. Laughton

Hull Kingston Rovers (white with red band): Hall, Hubbard, M. Smith, Hogan, Muscroft, Hartley, Harkin, Holdstock, Watkinson, Crooks, Lowe, Burton, Casey (captain). Substitutes: Proctor, Millington. Coach: R. Millward

Referee: D.G. Kershaw

Touch-judges: A.I. Barrow, W.J. Greenhalgh

Half-time: 11–4 Attendance: 92,496 Receipts: £591,117

Weather: sunny and cloudy, windy

Lance Todd Trophy: Burke (Widnes)

Cup presentation: Sir Douglas Bader CBE

Progressive score:

Widnes	score (min)	Hull Kingston Rovers
Burke try	3–0 (4)	
	3–2 (7)	Hubbard penalty
Burke penalty	5–2 (22)	
George try, Burke goal	10–2 (26)	
	10–4 (30)	Hubbard penalty
Adams drop-goal	11–4 (34)	
Gregory try, Burke goal	16–4 (42)	
Burke penalty	18–4 (45)	
	18–9 (55)	Burton try, Hubbard goal

Route to the final:

First round: Widnes 50 Doncaster 0, Hull Kingston Rovers 18 Barrow 13

Second round: Widnes 7 Castleford 5, Hull Kingston Rovers 23 York 7

Third round: Featherstone Rovers 5 Widnes 21, Hull Kingston R 19 Salford 8

Semi-finals: Widnes 17 Warrington 9 (Central Park, Wigan, 12,624), Hull Kingston Rovers 22 St Helens 5 (Headingley, Leeds, 17,073)

Head-to-head form guide:

Widnes 18 Hull Kingston Rovers 25 (League)

Hull Kingston Rovers 12 Widnes 4 (League)

Mick Burke grabs an early try for Widnes after recovering the ball following his own overhead kick

179

1982 RUGBY LEAGUE CHALLENGE CUP FINAL
Hull v Widnes

Hull bridged a 68-year gap after claiming the Challenge Cup in 1982 following two dramatic encounters with Widnes. With everything all-square at Wembley, the replay was scheduled for Leeds United's Elland Road ground 18 days later, Widnes defeating Hull 23–8 in the Premiership Trophy Final at Headingley in the interim. The Elland Road enclosure was dominated by Hull fans for the Wednesday evening clash, their team making several changes to the Wembley line-up. Injuries were responsible for the introduction of two veterans; 39-year-old Clive Sullivan and 37-year-old Tony Duke for Dane O'Hara (hamstring) and Ron Wileman (back), whilst Tony Dean and Keith Tindall were preferred to Kevin Harkin and Sammy Lloyd.

Hull—more composed than at Wembley—began strongly, Lee Crooks being just wide with a 15th minute drop-goal attempt. It was Widnes, however, that took first blood; Mick Burke landing a spectacular penalty from near halfway after Steve Norton was judged offside. Burke missed a further attempt seven minutes later then, as half-time beckoned, Hull got into their stride. Andy Gregory was penalised for illegal scrum-feeding and Dean's quick tap-penalty allowed Norton and David Topliss to put Gary Kemble through a gap to score near the posts. Crooks added

the goal and Hull led for the first time after an aggregate 113 minutes play. Spectators were still entering the ground as Hull struck again, Topliss racing 20 yards through a huge opening on the left—having performed a wrap-around with James Leuluai following a long pass from Dean—to cross the try-line despite Eric Hughes' tackle. With the half-time klaxon about to sound, Crooks' conversion just failed, hitting the outside of the far upright, Hull leading 8–2.

Widnes came back into contention after the interval, Burke kicking a penalty after Duke fouled Eric Prescott in a tackle, and Stuart Wright going over for a try in the right corner one minute later, following good work by Keith Elwell and Keiron O'Loughlin from a position set up by Gregory's 40-yard chip-and-chase. Burke just failed to nose his team ahead, shaving the outside of the far post as he tried to augment. Leading 8–7 Hull continued to press, getting close several times. Their reward came through tries from Topliss (jinking through four players to score near the left post off Norton's pass) and Crooks (going over from acting-halfback 12 yards out after some weak tackling), the latter player converting both. Burke split those scores with a penalty goal (Crooks kicking out at Brian Lockwood whilst being tackled) to set up an agonising last few minutes for Hull fans

Widnes' Brian Lockwood (with ball) makes eye contact with Hull's Keith Tindall (number 8) as he looks for an opening in the Elland Road replay

A sweet moment for Hull's players following the final whistle at Elland Road as they realise the Challenge Cup awaits them. Left to right is Steve Evans, captain David Topliss, Clive Sullivan, Paul Prendiville, whilst Gary Kemble (behind Topliss) looks equally pleased with himself

WINNING CAPTAIN

David Topliss (Hull 1982)

Born in Walton, near Wakefield, David Topliss was a stand-off with exceptional speed and side-stepping ability. Signing for Wakefield Trinity in 1968 from the Normanton amateur club, he was captain of Trinity's side that lost in the 1979 Rugby League Challenge Cup decider at Wembley. Transferring to Hull in 1981 for a £15,000 fee, he appeared twice more in Wembley Challenge Cup Finals, both as captain, drawing in 1982 (winning the replay against Widnes at Elland Road, Leeds) and losing in 1983. He also won the Championship (1982/83) and Yorkshire Cup (1982, 1983). After 127 Hull appearances he moved to Oldham in 1985, returning to Wakefield in 1987 as player-coach. He ended his playing career in 1988 after an aggregate 420 appearances with Trinity, continuing as coach until 1994. For Great Britain he was a 1979 tourist, and a member of their 1972 World Cup squad in France (although not called upon to play). He played in four Tests for Britain, twice for England and five times for Yorkshire. He had two spells in Australia with Penrith (1976) and Balmain (1977).

before they could celebrate their historic 18–9 victory.

Hull's magical night at Elland Road looked an unlikely proposition when they trailed 14–6 at Wembley with a quarter-hour remaining. Somehow, the Airlie Birds injected more urgency and, in a sensational finish, stormed back with two tries to force a replay. They built pressure with O'Hara almost scoring in the right corner and Terry Day being held on his back in the in-goal. Eventually, in the 67th minute, Topliss spun the ball out to Norton who broke through the defence for a try near the posts, O'Hara then going in at the corner for their second touchdown four minutes later, Crooks having squeezed the ball out to him despite being held. At 14–14, the tension was unbearable but Lloyd, having converted the first

effort, was wide with his kick, the match finishing level despite a late Widnes drop-goal attempt from Mick Adams that dropped beneath the crossbar.

The Widnes forwards had made a determined start at Wembley, powering their way downfield to enable Elwell to open the scoring with a 25-yard drop-goal. Five minutes later, Widnes grabbed the first try, Les Gorley sucking in two defenders before off-loading to Eddie Cunningham, who got over in the left corner, twisting out of a two-man tackle. Burke added a great

Disbelief on the face of the Widnes players (white jersey) as Dane O'Hara scores for Hull at Wembley to force a replay

STATS

Hull 14 Widnes 14

Saturday 1 May at Wembley Stadium, London (3.00 pm)

Hull (black and white irregular hoops): Kemble, O'Hara, Day, Evans, Prendiville, Topliss (captain), Harkin, Skerrett, Wileman, Stone, Crane, Lloyd, Norton. Substitutes: Leuluai (dnp), Crooks. Team manager: A. Bunting

Widnes (white with black stripes on sleeves): Burke, Wright, O'Loughlin, Cunningham, Basnett, Hughes, Gregory, M. O'Neill, Elwell, Lockwood, Gorley, Prescott, Adams (captain). Substitutes: A. Myler, S. O'Neill. Coach: D. Laughton

Referee: G.F. Lindop Touch-judges: W.H. Barker, G. Crisp

Half-time: 6–6 Attendance: 92,147 Receipts: £684,500

Weather: sunny and cloudy, windy

Lance Todd Trophy: Cunningham (Widnes)

Progressive score:

Hull	score (min)	Widnes
	0–1 (5)	Elwell drop-goal
	0–6 (10)	Cunningham try, Burke goal
Lloyd penalty	2–6 (15)	
Lloyd penalty	4–6 (25)	
Lloyd penalty	6–6 (40)	
	6–11 (51)	Cunningham try, Gregory goal
	6–14 (62)	Wright try
Norton try, Lloyd goal	11–14 (67)	
O'Hara try	14–14 (71)	

Replay: Hull 18 Widnes 9

Wednesday 19 May at Elland Road, Leeds (7.30 pm)

Hull (black and white irregular hoops): Kemble, Sullivan, Leuluai, Evans, Prendiville, Topliss (captain), Dean, Tindall, Duke, Stone, Skerrett, Crooks, Norton. Substitutes: Day (dnp), Crane

Widnes (white with black stripes on sleeves): unchanged except Whitfield replaced S. O'Neill. Substitutes: A. Myler (dnp), Whitfield (dnp)

Referee: G.F. Lindop Touch-judges: W.H. Barker, G. Crisp

Half-time: 8–2 Attendance: 41,171 Receipts: £180,525

Weather: overcast and cool

Man of the Match award: Topliss (Hull)

Cup presentation: The Rt Hon. Neil McFarlane MP, Minister for Sport

Progressive score:

Hull	score (min)	Widnes
	0–2 (18)	Burke penalty
Kemble try, Crooks goal	5–2 (33)	
Topliss try	8–2 (39)	
	8–4 (57)	Burke penalty
	8–7 (58)	Wright try
Topliss try, Crooks goal	13–7 (62)	
	13–9 (64)	Burke penalty
Crooks try, Crooks goal	18–9 (73)	

Route to the final:

First round: Hull 29 Salford 15, Cardiff City 8 Widnes 19

Second round: Fulham 5 Hull 11, Wigan 7 Widnes 9

Third round: Hull 16 Halifax 10, Bradford Northern 8 Widnes 8

Third round replay: Widnes 10 Bradford Northern 7

Semi-finals:
Hull 15 Castleford 11 (Headingley, Leeds, 21,207),
Widnes 11 Leeds 8 (Station Road, Swinton, 13,075)

Head-to-head form guide:

Widnes 16 Hull 2 (League)

Hull 21 Widnes 3 (League)

---

goal for an early 6–0 lead. Hull, although looking nervous and making errors, were level at 6–6 by half-time through three Lloyd penalties, all awarded for foul play, Hughes—one of three Widnes players involved in the first incident—being guilty for the latter two, resulting in him being 'booked' by referee Fred Lindop. Widnes, meanwhile, had a 30th minute 'try' by Wright disallowed, the player—who protested otherwise—appearing to bounce the ball down following Prescott's kick into the right corner.

Widnes added two further tries after the break through Cunningham (pushing through five defenders from acting-halfback eight yards out) and Wright (a thrilling 90 yard run down the right flank after

intercepting Kemble's pass). Gregory, taking over from Burke, who retired injured at half time, succeeded with the first of his two conversion attempts. With Adams being just wide with a drop-goal in between those efforts, the score stood at 14–6 to Widnes who appeared to have the trophy within reach, but Hull had clearly not read the script!

Widnes' two-try Wembley hero, Cunningham, was a shock late inclusion having missed over two months with a neck injury and previously being ruled out for the season. On the other hand, unlucky colleague and utility back John Myler succumbed to a troublesome knee cartilage in the Wembley build up after appearing in all the previous rounds, scoring two tries and 13 goals.

1983 RUGBY LEAGUE CHALLENGE CUP FINAL
Featherstone Rovers v Hull

Featherstone Rovers produced one of Wembley's great upsets in overcoming 4-to-1 odds-on favourites and Challenge Cup holders Hull 14–12 in the 1983 final, a disputed penalty three minutes from the end climaxing a sensational late rally. In a scrappy, though memorable, match their win owed much to the stirring performance of second-rower David Hobbs, the first forward to score two tries at Wembley.

His first, during the seventh minute, off a delayed Terry Hudson pass, followed a Rovers tap-penalty 10 yards out, brushing aside James Leuluai's vain tackle before placing the ball in the right corner. Steve Quinn was wide with the goal, succeeding later when Gary Kemble was penalised for 'lying on' at a play-the-ball. Lee Crooks, meanwhile, was off-target three times for Hull during the opening half, his failed 4th minute drop-goal being followed by two wide penalty strikes midway through the half. Hull's rhythm was disrupted through the 16th minute loss of Kevin Harkin who departed on a stretcher, his head connecting with Hudson's boot when he went down to collect the ball from a scrum. Skipper David Topliss took over at scrum half, substitute Terry Day coming on as stand-off. Five minutes before the

WINNING CAPTAIN

Terry Hudson (Featherstone Rovers 1983)

Terry Hudson signed for local club Featherstone Rovers in 1969, moving to Hull Kingston Rovers for £7,500 in 1971. His last match for them was in 1974, and he subsequently joined Wakefield Trinity (1975–78). In 1979 he played four matches on loan to Batley before transferring back to Featherstone later that year. His second spell at Post Office Road proved more fruitful, being appointed captain in 1982 and winning the Rugby League Challenge Cup (1983) and Second Division Championship (1979/80). A tenacious, workman-like scrum half, he concluded his career with Hunslet in the 1984/85 season. He represented Yorkshire once (in 1973).

break the Humbersider's were temporarily reduced to 12 men whilst Paul Rose served 10 minutes in the 'sin-bin'—the first to do so at Wembley—after his high tackle saw John Gilbert carried off with concussion.

Trailing 5–0, Hull began the second period with all guns blazing, their cohesion helped by Topliss' return to stand-off, Mick Crane—usually a loose forward—stepping off the bench to give an effective scrum half display. It looked ominous for Featherstone as the Airlie

David Hobbs touches down for Featherstone Rovers in the seventh minute, Hull's Keith Bridges powerless to stop him

183

Birds took a grip to lead 12–5 with 23 minutes remaining. Lee Crooks had registered their first points with a penalty-try, Topliss having obstructed him as he attempted to place a hand on the ball after playing it towards the try-line. Featherstone almost responded

Hobbs completes his brace of tries to bring Featherstone back into contention

STATS

Featherstone Rovers 14 Hull 12

Saturday 7 May at Wembley Stadium, London (3.00 pm)

Featherstone Rovers (blue with narrow white hoops): Barker, Marsden, Quinn, Gilbert, Kellett, Banks, Hudson (captain), Gibbins, Handscombe, Hankins, Hobbs, Slatter, Smith. Substitutes: Lyman, Siddall. Team manager: A. Agar

Hull (black and white irregular hoops): Kemble, O'Hara, Evans, Leuluai, Prendiville, Topliss (captain), Harkin, Skerrett, Bridges, Stone, Rose, Crooks, Norton. Substitutes: Day, Crane. Team manager: A. Bunting

Referee: R. Whitfield Touch-judges: J. Reed, H. Worth

Half-time: 5–0 Attendance: 84,969 Receipts: £655,510

Weather: cloudy

Lance Todd Trophy: Hobbs (Featherstone Rovers)

Cup presentation:

Lord Gormley of Ashton in Makerfield OBE

Progressive score:

Featherstone Rovers	score (min)	Hull
Hobbs try	3–0 (7)	
Quinn penalty	5–0 (32)	
	5–5 (42)	Crooks penalty-try, Crooks goal
	5–10 (53)	Leuluai try, Crooks goal
	5–12 (57)	Crooks penalty
Quinn penalty	7–12 (64)	
Hobbs try, Quinn goal	12–12 (72)	
Quinn penalty	14–12 (77)	

Route to the final:

First round: Featherstone Rovers 21 Batley 5, Blackpool Borough 11 Hull 19

Second round: Salford 11 Featherstone Rovers 17, Hull 32 Wakefield Trinity 15

Third round: St Helens 10 Featherstone Rovers 11, Warrington 4 Hull 10

Semi-finals: Featherstone R 11 Bradford Northern 6 (Headingley, Leeds, 10,784),

Hull 14 Castleford 7 (Elland Road, Leeds, 26,031)

Head-to-head form guide:

Hull 24 Featherstone Rovers 15 (League)

Featherstone Rovers 14 Hull 18 (John Player Trophy)

Featherstone Rovers 9 Hull 14 (League)

when Peter Smith crossed the whitewash but was recalled for a forward pass. Four minutes later, Leuluai grabbed Hull's second touchdown, racing between the posts after Rose burst through a gap following a wrap-around move from Topliss and Crane. Crooks, having converted both tries, added a penalty after Topliss was, allegedly, kneed during a tackle by Hudson, the latter consequently becoming the second visitor to the sin-bin.

In a tense, dramatic finish Rovers—trailing by seven points—began dominating scrum possession as they clawed their way back; Quinn booted over a 25-yard penalty after Kemble 'stole' the ball off Tim Slatter, then Hobbs exploited a gaping hole in Hull's tiring defence, racing over the try-line to the left of goal. Quinn converted to tie the score 12–12. Eight minutes remained and thoughts of a second successive replay loomed for Hull. A confident, inspired Hobbs sent a drop-goal sailing between the posts but Featherstone jubilation was cut short when referee Robin Whitfield ruled no goal, the ball not touching the ground before being struck. Three minutes later, butterflies flew around the stomachs of most supporters as the outcome was settled in dramatic fashion after touch-judge Jim Reed claimed Hull's Charlie Stone head-butted Smith, Hull disputing the decision. Quinn calmly slotted the match-winning penalty from 20 yards out, to the right of the posts.

The Rovers, who finished 12 positions below top-placed Hull in the First Division, had looked relegation candidates when Allan Agar took over as coach in mid-season. Without embellishing his squad, Agar rescued their senior status and steered them to shock wins over St Helens and Bradford Northern on their route to Wembley glory, the former halfback subsequently becoming the only non-player to receive the Man of Steel award.

Graham Morris

1984 RUGBY LEAGUE CHALLENGE CUP FINAL
Widnes v Wigan

The 1984 Widnes-Wigan Challenge Cup Final was lifted above the level of mundane through two breathtaking long-distance tries from the Chemics 20-year-old three-quarter Joe Lydon. The first came on the half-hour as Widnes protected a fragile 6–2 lead in their 25-yard area, second-row Les Gorley catching a ball that had been charged down by a colleague from an attempted Mark Cannon chip-kick. Gorley gave a short pass to Kevin Tamati who transferred smartly to

Widnes team manager Vince Karalius revives memories of his playing days as John Basnett (left) and Keiron O'Loughlin chair him with the Challenge Cup at Wembley

Lydon, the centre setting off down the left, accelerating past the cover before going under the posts following a thrilling 80-yard sprint. His second effort—with 10 minutes remaining—sealed victory. Wigan were again applying pressure inside the Widnes '25' only for the predatory Lydon to scoop up the ball after Gary Stephens lost possession in a tackle. Racing through a gap he handed off full back Shaun Edwards and avoided a despairing tackle from David Stephenson—who slid into touch—to score midway between the posts and left-hand corner, having covered 85 yards.

Wigan—minus full back Steve Hampson who sustained a broken leg the previous month—opened the scoring when Colin Whitfield, with his second penalty attempt—having missed a difficult touchline effort three minutes earlier—succeeded with a 45-yard kick in the 17th minute after Kevin Tamati interfered at a play-the-ball. Widnes' Keiron O'Loughlin claimed Wembley's first four-point try 10 minutes later after accepting John Basnett's inside pass following a break by Gorley. It was a near thing for O'Loughlin who somehow managed to retrieve the ball as he dived over after it squirted out of his grasp. With Mick Burke, who missed a penalty four minutes previous, adding the goal and augmenting Lydon's first

WINNING CAPTAIN

Eric Hughes (Widnes 1984)

Eric Hughes played 488 times for Widnes in a playing career that stretched from 1969 until 1984. Signed from Widnes rugby union club, the speedy stand-off shared many honours at Naughton Park, including the Rugby League Challenge Cup (1975, 1979, 1981, 1984), Premiership Trophy (1982, 1983), Championship (1977/78), Players' No.6 Trophy (1975/76), John Player Trophy (1978/79), BBC2 Floodlit Trophy (1978/79) and Lancashire Cup (1974, 1975, 1978, 1979). He was a tourist in 1979, appeared in eight Tests, and represented England (10 times—including 1975 World Cup) and Lancashire (11). During the 1976 close season he played in Australia with Canterbury-Bankstown. After retiring as a player, he held several coaching appointments; Widnes (1984–86), Rochdale Hornets (1987–88), St Helens (1994–96), Leigh (1996) and Wigan (1997). Elder brother Arthur was in Widnes' pack at Wembley in 1964.

Australian prop Kerry Hemsley—scorer of Wigan's only try—races through a gap in the Widnes defence

Edwards, meanwhile, took over the mantle of youngest Wembley finalist at 17 years, 202 days. Wigan fielded a record five overseas players including Australian prop Helmsley who flew back from his homeland after being on loan earlier in the season. With Widnes including New Zealander Kevin Tamati, it set an overall high of six.

strike three minutes afterwards, it put the Chemics 12–2 up at the break.

Mike O'Neill extended the lead with a 49th minute left-footed drop-goal from in front of the posts. Nine minutes later Lydon broke down the left but just failed to recover his own kick as it bounced into touch near the corner, making amends with his second try in the 70th minute. Burke just missed the goal, the scoreboard showing 17–2. Wigan, having given a lacklustre display in front of their vast army of fans, gained a consolation try when Stephens put Kerry Hemsley over in the 74th minute. John Pendlebury, taking over from the substituted Whitfield, missed the goal. Burke completed the 19–6 score-line with a 30-yard penalty three minutes later after Pendlebury was pulled up for an incorrect play-the-ball. In the final minute Wigan's Howie Tamati crossed the try-line from acting-halfback but was turned on his back.

In an afternoon of milestones, Widnes and Wigan shared a record 12th Wembley appearance, the former setting a new marker with a seventh win at the stadium. It was also a record seventh Wembley appearance for Widnes' Mick Adams, Keith Elwell and Eric Hughes, the trio equalling the four wins at the venue enjoyed by Brian Lockwood and Alex Murphy.

STATS

Widnes 19 Wigan 6

Saturday 5 May at Wembley Stadium, London (3.00 pm)

Widnes (white with black stripes on sleeves): Burke, Wright, Hughes (captain), Lydon, Basnett, O'Loughlin, Gregory, S. O'Neill, Elwell, K. Tamati, Gorley, M. O'Neill, Adams. Substitutes: D. Hulme, F. Whitfield. Team manager: V. Karalius

Wigan (cherry and white hoops): Edwards, Ramsdale, Stephenson, C. Whitfield, Gill, Cannon, Stephens, Hemsley, H. Tamati, Case, West (captain), Scott, Pendlebury. Substitutes: Elvin, Juliff. Coach: A. Murphy

Referee: W.H. Thompson

Touch-judges: B. Robinson, R. Parker

Half-time: 12–2 Attendance: 80,116 Receipts: £686,171

Weather: sunny and warm

Lance Todd Trophy: Lydon (Widnes)

Cup presentation: Lord Derby, Rugby League president

Progressive score:

Widnes	score (min)	Wigan
	0–2 (17)	C. Whitfield penalty
O'Loughlin try, Burke goal	6–2 (27)	
Lydon try, Burke goal	12–2 (30)	
M. O'Neill drop-goal	13–2 (49)	
Lydon try	17–2 (70)	
	17–6 (74)	Hemsley try
Burke penalty	19–6 (77)	

Route to the final:

Preliminary round: Carlisle 12 Widnes 20

First round: Widnes 54 Dewsbury 10, Bramley 10 Wigan 10

First round replay: Wigan 34 Bramley 4

Second round: Fulham 10 Widnes 12, Wigan 30 Oldham 6

Third round: Widnes 21 Hull Kingston Rovers 10, St Helens 7 Wigan 16

Semi-finals: Widnes 15 Leeds 4 (Station Road, Swinton, 14,046)

Wigan 14 York 8 (Elland Road, Leeds, 17,156)

Head-to-head form guide:

Widnes 36 Wigan 20 (Lancashire Cup)

Wigan 16 Widnes 31 (League)

Widnes 20 Wigan 15 (John Player Trophy)

Widnes 21 Wigan 14 (League)

Graham Morris

TELEVISION COVERAGE

Television today is crucial to rugby league's lifeblood, generating vital revenue through TV fees and sponsorship, but initial overtures by the BBC were treated with caution, the Rugby Football League wary of damaging attendances and gate receipts. The 1948 Challenge Cup Final was the first seen live although, with the medium in its infancy, in the London area only. George Duckworth, dubbed by the *Radio Times* as the 'famous English cricketer and rugby league expert' and Michael Henderson, who 'points out the differences between the two sets of rules (League and Union)' held the microphones. The same partnership commentated in 1949 and 1950, transmission extending to the Midlands by the time of the latter. All three matches were covered in full, scheduling being 2.45 pm until 4.40 pm.

The installation of BBC's Holme Moss transmitter on the Pennines brought television north in 1951 and, on 10 November that year, the Great Britain-New Zealand Test from Swinton was the first rugby league game transmitted in the area, followed by a Wigan-Wakefield Trinity league fixture in January and then the 1952 Challenge Cup Final, all shown in their entirety. The Wembley attendance, though, was 22,000 below the previous year and permission for further coverage was withheld until 1958 when another disappointing crowd—66,109—was the lowest since 1946.

In 1960 a coin toss at RFL headquarters was lost by Hull, who thus wore black shorts at Wembley instead of white, the BBC citing insufficient contrast between theirs and Wakefield's kit for the then monochrome coverage. Concerns over television eased in 1961 when over 94,000 attended and, in 1963, it seemed the occasion had gone international, the *Wakefield Express* reporting that it was broadcast on Belgian television from Brussels. Since 1958, the sequence of live coverage by the BBC has been broken just once, the 1982 Hull-Widnes replay at Elland Road, Leeds, being shown as 'highlights' only on the BBC1 Sportsnight programme later that Wednesday evening.

Today, television has a role in determining the outcome. Post-match controversy concerning the 1997 and 1998 finals prompted suggestions for a video referee, already being pioneered by Sky Television. A video referee was used for the first time at the 1999

WEMBLEY COMES NORTH

In 1952 many Workington Town fans decided against the longest trek yet to London, preferring the 'novelty' of watching on television instead, boosting trade for local dealers. *The Pontefract and Castleford Express*—which covered opponents Featherstone Rovers—carried a pre-Cup Final advert for television sets with the slogan: 'Bring Wembley into your home.' The following week, the same newspaper reported that 'people sorted themselves into television parties all over the town—eight, ten and twenty neighbours crowding into private sitting-rooms.'

Challenge Cup Final (replacing in-goal judges introduced in 1995), his verdict conveyed via a cluster of eight green or eight red lights. Since then video referees have sanctioned 20 of 79 tries scored, a big screen—mimicking Sky's example—being used since 2000.

Eddie Waring commentated on every final from 1958 until 1981, a total of 24. He was also involved in 1952 when Alan Dixon was lead commentator, and—according to Tony Hannan's excellent book *Being Eddie Waring*—had a supporting role in 1949. His successor, Ray French, led the commentary team for 27 consecutive years (1982–2008), Dave Woods taking over in 2009.

BBC TELEVISION CHALLENGE CUP FINAL LIVE COMMENTARY TEAMS

1948–50: Michael Henderson, George Duckworth
1951: no broadcast
1952: Alan Dixon, Eddie Waring
1953–57: no broadcast
1958–59: Eddie Waring, Bill Fallowfield
1960–75: Eddie Waring
1976–78: Eddie Waring, David Watkins
1979–81: Eddie Waring, Alex Murphy
1982: Ray French, Alex Murphy
1982 replay: no live broadcast
1983: Ray French, Alex Murphy, Keith Fielding
1984: Ray French, Allan Agar
1985–86: Ray French, Alex Murphy
1987: Ray French, Maurice Bamford
1988: Ray French, Alex Murphy
1989: Ray French, Peter Fox
1990: Ray French, Alex Murphy
1991–93: Ray French, Ross Strudwick
1994: Ray French, Steve Simms
1995: Ray French, Steve Simms, Terry Flanagan
1996–97: Ray French, Steve Simms, Joe Lydon
1998: Ray French, Joe Lydon
1999–2008: Ray French, Jonathan Davies
2009: Dave Woods, Jonathan Davies
(Note: First named is 'lead' commentator, others acting as 'summariser'. Broadcast was to London region only 1948–49, London and Midland regions only 1950.)

Gary Prohm starts the Hull Kingston Rovers fight back as he squeezes into the corner in the 65th minute for his second try

through the defence from 60 yards out off a peach of a pass from Ward, Martin Ketteridge adding the goal. Seven minutes later Dorahy opened Rovers' account with a penalty, awarded for interference at a play-the-ball, Bob Beardmore responding with a drop-goal to ease Castleford 7–2 ahead. With half-time on the horizon Rovers registered their first try when a misdirected pass on halfway by Castleford's Keith England found its way into Kelly's hands. The second-rower quickly handed on to Prohm who burst through a huge gap to make it 7–6, Dorahy missing the goal that would have given his team an unexpected interval lead.

It took three minutes of the second half for Castleford to increase their tally, Bob Beardmore, from just inside the Rovers 25-yard area, taking an

inside pass from his brother and acting-halfback Kevin before toe-poking a speculative kick through a melee of defenders towards the right corner. Following up through a static-looking Rovers defence, he dived on the ball at the feet of Prohm for the touchdown. In the 55th minute the match was put on hold whilst concussed Rovers forward Des Harrison was treated, eventually being taken off on a stretcher. Five minutes later, a third Castleford try resulted from a scrum on halfway, John Joyner breaking away before sending the diminutive Jamie Sandy on a 40-yard sprint. With defenders in hot pursuit, the winger crossed the try-line despite being tackled. With Ketteridge going wide with both his second half conversion attempts, Castleford led 15–6 and Rovers were looking a tired outfit until Prohm revived their spirits.

Castleford—the latest club to fly recently loaned players from Australia in Sandy and Ian French—included three men who had not figured in the previous rounds; Kevin Beardmore and Gary Hyde (both through injury problems), and Gary Lord (the 19-year-old's impressive recent form earning his place). Rovers, already missing unlucky second-row pair Chris Burton and Phil Hogan having both suffered broken arms in recent weeks, were further disrupted when loose forward Gavin Miller pulled a hamstring on the eve of the final. Although he played with his left thigh heavily strapped, it was soon apparent he was struggling. Despite Rovers matching Castleford's three tries, they lacked the desire that saw them overcome Leeds in the semi-final replay.

WINNING CAPTAIN

John Joyner (Castleford 1986)

John Joyner played for Castleford from 1972 until 1992, making a club record 613 appearances. A stylish, elusive centre, he also lined up at stand-off and loose forward in later years. Born in Leeds, he graduated through the Castleford under–17s side, his dazzling performances earning him selection for Great Britain (16 times), England (4) and Yorkshire (12). He was also a tourist three times (1979, 1984, 1988). His successes with Castleford included the Rugby League Challenge Cup (1986), Players' No.6 Trophy (1976/77), BBC2 Floodlit Trophy (1976/77) and Yorkshire Cup (1977, 1981, 1986). After retiring he took over as Castleford coach (1993–97) having previously been assistant-coach.

1987 RUGBY LEAGUE CHALLENGE CUP FINAL
Halifax v St Helens

Contrasting moods on the substitutes' bench as the match ends. St Helens' Paul Forber (foreground) looks downcast whilst the two Halifax players (wearing hoops) Graham Beevers (left) and Mick Scott leap into the air

For the third successive year the Challenge Cup Final conjured up a pulsating ending as Halifax hung on for victory over St Helens in a match that produced, arguably, the most crucial Wembley tackle of all. Its perpetrator was John Pendlebury, who had previously put the Thrum Hall's 19–12 ahead in the 64th minute with what ultimately proved a match-winning drop-goal.

Lance Todd Trophy winner Graham Eadie leaves St Helens' Phil Veivers (left) and Mark Elia grounded as he scores for Halifax in the 50th minute

St Helens had raised the temperature to boiling point with 12 minutes remaining, Paul Round, from acting-halfback, executing a wrap-around passing move with Graham Liptrot before cutting through to dive over the line with Graham Eadie hanging on. Loughlin added the goal to leave Halifax clinging on by one point. The tension was almost unbearable for the Yorkshire fans as Saints exerted tremendous pressure on their line, their worst fears seemingly realised as Mark Elia broke through in the 74th minute. But, as he dived over the try-line in the left corner, Pendlebury somehow grabbed him with a desperate lunge, his right fist knocking the ball from Elia's grasp for an incredible try-saver. The danger, though, was not over and, four minutes later, Elia dived in at the same spot but Andy Platt's pass was ruled forward. In the final minute Halifax's Paul Dixon was just held short and, seconds later, team-mate Colin Whitfield found an opening, but passed the ball to a St Helens player.

Halifax had taken an 11th minute lead when Wilf George went over in the corner, Gary Stephens having broken through on the left channel from 25 yards,

Mick Scott continuing the move and shrugging off three defenders before delivering the final pass. The try stood despite claims George hit touch in-goal before placing the ball. Whitfield, having missed a 30-yard penalty four minutes earlier, added an excellent goal. Paul Loughlin pulled two points back for Saints after Grant Rix was ruled offside. In the 23rd minute Kevin McCormack almost got St Helens' first try but was held up a yard short near the left corner, Whitfield missing his second penalty, from 30 yards, five minutes later. Halifax increased their lead to 12–2 when Seamus McCallion, from acting-halfback, threw himself between a group of defenders to score to the left of the posts, Whitfield augmenting.

Forty seconds into the second half St Helens obtained their elusive try, Elia taking a pass from Platt on his own 25-yard line to race down the left flank, bypassing Eadie on the outside with comparative ease, Loughlin adding the goal. Eadie made amends in the 50th minute, strolling in behind the posts after Pendlebury, breaking from the base of a scrum, found him in 'acres' of space. Whitfield augmented to restore the 10-point margin. St Helens, though, retaliated two minutes later when Elia sent Loughlin on his way from 25 yards out, dummying his way through two

defenders before scoring, although his goal effort went wide, Halifax leading 18–12. Five minutes later George almost had his second try but was pushed into touch, snapping the left-hand corner flag in the process.

When Pendlebury's one-pointer placed Halifax two scores ahead it looked as though the trophy was destined for Thrum Hall after a 48-year wait. But it was a close call in what was the first Challenge Cup Final to exceed £1m in receipts.

WINNING CAPTAIN

Chris Anderson (Halifax 1987)

Australian three-quarter Chris Anderson initially built his reputation as a quick, elusive wingman, bagging 92 tries in 232 matches for his first senior club, Canterbury-Bankstown (1971–84). During this period he played in three Grand Finals (winning in 1980) and represented Australia (11 times—including the 1975 World Cup) and New South Wales (8). He was in three Australian touring teams; to Great Britain and France (1978, 1982), New Zealand (1980). Born in Condoblin, New South Wales, and signed from the Forbes club of West Wyalong (New South Wales) in 1970, he spent part of the 1974/75 British season on loan to Widnes where, having played 18 times (October–February), he flew back for the Rugby League Challenge Cup Final, being rewarded with a winners' medal. In 1984 he transferred to Hull Kingston Rovers but, after only two appearances during November, joined Halifax. As player-coach at Thrum Hall, he moved to stand-off with great success winning the Rugby League Challenge Cup (1987), Championship (1985/86) and Charity Shield (1986). He finished playing after the 1986/87 campaign, continuing as coach in 1987/88 before returning home to take charge of Canterbury-Bankstown (1990–97), Melbourne Storm (1998–2001), Cronulla Sharks (2002–03) and Australia (1999–2003). Following his surprise appointment as coach of Welsh rugby union's Newport Gwent Dragons (2004–05), he returned to Australian rugby league, coaching Sydney Roosters in 2007.

STATS

Halifax 19 St Helens 18

Saturday 2 May at Wembley Stadium, London (3.00 pm)

Halifax (blue and white hoops): Eadie, Wilson, Whitfield, Rix, George, Anderson (captain), Stephens, Beevers, McCallion, Neller, Dixon, Scott, Pendlebury. Substitutes: Juliff, James. Player-coach: C. Anderson

St Helens (white with red chevron): Veivers, Ledger, Loughlin, Elia, McCormack, Clark, Holding, Burke, Liptrot, Fieldhouse, Platt, Haggerty, Arkwright (captain). Substitutes: Round, Forber (dnp). Coach: A. Murphy

Referee: J. Holdsworth
Touch-judges: D. Watson, A. Thornbury
Half-time: 12–2 Attendance: 91,267 Receipts: £1,009,206
Weather: sunny   Lance Todd Trophy: Eadie (Halifax)
Cup presentation: H.R.H. The Duke of Edinburgh

Progressive score:

Halifax	score (min)	St Helens
George try, Whitfield goal	6–0 (11)	
	6–2 (20)	Loughlin penalty
McCallion try, Whitfield goal	12–2 (33)	
	12–8 (41)	Elia try, Loughlin goal
Eadie try, Whitfield goal	18–8 (50)	
	18–12 (52)	Loughlin try
Pendlebury drop-goal	19–12 (64)	
	19–18 (68)	Round try, Loughlin goal

Route to the final:

Preliminary round: St Helens 18 Swinton 16
First round: Fulham 10 Halifax 38, Dewsbury 12 St Helens 48
Second round: Halifax 29 Hunslet 10, Oldham 14 St Helens 24
Third round: Halifax 35 Hull Kingston Rovers 7, St Helens 41 Whitehaven 12
Semi-finals:
Halifax 12 Widnes 8 (Headingley, Leeds, 16,064),
St Helens 14 Leigh 8 (Central Park, Wigan, 13,105)

Head-to-head form guide:

St Helens 38 Halifax 16 (League)
Halifax 20 St Helens 19 (League)

Graham Morris

1988 RUGBY LEAGUE CHALLENGE CUP FINAL
Wigan v Halifax

Wigan produced a display of supreme quality in overcoming holders Halifax 32–12 to win the 1988 Challenge Cup Final, setting new Wembley records of eight wins and 14 appearances. Despite the Cherry and Whites phoenix-like emergence as Britain's outstanding rugby league combination, few in the crowd would dare think they were witnessing the beginning of an unprecedented Wembley dynasty. On paper, Wigan's side—which now included big name signings like Dean Bell, Andy Goodway, Andy Gregory, Ellery Hanley, Kevin Iro and Joe Lydon—looked a more formidable adversary than on their last visit three years earlier, although unlucky full back, Steve Hampson, missed out a third time, having broken an arm 17 days earlier. Hampson took his setback bravely, saying: 'I can cope, I am used to it by now. Somebody up there does not want me to appear

at Wembley, but one day I will be there.' Happily his prediction would be realised.

Wigan did not find top gear until the 24th minute, scoring the first of four unconverted pre-interval tries. Gregory was the initiator, creating an opening for Shaun Edwards to go on a thrilling 75-yard run before being hauled down yards from the Halifax posts. His quick play-the-ball saw acting-halfback Kevin Iro thrust his way between two defenders to go over. Minutes later, a wonderful 45-yard breakaway by Hanley almost led to another try but Tony Iro's inside pass to brother Kevin was dropped with a try begging. But further touchdowns soon followed from Henderson Gill (in the left corner off Bell's pass following a Gregory break), Kevin Iro (again in the left corner following brother Tony's tremendous 50-yard run from the restart to set up the position), and Lydon (finishing off a great bout of inter-passing down the left between Gill, Bell and Edwards). With no specialist marksman, Gill (an easy kick), Lydon (twice), and Gregory (hit the upright) all failed to augment, the score standing at 16–0.

Seven minutes into the second half, Tony Iro went over in the right corner from 10 yards out off Gregory's wide pass, Gill missing the conversion. From the restart, Lydon caught the ball, racing 70 yards before transferring to Hanley on the Halifax 25-yard line, the loose forward scoring the try of the afternoon under the posts. At last the extra points were obtained, Gregory being on target for a 26–0 lead. Halifax—disrupted by the loss of two of their most creative players in Les Holliday (knee ligaments in

Joe Lydon finishes off a spectacular Wigan move by diving over for a try shortly before half-time

the 20th minute) and scrum half Steve Robinson (concussion in the 48th)—gained some respectability when Tony Anderson recorded a try near the right corner-flag off Ian Wilkinson's pass, Colin Whifield adding a great touchline goal. It led to their best spell of the game, twice more coming close to crossing Wigan's try-line. But it was short-lived, Gregory, with a great dummy, breaking from just inside his own half to send Edwards on a lengthy run, his pass to Hanley (which looked forward) allowing the latter to send Bell in near the posts, Lydon converting. Two minutes later Gregory's kick into the right corner was followed up by Tony Iro who touched down, repeating a move executed by the pair in the 13th minute, the winger being ruled offside each time. Halifax scored the final try, prop Neil James dummying his way over, Whitfield adding the goal.

Shaun Edwards—Wembley's youngest ever captain at 21 years 195 days—played with a hamstring problem (Ged Byrne replacing him five minutes from time), although still making a major contribution. After defeating Salford 34–4 in the semi-final at rain-soaked Burnden Park—an occasion sullied by crowd violence from an army of trouble-making youths who, it transpired, were not rugby league supporters—cup-tie 'fever' hit Wigan. Their 17,000 allocation of tickets sold

within hours, chairman Maurice Lindsay displaying enterprise by travelled to Wembley to 'negotiate' an extra 500 tickets, a move that, apparently, displeased Rugby Football League officials!

STATS

Wigan 32 Halifax 12

Saturday 30 April at Wembley Stadium, London (3.00 pm)

Wigan (cherry and white hoops): Lydon, T. Iro, K. Iro, Bell, Gill, Edwards (captain), Gregory, Case, Kiss, Shelford, Goodway, Potter, Hanley. Substitutes: Byrne, Wane. Coach: G. Lowe

Halifax (blue and white hoops): Eadie (captain), Meredith, T. Anderson, Wilkinson, Whitfield, Grogan, Robinson, James, McCallion, Neller, Holliday, Dixon, Pendlebury. Substitutes: Fairbank, Scott. Coach: C. Anderson

Referee: G.F. Lindop Touch-judges: J. Easter, W. Walker

Half-time: 16–0 Attendance: 94,273 Receipts: £1,102,247

Weather: cloudy and dry, slight breeze

Lance Todd Trophy: Gregory (Wigan)

Cup presentation: The Hon. Douglas McClelland AC, High Commissioner for Australia

Progressive score:

Wigan	score (min)	Halifax
K. Iro try	4–0 (24)	
Gill try	8–0 (27)	
K. Iro try	12–0 (29)	
Lydon try	16–0 (38)	
T. Iro try	20–0 (47)	
Hanley try, Gregory goal	26–0 (49)	
	26–6 (56)	T. Anderson try, Whitfield goal
Bell try, Lydon goal	32–6 (66)	
	32–12 (69)	James try, Whitfield goal

Route to the final:

First round:
Wigan 2 Bradford Northern 0, Heworth (York) 4 Halifax 60

Second round:
Wigan 30 Leeds 14, Halifax 30 Rochdale Hornets 6

Third round:
Wigan 10 Widnes 1, Hull Kingston Rovers 4 Halifax 26

Semi-finals:
Wigan 34 Salford 4 (Burnden Park, Bolton, 20,783),

Halifax 0 Hull 0 (Headingley, Leeds, 20,534)

Semi-final replay: Halifax 4 Hull 3 (Elland Road, Leeds, 25,117)

Head-to-head form guide:

Wigan 44 Halifax 12 (Charity Shield, Douglas, Isle of Man)

Wigan 14 Halifax 17 (League)

Halifax 14 Wigan 16 (League)

Wigan's Ellery Hanley evades the tackle of Halifax's Martin Meredith on his way to scoring the best try of the match following a dazzling break from Joe Lydon

1989 RUGBY LEAGUE CHALLENGE CUP FINAL
Wigan v St Helens

Gary Connolly of St Helens tries to outmanoeuvre Wigan's Tony Iro (number 2)

Wigan graced Wembley for a fourth time in six seasons, taking on arch rivals St Helens in the third meeting of the two Lancashire giants at the venue. Wigan reversed the previous two Challenge Cup Final results with a resounding 27–0 victory watched by a crowd limited to 78,000 due to the stadium's ongoing redevelopment towards becoming an all-seated facility.

St Helens included 17-year-old Gary Connolly—still registered as an amateur—at full back, but inside the first minute, he dropped the ball fielding a deep clearance kick from Wigan's Joe Lydon, placing Saints under early pressure. In only the second minute, from a St Helens drop-out under the posts, Wigan's Ellery Hanley ran the ball back from midfield and, moving right, he connected with Kevin Iro who beat four players on a great touchline burst to score near the right corner. Lydon just missed the goal but was on the mark with a 19th minute 45-yard penalty, Paul Groves being guilty of 'lying on' after a tackle. Seven minutes later Hanley scored one of Wembley's greatest tries, Andy Gregory and Shaun Edwards combining to send

him on a mesmerising 40-yard run, beating five defenders with power and pace to go behind the posts virtually untouched. Lydon's goal made it 12–0. Nine minutes before the break, St Helens provided a rare threat, Neil Holding's high kick into Wigan's in-goal being dealt with by Steve Hampson as Phil Veivers breathed down his neck.

Four minutes into the second half, Gregory—back after a month out with an ankle ligament injury—coolly landed a drop-goal from in front of the posts, pushing St Helens three scores behind at 13–0. Three minutes later Kevin Iro got his second try, going over in the right corner after evading two defenders to conclude a seven-man move that covered the width of the pitch. Lydon was well wide with his goal effort. St Helens then had their best spell of the match but could not create an opening and, in the 65th minute, Edwards—from just inside Wigan's half—dummied through a gap from acting-halfback, racing downfield to send Gregory over with a short inside pass in front of the posts. Lydon converted for a 23–0 lead.

Connolly produced a last-ditch tackle on Lydon when a try looked certain before, four minutes later, Hampson—celebrating his Wembley debut at last—came up with the most popular try of the match, taking Lydon's pass after a passing move that stretched across the field. Lydon missed the goal but Hampson's smile was the biggest of the afternoon! In the final minute Tony Iro almost scored in the right corner but a forward pass was ruled.

Although the match disappointed as a contest, there was much to admire in Wigan's excellent display.

It was a record ninth Wembley success, their overall total of 10 victories equalling that of Leeds, whilst Gregory became the sixth player to win four Wembley winners' medals. St Helens—who flew in Michael O'Connor and Paul Vautin from Australia for the occasion—was the first scoreless side at Wembley since 1951.

Steve Hampson scores the concluding try for Wigan—the most warmly applauded of the match

STATS

Wigan 27 St Helens 0

Saturday 29 April at Wembley Stadium, London (3.00 pm)

Wigan (blue and white hoops): Hampson, T. Iro, K. Iro, Bell, Lydon, Edwards, Gregory, Lucas, Kiss, Shelford, Platt, Potter, Hanley (captain). Substitutes: Betts, Goodway. Coach: G. Lowe

St Helens (white with red chevron): Connolly, O'Connor, Veivers, Loughlin, Quirk, Cooper, Holding, Burke, Groves, Forber, Dwyer, Haggerty, Vautin (captain). Substitutes: Bloor, Evans. Coach: A. Murphy

Referee: R. Tennant Touch-judges: S. Jackson, J. Ward

Half-time: 12–0 Attendance: 78,000 Receipts: £1,121,293

Weather: cloudy Lance Todd Trophy: Hanley (Wigan)

Cup presentation: The Rt Hon. Viscount Whitelaw

Progressive score:

Wigan	score (min)	St Helens
K. Iro try	4–0 (2)	
Lydon penalty	6–0 (19)	
Hanley try, Lydon goal	12–0 (26)	
Gregory drop-goal	13–0 (44)	
K. Iro try	17–0 (47)	
Gregory try, Lydon goal	23–0 (65)	
Hampson try	27–0 (75)	

Route to the final:

First round: Doncaster 6 Wigan 38, Swinton 5 St Helens 16

Second round: Bradford Northern 4 Wigan 17, St Helens 28 Barrow 6

Third round: Oldham 4 Wigan 12, St Helens 32 Featherstone Rovers 3

Semi-finals: Wigan 13 Warrington 6 (Maine Road, Manchester, 26,529), St Helens 16 Widnes 14 (Central Park, Wigan, 17,119)

Head-to-head form guide:

St Helens 11 Wigan 18 (League)

Wigan 14 St Helens 7 (League)

Wigan 2 St Helens 4 (Premiership Trophy)

WINNING CAPTAIN

Ellery Hanley (Wigan 1989, 1990, 1991)

Ellery Hanley was, arguably, the most outstanding British player of the late-1980s/early-1990s, his power and pace creating an imposing on-field presence. He signed with Bradford Northern as a 17-year-old in 1978 from the Corpus Christi club of Leeds, playing mostly at stand-off. His reputation grew and during the 1984/85 season he scored 55 tries, the highest in Britain since 1960/61. He moved to Wigan in 1985 for a record £85,000, taking over as club captain during the 1986/87 campaign when he also relocated to loose forward and scored 63 tries. With Wigan he won the Rugby League Challenge Cup (1988, 1989, 1990, 1991), World Club Challenge (1987), Premiership Trophy (1987), Championship (1986/87, 1989/90, 1990/91), John Player Trophy (1985/86, 1986/87, 1988/89), Regal Trophy (1989/90) and Lancashire Cup (1985, 1986, 1987, 1988). A £250,000 move to Leeds in 1991 set another transfer record, his final match being in 1995. He had several short-term spells in Australia with Balmain (1988, 1996, 1997) and Western Suburbs (1989). A tourist in 1984, 1988 and 1992, the latter two as captain (injury costing him a third tour captaincy in 1990), he made 36 Test appearances (19 as captain), played for England (twice) and Yorkshire (5 times). He coached Great Britain (1994–95), England (1994–95) and St Helens (1998–2000), later moving to rugby union, being on the coaching staff for England, Bristol and Bath. Returning to rugby league, he briefly joined Castleford Tigers as a coaching consultant during 2004 and was Doncaster coach in 2008. He received the MBE in 1990 and was elected to the Rugby League Hall of Fame in 2005.

Graham Morris

1990 RUGBY LEAGUE CHALLENGE CUP FINAL
Wigan v Warrington

Wigan celebrated a record third consecutive Challenge Cup Final victory in 1990, watched for the first time by an all-seated Wembley audience. They achieved it with another emphatic Wembley score, this time by 36–14 over an edgy-looking Warrington. Wigan fielded several players below full fitness who required pain-killing injections, in particular Andy Gregory (groin), Ellery Hanley (pelvic) and Shaun Edwards (broken hand). Warrington were without injured centre Tony Thorniley and stand-off Robert Turner. The latter—the club's regular marksman—lost his bid to recover from a knee ligament problem, the goal-kicking duties falling to Paul Bishop.

Warrington, tackling robustly, gave away two penalties in the opening minute, setting the standard for a match that contained several disagreeable moments as players faced up to each other. Bishop missed penalty kicks in the sixth and 14th minutes, Wigan's Joe Lydon making no mistake with an angled 35-metre shot in the 10th, awarded after a foul on Edwards, his kick being delayed whilst the player received treatment. Edwards' injury, from a Bob Jackson blow, was later diagnosed as a depressed cheekbone and fractured eye socket, costing his place in the forthcoming Great Britain tour. Incredibly, he remained on the field until the final few minutes.

Warrington almost claimed the first try in the 15th minute when Paul Darbyshire followed up Bishop's cross-field kick into the left corner but Mark Forster had already fumbled the ball during the chase. Five minutes later, Wigan's Denis Betts scored, grabbing the ball and resisting Des Drummond's challenge after Edwards charged down a David Lyon clearance near his own line. Lydon converted. Bishop finally registered Warrington's first points with a penalty just to the side of the posts, Duane Mann having been held down following a tackle, making it 8–2 to Wigan. Warrington, inspired by Bishop's smart kicking, began to threaten but disaster struck in the 32nd minute when Gary Mercer's attempted short overhead kick landed in speedster Mark Preston's arms, the Wigan winger racing 80 metres down the left touchline, escaping Lyon's despairing tackle to score. Lydon added the extra points, plus a 40-metre penalty after Gary Sanderson held down Hanley following a tackle to make it 16–2. Warrington put a more positive spin on their half-time team-talk when Bishop's jinking run and pass sent Mike Gregory through a hole, beating off four defenders to go under the posts. Bishop obliged with the conversion.

Trailing 16–8, any idea of a

Determination is etched on the face of Wigan skipper Ellery Hanley as he breaks away against Warrington

Wires comeback was dispelled by a 14-minute three-try Wigan blitz. Kevin Iro got the first nine minutes after the resumption, powering past two defenders to go behind the posts after being set up by Edwards and Hanley. Six minutes later came the try of the match; Steve Hampson broke out of his 22-metre area, Hanley taking over with a terrific run before transferring to Edwards whose inside pass sent Preston racing over in the left corner. Next up was Hanley, charging in behind the posts as Mann and Lyon failed to detain him, following a great break and overhead pass from Andy Gregory. With Lydon succeeding with two of the three conversion attempts the score shot up to 32–8 and the cup was as good as in the Central Park trophy cabinet. Lyon got one back for Warrington, his 40-metre run to the posts, pulling out of Lydon's tackle on the way, being set up by Mike Gregory who broke from the scrum base, off-loading as the tackle came in. With Bishop leaving concussed midway through the second half, Darbyshire added the goal. Iro completed the scoring four minutes later with a try in the corner off Ian Gildart's pass. An altercation followed, Iro throwing the ball into the face of Drummond, after taking exception to his tackle. For the third year running Iro fell one short of Wembley's first try hat-trick, having a 68th minute score disallowed through Andy Goodway's forward pass.

Andy Gregory became the second player to win the Lance Todd Trophy twice following Gerry Helme in the 1950s, whilst claiming a record fifth Wembley Challenge Cup win.

Prop Neil Harmon races through a gap for Warrington

STATS

Wigan 36 Warrington 14

Saturday 28 April at Wembley Stadium, London (3.00 pm)

Wigan (cherry and white irregular hoops): Hampson, Lydon, K. Iro, Bell, Preston, Edwards, A. Gregory, Shelford, Dermott, Platt, Betts, Goodway, Hanley (captain). Substitutes: Goulding, Gildart. Coach: J. Monie

Warrington (primrose and blue hoops): Lyon, Drummond, Mercer, Darbyshire, Foster, Crompton, Bishop, Burke, Mann, Harmon, Jackson, Sanderson, M. Gregory (captain). Substitutes: McGinty, Thomas. Coach: B. Johnson

Referee: J. Holdsworth

Touch-judges: W. Goulding, G. Wheatley

Half-time: 16–8 Attendance: 77,729 Receipts: £1,360,000

Weather: sunny and warm

Lance Todd Trophy: Gregory (Wigan)

Cup presentation: Sir Peter Harding, Air Chief Marshall

Progressive score:

Wigan	score (min)	Warrington
Lydon penalty	2–0 (10)	
Betts try, Lydon goal	8–0 (20)	
	8–2 (24)	Bishop penalty
Preston try, Lydon goal	14–2 (32)	
Lydon penalty	16–2 (35)	
	16–8 (40)	M. Gregory try, Bishop goal
K. Iro try, Lydon goal	22–8 (49)	
Preston try	26–8 (55)	
Hanley try, Lydon goal	32–8 (62)	
	32–14 (74)	Lyon try, Darbyshire goal
K. Iro try	36–14 (78)	

Route to the final:

First round: Hull Kingston Rovers 4 Wigan 6, Warrington 20 Featherstone Rovers 12

Second round: Wigan 30 Dewsbury 6, Warrington 20 Trafford Borough 11

Third round: Wakefield Trinity 14 Wigan 26, Bradford Northern 10 Warrington 12

Semi-finals:

Wigan 20 St Helens 14 (Old Trafford, Manchester, 26,489),

Warrington 10 Oldham 6 (Central Park, Wigan, 15,631)

Head-to-head form guide:

Wigan 6 Warrington 18 (League)

Warrington 2 Wigan 8 (League)

Wigan 28 Warrington 26 (Premiership Trophy)

1991 RUGBY LEAGUE CHALLENGE CUP FINAL
Wigan v St Helens

For the second time in three seasons Wigan defeated St Helens at Wembley but, as with its predecessor, their meeting fell short of its pre-match hype. The score-line of 13–8—the closest call during Wigan's record run of four Wembley victories—suggests an enthralling edge-of-your-seat contest but, for the most part, reality was otherwise. Both gave the impression it was a match too far giving a weary display at the end of a hectic season, Wigan having played 10 times in 33 days to retain their Championship title.

As a contest, the occasion was rescued by an unexpected second half fight back by St Helens who—having struggled to retain possession in the opening period—came close to stealing the cup from Wigan's tiring grasp. The Cherry and Whites fielded several players patched up with pain killing injections, Ellery

St Helens' robust prop Kevin Ward tries to find a route between Wigan's Bobbie Goulding (14) and Denis Betts

Hanley testing his torn thigh muscle on the pitch ahead of kick-off before deciding to play, Joe Lydon withdrawing the previous day with a hamstring injury, David Myers replacing him. Meanwhile, prop Kelvin Skerrett missed out through suspension.

Early Wigan pressure was rewarded by a 12–0 lead in as many minutes, a 35-metre angled Frano Botica penalty (Duane Mann straying offside at a scrum) being followed by tries from Myers and Botica. Myers scored in unfortunate circumstances; Andy Gregory's long downfield kick was gathered by St Helens' Phil Veivers near his own try-line but, as Shaun Edwards

came in to tackle they appeared to clash heads, the Saints full back falling pole-axed to the ground. Kevin Iro recovered the loose ball to feed Myers who stepped inside Les Quirk to cross the whitewash near

STATS

Wigan 13 St Helens 8

Saturday 27 April at Wembley Stadium, London (2.30 pm)

Wigan (blue and white irregular hoops): Hampson, Myers, K. Iro, Bell, Botica, Edwards, Gregory, Lucas, Dermott, Platt, Betts, Clarke, Hanley (captain). Substitutes: Goulding, Goodway. Coach: J. Monie

St Helens (white with red chevron): Veivers, Hunte, Ropati, Loughlin, Quirk, Griffiths, Bishop, Neill, Dwyer, Ward, Harrison, Mann, Cooper (captain). Substitutes: Connolly, Groves. Coach: M. McClennan

Referee: J. Smith Touch-judges: R. Carter, J.E. Chamberlain

Half-time: 12–0 Attendance: 75,532 Receipts: £1,610,447

Weather: sunshine followed by heavy rain

Lance Todd Trophy: Betts (Wigan)

Cup presentation: The Rt Hon. Kenneth Clarke MP, Secretary of State for Education and Science

Progressive score:

Wigan	score (min)	St Helens
Botica penalty	2–0 (5)	
Myers try	6–0 (7)	
Botica try, Botica goal	12–0 (12)	
Gregory drop-goal	13–0 (47)	
	13–6 (61)	Hunte try, Bishop goal
	13–8 (71)	Bishop penalty

Route to the final:

First round: Castleford 4 Wigan 28, Swinton 8 St Helens 18

Second round: Rochdale Hornets 4 Wigan 72, St Helens 16 Wakefield Trinity 2

Third round: Wigan 12 Bradford Northern 2, Halifax 16 St Helens 24

Semi-finals: Wigan 30 Oldham 16 (Burnden Park, Bolton, 19,057), St Helens 19 Widnes 2 (Central Park, Wigan, 16,109)

Head-to-head form guide:

St Helens 15 Wigan 28 (League)

Wigan 28 St Helens 14 (League)

Two Wigan greats show of their winners' medals, Andy Gregory (left) and Ellery Hanley

the right corner. Vievers, meanwhile, was assisted, rubber-legged, from the field. Botica's try came five minutes later as rampant Wigan cashed in on Saints inability to retain possession. Dean Bell was the instigator, his neat sidestep taking him through the defence, Denis Betts continuing the move with a powerful run before off-loading to Botica who dived into the left corner. Having been just wide with the first conversion attempt, Botica tagged on a great goal.

Five minutes before the interval, Gregory's 40-metre drop-goal fell short. Then, on the stroke of half-time, St Helens almost scored, Bernard Dwyer's tremendous break from acting-halfback taking him from one end of the field to the other. He transferred to Gary Connolly who kicked over the remnants of Wigan's scattered defence, Botica—who had raced across from his wing—just beating Quirk to a ball that landed behind the posts.

Seven minutes into the second half, Gregory—mimicking his strategy of two years earlier—succeeded with his second drop-goal effort making it 13–0, Saints, therefore, having to score three times. Two minutes later St Helens' Paul Bishop made a break down the middle from his own half and, with just Steve Hampson to beat, kicked towards the try-line only for the full back to bring him down. It earned

Hampson 10 minutes in the sin-bin, but Bishop—covering for regular marksman Paul Loughlin (withdrawn at half-time through concussion)—failed with the resultant penalty kick, hitting the near post. Saints were having their best period and John Harrison, after a surging burst, was stopped near the posts, losing the ball in the process. Three minutes later, St Helens knocked on the door again, Dwyer almost going over. Their break came through a wayward Wigan pass near their own line which found Veivers (who had returned seven minutes earlier), the ball being whipped across to the right, Jonathan Griffiths' long pass putting Alan Hunte over in the corner. Bishop added the touchline goal plus a penalty 10 minutes later (Edwards holding down Quirk after a tackle) and, with a score of 13–8, the first real buzz of excitement went around the stadium. But there was no further scoring, Saints finishing with 12 men after Dwyer suffered a bad ear injury, departing in the dying seconds.

Hanley equalled Derek Turner, Eric Ashton and Alex Murphy in captaining three winning teams at Wembley, being the first to do so in consecutive years. Meanwhile Gregory, who equalled the record of seven Wembley appearances, set a standalone record of six wins.

202

1992 RUGBY LEAGUE CHALLENGE CUP FINAL
Wigan v Castleford

Wigan's Challenge Cup dominance continued unabated in 1992 and—judging by their 71–10 semi-final trouncing of Bradford Northern—looked set to continue for some time. As in their recent Wembley past, Wigan's assuredness and confidence at what was becoming a 'second home' contrasted with the early uncertainty and nerves of their opposition. This time their victims were Castleford, losing at Wembley for the first time after four previous successes, by 28–12. But, as Wigan re-wrote the record book yet again, there was one person in the camp who had set his heart on a little bit more; Martin Offiah.

Appearing in his first Challenge Cup Final, following a record £440,000 transfer from Widnes four months earlier, the prolific try scorer had ambition to be the first to score three touchdowns in a Wembley final, his narrow failure being one of the game's talking points. It took five minutes for him to obtain his first after taking a wide cut-out pass from Andy Gregory, the winger's harmless looking kick towards Castleford's

try-line being fumbled by Graham Steadman. Offiah sped past two defenders, kicking the ball from Steadman's tenuous grasp as he lay on the ground and dropping on it for the touchdown. His second and Wigan's third, just before the interval, again looked a forlorn cause. Shaun Edwards, from 50 metres out, sent a perfect kick into Castleford's in-goal area, Offiah's incredible pace enabling him to overhaul the better placed Mike Ford and Jon Wray to dive between them and score to the left of the posts.

Offiah almost got another in the 51st minute, dropping on the ball following an Edwards up-and-under but Steve Hampson had knocked-on as it came down. A minute later Offiah's angst was raised when, picking up a loose ball on halfway, he raced over the try-line unopposed. Referee Robin Whitfield was set to award the score but touch-judge Mike Singer claimed Offiah knocked the ball forward in the tackle that loosened it from Wray's grip. Interviewed afterwards by BBC television's Ray Stubbs, Offiah said:

Castleford's Graham Steadman brings the ball away watched by colleagues Dean Sampson (left) and Martin Ketteridge as Wigan's Phil Clarke (extreme left) moves across to cover

203

'I would like to have got the three tries. I was a little disappointed. I suppose you can't be too upset if you've won the Lance Todd (Trophy).' He also earned that accolade for his crucial try-saving feat in the 55th minute when Castleford, down 19–6, threatened a revival; catching and outpacing the speedy St John

Dean Bell lifts the Challenge Cup in triumph as team-mate Joe Lydon shakes hands with guest of honour Lord Derby and Steve Hampson raises his hands with delight

STATS

Wigan 28 Castleford 12

Saturday 2 May at Wembley Stadium, London (2.30 pm)

Wigan (cherry and white irregular hoops): Lydon, Botica, Bell (captain), Miles, Offiah, Edwards, Gregory, Skerrett, Dermott, Platt, Betts, McGinty, Clarke. Substitutes: Hampson, Cowie. Coach: J. Monie

Castleford (white with amber and black patterned chevron): Steadman, Wray, Ellis, Blackmore, Nelson, Anderson, Ford, Crooks (captain), Southernwood, England, Bradley, Ketteridge, Nikau. Substitutes: Smith, Sampson. Coach: D. van de Velde

Referee: R. Whitfield Touch-judges: A. Brown, M. Singer

Half-time: 19–0 Attendance: 77,286 Receipts: £1,877,564

Weather: mixture of bright periods and heavy rain

Lance Todd Trophy: Offiah (Wigan)

Cup presentation: Lord Derby, Rugby League president

Progressive score:

Wigan	score (min)	Castleford
Offiah try, Botica goal	6–0 (5)	
Edwards try, Botica goal	12–0 (21)	
Lydon drop-goal	13–0 (37)	
Offiah try, Botica goal	19–0 (39)	
	19–6 (44)	Blackmore try, Ketteridge goal
Hampson try, Botica goal	25–6 (59)	
	25–12 (68)	England try, Ketteridge goal
Botica penalty	27–12 (72)	
Lydon drop-goal	28–12 (78)	

Route to the final:

First round: Salford 6 Wigan 22,
Trafford Borough 0 Castleford 50 (at Headingley, Leeds)
Second round:
Wigan 14 Warrington 0, Hunslet 12 Castleford 28
Third round:
St Helens 6 Wigan 13, Castleford 19 Featherstone Rovers 12
Semi-finals:
Wigan 71 Bradford Northern 10 (Burnden Park, Bolton, 18,027)
Castleford 8 Hull 4 (Headingley, Leeds, 14,636)

Head-to-head form guide:

Castleford 38 Wigan 26 (League)

Wigan 10 Castleford 6 (League)

Ellis, who was chasing his own kick towards Wigan's line, Offiah got the first touch as they both dived, pushing the ball dead.

Edwards scored Wigan's second try in the 21st minute after supporting a midfield break by Martin Dermott. Ten minutes later, Steadman atoned for his earlier error with a try-saving tackle on Frano Botica as he headed for the right corner but, with Joe Lydon landing a 37th minute 30-metre drop-goal and Botica converting all three first half tries, Wigan held a secure looking 19–0 interval lead.

Despite losing skipper Lee Crooks, who limped off with a groin injury in the 34th minute, Castleford were more competitive after the break, scoring after four minutes through Richie Blackmore, who was provided with space by Tawera Nikau and Dean Sampson to go over near the posts. Martin Ketteridge added the goal. Hampson restored the 19-point margin with a try in the right-hand corner, collecting a reverse pass from Botica who also augmented. Castleford, showing sterner stuff, got a second try, Keith England diving over near the uprights off Steadman's 'back door' flip-pass, Ketteridge again converting. Wigan had the last words through a Botica penalty (England offside at a play-the-ball), and another Lydon drop-goal, both from 35-metres.

Wigan scrum half Andy Gregory extended his Wembley records to seven victories and eight appearances, although, having fought a week-long treatment battle on a groin injury, he was below par after taking a first half knock from the boot of Crooks, being substituted in the 49th minute with a 'dead leg'.

1993 RUGBY LEAGUE CHALLENGE CUP FINAL
Wigan v Widnes

Wigan celebrated a sixth successive Challenge Cup win in 1993, but the 5-to-1 odds-on favourites were given their sternest test of that run in subduing a determined Widnes 20–14. The first final under the 10-metre rule (previously defences retreated five metres at a play-the-ball), it was a competitive, absorbing match although Widnes blemished their performance through the 65th minute dismissal of Richie Eyres, following a touch-judge's intervention, his elbow having made contact with the side of Martin Offiah's head. And there could have been a second sending off, Bobbie Goulding escaping with a warning from referee Russell Smith after a high tackle on Wigan's Jason Robinson four minutes from the end, prompting BBC television co-commentator Ross Strudwick to say 'He's a very lucky boy!', the Widnes scrum half being subsequently fined £1,000 for his misdemeanour.

The under-fire pair was involved in the first score, Goulding creating the gap for Eyres, who twisted his way over for a try despite two defenders holding on. Jonathan Davies added a great conversion. It gave an early warning to Wigan that it was not to be an afternoon stroll, although the lead was short-lived. Three minutes later Robinson crossed the Widnes try-line on the right, having taken a return pass off Denis Betts, although with three defenders in attendance he

Wigan's Shaun Edwards skips out of a Widnes tackle

STATS

Wigan 20 Widnes 14

Saturday 1 May at Wembley Stadium, London (2.30 pm)

Wigan (cherry and white hoops): Hampson, Robinson, Lydon, Farrar, Offiah, Botica, Edwards, Skerrett, Dermott, Platt, Betts, Clarke, Bell (captain). Substitutes: Panapa, Farrell. Coach: J. Monie

Widnes (white with black and red chevrons): Spruce, Devereux, Currier, Wright, Myers, Davies, Goulding, Sorenson, P. Hulme (captain), Howard, Eyres, Faimalo, D. Hulme. Substitute: O'Neill, McCurrie. Coach: P. Larder

Referee: R. Smith Touch-judges: J. Beech, K. Spencer

Half-time: 14–12 Attendance: 77,684 Receipts: £1,981,591

Weather: sunny, very warm

Lance Todd Trophy: Bell (Wigan)

Cup presentation: Lord Derby, Rugby League president

Progressive score:

Wigan	score (min)	Widnes
	0–6 (7)	Eyres try, Davies goal
Skerrett try, Botica goal	6–6 (11)	
	6–12 (17)	Sorenson try, Davies goal
Bell try, Botica goal	12–12 (23)	
Botica penalty	14–12 (40)	
Panapa try, Botica goal	20–12 (42)	
	20–14 (49)	Davies penalty

Route to the final:

Preliminary round: Wigan 40 Hull 2, Widnes 62 Swinton 14

First round: Dewsbury 4 Wigan 20, Whitehaven 8 Widnes 20

Second round:
Wigan 23 St Helens 3, Sheffield Eagles 6 Widnes 52

Third round:
Halifax 18 Wigan 19, Hull Kingston Rovers 4 Widnes 4

Third round replay: Widnes 16 Hull Kingston Rovers 11

Semi-finals:
Wigan 15 Bradford Northern 6 (Elland Road, Leeds, 20,085), Widnes 39 Leeds 4 (Central Park, Wigan, 13,823)

Head-to-head form guide:

Wigan 14 Widnes 2 (League)

Widnes 6 Wigan 18 (League)

was unable to ground. But, within a minute, team-mate Kelvin Skerrett brushed aside Andy Currier to charge over despite Stuart Spruce's vain tackle, Frano Botica's goal tying the score, 6–6. But un-fancied Widnes had a surprise in store. Instead of the Cherry and Whites grasping the nettle and building their usual half-time winning lead, it was the Chemics that claimed the next try through 36-year-old prop Kurt Sorenson, who roared in from 25 metres out, Botica and Steve Hampson unable to repel him. Davies again converted and although less than a quarter of the match had been played, the neutrals in the crowd sprung to life at the prospect on an upset.

The second half was equally close, with only one try scored. It fell to Wigan's Sam Panapa two minutes after the resumption, Bell putting him through under the posts following an earlier break by Betts, Botica adding the extras. A 35-metre Davies penalty (Martin Dermott interfering at a play-the-ball) closed the scoring, although there was still a tense, incident-filled half-hour remaining in the energy-sapping heat of a sunlit afternoon during which time Botica was wide with a drop-goal and missed two penalties (one striking a post), and a late Hampson drop-goal attempt fell beneath the crossbar.

Wigan's victory was aided by the 30th minute switch

Widnes' Stuart Spruce tries in vain to prevent Kelvin Skerrett scoring for Wigan

When Widnes' John Devereux shoved Offiah into the side hoarding after the latter kicked the ball towards the Chemics try-line in the 20th minute, the pair squared up to each other. Three minutes later Devereux collected a kick by Wigan's Shaun Edwards into the corner but lost possession when tackled by Dean Bell and Offiah, the latter picking up to send Bell in for a simple touchdown with an over-arm pass. Botica's goal was his 177th of the season, overtaking Fred Griffiths' 1958/59 club record. Goulding was just wide with a drop-goal and Botica missed a penalty, making amends through a 20-metre effort right on half-time (Currier tackling from an offside position), placing Wigan ahead for the first time, 14–12.

of skipper Bell from his starting position of loose forward to his usual centre spot, allowing Phil Clarke to take over that role, giving the team a more balanced, familiar look. Substitute forward Andrew Farrell, who joined the action in the 55th minute, became Wembley's youngest winner at 17 years, 336 days. Edwards, meanwhile, equalled the Wembley records of Andy Gregory with seven wins and eight appearances whilst Australian coach John Monie set his own marker, having managed four winning teams at Wembley. Widnes, who were missing forwards Paul Moriarty (broken arm) and Emosi Koloto (back injury), flew previously on-loan Australian Julian O'Neill back from the Brisbane Broncos for the final.

Graham Morris

1994 RUGBY LEAGUE CHALLENGE CUP FINAL
Wigan v Leeds

Wigan extended their Wembley run to seven wins, defeating Leeds on a hot, sunny afternoon by 26–16. It was their winger Martin Offiah who raised the temperature higher than most, providing the highlights in the most entertaining of the Cherry and Whites' conveyor belt of London victories, earning plaudits through two spectacular tries, both at key moments. Many critics rated his first—in the 13th minute—to be the finest at the historic venue. Taking a pass from acting-halfback Frano Botica in front of his own posts, he raced through a gap to go haring along the right touchline, taking on and outmanoeuvring

Leeds' Alan Tait on the outside for a breathtaking try in the right corner. Offiah, sinking to his knees, looked towards the heavens almost in disbelief, after scoring the most memorable try of his career.

Botica was wide with the goal attempt, Wigan leading 4–0 after a frantic end-to-end opening that continued throughout the match, Leeds having been close to claiming the first score one minute earlier when Garry Schofield was stopped from placing the ball after crossing Wigan's try-line. Leeds' defence cracked again in the 25th minute, a high ball off Shaun Edwards' boot bouncing off Tait's chest into the arms of Andrew Farrell, who ran 15 metres before placing it beneath the posts. Botica's goal, and a penalty 11 minutes later (James Lowes offside), made it 12–0. Leeds, inspired by ex-Wigan icon Ellery Hanley, threatened several times, but there was no further scoring before half-time.

A moment of contemplation for Martin Offiah after the Wigan flyer had scored one of Wembley's most sensational tries in the 13th minute

WINNING CAPTAIN

Dean Bell (Wigan 1992, 1993, 1994)

New Zealand centre Dean Bell was born in Otara, Auckland, and played for Manukau. He came to England in 1982/83 to join Carlisle, returning the following campaign with the New Zealand Maoris, who opposed several amateur sides. He concluded that season with Leeds, winning the John Player Trophy. He rejoined Manukau, transferring to Australian club Eastern Suburbs for 1985 and 1986 (he returned there on loan in 1988). Wigan signed him during September 1986, the talented, tough opponent—known as 'Mean Dean'—inheriting the captaincy in 1991/92. With Wigan he won the Rugby League Challenge Cup (1988, 1989, 1990, 1991, 1992, 1993, 1994), Championship (1986/87, 1989/90, 1990/91, 1991/92, 1992/93, 1993/94), Premiership Trophy (1987, 1992), John Player Trophy (1986/87, 1988/89), Regal Trophy (1989/90, 1992/93), Lancashire Cup (1986, 1987, 1988, 1992) and Charity Shield (1987, 1991), missing the 1987 and 1991 World Club Challenge wins through injury. His last Wigan match was in 1994, joining Auckland Warriors as skipper for their inaugural 1995 season, after which he retired. Back in England he coached Leeds (1995–97), later concentrating on youth development at the club, followed by a similar role at Wigan (1999–2007) before returning to his homeland. He made 26 New Zealand Test appearances (four as captain) and was a Kiwi tourist three times (including captain in 1987 to Australia and Papua New Guinea).

207

Andrew Farrell has plenty of space as he touches down for Wigan

Leeds looked more purposeful after the break, Graham Holroyd landing a penalty (Farrell interference at a play-the-ball), followed by two quick tries—both after Wigan fumbled the ball—through Jim Fallon (on the right off Lowes' over-arm pass) and Schofield (escaping Offiah and Martin Dermott to score in the right corner). Holroyd missed both conversions, but Leeds only trailed 12–10. The momentum swung back to Wigan through a Botica 30-metre penalty (Harvey Howard fouling Mick Cassidy) and Offiah's second try four minutes later (Cassidy—escaping Leeds' cover—sending him sprinting from halfway). Sam Panapa sealed the win with Wigan's fourth try, crossing the whitewash left of the posts off Botica's pass, the ball having been swung quickly from the right after Va'aiga Tuigamala was held short. With Botica converting both efforts, Wigan led 26–10. Leeds' Francis Cummins—Wembley's youngest finalist at 17 years 200 days who had set the stadium alight with his 65 metre sprint down the left flank in the 2nd minute— raced 80 metres for a try after recovering the ball when Offiah knocked forward Phil Clarke's poor pass. Holroyd's conversion completed the scoring.

Wigan's post-match celebrations were sullied by an alleged altercation between coach John Dorahy and club chairman Jack Robinson on the team bus returning to Wigan. Whatever the truth, Dorahy was dismissed within two days. There was also pre-match controversy after Dorahy had omitted Jason Robinson

in favour of recent signing Tuigamala. Allegedly, Dorahy asked Robinson to prove his fitness in the reserves following a shoulder injury, which Robinson claimed he did but to no avail. Meanwhile, Dean Bell equalled Hanley's feat of leading three consecutive Challenge Cup winning sides and receipts exceeded £2m for the first time.

STATS

Wigan 26 Leeds 16

Saturday 30 April at Wembley Stadium, London (2.30 pm)

Wigan (cherry and white design): Connolly, Tuigamala, Bell (captain), Mather, Offiah, Botica, Edwards, Skerrett, Dermott, Platt, Betts, Farrell, Clarke. Substitutes: Panapa, Cassidy. Coach: J. Dorahy

Leeds (blue with amber bands): Tait, Fallon, Iro, Innes, Cummins, Holroyd, Schofield, Harmon, Lowes, Howard, Mercer, Eyres, Hanley (captain). Substitutes: Vassilakopoulos, O'Neill. Coach: D. Laughton

Referee: D. Campbell Touch-judges: W. Blunden, M. Haigh

Half-time: 12–0 Attendance: 78,348 Receipts: £2,032,839

Weather: sunny and hot

Lance Todd Trophy: Offiah (Wigan)

Cup presentation: The Rt. Hon. Betty Boothroyd MP, Speaker of the House of Commons

Progressive score:

Wigan	score (min)	Leeds
Offiah try	4–0 (13)	
Farrell try, Botica goal	10–0 (25)	
Botica penalty	12–0 (36)	
	12–2 (43)	Holroyd penalty
	12–6 (48)	Fallon try
	12–10 (51)	Schofield try
Botica penalty	14–10 (58)	
Offiah try, Botica goal	20–10 (62)	
Panapa try, Botica goal	26–10 (67)	
	26–16 (73)	Cummins try, Holroyd

Route to the final:

Fourth round: Wigan 24 Wakefield Trinity 16, Rochdale Hornets 18 Leeds 40

Fifth round: Hull 21 Wigan 22, Leeds 38 Warrington 4

Sixth round: Wigan 32 Featherstone Rovers 14, Leeds 33 Bradford Northern 10

Semi-finals:

Wigan 20 Castleford 6 (Headingley, Leeds, 17,049), Leeds 20 St Helens 8 (Central Park, Wigan, 20,771)

Head-to-head form guide:

Wigan 32 Leeds 18 (League)

Leeds 14 Wigan 26 (League)

Graham Morris

1995 RUGBY LEAGUE CHALLENGE CUP FINAL
Wigan v Leeds

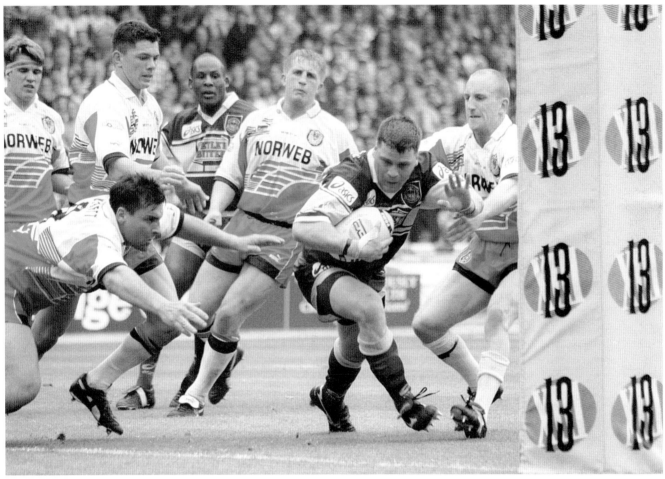

Leeds hooker James Lowes claims the last try despite the Wigan ensemble of Kelvin Skerrett (diving) and (from left) Gary Connolly, Henry Paul, Denis Betts and Shaun Edwards

Wigan and Leeds became the first clubs to meet in consecutive Wembley Challenge Cup Finals, the Headingley team having emerged as the closest challengers to the Cherry and Whites dominance. Leeds confidently entered the 1995 decider having beaten Wigan four months earlier and finished runners-up to them in the League. The outcome, though, was the same, Wigan winning their rematch convincingly, by 30–10, the 5–1 try-count being more emphatic than the previous year's 4–3. The Yorkshire side suffered through a subdued performance from Ellery Hanley who played with a shoulder injury that ultimately dictated it would be his last match of a glittering career.

Graham Holroyd opened the scoring with a penalty

TO AUSTRALIA AND BACK!

The following players were brought back from their parent Australian club for the Challenge Cup Final having returned home several months earlier for the Australian season.

- 1975: Chris Anderson (Widnes—from Canterbury-Bankstown)
- 1984: Kerry Helmsley (Wigan—Balmain)
- 1985: John Ferguson (Wigan—Eastern Suburbs)
- 1986: Jamie Sandy (Castleford—Brisbane Easts), Ian French (Castleford—Wynnum-Manly)
- 1989: Michael O'Connor (St Helens—Manly-Warringah), Paul Vautin (St Helens—Manly-Warringah)
- 1993: Julian O'Neill (Widnes—Brisbane Broncos)

for Leeds, Kelvin Skerrett being guilty of 'lying on' after a tackle before, moments later, the game was suspended when Mick Cassidy took a bad knock to the head tackling Richie Eyres, his afternoon ending prematurely when taken off on a stretcher. Wigan almost scored when Shaun Edwards sent a cross-field

Phil Clarke of Wigan attempts to resist the challenge of Leeds full back Alan Tait

STATS

Wigan 30 Leeds 10

Saturday 29 April at Wembley Stadium, London (2.30 pm)

Wigan (cherry and white design): Paul, Robinson, Tuigamala, Connolly, Offiah, Botica, Edwards (captain), Skerrett, Hall, Cowie, Betts, Cassidy, Clarke. Substitutes: Atcheson, Farrell. Coach: G. West

Leeds (blue with amber bands): Tait, Fallon, Iro, Innes, Cummins, Schofield, Holroyd, Howard, Lowes, Faimalo, Mercer, Eyres, Hanley (captain). Substitutes: Mann, Harmon. Coach: D. Laughton

Referee: R. Smith

Touch-judges: A. Brown, P. Hewitt

In-goal judges: R. Duckworth, W. Blunden

Half-time: 12–4 Attendance: 78,550 Receipts: £2,040,000

Weather: cloudy and dry

Lance Todd Trophy: Robinson (Wigan)

Cup presentation: H.R.H. The Duke of Edinburgh

Progressive score:

Wigan	score (min)	Leeds
	0–2 (4)	Holroyd penalty
Robinson try, Botica goal	6–2 (14)	
Paul try	10–2 (23)	
	10–4 (31)	Holroyd penalty
Botica penalty	12–4 (37)	
Robinson try, Botica goal	18–4 (45)	
Hall try, Botica goal	24–4 (52)	
Tuigamala try, Botica goal	30–4 (64)	
	30–10 (78)	Lowes try, Holroyd goal

Route to the final:

Fourth round: Wigan 16 St Helens 16, Leeds 31 Bradford Northern 14

Fourth round replay: St Helens 24 Wigan 40

Fifth round: Batley 4 Wigan 70, Leeds 44 Ryedale-York 14

Sixth round: Widnes 12 Wigan 26, Leeds 50 Workington Town 16

Semi-finals: Wigan 48 Oldham 20 (McAlpine Stadium, Huddersfield, 12,749)

Leeds 39 Featherstone Rovers 22 (Elland Road, Leeds, 21,485)

Head-to-head form guide:

Wigan 38 Leeds 6 (League)

Leeds 33 Wigan 28 (League)

kick into the right corner that just bounced out of Jason Robinson's reach as he dived. Six minutes later, the winger was more successful after colleague Martin Offiah popped up on the right-hand side of Wigan's attack to launch him on a 40-metre dash to score near the corner, evading Francis Cummins' tackle and outsmarting three other defenders. Frano Botica's excellent goal made it 6–2.

A moment of controversy appeared midway through the opening period when, from a couple of metres inside his own half, Leeds' Garry Schofield, at

PERIMETER FENCING

Tall metal railings were placed around the perimeter of Wembley's playing area in front of the lower terracing at Challenge Cup Finals from 1980 until 1988. This was a consequence of events following the England-Scotland soccer international at the stadium in June 1977 when supporters invaded the pitch damaging both goals, fencing subsequently being erected at the FA Cup Final from 1978. In the wake of the 1989 'Hillsborough Disaster' when 95 lives were lost at an FA Cup semi-final when perimeter fencing stopped supporters escaping a congested terrace, the railings were removed for that year's St Helens-Wigan Challenge Cup Final at the Rugby Football League's request. Unfortunately that match concluded with a (non-violent) pitch invasion by excitable fans, police having to clear the area, less imposing new barriers being introduced from 1990 until 1993.

a Wigan play-the-ball, nipped in quickly to intercept acting-halfback Botica's pass and race unopposed towards the try-line. Referee Russell Smith brought Schofield back, awarding a penalty against him for not being 'square', to which 10 metres were added for 'back chat', Botica being just wide with the resulting goal attempt.

Leeds had looked the more potent side in the opening 10 minutes but Wigan gained the ascendancy, Henry Paul twisting through the defence for their second touchdown off Phil Clarke's transfer, the latter player drawing the opposition after collecting a long pass from Edwards that cut out three attackers. The score had followed a great 40-metre midfield break by Denis Betts. Botica was just wide with the goal attempt, Wigan leading 10–2. The first half concluded with a penalty each from Holroyd and Botica, both for offside.

The second half began with near misses at both ends; Eyres dabbing the ball over Wigan's try-line but it just went dead before he could touch down, and Gary Connolly's high inside pass to Offiah was dropped by the wingman as he reached up for it with a try looking certain. But it took just five minutes of the half for Robinson to complete his brace when, from acting-halfback, he took advantage of poor Leeds marking to burst from halfway through a group of defenders—who seemed rooted to the spot—for a brilliant try under the pots. Wigan added two more over the next 20 minutes; Martin Hall taking advantage of poor marking at a play-the-ball to dummy his way over the try-line from acting-halfback after Andy Farrell was held short, and Va'aiga Tuigamala, powering past four defenders off a wide pass from Edwards to cross the whitewash. With Botica converting all three tries, the score became frighteningly one-sided at 30–4. With two minutes remaining, Botica was penalised for punching James Lowes following an altercation at a Leeds play-the-ball. From the resulting tap-penalty 15 metres out, Neil Harmon made the break before transferring to Lowes who worked his way through five defenders to score to the right of the posts, Holroyd kicking the goal.

In what had been the first Wembley occasion to employ rugby league's latest innovation of in-goal judges, Wigan's success would be the last in their phenomenal sequence of eight victories in front of the Twin Towers. During that run they won 41 successive ties, including a replay, and incorporated six Challenge Cup and League doubles. Wigan could also boast the record number of wins (15 at Wembley, 16 overall), and most appearances in the final (21 at Wembley, 25 overall). Edwards, meanwhile, expanded his personal Wembley tally to 9 wins and 10 visits. As a footnote and a chilling reminder of Wigan's supremacy at the time, they defeated Leeds three weeks later, 69–12, in the Premiership Trophy Final at Old Trafford.

WINNING CAPTAIN

Shaun Edwards (Wigan 1988, 1995)

Shaun Edwards signed for Wigan in a blaze of publicity in 1983. A brilliant halfback, destined to win more honours than anyone in the Rugby League's history, the former Wigan St Patrick's starlet was one of the most influential and committed players the game has seen. His penchant for supportive play brought him 274 tries in 467 appearances for Wigan including a record-equalling 10 tries in one match during 1992. He was 17 years old when he appeared in the 1984 Challenge Cup Final at Wembley and still only 21 when he captained Wigan there in 1988. His trophy haul with Wigan covers the Rugby League Challenge Cup (1985, 1988, 1989, 1990, 1991, 1992, 1993, 1994, 1995), World Club Challenge (1987, 1991, 1994), Premiership Trophy (1987, 1992, 1994, 1995, 1996), Championship (1986/87, 1989/90, 1990/91, 1991/92, 1992/93, 1993/94, 1994/95, 1995/96), John Player Trophy (1985/86, 1986/87, 1988/89), Regal Trophy (1989/90, 1992/93, 1994/95, 1995/96), Lancashire Cup (1985, 1986, 1987, 1988, 1992) and Charity Shield (1985, 1987, 1991). He represented Great Britain in 36 Tests, England (3 times, including the 1995 World Cup), Ireland (1), Lancashire (4), and was a tourist in 1988 and 1992. London Broncos signed him for £60,000 in 1997, although he moved to Bradford Bulls later that year for £40,000. Returning to the Broncos in 1998, he concluded his playing career there in 2000. During 1989, he played for Balmain in Australia. He later moved to rugby union, coaching London Wasps and Wales. In 1996, he received the OBE.

Kevin Iro breaks for Leeds closely watched by Wigan duo Va'aiga Tuigamala (left) and Lance Todd Trophy winner Jason Robinson

THAT'S ENTERTAINMENT!

Before the Wembley years

At the earlier Challenge Cup Finals supporters were usually entertained beforehand by a local band that normally played a 'selection' for an hour before the match and again during the interval. Often there would be an enterprising individual, for example a trick cyclist, juggler or contortionist, who would pay the host club to allow him on the field to amuse the crowd, and then make a collection afterwards. In 1913 when Huddersfield met Warrington at Headingley, a bugle band gathered on the terraces and proceeded to blast away during the game to the consternation of the *Warrington Guardian* writer who said: 'During the interval the Kingston Unity Band played a selection, but what with the Bugle Band and the din of the (supporters) rattles, one was at a loss to know whether the Yorkshire band was playing a ragtime medley or a selection from some great work.' As a forerunner to today's drums, trumpets and kazoos, it proves nothing is ever new under the sun!

Over the years entertainment became more streamlined and, when Wembley arrived on the scene, regimental marching bands and community singing would become the norm, spectators being supplied with a song sheet courtesy of the *News Chronicle* and, from 1953, the *Daily Express*. Interestingly the 1927 Football Association Cup Final (their fifth at Wembley) was the first to include community singing, and the first where 'Abide With Me' was sung. Two weeks later community singing was on the agenda at Wigan's Central Park before the Rugby League Challenge Cup Final (the RFL having given the *Daily Dispatch* permission to organise it). However, at 3.00 pm—30 minutes before kick-off—a man 'wearing a white coat' (the conductor) mounted the rostrum and announced the band had not arrived! He began leading the crowd unaccompanied but there was 'only silence' although, to his relief, the musicians then arrived.

In the Wembley era

The first Wembley Challenge Cup Final of 1929 included a regimental marching band—The Band of His Majesty's Welsh Guards—that also accompanied the community singing conducted by Arthur C. Caiger who was mounted on a rostrum wearing the white coat that was to become such a familiar item. The repertoire included the hymn 'Abide with Me', the singing of which—prior to the entry of the two teams—has remained such a poignant moment ever since. Regimental bands have continued to play a part, whilst community singing—in its original mode—carried through until 1971, led by T.P. Ratcliff during the pre-war years of 1930 to 1939, the aforementioned Caiger returning in 1947 and continuing until 1962, Bill Scott-Coomber carrying the tradition through from 1963 to 1971.

Until then the crowd was encouraged to 'wave your song sheets in the air', but, in 1972, a wind of change blew through the ether. The traditional, white coated conductor gave way to popular entertainers and television stars such as Ed Stewart, Bernard Manning, Ken Dodd and even Cannon and Ball, who all took up the conductor's baton to lead their audience in a lighter, more humorous and 'modern' approach to the pre-match sing-a-long. A subtle change for 1972 was that the song sheet was superseded by the more sensible option of printing the words in the match programme.

The desire for change continued when, in 1973 and 1974, the community singing was preceded with a Women's League of Health and Beauty display entitled 'Exercises for Sport for All'. This gave way, in 1975, to the Schoolboy Under-11s curtain raiser, providing an opportunity for well-known children's entertainers such as Bernie Clifton and Stu Francis of Crackerjack fame to greet the crowd and present mementoes to the boys after their exploits. The schools curtain raiser, albeit with a few changes along the way, has continued ever since.

Community singing ended in 1991 with Vince Miller being the last to climb the rostrum steps. The crowd, though, were still invited to rise to their feet and sing 'Abide with Me' as the teams await their entrance in the tunnel and occasionally, an extra song or two has been added to the list, for example 'Maybe it's because I'm a Londoner' in 1999 acknowledged London Broncos involvement that year, 'Flower of Scotland' at the Murrayfield events, and 'Bread of

Renowned BBC commentators Eddie Waring and Ray French have led the way in capturing the entertainment and spectacle of Challenge Cup Final day for television viewers for over 50 years. Waring (left) covered every final from 1958 until 1981, whilst French (seen with co-commentator Steve Simms in background) did so from 1982 until 2008

Heaven' and the Welsh National Anthem in Cardiff. Another dimension was added in 1992 with the 'Entertainment Showcase', a format that, whilst no longer called as such, still exists, providing slick, professional entertainment with star performers featured, ranging from Atomic Kitten to Katherine Jenkins. Everything, in fact, designed to put the crowd in good spirits before the singing of the National Anthem, the appearance of the guest of honour and, of course, the entry of the two teams.

Pomp and ceremony

The return to Wembley in 2007 saw a nice touch with banners encircling the arena from an upper tier displaying the name of every Challenge Cup finalist in chronological order of their first appearance. Beginning with '1897 Batley' and '1897 St Helens', the exercise was repeated for 2008 with the addition of '2007 Catalans Dragons'.

The Rugby Football League also chose 2008 to launch an annual pre-match 'Parade of Legends', inviting players from a previous final to appear, the inaugural occasion marking the 40th Anniversary of the famous Leeds-Wakefield Trinity 'Watersplash'

final. Players from both sides were introduced to the crowd, poignancy being added through a one minute silence in memory of Don Fox, winner of the Lance Todd Trophy in that match, who passed away days earlier.

Pre-match parades had taken place on previous occasions at Wembley. In 1979 'Fifty Years at Wembley' was celebrated through the introduction of players from the 1929 Dewsbury and Wigan teams. Six years later, in 1985, the '50th Rugby League Final at Wembley' provided an excuse to present one player from each of the Wembley deciders thus far, ranging from Henry Coates (Dewsbury, 1929) to Joe Lydon (Widnes, 1984). The 1997 'Centenary Final' was preceded by a parade of rugby league personalities (including officials and ex-players such as Hubert Lockwood, Trevor Foster, Neil Fox and Eric Ashton) each representing a decade and transported around the outer track in a vintage car. The farewell to the 'old' Wembley in 1999 embraced a 'Parade of Wembley Greats' with every club that graced the stadium from 1929 represented, whilst the first match at the 'new' Wembley in 2007 was preceded by a presentation of 'Lance Todd Trophy Winners' to the crowd.

213

1996 RUGBY LEAGUE CHALLENGE CUP FINAL
St Helens v Bradford Bulls

The 1996 Challenge Cup Final is a serious candidate to be rated as Wembley's best ever, St Helens staging a magnificent fight back to overcome a gallant, talented Bradford Bulls outfit 40–32. Saints trailed 26–12 with 23 minutes left, as Bradford, inspired by Robbie Paul—Wembley's youngest captain at 20 years 84 days—appeared to be cruising to their first Challenge Cup success since 1949. It was Paul's opposite number—as both scrum half and skipper—that led Wembley's greatest ever comeback, Saints' Bobbie Goulding exploiting a chink in the Bulls armour with his towering, unsettling kicks.

The revival began when Goulding's 57th minute sky-rocket of a kick was not defused by Bulls' full back Nathan Graham, who allowed the ball to bounce in his in-goal area, Saints' Keiron Cunningham jumping up for it as it rebounded to bring it down behind the posts.

It was the start of a torrid seven-minute spell for Graham as two more Goulding specials caught out the luckless defender to produce tries. The scorers were Simon Booth (grabbing the ball and diving over the try-line after Paul Loughlin and Graham both failed to make the catch in front of their posts) and Ian Pickavance (diving onto the ball in the in-goal after Graham and Saints' Alan Hunte jumped together with neither taking it cleanly). With Goulding—whose 'bombs' were all launched from 20 to 30 metres out—adding all three goals, it put St Helens ahead 30–26 after the most dramatic of Wembley turnarounds. Four minutes later, the rampant Saints scored again, a mesmerising passing move ending with a great dummy and break from 40 metres out by Karle Hammond who, as Paul Medley challenged, off-loaded to the supporting Danny Arnold who dived over from close

St Helens full back Steve Prescott is unable to stop Bradford Bulls captain Robbie Paul from commencing his try hat-trick just before half-time

214

Unfortunate Bradford Bulls full back Nathan Graham (in foreground, left) was subjected to a frantic period of aerial bombardment during the second half from St Helens captain Bobbie Goulding. Here he loses the ball during a challenge from Alan Hunte, an incident that led to Ian Pickavance's try

in. Goulding missed the kick at goal.

There was still time for uncertainty when, with nine minutes left, Paul completed Wembley's first try hat-trick—earning a £10,000 prize from sponsors Silk Cut—with one of the best solo efforts witnessed inside the venue. Collecting a pass from five metres inside his own half, he embarked on a bewildering run that took him past four defenders before planting the ball under the posts. Paul Cook added the goal and, at 34–32 to St Helens, a breathless crowd awaited more sensations in a 'roller-coaster' of a final. Five minutes from the end, though, Apollo Perelini ensured the lead would not change hands a third time, his 10 metre burst ending with him diving over to the left of the posts off Goulding's reverse pass, the scrum half adding the goal to complete the scoring.

Goulding's boot had been to the fore as St Helens built up an eight-point lead in the opening 18 minutes through two Steve Prescott tries. His kick to the right flank was collected by Scott Gibbs who escaped Loughlin's clutches to put the full back over for the first with an inside pass, the second coming after Prescott got his foot to a Goulding chip-kick that had cascaded over the defensive wall from 40-metres out, diving on it as it crossed the try-line. Jon Scales replied with a great try, racing down the left touchline from near halfway off Loughlin's pass, Paul Cook adding the goal, followed by a penalty (Andy Leathem interference at a play-the-ball) to tie the score. But,

STATS

St Helens 40 Bradford Bulls 32

Saturday 27 April at Wembley Stadium, London (2.30 pm)

St Helens (red with broad white bands and chevron): Prescott, Arnold, Gibbs, Newlove, Sullivan, Hammond, Goulding (captain), Perelini, Cunningham, Leathem, Joynt, Booth, Northey. Substitutes: Martyn, Pickavance, Matautia, Hunte. Coach: S. McRae

Bradford Bulls (white with black, amber and red epaulette): Graham, Cook, Calland, Loughlin, Scales, Bradley, Paul (captain), McDermott, Dwyer, Hamer, Donougher, Nickle, Knox. Substitutes: Fairbank, Medley, Donohue, Hassan. Coach: B. Smith

Referee: S. Cummings Touch-judges: J. Glover, F. Hawley In-goal judges: K. Leyland, A. Randerson

Half-time: 12–14 Attendance: 75,994 Receipts: £1,893,000

Weather: sunny and hot

Lance Todd Trophy: Paul (Bradford Bulls)

Cup presentation:
The Rt Hon. Iain Sproat MP, Minister for Sport

Progressive score:

St Helens	score (min)	Bradford Bulls
Prescott try	4–0 (3)	
Prescott try	8–0 (18)	
	8–6 (25)	Scales try, Cook goal
	8–8 (32)	Cook penalty
Arnold try	12–8 (33)	
	12–14 (38)	Paul try, Cook goal
	12–20 (48)	Dwyer, Cook goal
	12–26 (54)	Paul try, Cook goal
Cunningham try, Goulding goal	18–26 (57)	
Booth try, Goulding goal	24–26 (60)	
Pickavance try, Goulding goal	30–26 (63)	
Arnold try	34–26 (67)	
	34–32 (71)	Paul try, Cook goal
Perelini try, Goulding goal	40–32 (75)	

Route to the final:

Fourth round: Castleford Tigers 16 St Helens 58, Bradford B 60 Batley Bulldogs 18

Fifth round: Rochdale Hornets 20 St Helens 58, Leigh Centurions 12 Bradford B 44

Sixth round: Salford Reds 26 St Helens 46, Bradford Bulls 30 Wakefield Trinity 18

Semi-finals:
St Helens 24 Widnes 14 (Central Park, Wigan, 13,424),

Bradford Bulls 28 Leeds 6 (McAlpine Stadium, Huddersfield, 17,139)

Head-to-head form guide:

St Helens 26 Bradford Bulls 20 (League)

the following minute, Arnold scored his first try, cutting inside three defenders near the right corner from a lobbed one-handed pass off John Newlove, who had broken through the middle. Although Goulding missed his third conversion, Saints led 12–8.

Whilst most observers expected Saints to go 'marching on' to victory, the Bulls brought the stadium alive with three unanswered tries, Paul getting the first just two minutes before the interval, stretching over beneath the crossbar after taking a pass close to the try-line from acting-halfback Bernard Dwyer. Eight minutes into the second half, Dwyer got the next, finding a gap to

WELSH CONNECTIONS

The participation of Welshmen in the Challenge Cup Final began at the first in 1897, Wattie Davies and Dai Fitzgerald appearing for Batley. From then until (and including) the 1985 final only six occasions were bereft of a Welsh presence; 1909, 1951, 1962, 1964, 1968, 1973. Wales' highest representation in a final is 13 in 1947 (Bradford Northern v Leeds), the most in one team being eight; Wigan (1924), Keighley (1937), Salford (1938) and Leeds (1947). From 1986 until 1996 the contribution of players from the Principality diminished, just five of those 11 finals having a representative, the last being Scott Gibbs (St Helens) in 1996. The introduction of professionalism in rugby union in 1996 virtually ended the flow of Welsh talent into rugby league and no Welsh-born player has appeared from 1997. There have, however, been several since then who have represented Wales at rugby league but born outside that country having qualified through a Welsh parent or grandparent. Notable examples are Keiron Cunningham and Anthony Sullivan (both St Helens) and Iestyn Harris (Leeds Rhinos). The first Welsh-born Challenge Cup winning captain was Jim Bacon (Leeds, in 1923), followed by Jim Sullivan (Wigan, 1929), Dai Rees (Halifax, 1931), Gus Risman (Salford, 1938, and Workington Town, 1952), Trevor Foster (Bradford Northern, 1944—second leg) and Kel Coslett (St Helens, 1972 and 1976). Note: Jack Evans (Swinton, 1926) was born in Wales although raised in England, whilst former Wales rugby union international Joe Thompson (Leeds, 1932) was born in England.

race 10 metres and put the ball down to the right of the posts, Paul registering his second six minutes later, twisting his way through three defenders from acting-halfback before placing the ball on the try-line. Cook added all three goals and Bradford held a commanding 14-point lead, but it was not enough!

St Helens' 40 points and Bradford's 32 were the highest recorded for both winner and runner-up in a Challenge Cup Final, resulting in a record aggregate 72. It was also the first time four substitutes were allowed, rather than two.

WINNING CAPTAIN

Bobbie Goulding (St Helens 1996, 1997)

Widnes-born Bobbie Goulding was an audacious, creative scrum half whose promptings and kicking ability often dictated the outcome of a match. Wigan signed him from Widnes St Marie's in 1988, following which he helped them win the Rugby League Challenge Cup (1990, 1991) and Championship (1989/90, 1990/91). He transferred to Leeds in 1991 for £90,000 but moved to Widnes in 1992 in a player-exchange deal involving full back Alan Tait. St Helens signed him in 1994 for £135,000 and, as skipper, he led them to success in the Rugby League Challenge Cup (1996, 1997) and was a member of their 1996 Super League Championship winning team. Leaving St Helens on a free transfer in 1998 he completed his playing career with Huddersfield Giants (1998–99), Wakefield Trinity Wildcats (2000), Salford City Reds (2001–02), Leigh Centurions (2002) and Rochdale Hornets (2004–05). Player-coach at the latter, he returned to Hornets as coach (2007-08) before taking charge of the France national side in 2009. He was a tourist twice (1990, 1996), represented Great Britain (15 Tests), England (5 times—including the 1995 World Cup) and Lancashire (once).

Ian Pickvance touches down for St Helens in the 63rd minute

Graham Morris

1997 RUGBY LEAGUE CHALLENGE CUP FINAL
St Helens v Bradford Bulls

The Rugby Football League celebrated its Centenary Challenge Cup Final in 1997, St Helens again denying Bradford Bulls in a repeat of the previous year's encounter. Although not as spectacular as its predecessor it was still a memorable final, the Saints—despite only extending their victory margin by two points—being more comfortable winners the second time around. In a match containing several debateable decisions, St Helens were well ahead of their rivals, 30–10, with just over an hour played, a late Bulls rally making the final score-line look respectable at 32–22.

Tommy Martyn snared St Helens' opening two tries, both through dropping on well-judged kicks to the in-goal area from halfback partner Bobbie Goulding. The first was propelled along the ground close to the try-line, the second travelling some 20 metres across the face of goal. Goulding hit the upright with his first conversion attempt, the second clocking up his 1,000th point for the club. It tied the scores at 10–10 after Bradford had responded to Martyn's first touchdown by taking a 10–4 lead through tries from Danny Peacock (shrugging off Steve Prescott's tackle to

THE SILK CUT PLATE

The Silk Cut Plate Final—named after the sponsor of that year's Rugby League Challenge Cup—took place for the only time in 1997. Played at Wembley after the schools match as a curtain-raiser to the Challenge Cup Final, the competition was open to the 16 clubs knocked out in the fourth round of the Challenge Cup, excepting any Super League clubs (there were two), who were replaced by the highest placed non-Super League clubs (based on the League tables). Having had poor attendances in earlier rounds, the Final, in which Hull Kingston Rovers defeated Hunslet Hawks 60–16, was played in front of a sparsely filled stadium, possibly as a consequence of an earlier bomb alert that had delayed the Wembley gates being opened.

race into the right corner after receiving from Sonny Nickle who broke from halfway) and Paul Loughlin (intercepting Karle Hammond's pass 20 metres out). Steve McNamara—wide with his first attempt—augmented the second. In the final minute of the half Hammond put St Helens back in front, somehow squeezing through five defenders to reach out and

St Helens captain Bobbie Goulding (extreme right, number 7) applauds his players after inviting vice-captain Chris Joynt (extreme left)—who led the team through most rounds in Goulding's absence—to receive the Challenge Cup from Lord Derby. The player taking his turn to hold the trophy is Keiron Cunningham

217

Tommy Martyn scores St Helens' opening try to disappoint the Bradford Bulls trio of Danny Peacock (left), Stuart Spruce (28) and Abi Ekoku

place the ball on the try-line, Goulding adding the goal.

A hectic opening to the second half saw several near-misses; Prescott being pushed into touch near the corner by Matt Calland after a 20-metre break whilst, at the opposite end, Martyn's ankle tap denied Peacock before, seconds later, Abi Ekoku was grounded just short. St Helens, though, increased their lead with further tries from Chris Joynt (Martyn's reverse pass prising an opening 30 metres out), and Anthony Sullivan (winning the race to dive on the ball after Martyn's 45-metre kick to the left corner, although video replays showed a clear knock-on by the winger). With Goulding adding both goals, plus a 62nd minute penalty (James Lowes' interference at a play-the-ball), St Helens led by 20 points. Bradford hauled themselves back through tries from Glen Tomlinson (diving on the ball after a great kick and chase from Lowes) and Lowes (from acting-halfback, beating three opponents to score to the right of the posts). McNamara tagged both goals, Goulding splitting their efforts with his second penalty (Bernard Dwyer offside when making a tackle).

For Saints—who were without international three-quarter Alan Hunte who sustained a torn hamstring two weeks earlier—it was the first time they had gained consecutive Challenge Cup wins. The Bulls, meanwhile, missed the second half influence of skipper Robbie Paul (back from Sydney after representing New Zealand against Australia the previous weekend) who limped off in the 47th minute, returning on the hour as a mere passenger. St Helens skipper Goulding invited Joynt to receive the cup having led the team through the competition after Goulding was suspended for six matches following his dismissal during the fourth round win over Wigan Warriors.

STATS

St Helens 32 Bradford Bulls 22

Saturday 3 May at Wembley Stadium, London (2.45 pm)

St Helens (black with red web design and white filled chevron): Prescott, Arnold, Haigh, Newlove, Sullivan, Martyn, Goulding (captain), Perelini, Cunningham, O'Neill, Joynt, McVey, Hammond. Substitutes: Pickavance, Matautia, Northey, Morley. Coach: S. McRae

Bradford Bulls (amber with black and red bands on sleeves): Spruce, Ekoku, Peacock, Loughlin, Cook, Bradley, Paul (captain), McDermott, Lowes, Reihana, Nickle, Dwyer, McNamara. Substitutes: Medley, Calland, Tomlinson, Knox. Coach: M. Elliott

Referee: S. Cummings
Touch-judges: P. Hewitt, J. Molyneux
In-goal judges: W. Blunden, F. Hawley
Half-time: 16–10 Attendance: 78,022 Receipts: £2,033,426
Weather: overcast, light rain during second half
Lance Todd Trophy: Martyn (St Helens)
Cup presentation: Lord Derby, Rugby League president

Progressive score:

St Helens	score (min)	Bradford Bulls
Martyn try	4–0 (10)	
	4–4 (12)	Peacock try
	4–10 (20)	Loughlin try, McNamara goal
Martyn try, Goulding goal	10–10 (28)	
Hammond try, Goulding goal	16–10 (40)	
Joynt try, Goulding goal	22–10 (49)	
Sullivan try, Goulding goal	28–10 (53)	
Goulding penalty	30–10 (62)	
	30–16 (64)	Tomlinson try, McNamara goal
Goulding penalty	32–16 (76)	
	32–22 (78)	Lowes try, McNamara goal

Route to the final:

Fourth round:
St Helens 26 Wigan Warriors 12,
Hunslet Hawks 10 Bradford Bulls 62

Fifth round:
St Helens 54 Hull Sharks 8,
London Broncos 12 Bradford Bulls 34

Sixth round:
Keighley Cougars 0 St Helens 24,
Oldham Bears 12 Bradford Bulls 38

Semi-finals:
St Helens 50 Salford Reds 20 (Central Park, Wigan, 12,580),
Bradford B 24 Leeds Rhinos 10 (McAlpine Stadium, Huddersfield, 18,193)

Head-to-head form guide:

No previous meetings during season

1998 RUGBY LEAGUE CHALLENGE CUP FINAL
Sheffield Eagles v Wigan Warriors

Sheffield Eagles—founded in 1984—pulled off one of the Challenge Cup Final's biggest shocks in defeating 14-to-1 odds-on favourites Wigan Warriors 17–8 in 1998. Their success owed much to skipper Paul Broadbent and fellow-prop Dale Laughton whose solid drives up the middle laid the foundations, with Mark Aston's long kicks to the left touchline (avoiding Jason Robinson's potential threat on the opposite flank) continually forcing the Warriors back. It was all part of a game plan that denied the opposition any opportunity to demonstrate their superior pace.

It started perfectly for the Eagles, Aston's high kick being caught in the right corner by Nick Pinckney, who out-jumped an uncertain Robinson for the opening score. Wigan injected more urgency into their play and for the next 10 minutes piled on the pressure, but without success; Waisale Sovatabua saved twice (reaching high to intercept a potential try-scoring pass from Gary Connolly to Simon Haughton, and then palming away the ball when Tony Smith looked set to capitalise on Andrew Farrell's kick to the in-goal), whilst Henry Paul was also stopped short of the try-line.

Wigan, though, paid a high price for a temporary lapse near their try-line. Their centre Danny Moore played the ball, but acting-halfback Robinson (who seemed temporarily concussed) was looking away, Aston nipping in to grab the ball. From the ensuing play, Sheffield's Matt Crowther—despite Connolly's

desperate tackle attempt—dived into the left corner for a sensational try, having collected a long cut-out pass from Rod Doyle that bounced off the ground into his arms. Aston, having missed the earlier conversion, was on target this time. Five minutes later Farrell pulled two points back with a penalty, Dave Watson being guilty of 'lying on' at a play-the-ball. Aston, though, sent his colleagues back to the changing rooms in a positive mood, his last-minute drop-goal in front of goal making it 11–2.

Those anticipating a Wigan revival were stunned 12 minutes into the second period; Darren Turner—after Broadbent was tackled just short—stretching over from acting-halfback through a melee of defenders to place the ball on the try-line. Referee Stuart Cummings confirmed the touchdown after consulting the in-goal judge amidst claims of a double-movement. Aston converted, the 17–2 score-line being greeted

Darren Turner stretches Sheffield's lead with a crucial try even though Wigan seemed to have plenty of bodies available

with disbelief inside the stadium. The try roused a Wigan side facing the reality of unexpected defeat, their increased tempo producing a Mark Bell try, the winger planting the ball firmly on the whitewash in the right corner after it was passed swiftly across by Paul, Denis Betts and Lee Gilmour. Farrell added the difficult kick but Wigan still trailed by nine points.

Wigan were unrelenting, Robinson—after

recovering a loose ball—having a 60th minute try in the left corner struck off when Paul was judged to have knocked-on when being tackled. Five minutes later Farrell was held up over the try-line although claiming he got the ball down (video replays seemed to indicate Aston got his hand underneath it), Wigan subsequently being penalised for debating the verdict. Somehow Sheffield weathered the Wigan storm, and Aston was wide with a 72nd minute drop-goal, team mate Paul Carr being held up over the try-line two minutes before full time.

A jubilant John Kear had the distinction of being the first successful English coach since Malcolm Reilly in 1986, the final containing a high of 11 overseas players, including a club record equalling six for Sheffield. Henry Paul emulated his brother Robbie from a year earlier, playing in the final one week after representing New Zealand in a one-off Test versus Australia, this time in Auckland.

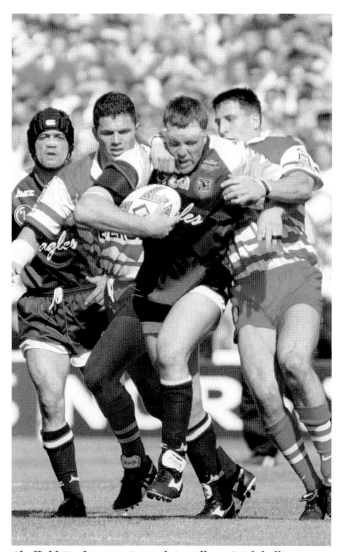

Sheffield Eagles captain Paul Broadbent (with ball) set an example with his charges through the Wigan ranks

---

STATS

Sheffield Eagles 17 Wigan Warriors 8

Saturday 2 May at Wembley Stadium, London (2.45 pm)

Sheffield Eagles (blue with white sleeves): Sovatabua, Pinkney, Taewa, Senior, Crowther, Watson, Aston, Broadbent (captain), Lawless, Laughton, Carr, Shaw, Doyle. Substitutes: Turner, Jackson, Wood, Stott (dnp). Coach: J. Kear

Wigan Warriors (white with cherry filled W-shape chest and bands): Radlinski, M. Bell, Moore, Connolly, Robinson, Paul, Smith, Holgate, McCormack, Mestrov, Betts, Haughton, Farrell (captain). Substitutes: Cowie, Cassidy, O'Connor, Gilmour. Coach: J. Monie

Referee: S. Cummings Touch-judges: F. Hawley, P. Hewitt In-goal judges: P. Walton, S. Wright

Half-time: 11–2 Attendance: 60,669 Receipts: £1,557,150

Weather: sunny with strong wind

Lance Todd Trophy: Aston (Sheffield Eagles)

Cup presentation: The Rt Hon. Chris Smith MP, Secretary of State for Culture, Media and Sport

Progressive score:

Sheffield Eagles	score (min)	Wigan Warriors
Pinkney try	4–0 (5)	
Crowther try, Aston goal	10–0 (29)	
	10–2 (34)	Farrell penalty
Aston drop-goal	11–2 (40)	
Turner try, Aston goal	17–2 (52)	
	17–8 (57)	M. Bell try, Farrell goal

Route to the final:

Fourth round: Leigh Centurions 11 Sheffield E 66, Keighley Cougars 0 Wigan W 76

Fifth round: Sheffield E 84 Egremont Rangers 6, Dewsbury Rams 0 Wigan W 56

Sixth round: Castleford Tigers 22 Sheffield E 32, Wigan W 22 St Helens 10

Semi-finals: Sheffield E 22 Salford Reds 18 (Headingley, Leeds, 6,961), Wigan W 38 London Broncos 8 (McAlpine Stadium, Huddersfield, 11,058)

Head-to-head form guide:

No previous meetings during season

1999 RUGBY LEAGUE CHALLENGE CUP FINAL
Leeds Rhinos v London Broncos

Leeds Rhinos lifted the Challenge Cup for the first time since 1978 in an historic, record-making farewell to the old Wembley Stadium. Held three days short of the 70th anniversary of the first Wembley final in 1929, it seemed appropriate the capital city should have its own representative in London Broncos. The first team outside the so-called 'Northern Heartlands' to reach the final, evolving from the Fulham club that began life in 1980, they contributed to an enjoyable afternoon's entertainment, despite a Leeds second-half onslaught that ended with a 52–16 score-line. A carnival-like atmosphere was reflected through entrepreneurial Broncos chairman Richard Branson foregoing the usual suit and tie to lead his troops out in open-neck dark blue shirt and jeans.

Leeds produced the biggest ever Challenge Cup Final score (52) and winning margin (36), whilst team captain Iestyn Harris—despite missing two conversions—equalled the eight goals of Cyril Kellett (1973) and 20 points of Neil Fox (1960). Meanwhile, London skipper Shaun Edwards extended his incredible appearance record to 11 finals. The most notable individual achievement, though, was that of Rhinos right wingman Leroy Rivett in scoring a

Martin Offiah of London Broncos notches the opening try with Leeds' Leroy Rivett failing to reach him in time

Challenge Cup Final record four tries to claim the Lance Todd Trophy (the award was announced before his fourth touchdown, the last to be scored at the stadium). He began his quartet with Leeds' first try in the 25th minute, created by a superb dummy and break from Daryl Powell 40 metres out, despatching Rivett on a 15-metre run that ended when he reached out of a tackle to place the ball 10 metres in from the right-hand flag. His remaining three came after the interval. The first was on the overlap following quick passing (including a glorious cut-out pass by Harris) after Ryan Sheridan's tremendous break set up the position, the next after he intercepted Karle Hammond's long pass to sprint 90 metres. He completed his foursome in the 76th minute after evading two defenders on a 30-metre sprint to the right corner off Richie Blackmore's pass.

Leeds almost scored in the second minute of the match, hooker Terry Newton making a 40-metre burst from acting-halfback before being hauled down by Tulsen Tollett at the corner. But it was the Broncos that caused the early excitement through two tries,

WINNING CAPTAIN

Iestyn Harris (Leeds Rhinos 1999)

Iestyn Harris built his reputation as a danger-man through his adept passing and sidestepping ability, be it from full back, centre or stand-off. He has represented Wales 16 times including the 2000 World Cup as captain. Born and raised in Oldham, he qualified through his grandfather, Norman Harris, who left Cross Keys rugby union club to join Oldham in 1945. Due to his ancestry, the Welsh Rugby Union tempted him to the valleys in 2001, where he joined Cardiff and played 25 times for Wales in the 15-a-side code. He began his senior rugby league career when Warrington signed him from Oldham St Anne's in 1993, transferring to Leeds in 1997 in a deal reportedly worth £375,000 (including a player-exchange). Appointed captain he led them to victory in the 1999 Rugby League Challenge Cup Final. Following his rugby union sabbatical, he returned to rugby league in 2004 with Bradford Bulls, where he enjoyed success in the Super League Grand Final (2005) and World Club Challenge (2006) before transferring to Featherstone Rovers for 2009. He has appeared in 15 Tests for Great Britain and was a tourist in 1996.

Barrie McDermott burst the dam for Leeds Rhinos with this 49th minute try, London captain Shaun Edwards and Robbie Beazley (on ground) unable to stop him

from Martin Offiah and Robbie Simpson, that put them 10–0 ahead after 10 minutes' play. Offiah's was a vintage 40-metre burst down the left channel, neatly sidestepping Harris after collecting a ball that ricocheted off Blackmore from a misguided John Timu kick. There was a two-minute delay as Wembley's first video refereeing decision—by David Asquith—determined Offiah was onside. Simpson's effort came about when Hammond sent him clean through a gap into the right corner. Rob Smyth made two magnificent conversion attempts, the first succeeding.

Harris clawed two points back with a simple penalty after Edwards went high on Sheridan. Following Rivett's first touchdown there were near misses at both ends; from Sheridan (his 'try' under the posts disallowed through obstruction by colleague Powell) and Edwards (brought down from behind by Sheridan within 10 metres of the posts). In the final minute

UNLUCKY FOR SOME!

Six current British professional clubs—all founded since the Second World War—have yet to reach a Challenge Cup Final. They are Blackpool Panthers (debut year 2005), Celtic Crusaders (2006), Doncaster (1951), Gateshead Thunder (reformed 2001), London Skolars (2003) and Whitehaven (1948). Whitehaven almost made it to Wembley in 1957, losing 10–9 to Leeds in the semi-final through a late 35-yard drop-goal from Jeff Stevenson. Four other, long established clubs have appeared in a final but are still chasing their Wembley dream; Batley Bulldogs, Oldham, Rochdale Hornets and Swinton Lions. Of those, the unluckiest are Oldham (four consecutive finals from 1924 to 1927 before the switch to Wembley in 1929) and Swinton (appeared in the last three pre-Wembley finals and again in 1932 when Wembley was unavailable). The name of Harlequins RL is yet to grace the final, although predecessors London Broncos reached Wembley in 1999.

STATS

Leeds Rhinos 52 London Broncos 16

Saturday 1 May at Wembley Stadium, London (2.45 pm)

Leeds Rhinos (blue with amber bands): Harris (captain), Rivett, Blackmore, Godden, Cummins, Powell, Sheridan, McDermott, Newton, Fleary, Morley, Farrell, Glanville. Substitutes: Jackson, St Hilaire, Hay, Mathiou. Coach: G. Murray

London Broncos (red with black, yellow and white trim): Tollett, Smyth, Fleming, Timu, Offiah, Hammond, Edwards (captain), Retchless, Beazley, Salter, Millard, Simpson, Gill. Substitutes: Ryan, Toshack, Callaway, Air. Coach: D. Stains

Referee: R. Smith Touch-judges: J. Molyneux, F. Hawley Video referee: D. Asquith

Half-time: 12–10 Attendance: 73,242

Weather: sunny and warm

Lance Todd Trophy: Rivett (Leeds Rhinos)

Cup presentation:
The Rt. Hon. Frank Dobson MP, Secretary of State for Health

Progressive score:

Leeds Rhinos	score (min)	London Broncos
	0–6 (6)	Offiah try*, Smyth goal
	0–10 (10)	Simpson try
Harris penalty	2–10 (18)	
Rivett try	6–10 (25)	
Godden try, Harris goal	12–10 (40)	
	12–16 (43)	Fleming try*, Smyth goal
McDermott try, Harris goal	18–16 (49)	
Rivett try, Harris goal	24–16 (56)	
St Hilaire try, Harris goal	30–16 (59)	
Rivett try	34–16 (65)	
Harris try, Harris goal	40–16 (68)	
Cummins try, Harris goal	46–16 (71)	
Rivett try, Harris goal	52–16 (76)	

Route to the final:

Fourth round: Leeds R 28 Wigan Warriors 18, London B 64 Doncaster Dragons 0

Fifth round: Leeds R 24 St Helens 16, Hull Kingston Rovers 0 London B 6

Sixth round: Widnes Vikings 10 Leeds R 46, London B 54 Whitehaven Warriors 6

Semi-finals: Leeds R 23 Bradford B 20 (McAlpine Stadium, Huddersfield, 23,438),

London B 33 Castleford Tigers 27 (Headingley, Leeds, 7,561)

Head-to-head form guide:

Leeds Rhinos 38 London Broncos 12 (League)

Leeds' Leroy Rivett scores his record making fourth try

before the break, Leeds went ahead for the first time, 12–10, after Darren Fleary made a terrific break, handing over to Brad Godden from 30 metres out, the centre exchanging passes with Lee Jackson near the posts before touching down.

London—not favoured in the pre-match forecasts—produced a surprise by hitting back in the 43rd minute; the bounce off Matt Toshack's high kick to the right deceived Francis Cummins but fell kindly for Greg Fleming, who raced over, the video referee, after a three-minute scrutiny, confirming he was onside. Smyth added the goal and the Broncos led once more, 16–12.

In the 47th minute Hammond took advantage of one of rugby league's newest rules to produce Wembley's inaugural '40–20' kick into touch. But that was soon followed by Leeds notching the first of their seven second half tries, the scorer Barrie McDermott being clearly elated after his neat sidestep and charge took him under the posts from a tap-penalty, awarded when Rivett was obstructed after kicking towards the London try-line. Leeds—having made their customary half-time change of introducing Marcus St Hilaire at full back and moving Harris to stand-off—were looking far more potent and, apart from Rivett, there were further tries from St Hilaire (left of the posts after some awesome passing), Harris (under the crossbar after supporting St Hilaire's break through a melee of defenders) and Cummins (off Harris after Godden broke from midfield). Prior to Rivett's concluding try a third video decision was required when London's Shane Millard forced his way over the line, but was adjudged to have lost the ball.

CHALLENGE CUP FINAL VENUES
Apart from Wembley, the following 17 venues have staged Challenge Cup Finals:

Headingley, Leeds (1897, 1898, 1901, 1903, 1905, 1906, 1909, 1912, 1913, 1920, 1922, 1925, 1943 2nd leg)

Hosted the first Challenge Cup Final and staged 13 altogether, the most outside Wembley. Opened in 1890, it has been home to Leeds/Leeds Rhinos ever since and now shared with Leeds Carnegie rugby union. The attendance record of 40,175 was set on 21 May 1947 at a League match against Bradford Northern, the current capacity being 22,500. Adjoining is Yorkshire county cricket ground.

Fallowfield Stadium, Manchester (1899, 1900)

Built for Manchester Athletic Club who transferred from Old Trafford in 1892, staging athletics and track cycling. In 1893 it hosted the FA Cup Final, watched by 45,000, an occasion blighted by crowd problems. The England-Scotland rugby union international was held in 1897 and, from 1945, was home to Broughton Park rugby union for several seasons. Renamed 'The Reg Harris Stadium' in the early 1950s (honouring the former world sprint cycling champion) it was demolished in 1994.

Athletic Grounds, Rochdale (1902, 1924, 1926)

Rochdale Hornets moved there permanently in 1900 having already played several matches (the first being 1894) at what was then an athletic and track cycling arena. The outer track remained throughout Rochdale's time there, providing a home for speedway in the late 1920s and early 1970s when stock car racing also took place. Greyhound racing was hosted from 1932 until the late 1960s. The record 41,831 attendance was set at the 1924 Challenge Cup Final. Hornets moved to Spotland in 1988 to ground-share with Rochdale AFC, the Athletic Grounds making way for a supermarket.

The Willows, Salford (1904, 1911)

Salford (now Salford City Reds) first played there in 1901 but plan to relocate to a new stadium in 2010. The playing area was originally surrounded by a cycling track, dispensed with during the early 1930s as the venue took on its more familiar rectangle shape. On 13 February 1937 the ground record of 26,470 was set in a Challenge Cup match against Warrington (another tie between the two on 17 March 1951 reportedly drew nearly 28,000, an exact figure proving difficult to verify). The current capacity is 11,363.

Wheater's Field, Broughton (1907)

The home ground of the former Broughton Rangers club from 1892 until 1913, the area is now covered by a housing estate. The highest attendance reported was 23,000 for a Lancashire League match against Swinton on 29 January 1898.

Fartown, Huddersfield (1908, 1910, 1910 replay, 1945 1st leg)

Providing a base for Huddersfield from 1878, Fartown—with its adjoining cricket ground—was drastically altered and reopened in 1891, taking on the more recognisable look of later years. On 19 April 1947 the attendance record of 35,136 was set at the Leeds v Wakefield Trinity Challenge Cup semi-final. The club last played there in 1992 and now—as Huddersfield Giants—share Galpharm Stadium with Huddersfield Town AFC.

Thrum Hall, Halifax (1914)

Halifax transferred there in 1886, its record attendance of 29,153 being set on 29 March 1959 for a Challenge Cup match against Wigan. During 1998 they transferred to The Shay to ground-share with Halifax Town AFC, the latter being liquidated in 2008, reforming as FC Halifax Town.

Watersheddings, Oldham (1915)

The former home of Oldham from 1889, the ground record of 28,000 being created on 24 February 1912 at a League match against Huddersfield. Oldham moved to Boundary Park in 1997, sharing with Oldham Athletic AFC, Watersheddings since being demolished for housing.

The Cliff, Broughton (1921)

Broughton Rangers relocated there from Wheater's

Field in 1913, remaining until 1933 when they moved to Belle Vue speedway stadium in Manchester, being known as Belle Vue Rangers from 1946 until folding in 1955. The Cliff's record attendance was on 21 November 1931, 26,471 attending the Salford v Swinton Lancashire Cup Final. In 1951 Manchester United AFC purchased The Cliff as a training facility and still use it today.

Belle Vue, Wakefield (1923)
Since 1879 it has been the ground of Wakefield Trinity/Wakefield Trinity Wildcats. Its record attendance is 37,906 for the Leeds-Huddersfield Challenge Cup semi-final on 21 March 1936, the current capacity being 11,000. At present, the Wildcats are pursuing a new facility.

Central Park, Wigan (1927, 1928, 1932, 1944 1st leg)
Used by Wigan/Wigan Warriors from 1902, the record attendance being 47,747 for a League fixture versus St Helens on 27 March 1959. Now the site of a supermarket, the club played its last match there in 1999 before sharing the JJB Stadium (DW Stadium from 2009) with Wigan Athletic AFC.

Odsal Stadium, Bradford (1941, 1942, 1944 2nd leg, 1945 2nd leg, 1954 replay)
Bradford Bulls—then Bradford Northern—moved there in 1934. A former quarry that became a waste disposal site, the playing area is well below ground level. Once the biggest ground in England outside Wembley, an official attendance record of 102,569 was set at the 1954 Challenge Cup Final replay. During 2001 and 2002 Bradford Bulls played at Valley Parade, home of Bradford City AFC to allow renovation at Odsal, its present capacity being 27,500. Speedway was held from 1945 until 1997 and stock car racing has also been staged.

Crown Flatt, Dewsbury (1943 1st leg)
Opened in 1876, its first occupant was Dewsbury Athletic rugby club (Dewsbury and Savile from 1886) who departed in 1898 to take up soccer as Savile Town. A new Dewsbury was founded, playing their first match there in September 1898, a record 26,584 witnessing a Yorkshire Cup match against Halifax on 30 October 1920. A fire destroyed the main stand in 1988 leading to financial problems and the ground was sold for housing, its last match being 1991. Dewsbury shared Batley's Mount Pleasant until 1994 before moving to a 'new' Crown Flatt home. The original

venue hosted an England-Wales rugby union international in 1890.

Elland Road, Leeds (1982 replay)
Leeds United AFC's ground is the largest stadium in Yorkshire with a current 40,242 capacity, the record attendance of 57,892 being set for an FA Cup match against Sunderland on 15 March 1967. Opened in 1897, it has provided a base for the Holbeck (Northern Union) club (1897–1904), Leeds City AFC (1904–1919) and Leeds United (1920 to present). Hunslet rugby league club shared the ground from 1982 until 1994.

Murrayfield, Edinburgh (2000, 2002)
Opened in 1925 as a home for Scottish rugby union. Today, it is the largest stadium in Scotland, once holding the world record rugby union attendance of 104,000 for Scotland v Wales in 1975. Its present capacity is 67,800, all seated.

Twickenham, London (2001, 2006)
The headquarters of England rugby union since 1907, its current 82,000 capacity is the second largest in the United Kingdom after the 'new' Wembley. Initially, Harlequins rugby union were invited to move in on a permanent basis, their game against Richmond on 2 October 1909 being the first held. Harlequins relocated to The Stoop in 1963, a ground since shared with rugby league clubs London Broncos (1997 to 1999) and Harlequins RL (2006 to present).

Millennium Stadium, Cardiff (2003, 2004, 2005)
Opened in 1999 on the site of the former Cardiff Arms Park ground, and the national stadium of Wales for rugby union and soccer, its capacity being 74,500. During Wembley's absence it staged six FA Cup Finals (2001–2006). Cardiff rugby union play on an adjoining ground that retains the name of Cardiff Arms Park.

2000 RUGBY LEAGUE CHALLENGE CUP FINAL
Bradford Bulls v Leeds Rhinos

Bradford Bulls—at the forefront of Super League since its inception in the mid-1990s—won their first major final of the summer era in capturing the 2000 Challenge Cup. Their 24–18 victory over Leeds Rhinos at Murrayfield was also their first success in the competition for 51 years. The Rugby Football League's decision to take the event to the Scottish rugby union stronghold almost backfired when, the preceding Thursday, the playing area was under almost three feet of water after the River Leith overflowed following several days' heavy rainfall. It also flooded the changing areas and affected the power systems, so it was with some relief, following a colossal effort, that it was announced on Friday noon that the match could go ahead. Bradford's Paul brothers—Henry and Robbie—had played in Sydney that previous Thursday, representing New Zealand against Australia in the annual Anzac Test, an experience developing into a pre-Cup Final ritual for the pair.

With their big pack taking an early grip, the Bulls built a 10–0 lead, Henry Paul's 35-metre penalty (he was caught off the ball by a Barrie McDermott elbow to his face—an incident spotted by a touch-judge) being followed by two tries from Michael Withers. Both touchdowns resulted from Henry Paul's high

kicks towards the left corner; the first caught by Tevita Vaikona who provided the scoring pass, the second recovered by Withers himself after it rebounded off Leeds' Richie Blackmore. Henry Paul was just wide with both conversions.

Iestyn Harris replied with a Leeds penalty (Bradford failed to retreat 10 metres at a play-the-ball) but the Bulls continued to press; James Lowes was stopped a metre short and then set up a chance for Robbie Paul moments later, his grubber kick into the in-goal being fumbled by his skipper. Nathan McAvoy claimed Bradford's next touchdown, receiving the ball 40 metres out after slick passing from Lowes and Paul Anderson before racing down the flank, chipping it neatly over Harris' head and catching it in mid-air for a try he made look easy. Henry Paul's kick hit the upright, subsequently being wide with a 39th minute penalty, the Bulls leading 14–2 at the break.

Having looked poor defensively during the opening half, Leeds demonstrated a more competitive streak after the interval, initial pressure leading to a second Harris penalty (Stuart Fielden obstructed him after he kicked the ball). But, one minute later, Fielden got Bradford's fourth try, taking another high ball from Henry Paul on the try-line to go over, a score endorsed

Michael Withers performs a spectacular dive into the corner to score Bradford Bulls' first try in the 10th minute

226

Try-scorer Stuart Fielden (with ball) works hard to make progress for Bradford against a stubborn Leeds defence

by video referee, Gerry Kershaw. Henry Paul's conversion placed the Bulls comfortably ahead at 20–4. A few minutes later, Leeds notched their opening try, Ryan Sheridan's kick from his own 20-metre line resulting in the ball being collected by colleague Francis Cummins who off-loaded to Andy Hay, the latter scoring with two defenders in attendance. Kershaw again sanctioned the touchdown, Harris adding an excellent goal plus a penalty (Brian McDermott not playing the ball correctly—Henry Paul's subsequent dissent added 10 metres for a kickable 31-metre strike).

At 20–12 Bradford's lead looked less secure, but a high Anthony Farrell tackle on Robbie Paul resulted in another Henry Paul penalty goal. Leeds then put everything back into the melting pot when Marcus St Hilaire followed up Harris' grubber kick from in front of the posts to place a hand on the ball, Kershaw again concurring. Harris' goal reduced the deficit to four points but, despite his last second 'up-and-under' on Bradford's try-line, that was safely gathered by Lowes, the only remaining score was Henry Paul's third penalty (stealing the ball in a three-man tackle).

The occasion was hailed a success, most visitors to Edinburgh enjoying the hospitality offered whilst around 10,000 Scots also attended the final. It was a far cry from the Leeds-Hull semi-final when, reportedly, around 500 so-called Hull supporters invaded the pitch, clashing with police and pulling the posts down, an incident leading to many arrests.

STATS

Bradford Bulls 24 Leeds Rhinos 18

Saturday 29 April at Murrayfield, Edinburgh (2.45 pm)

Bradford Bulls (white with narrow amber, black and red chest band): Spruce, McAvoy, Naylor, Withers, Vaikona, H. Paul, R. Paul (captain), Brian McDermott, Lowes, Anderson, Peacock, Forshaw, Mackay. Substitutes: Pryce, Boyle, Dwyer, Fielden. Coach: M. Elliott

Leeds Rhinos (blue with amber bands): Harris (captain), Rivett, Blackmore, Senior, Cummins, Powell, Sheridan, Fleary, Lawford, Barrie McDermott, Morley, Farrell, Hay. Substitutes: Jackson, Barnhill, St Hilaire, Mathiou. Coach: D. Lance

Referee: S. Presley
Touch-judges: S. Taylor, P. Hewitt
Video referee: G. Kershaw

Half-time: 14–2   Attendance: 67,247

Weather: overcast with slight breeze, ground very damp

Lance Todd Trophy: H. Paul (Bradford Bulls)

Cup presentation: Kate Hoey MP

Progressive score:

Bradford Bulls	score (min)	Leeds Rhinos
H. Paul penalty	2–0 (8)	
Withers try	6–0 (10)	
Withers try	10–0 (17)	
	10–2 (21)	Harris penalty
McAvoy try	14–2 (29)	
	14–4 (47)	Harris penalty
Fielden try*, H. Paul goal	20–4 (48)	
	20–10 (51)	Hay try*, Harris goal
	20–12 (57)	Harris penalty
H. Paul penalty	22–12 (66)	
	22–18 (72)	St Hilaire try*, Harris goal
H. Paul penalty	24–18 (79)	

Route to the final:

Fourth round:
Bradford B 32 Huddersfield-Sheffield Giants 4, Featherstone Rovers 12 Leeds R 48

Fifth round:
Wakefield Trinity Wildcats 0 Bradford B 46, Leeds R 26 St Helens 20

Sixth round:
Halifax Blue Sox 18 Bradford B 28, Leeds R 42 Dewsbury Rams 10

Semi-finals:
Bradford Bulls 44 Warrington Wolves 20 (Headingley, Leeds, 11,894),

Leeds Rhinos 28 Hull FC 22 (McAlpine Stadium, Huddersfield, 18,068)

Head-to-head form guide:

No previous meeting during season

2001 RUGBY LEAGUE CHALLENGE CUP FINAL
St Helens v Bradford Bulls

There was a time when playing the Rugby League Challenge Cup Final at Twickenham—the bastion of English rugby union—would have been unthinkable, but in 2001 it finally happened, St Helens and Bradford Bulls contesting the outcome of the 100th competition. It was their third meeting over the last six finals, Saints again being triumphant, 13–6, on an occasion marred by heavy rain that made handling difficult. Nonetheless, both teams provided an entertaining match, although hardly the classic encounter anticipated. The Bulls were without full back Stuart Spruce, his shoulder injury the previous week keeping him out for the rest of the season.

The deeper than usual in-goal area led to a profusion of kicks into that zone from St Helens' Sean Long and Bradford's Henry Paul, the former being particularly fruitful by producing the only two tries of the afternoon, both in the opening half. Henry Paul attempted an early, fourth minute grubber kick, the ball just evading brother, Robbie, Long getting into the act with a couple of testing efforts in the 10th and 11th minute. The second rebounded back off the upright,

whilst the first resulted in a 10-minute sin-bin for Bradford's Shane Rigon after he tackled Tommy Martyn off the ball. Long's persistence succeeded in the 12th minute, Martyn following up his neat kick into the in-goal to dive on the ball. In the 26th minute, another Long effort ricocheted of a Bulls player,

---

WINNING CAPTAIN

Chris Joynt (St Helens 2001)

Chris Joynt signed for Oldham in 1989 from his local amateur club, Wigan St Patrick's, joining St Helens in 1992. In 1993 the skilful, all-action second-row forward made his Great Britain debut, the first of 25 Tests. A member of the 1996 touring side to New Zealand and the South Pacific, he also represented England (6 times—including the 1995 World Cup), Ireland (4—all in the 2000 World Cup) and Lancashire (1). At St Helens, where he became captain in 1997, he won the Rugby League Challenge Cup (1996, 1997, 2001, 2004), Super League Grand Final (1999, 2000, 2002), Super League Championship (1996), World Club Challenge (2001) and Premiership Trophy (1993). He played in Australia for Newcastle Knights during 1995. Following the 2004 season, he decided to retire after 383 appearances for St Helens.

Not a Bradford Bulls player in sight as Keiron Cunningham races over for his try watched by four St Helens colleagues and referee Russell Smith

Keiron Cunningham picking up and escaping two defenders to go over behind the posts. As with the first try, video referee Steve Cross confirmed the score. Long converted both efforts and, with Henry Paul booting over a 20th minute penalty after Paul Anderson was stripped of the ball in a three-man tackle, Saints led 12–2. Shortly before half-time Martyn contributed a drop-goal, whilst Henry Paul claimed his second penalty, from 34 metres through

Saints' Vila Matautia 'holding down' after a tackle.

The second half opened with a deluge of rain as the skies darkened, pouring down as it had 30 minutes before kick-off, the heavens having deceived everyone with a short-lived burst of sunlight shortly after the match commenced. Apart from the pitch becoming completely sodden, causing unavoidable handling errors, gaps began appearing beneath an uncovered section of the stadium as spectators vacated their seats to search for shelter elsewhere. The only second half score was a third Henry Paul penalty given for offside at a play-the-ball. Most of the try scoring chances went to St Helens, video replays denying them three times; Martyn in the 53rd minute (given offside after winning the scramble to claim a touchdown following a kick by Long), Sean Hoppe in the 60th (ruled to have dived on the ball after it went dead having been hacked on its way from midfield by Martyn when Bradford lost possession), and Tim Jonkers in the 70th (Henry Paul flicking the ball away to safety ahead of his dive following another grubber by Long). The disallowed Hoppe try led to a 33-metre penalty attempt from Long that went wide, Bradford's Joe Vagana having brought down Martyn after he kicked ahead. In the final minute St Helens' Chris Joynt and Peter Shiels were both halted short of the try-line.

STATS

St Helens 13 Bradford Bulls 6

Saturday 28 April at Twickenham, London (2.45 pm)

St Helens (black with red and white trim): Wellens, Hoppe, Iro, Newlove, Sullivan, Martyn, Long, Nickle, Cunningham, Fairleigh, Joynt (captain), Shiels, Sculthorpe. Substitutes: Jonkers, Matautia, Hall, Stewart (dnp). Coach: I. Millward

Bradford Bulls (white with red, amber and black chevron): Withers, Vaikona, Naylor, Rigon, Pryce, H. Paul, R. Paul (captain), Vagana, Lowes, McDermott, Peacock, Gartner, Forshaw. Substitutes: Deacon, Anderson, Gilmour, Fielden. Coach: B. Noble

Referee: R. Smith Touch-judges: F. Hawley, A. Martin Video referee: S. Cross

Half-time: 13–4 Attendance: 68,250

Weather: cloudy with brief sunshine, cool and windy, heavy rain during second half

Lance Todd Trophy: Long (St Helens)

Cup presentation: The Rt Hon. Tony Blair, Prime Minister

Progressive score:

St Helens	score (min)	Bradford Bulls
Martyn try*, Long goal	6–0 (12)	
	6–2 (20)	H. Paul penalty
Cunningham try*, Long goal	12–2 (26)	
Martyn drop-goal	13–2 (38)	
	13–4 (40)	H. Paul penalty
	13–6 (48)	H. Paul penalty

Route to the final:

Fourth round: St Helens 22 Wigan Warriors 8, Bradford Bulls 54 Widnes Vikings 10

Fifth round: Whitehaven 22 St Helens 34, Halifax Blue Sox 18 Bradford Bulls 68

Sixth round: St Helens 54 Huddersfield G 16, Wakefield T Wildcats 0 Bradford B 38

Semi-finals: St Helens 27 Leeds Rhinos 22 (JJB Stadium, Wigan, 16,416), Bradford B 39 Warrington W 22 (McAlpine Stadium, Huddersfield, 13,856)

Head-to-head form guide:

Bradford Bulls 31 St Helens 24 (League)

Bradford captain Robbie Paul attempts to bring the ball away from his own line

2002 RUGBY LEAGUE CHALLENGE CUP FINAL
Wigan Warriors v St Helens

Gary Connolly is about to score for Wigan Warriors after covering 30 metres

WINNING CAPTAIN

Andrew Farrell (Wigan Warriors 2002)

Andrew Farrell first played in Wigan's senior side as a 16-year-old during 1991, being formally signed from local club, Orrell St James, in January 1992. He made 370 appearances for the Cherry and Whites, becoming captain in 1996, aged 21. His list of club honours cover the Championship (1993/94, 1994/95, 1995/96), Super League Grand Final (1998), Rugby League Challenge Cup (1993, 1994, 1995, 2002), World Club Challenge (1994), Premiership Trophy (1994, 1995, 1996, 1997) and Charity Shield (1995). Wigan's regular goal-kicker from 1995, he created a new club record for the season of 429 points (183 goals including five drop-goals, 17 tries) in 2001. His totals of 1,355 goals and 3,135 points places him second on both counts behind Jim Sullivan in the club's all-time list. One of Great Britain's most outstanding back-row forwards, he displayed pace, power, wonderful distribution and solid defence, becoming his country's youngest Test forward at 18 years, five months, against New Zealand in November 1993. For his remaining rugby league career he never missed a Test match, setting a record run of 34 appearances, creating another milestone by being skipper for the latter 29, beginning his sequence as Britain's youngest tour captain in 1996. He represented England (11 times, including the World Cups of 1995—being in the team beaten by Australia in the final—and 2000) and Lancashire (3). Awarded the OBE in the 2005 New Years Honours, it was announced in March 2005 that he was departing for rugby union, joining Saracens and making his England debut in 2007.

Whenever the 2002 Challenge Cup Final is recalled the name of Wigan full back Kris Radlinski is certain to be mentioned, such was his contribution to the 21–12 win over favourites St Helens. In hospital the preceding week with a badly swollen foot—believed through an insect bite—he decided 90 minutes before kick-off to play following consultation with Wigan's club doctor. If Radlinski had personal doubts it was not revealed in a fearless display that won him the Lance Todd Trophy, an award owing much to his defensive commitment.

He made his first key tackle in the 10th minute, thwarting Tim Jonkers—who consequently lost possession—as he was about to cross the try-line. During the next five minutes Wigan raced over the whitewash for two tries through Brett Dallas (in the right corner after quick passing by Terry Newton, Adrian Lam and Gary Connolly—set up by Radlinski's off-load in a two-man tackle) and Adrian Lam (left of the posts after sidestepping Paul Wellens and evading Keiron Cunningham). Andrew Farrell added both goals to place Wigan 12–0 ahead, although his subsequent 21st minute drop-goal attempt was poor, hardly rising above ground level.

St Helens responded, piling on the pressure and being rewarded with two tries; from Darren Albert

Wigan's Lance Todd Trophy winner Kris Radlinski (on ground) cannot prevent Martin Gleeson scoring for St Helens

Saints' line, Farrell concluded the scoring with a penalty.

The following month, St Helens' misery was compounded through a £25,000 fine for fielding a weakened team against Bradford Bulls one week before the final.

(jumping to catch Sean Long's high kick into the right corner and grounding it despite Jamie Ainscough's presence) and Martin Gleeson (racing in from 10 metres after avoiding Paul Johnson to stretch over the try-line with Radlinski hanging on). Both Long's goal efforts—from similar positions on the right—just went wide of the far upright, the score standing at 12–8. Saints could have had more; Albert being shunted into touch near the corner flag, and Paul Newlove being brought down by Connolly short of the try-line. In the 25th minute controversy surfaced after Cunningham burrowed his way through four Wigan defenders and appeared to place the ball down under the posts, but the video referee ruled Radlinski's leg prevented the grounding, the hooker being adamant he scored.

After the interval, Saints' Paul Sculthorpe had a 50th minute try scrubbed after diving over from acting-halfback through Gleeson not playing the ball correctly. Farrell's resultant penalty kick into touch swung the momentum to Wigan, Julian O'Neill's break from just inside his own half allowing Johnson to send Connolly sprinting behind the posts. Farrell's conversion made it 18–8. Nine minutes later, Sculthorpe stretched his right arm over the try-line to score after twisting his way through three defenders. Long again missed the goal, his easiest so far, almost making amends a minute later with a searing break through the middle only to be brought down by Ainscough 18 metres from the try-line. A Lam drop-goal gave Wigan valuable breathing space and, when Newton had the ball 'stolen' in a three-man tackle on

STATS

Wigan Warriors 21 St Helens 12

Saturday 27 April at Murrayfield, Edinburgh (2.45 pm)

Wigan Warriors (blue with white rim): Radlinski, Dallas, Connolly, Ainscough, Johnson, O'Neill, Lam, O'Connor, Newton, C Smith, Cassidy, Furner, Farrell (captain). Substitutes: Carney, Hodgson, M. Smith, Bibey. Coach: S. Raper

St Helens (white with red chevrons): Wellens, Albert, Gleeson, Newlove, Stewart, Martyn, Long, Britt, Cunningham, Shiels, Joynt (captain), Jonkers, Sculthorpe. Substitutes: Hoppe, Ward, Stankevitch, Higham. Coach: I. Millward

Referee: S. Cummings Touch-judges: S. Wright, P. Hewitt Video referee: R. Tennant

Half-time: 12–8 Attendance: 62,140

Weather: sunny and warm after early light rain, some cloud, strong breeze

Lance Todd Trophy: Radlinski (Wigan Warriors)

Cup presentation:
The Rt Hon. Richard Caborn MP, Minister for Sport

Progressive score:

Wigan Warriors	score (min)	St Helens
Dallas try, Farrell goal	6–0 (11)	
Lam try, Farrell goal	12–0 (15)	
	12–4 (22)	Albert try
	12–8 (31)	Gleeson try
Connolly try, Farrell goal	18–8 (51)	
	18–12 (60)	Sculthorpe try
Lamb drop-goal	19–12 (66)	
Farrell penalty	21–12 (76)	

Route to the final:

Fourth round:
Wigan Warriors 34 Hull FC 10, Oldham 6 St Helens 40

Fifth round:
Union Treiziste Catalane (France) 6 Wigan Warriors 72, Warrington Wolves 14 St Helens 36

Sixth round: Leigh Centurions 16 Wigan W 30, Halifax Blue Sox 20 St Helens 26

Semi-finals: Wigan Warriors 20 Castleford Tigers 10 (Headingley, Leeds, 10,380), St Helens 42 Leeds Rhinos 16 (JJB Stadium, Wigan, 17,475)

Head-to-head form guide:

St Helens 19 Wigan Warriors 0 (League)

2003 RUGBY LEAGUE CHALLENGE CUP FINAL
Bradford Bulls v Leeds Rhinos

Bradford Bulls and Leeds Rhinos fought out a thrilling duel at Cardiff's Millennium Stadium to settle the destination of the Challenge Cup in 2003, a match that—apart from an eight-minute spell in the latter stages—never had more than one score separating the teams. It was an afternoon full of incident and talking points—not least the decision by Leeds captain Kevin Sinfield to spurn a kickable 73rd minute penalty goal opportunity that could have tied the score at 22–22. Clearly feeling a try was imminent he decided his team should run with the ball instead, but Bradford's line could not be dented and they held on to seal a 22–20 victory. For the first time, the final was played 'indoors', the stadium roof being closed due to inclement weather. The absence of wind and rain provided ideal conditions for Sinfield and Bradford's Paul Deacon—who both claimed 100% goal-kicking success—the 'trapped' noise from the vociferous supporters being described as 'incredible' by those who experienced it.

The teams shared six tries although only two—the opening score by Bradford's Robbie Paul and the afternoon's last try from Leeds' David Furner—were awarded without confirmation from the video referee. Paul's effort in the sixth minute was an all-New Zealand affair, Joe Vagana sucking in the opposition and transferring to Tevita Vaikona who then beat two men in a 25-metre break prior to sending his skipper

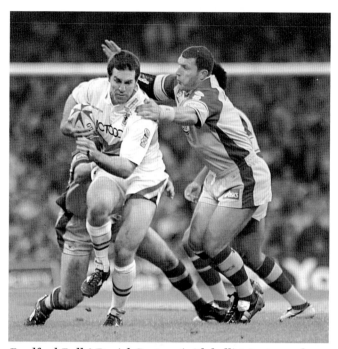

Bradford Bulls' Daniel Gartner (with ball) tries to evade the clutches of Leeds Rhinos prop Barrie McDermott

over near the posts off an inside pass. The following two touchdowns went to Leeds as they moved into a 14–8 lead. Gary Connolly got the first, a brilliant solo run across the face of goal, using a dummy pass as he burst through the defensive line from acting-halfback to slide over to the left of the posts with two Bulls players clinging on. Chris McKenna claimed the next, awarded despite suspicion that defender Shontayne Hape had his arm underneath the ball as it was grounded. The chance had been created by Sinfield's kick into the right corner, the ball going loose after a mid-air contest between Mark Calderwood and Lesley Vainikolo, McKenna catching it and grounding. Vainikolo brought the scores level at 14–14 just before half-time, winning the race to dive onto Deacon's chip into the left corner.

Three minutes after the interval, Bradford scored their third try, Jamie Peacock crossing the whitewash in the right corner despite the attentions of three Leeds defenders. Barrie McDermott's reverse inside-pass set up Furner's concluding try, the loose forward charging through several defenders to score near the posts. It brought Leeds tantalisingly close and the

WINNING CAPTAIN

Robbie Paul (Bradford Bulls 2000, 2003)

Robbie Paul was aged 18 when he joined Bradford Bulls (then 'Bradford Northern') in 1994, becoming club captain in the 1995/96 season. A powerful, inspirational scrum half, he won the Rugby League Challenge Cup (2000, 2003), Super League Grand Final (2001, 2003, 2005), Super League Championship (1997), League Leaders' Shield (2003) and World Club Challenge (2002—missing the 2004 success through injury) with the Bulls. Born in Tokoroa, New Zealand, he played for Waitakere, representing his country 27 times, including the 2000 World Cup. After 305 Bradford matches he assisted Huddersfield (2006–07) and Salford (2008–09, winning the 2008 Northern Rail Cup and National League One Grand Final), joining Leigh for 2010. During the 1995/96 close season, he played rugby union for Harlequins.

232

tension steadily mounted as they made a concerted effort to close the two-point gap and take the spoils. When their hooker Matt Diskin propelled the ball towards the in-goal with his boot, Paul was unable to get a proper grip, colleague Hape instinctively dropping on it from an offside position. But Sinfield's

another heart-stopping moment; Deacon's attempted clearance-kick 25 metres from his own line being charged down by Andrew Dunemann, who then hacked it towards the Bradford posts. Peacock somehow managed to get back and scuff-kick the ball dead, the Bulls surviving to acclaim a slide-rule victory.

David Furner scores for Leeds after one hour's play. The Bradford player is Mike Forshaw

resultant aforementioned decision to take a tap-penalty rather than go for the two points on offer did not pay the anticipated dividend, their siege ending with Connolly watching the ball bounce out of play as he followed up another Diskin kick, this time towards the right corner. Minutes later came another testing moment for the Bulls defence when Sinfield's kick bounced awkwardly towards their in-goal, deceiving Paul who recovered just in time to dive on it ahead of Calderwood.

Two minutes still remained when the Bradford players threw up their arms in celebration, not realising the stadium clock—which showed 80 minutes was up—did not reflect the official time-keeper's watch! Less than half a minute later Leeds produced

Deacon landed two penalty goals (McDermott reported by a touch-judge for an off-the-ball tackle on Daniel Gartner, and Leeds not retiring 10 metres at a play-the-ball—the latter effort stretching the Bulls lead to 22–14), and Sinfield one (Bradford's James Lowes ripping the ball out in a two-man tackle on Diskin—an extra 10 metres being conceded for 'back chat'). In a match full of misses and near misses Leeds had two first half tries disallowed; by Furner (obstruction) and Calderwood (knock-on). Video referee Geoff Berry adjudicated five times, ruling out just one try, 'scored' after 80 seconds, Bradford's Lee Radford being denied after covering 38 metres when the ball was stolen from Leeds' Ryan Bailey in a four-man tackle. There was another contentious incident in the 46th minute when Sinfield sent a high kick downfield from inside his own 20-metre area, Vainikolo appearing to impede Calderwood as the pair pursued the ball inside Bradford's 20-metre zone but, after Peacock had retrieved possession and was tackled in his own in-goal, referee Russell Smith ruled a drop-out from under the posts.

Bradford triumphed without suspended prop Stuart Fielden (he would have missed the final anyway with a cruciate injury) and full back Michael Withers, who withdrew with a groin problem in the morning, opening the way for Scott Naylor to receive a late call-up. Although clearly upset after the match, Sinfield could take some comfort from his performance in the semi-final win over St Helens two weeks earlier that included a tremendous touchline goal to take the match—described as one of the greatest Challenge Cup semi-finals ever—into a tension-packed extra 20 minutes. It was during that contest that Leeds' Matt Adamson broke his cheekbone, showing courage by still turning out in Cardiff.

STATS

Bradford Bulls 22 Leeds Rhinos 20

Saturday 26 April at Millennium Stadium, Cardiff (2.30 pm)

Bradford Bulls (white with red, amber and black chevron): R. Paul (captain), Vaikona, Naylor, Hape, Vainikolo, L. Pryce, Deacon, Vagana, Lowes, Gartner, Radford, Peacock, Forshaw. Substitutes: Anderson, Gilmour, Pratt, Parker. Coach: B. Noble

Leeds Rhinos (amber with blue shoulders and stripe down side): Connolly, Calderwood, McKenna, Senior, Cummins, Sinfield (captain), Dunemann, Bailey, Diskin, McDermott, Walker, Adamson, Furner. Substitutes: Burrow, Ward, Poching, McDonald. Coach: D. Powell

Referee: R. Smith Touch-judges: A. Martin, S. Marshall
Video referee: G. Berry

Half-time: 14–14 Attendance: 71,212

Weather: stadium roof closed

Lance Todd Trophy: Connolly (Leeds Rhinos)

Cup presentation: The Rt Hon. Neil Kinnock, Vice-President of the European Commission

Progressive score:

Bradford Bulls	score (min)	Leeds Rhinos
Paul try, Deacon goal	6–0 (6)	
	6–6 (10)	Connolly try*, Sinfield goal
Deacon penalty	8–6 (16)	
	8–8 (19)	Sinfield penalty
	8–14 (22)	McKenna try*, Sinfield goal
Vainikolo try*, Deacon goal	14–14 (39)	
Peacock try*, Deacon goal	20–14 (43)	
Deacon penalty	22–14 (52)	
	22–20 (60)	Furner try, Sinfield goal

Route to the final:

Fourth round: Warrington Wolves 12 Bradford B 38, Leeds R 46 Whitehaven 6

Fifth round: Hunslet Hawks 0 Bradford B 82, Leeds R 21 London Broncos 12

Sixth round: Widnes Vikings 28 Bradford Bulls 38, Leeds Rhinos 41 Hull FC 18

Semi-finals: Bradford B 36 Wigan W 22 (McAlpine Stadium, Huddersfield, 15,359),

Leeds R 33 St Helens 26 (after extra time, McAlpine Stadium, Huddersfield, 19,118)

Head-to-head form guide:

No previous meetings during season

This dramatic sprint for the ball between Leeds' Mark Calderwood (nearest camera) and Bradford's Lesley Vainikolo almost resulted in a 46th minute try for the former

Graham Morris

2004 RUGBY LEAGUE CHALLENGE CUP FINAL
St Helens v Wigan Warriors

The 2004 Challenge Cup competition pitched St Helens and Wigan Warriors together in the final for a record sixth time, Saints emerging victorious to tie the 'rubber' at three wins apiece. Played in baking heat inside the Millennium Stadium, St Helens won comfortably in the end, 32–16, but it was not until the final minute of the opening half that the margin became stretched when Paul Wellens' try opened up a 20–10 lead. Squeezing through two defenders he reached out to get the ball down near the posts following some tremendous attacking play on Wigan's line.

Lee Gilmour's 3rd minute try in the left corner had

A big moment in the careers of three great St Helens players as Paul Sculthorpe (left) shares the joy of lifting the cup with Paul Wellens (centre) and Keiron Cunningham

put St Helens ahead after Wigan's Kris Radlinski tried a clearance kick 35 metres from his own line which went nowhere due to Jason Hooper's attempted leg tackle. It threw the full back off balance and the ball went loose, Saints' Willie Talau picking up to race for the try-line before despatching the scoring pass, Sean Long converting. In the ninth minute, Andrew Farrell almost got Wigan on the scoreboard when he flung himself over the try-line in a three-man tackle, the video referee denying him through a knock-on. Farrell later claimed Saints' Paul Sculthorpe dislodged the ball and that Wigan colleague Terry Newton should have been credited with a try after diving over them for the touch down. Four minutes later, though, Newton did score, juggling the ball as he dropped

LEADING THE WAY

In recent years the honour of leading out the team at the Challenge Cup Final has been bestowed by the club chairman—who traditionally has that honour—to a former player. Welshmen Trevor Foster (Bradford Bulls in 2003) and Billy Boston (Wigan Warriors, 2004) did so in Cardiff, whilst South African Tom van Vollenhoven fronted St Helens at Twickenham in 2006. There have been other instances when ex-players have done so, but in their capacity as chairman, most notably Eric Ashton with St Helens in 1996 and 1997, having played in six Challenge Cup Finals and coached in five (two as player-coach). The current practice of the coach/team manager following his chairman onto the field, followed by the team, started in 1975 with Vince Karalius (Widnes) and Alex Murphy (Warrington). Previously this had only occurred in instances where the team captain was also player-coach.

beneath the posts after collecting a kick from Adrian Lam (who appeared to be obstructed). Farrell's goal levelled the score, 6–6.

Video evidence cancelled another Wigan try in the

STATS

St Helens 32 Wigan Warriors 16

Saturday 15 May at Millennium Stadium, Cardiff (2.30 pm)

St Helens (white with red chevrons): Wellens, Gardner, Gleeson, Talau, Albert, Hooper, Long, Fozzard, Cunningham, Mason, Joynt, Gilmour, P. Sculthorpe (captain). Substitutes: Edmondson, Bibey, Wilkin, Feaunati. Coach: I. Millward

Wigan Warriors (blue with black trim): Radlinski, Hodgson, O'Loughlin, Brown, Dallas, Orr, Lam, C. Smith, Newton, Pongia, Tickle, Hock, Farrell (captain). Substitutes: O'Connor, Cassidy, D. Sculthorpe, Wild. Coach: M. Gregory

Referee: K. Kirkpatrick Touch-judges: P. Johnson, S. Marshall Video referee: D. Campbell

Half-time: 20–10 Attendance: 73,734

Weather: very hot and sunny

Lance Todd Trophy: Long (St Helens)

Cup presentation: Lord Derby, Rugby League president

Progressive score:

St Helens	score (min)	Wigan Warriors
Gilmour try, Long goal	6–0 (3)	
	6–6 (13)	Newton try, Farrell goal
Long penalty	8–6 (19)	
Talau try, Long goal	14–6 (24)	
	14–10 (33)	Dallas try
Wellens try, Long goal	20–10 (40)	
P. Sculthorpe try, Long goal	26–10 (51)	
Long penalty	28–10 (55)	
	28–16 (66)	Dallas try, Farrell goal
Talau try	32–16 (69)	

Route to the final:

Fourth round: Bradford Bulls 10 St Helens 30, Wigan Warriors 38 Widnes Vikings 12

Fifth round: St Helens 24 Leeds Rhinos 14, Limoux (France) 20 Wigan Warriors 80

Sixth round: St Helens 31 Hull FC 26, Wigan Warriors 20 Wakefield T Wildcats 4

Semi-finals: St Helens 46 Huddersfield Giants 6 (Halliwell Jones Stadium, Warrington, 13,134),

Wigan Warriors 30 Warrington Wolves 18 (Halton Stadium, Widnes, 11,175)

Head-to-head form guide:

St Helens 21 Wigan Warriors 21 (League)

17th minute after Kevin Brown raced under the posts from halfway, team-mate Craig Smith having knocked-on as he tried to grab a wayward pass by Saints' Keiron Cunningham. A high tackle by Quentin Pongia on Wellens resulted in Long's penalty giving St Helens an 8–6 advantage, the Saints scrum half providing a grubber-kick five minutes later that bounced up perfectly in the left corner for Talau to latch on to before touching down. Long's conversion made it 14–6 and it looked like they would increase that lead when a wonderful passing move sent Darren Albert sprinting down the left touchline to go over for a spectacular 'try' in the 30th minute. But, with touch-judge Stuart Marshall convinced Albert had stepped on the touchline in avoiding Danny Orr's tackle, it was referred for video analysis that endorsed the flag-waver's opinion.

A thrilling opening half continued, a cut-out pass from Farrell enabling Lam to send Brett Dallas diving over on the left, a position created moments earlier when St Helens centre Martin Gleeson had lost possession near his own line. Farrell's goal attempt hit the near upright leaving Wigan just four points adrift, the first half scoring concluding with Long's conversion of Wellens' aforementioned try.

Six minutes after the break Hooper made a poor drop-goal attempt that hardly left his boot before, a minute later, video referee David Campbell was called upon a fourth time, again rejecting a try claim from Albert, his foot entering touch following an incredible Radlinski tackle in the left corner. St Helens' next try, though, was not far away and came after a few

WINNING CAPTAIN

Paul Sculthorpe (St Helens 2004, 2006)

Paul Sculthorpe was one of the most talented ball-playing loose forwards produced by British rugby league, his pace and eye for an opening seeing him utilised at stand-off on many occasions by club and country. Born in Burnley and raised in Oldham, he signed for Warrington from Waterhead amateur club in 1994, making his debut the following year. St Helens paid a reported £300,000 (plus a player-exchange) for him in December 1997, where he was to win the Rugby League Challenge Cup (2001, 2004, 2006, 2008—dislocating his shoulder in the opening minutes of the latter in what would prove to be the last of 261 St Helens appearances), Super League Grand Final (1999, 2000, 2002), League Leaders' Shield (2005, 2006, 2007, 2008) and World Club Challenge (2001, 2007). He appeared in 26 Tests and represented England (4 times) and Lancashire (3). Knee injury problems caused him to miss St Helens' 2006 Super League Grand Final and 2007 Challenge Cup Final wins and the chance to lead Great Britain in the 2005 and 2006 Tri-Nations series.

A wonderful action shot capturing the vital first try of the second half from St Helens captain Paul Sculthorpe, Wigan's Gareth Hock being unable to keep him out

moments of 'jitters' as both teams spilled the ball, Paul Sculthorpe regaining possession after a pass by Brown went astray. After playing the ball to acting-halfback Long—who scooted towards the try-line—Paul Sculthorpe was on hand to accept the pass and score despite Gareth Hock's tackle. Long added the extras plus a penalty a few minutes later when Smith went high on Mark Edmondson, St Helens going 28–10 in front.

Dallas claimed his second try, scoring behind the posts off an inside pass by Brown, who had broken through the left channel. With Farrell adding the goal it gave Wigan—trailing by 12 points with 14 minutes left—an outside chance but that hope faded when, a few minutes later, Long raced away from inside his own half. Chipping the ball through and re-gathering, he supplied the supporting Gilmour who sent Talau tearing over the try-line. Long was wide with the conversion, his only miss from seven goal attempts.

The match took place against a background of sub-plots. At St Helens it centred on Long and Gleeson being investigated by a Rugby Football League committee for allegedly betting against their own club when fielding a weakened team (that included Gleeson) in losing to Bradford Bulls the previous month in a League fixture. Both players were later banned for several months. For Wigan—who played without three-quarters Brian Carney (broken ankle) and centre Martin Aspinwall (pulled hamstring)—it

concerned the debilitating illness that had begun to afflict their coach Mike Gregory. He flew to the United States for specialist treatment two days after the final, but, tragically, it claimed his life in 2007.

Australian wingman Brett Dallas outpaces St Helens' Martin Gleeson to register the first of his two tries for Wigan Warriors

2005 RUGBY LEAGUE CHALLENGE CUP FINAL
Hull FC v Leeds Rhinos

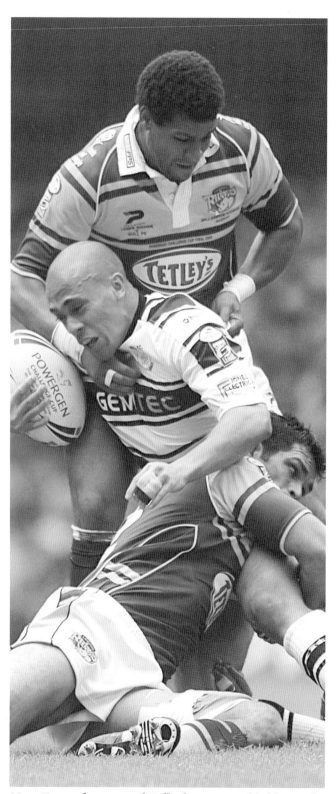

Motu Tony—the scorer of Hull's first try—tackled by Leeds Rhinos' Ryan Bailey (top) and Chris McKenna

The 2005 Challenge Cup Final, held for a third consecutive year at Cardiff's Millennium Stadium, produced one of the most dramatic finishes in the history of the competition. With only three minutes remaining, favourites Leeds Rhinos were holding on to a 24–19 lead, with opponents Hull—having conceded tries in the 65th and 68th minutes—starting to look weary. But looks can so often be deceptive and, when Hull's Richard Horne—10 metres from the Leeds try-line—switched the direction of attack from right to left with a pass to the predatory Paul Cooke, the unexpected happened. Cooke's quick dummy took him bursting through between Danny Ward and Kevin Sinfield to cross the try-line behind the posts. Danny Brough's simple, but crucial goal put Hull on course for their first Challenge Cup success in 23 years.

Leeds had sprung a surprise in omitting prop Barrie McDermott, considered by many as just the player to take on Hull's forwards, and they also took a gamble by including centre Keith Senior, the player having injured his ankle the previous weekend. It became clear within minutes of the start that Senior was having difficulty moving and he retired at the interval. Hull full back Shaun Briscoe also suffered bitter disappointment, withdrawing the previous day with appendicitis.

The Rhinos' took the lead when Sinfield's lofty kick

KANGAROOS AND KIWIS

Australian and New Zealand players made their mark on the Challenge Cup Final following inaugural tours to this country by New Zealand (1907) and Australia (1908). Consequently three of those tourists appeared in the 1910 final; Australians Jimmy Devereux and Andy Morton with Hull, and—in the replay for Leeds—New Zealander Harold Rowe. The first Challenge Cup winning Australian captain was Bert Gilbert (Hull, 1914), followed by Vic Hey (Leeds, 1941 and 1942), Harry Bath (Warrington, 1950), Keith McLellan (Leeds, 1957) and Chris Anderson (Halifax, 1987). Successful New Zealand-born skippers have been Cec Mountford (Wigan, 1951), Graeme West (Wigan, 1985), Dean Bell (Wigan, 1992, 1993 and 1994) and Robbie Paul (Bradford Bulls, 2000 and 2003), whilst Richard Swain (Hull, 2005) was an Australian-born New Zealand international.

Clash of the captains as Leeds' Kevin Sinfield—wearing a bloodied head bandage—is lifted in the tackle by Hull's Richard Swain, for whom colleague Stephen Kearney prepares to lend a hand

into Hull's in-goal area on the right was not defused by Gareth Raynor who, having been unable to take the ball cleanly, tugged at Mark Calderwood's shorts as the Leeds winger attempted to get a hand on the bouncing ball. Referee Steve Ganson referred it to video referee Robert Connolly who awarded a penalty-try, Sinfield adding the goal. Unfazed by that setback, Hull came close in the 17th minute when Horne's kick into the Leeds in-goal just went dead with colleague Richard Whiting and Leeds' Marcus Bai in pursuit. One minute later, Horne was prevented from making a touchdown when Leeds' Ali Lauitiiti got his legs beneath the ball in a two-man tackle.

Hull eventually scored following Shayne McMenemy's kick to the right corner, Whiting out-jumping the Rhinos' defenders to knock the ball back to Motu Tony, the winger chipping it over Bai and recovering it on the rebound to dive over. Brough added a great conversion to tie the score at 6–6. Hull continued to worry Leeds but video evidence ruled out two potential tries; Kirk Yeaman in the 30th minute (Chev Walker knocking the ball from his grip as he crossed the line), and Nathan Blacklock in the 35th (diving ahead of Bai as he attempted to touch the ball down in the right corner but being ruled offside when Horne directed the kick—Blacklock not grounding

correctly in any case).

Six minutes into the second half, Hull scored again after Garreth Carvell was tackled just short of the posts. The resultant play-the-ball saw possession move swiftly to the left, Blacklock sending Raynor in on the overlap near the corner flag. Brough added another tremendous goal and Hull led 12–6. In what was developing into a thrilling contest, Leeds hit back four

WINNING CAPTAIN

Richard Swain (Hull FC 2005)

New Zealand international Richard Swain was actually born in Australia in Tamworth, New South Wales. Having played for the Raymond Terrace club at under-18 level in the Newcastle competition and Newcastle Knights at junior grade he was signed by Hunter Mariners for the 1997 season, subsequently playing for Melbourne Storm (1998–2002, winning the Australian Grand Final in 1999) and Brisbane Broncos (2003) before joining Hull FC for 2004. An alert hooker in loose play, his mesmerising runs from dummy half and opportunity awareness helped take Hull to Rugby League Challenge Cup victory (2005) and runners-up slot in the Super League Grand Final (2006). He retired after the 2007 season having appeared 19 times for New Zealand (qualifying through his New Zealand-born mother), including five in the 2000 World Cup, and was a member of the Kiwi side that visited England and Wales in 2002.

minutes later when Sinfield took a tap-penalty after Hull stole the ball in a tackle. He was rewarded two plays later when he cut through two defenders to send Ward diving over, two would-be tacklers failing to stop him. Connolly confirmed the grounding and Sinfield added the goal to level the scores once more. Hull were giving as good as they got and, minutes later, regained the lead with a bizarre try. Horne chipped into the Leeds in-goal on the right, Bai appearing to avert any danger by recovering the ball. But then Bai, who was being held by Whiting, inexplicably attempted to back-flip the ball to colleague Richie Mathers, Whiting immediately releasing his grip to catch hold of it and score. Brough converted, adding what would prove a decisive drop-goal five minutes later, stretching the lead to 19–12, the widest margin so far.

The action continued at a hectic pace but Leeds appeared to turn the match in their favour with two tries in a four-minute spell through Calderwood (racing from halfway after cutting between two defenders off Sinfield's pass) and Bai (out-jumping Tony to collect Mathers' kick in the left corner before running behind the posts). Sinfield added both goals and Leeds led by five points. Following Cooke's late winner there was still a few moments of drama as Hull nervously clung to their 25–24 lead after Jamie Thackray spilled Sinfield's restarting kick-off, forcing a drop-out from under their posts. Brough's kick went deep into Leeds territory but the Rhinos worked the ball back up the field and, with 30 seconds left, Sinfield's attempt to force a draw with a 28-metre drop-kick was met by a Richard Swain 'charge down' and Hull could start to relax.

The first final played in the new calendar slot of

August, it was a personal triumph for Hull's jubilant coach John Kear who proved lightening can, indeed, strike twice by repeating his miracle of 1998 with Sheffield Eagles.

STATS

Hull FC 25 Leeds Rhinos 24

Saturday 27 August at Millennium Stadium, Cardiff (2.30 pm)

Hull FC (black and white irregular hoops): Blacklock, Tony, Whiting, Yeaman, Raynor, R. Horne, Brough, Dowes, Swain (captain), Carvell, McMenemy, Kearney, Cooke. Substitutes: King, Thackray, Saxton, Chester. Coach: J. Kear

Leeds Rhinos (blue with amber bands): Mathers, Calderwood, Walker, Senior, Bai, Sinfield (captain), Burrow, Bailey, Diskin, Ward, Lauitiiti, McKenna, Ellis. Substitutes: McGuire, Dunemann, Poching, Jones-Buchanan. Coach: T. Smith

Referee: S. Ganson Touch-judges: P. Bentham, S. Wright Video referee: R. Connolly

Half-time: 6–6 Attendance: 74,213

Weather: cloudy and humid

Lance Todd Trophy: Sinfield (Leeds Rhinos)

Cup presentation:
The Rt Hon. The Lord Jack Ashley of Stoke

Progressive score:

Hull FC	score (min)	Leeds Rhinos
	0–6 (12)	Calderwood penalty-try*, Sinfield goal
Tony try, Brough goal	6–6 (20)	
Raynor try, Brough goal	12–6 (46)	
	12–12 (50)	Ward try*, Sinfield goal
Whiting try, Brough goal	18–12 (53)	
Brough drop-goal	19–12 (58)	
	19–18 (65)	Calderwood try, Sinfield goal
	19–24 (68)	Bai try, Sinfield goal
Cooke try, Brough goal	25–24 (77)	

Route to the final:

Fourth round: Wakefield T Wildcats 12 Hull FC 36, Leeds Rhinos 26 Warrington W 22

Fifth round: Hull FC 26 Bradford Bulls 24, Leeds Rhinos 70 Pia Donkeys (France) 0

Sixth round: Hull FC 46 Leigh Centurions 14, Leeds Rhinos 32 London Broncos 12

Semi-finals: Hull FC 34 St Helens 8 (Galpharm Stadium, Huddersfield, 16,171), Leeds Rhinos 56 Toulouse Olympique (France) 18 (Galpharm Stadium, Huddersfield, 10,553)

Head-to-head form guide:

Hull FC 12 Leeds Rhinos 16 (League)
Leeds Rhinos 34 Leeds FC 14 (League)

Hull's Garreth Carvell (left), Jamie Thackray (holding cup) and Ewan Dowes relish their success

2006 RUGBY LEAGUE CHALLENGE CUP FINAL
St Helens v Huddersfield Giants

Huddersfield Giants turned back the clock in 2006, appearing in their first Challenge Cup Final for 44 years. Although losing 42–12 to a speedier, classier St Helens, the Giants were still in with a shout until Jon Wilkin (his broken nose, sustained early on, provided a memorable image, bandaged in what could be best described as a sling) scored a 44th minute try that lowered the drawbridge leading to their try-line.

Despite St Helens being installed as 9-to-1 odds-on favourites, Huddersfield took up their task with gusto, almost scoring Wembley's quickest points after just 20 seconds following captain Chris Thorman's deep kick-off. St Helens' Leon Pryce looked nervy as the ball ricocheted with some force off his leg, being gratefully collected by Huddersfield's Stephen Wild inside Saints' 20-metre area, Brad Drew just being held on the try-line two plays later. It was a let-off for St Helens but the danger continued, Thorman attempting a chip-kick on the next play, Huddersfield regaining possession after Pryce appeared to poke a

boot at the ball although the tackle count was not wiped clean. Drew attempted a drop-goal at the end of the 'set' but, under pressure from Jason Hooper, he hopelessly miscued. St Helens' defence eventually cracked in the sixth minute after Drew made a tremendous break from acting-halfback 40 metres out. Running diagonally to the right, he dummied through four opponents before passing to Michael de Vere who sent Martin Aspinwall diving over at the corner. The goal strike from de Vere saw the ball squeeze inside the near post for a 6–0 lead.

St Helens became more assertive, Hooper knocking on in the 17th minute when a chance presented itself after Sean Long's kick to the posts caused mayhem in the Huddersfield ranks. Four minutes later, Paul Sculthorpe dabbed the ball towards the Giants try-line, rebounding off Huddersfield's Steve Snitch and Drew on its way to the in-goal, Willie Talau collecting to dive over. Jamie Lyon added the goal, tying the score 6–6. There was several minutes

Huddersfield's Brad Drew can only look on as St Helens' Jon Wilkin (complete with bandaged nose) goes over for his second try in the 67th minute

Destination Wembley

A tremendous start for Huddersfield Giants as Martin Aspinwall slides over the St Helens try-line in the sixth minute

delay whilst Hooper, having suffered an injury following a 25th minute clash of heads with Huddersfield's Eorl Crabtree, received attention. Play resumed and, in the 29th minute, St Helens' Ade Gardner got clear off a Lyon pass sprinting 55 metres down the right touchline, but Paul Reilly dashed across, his awesome tackle putting the winger in touch 15 metres from the try-line. Seven minutes later Lyon—making a break from halfway, near the right touchline—was again Gardner's provider with an inside pass, the latter transferring the ball outside for Long, who scooted in from 20 metres out. Lyon added an excellent goal.

St Helens—relieved to go in at half-time leading 12–6—did not hang around in the second half, adding five glorious tries, all augmented by Lyon. The crucial first from Wilkin—which opened up a 12-point gap—was set up by a 45-metre Maurie Fa'asavalu break and continued by James Roby, the latter's quick play-the-ball being picked up by Paul Wellens, who sent Wilkin diving over to the left of the posts. Tries followed from Fa'asavalu (diving in after Roby's kick to the left of the posts), Lyon (collecting Long's kick to dive over near the right corner following the scrum half's dummy and break from halfway), Wilkin (under the posts off Keiron Cunningham's pass following a 35-metre run from acting-halfback) and Jason Cayless (crawling towards the ball for the touch amidst a melee of defenders after another kick to the in-goal by Long). Huddersfield weighed in with a 70th minute consolation try, Robbie Paul diving on the ball near the posts following a neat chip-kick from Drew after St Helens lost the ball, de Vere augmenting.

St Helens skipper Sculthorpe received the trophy from Martin Offiah, the former wing star being a late

deputy for ex-England soccer manager, Sir Bobby Robson, who required an operation the preceding week, Long being awarded the Lance Todd Trophy a record third time.

STATS

St Helens 42 Huddersfield Giants 12

Saturday 26 August at Twickenham, London (2.45 pm)

St Helens (white with red chevron and trim): Wellens, Gardner, Lyon, Talau, Meli, Pryce, Long, P. Anderson, Cunningham, Cayless, Wilkin, Sculthorpe (captain), Hooper. Substitutes: Gilmour, Roby, Graham, Fa'asavalu. Coach: D. Anderson

Huddersfield Giants (claret and gold irregular hoops): Reilly, Aspinwall, Nero, de Vere, Donlan, Thorman (captain), Paul, Jackson, Drew, Gannon, Crabtree, Raleigh. Wild. Substitutes: Snitch, Jones, Smith, McDonald. Coach: J. Sharp

Referee: R. Silverwood Touch-judges: J. Child, A. Martin Video referee: I. Ollerton

Half-time: 12–6 Attendance: 65,187

Weather: sunny and hot

Lance Todd Trophy: Long (St Helens)

Cup presentation: Martin Offiah MBE

Progressive score:

St Helens	score (min)	Huddersfield Giants
	0–6 (6)	Aspinwall try, de Vere goal
Talau try, Lyon goal	6–6 (21)	
Long try, Lyon goal	12–6 (36)	
Wilkin try, Lyon goal	18–6 (44)	
Fa'asavalu try, Lyon goal	24–6 (51)	
Lyon try*, Lyon goal	30–6 (57)	
Wilkin try, Lyon goal	36–6 (67)	
	36–12 (70)	Paul try, de Vere goal
Cayless try*, Lyon goal	42–12 (74)	

Route to the final:

Fourth round: St Helens 56 Doncaster Lakers 6, Halifax 8 Huddersfield Giants 40

Fifth round: St Helens 42 Bradford Bulls 18, Huddersfield G 38 York City Knights 4

Sixth round: St Helens 56 Catalans D 10, Huddersfield G 44 Salford City Reds 14

Semi-finals: St Helens 50 Hull KR 0 (Galpharm Stadium, Huddersfield, 12,868),

Huddersfield G 30 Leeds Rhinos 12 (Grattan Stadium, Bradford, 12,574)

Head-to-head form guide:

Huddersfield Giants 16 St Helens 18 (League)

Huddersfield Giants 19 St Helens 16 (League)

St Helens 56 Huddersfield Giants 8 (League)

Graham Morris

NEW WEMBLEY

In 1994, the Genesis Corporation submitted plans to take over and redevelop Wembley Stadium. With Wembley designated by English Heritage as a Grade 2 listed building, the demolition was agreed in principle with the stipulation that its famous twin towers be incorporated in any new design. English Heritage did not, however, like the submitted plans and a rethink was ordered. Subsequently, there was wider debate, led by the Sports Council, proposing Wembley be replaced by a 'national' stadium. (Although Wembley was already thought of by most as a national stadium it was privately owned and leased out for major events.) Wembley was joined as a candidate by other potential sites such as at Manchester and Birmingham, the list including Bradford's Odsal Stadium. The decision eventually went to Wembley.

In September 2000 the Football Association, who would own the new stadium, struck a deal with Australian company Multiplex to build it at an estimated cost of £326 million. The work, following several delays which included an FA request in 2001 for government help with the funding, began two years later. But it was beset with problems, including workers' strikes and reported financial losses by Multiplex. A planned opening for 2006 that was to have included the staging of that year's FA Cup and Challenge Cup finals had to be shelved (there had been a two-page feature promoting the latter in the 2005 Challenge Cup Final programme). With many fans having already organised their 2006 London trip, the Rugby Football League decided to stick with the capital and return to Twickenham, although it's South Stand, which was being rebuilt, was out of use.

The new Wembley Stadium, owned by the Football Association through its subsidiary, Wembley National Stadium Limited, eventually opened its doors on 24 March 2007 for an under-21 soccer international between England and Italy having finally cost almost £800 million. Two months later a bronze statue of Bobby Moore was unveiled in front of the main entrance, celebrating the former England soccer captain's role in the defeat of West Germany 4–2 in the 1966 World Cup Final at Wembley. In 2005, before the pitch was laid, a 'time capsule' was buried

Fans converge on Wembley for the 2008 final

underneath it measuring one metre in diameter. It contained several items relating to sport and entertainment at the former stadium, rugby league's contribution being a Great Britain shirt, a book containing the laws of the game, and a photograph from the 1999 final. The all-seated stadium, complete with its retractable roof, boasts a striking 315-metre long, 133-metre tall steel archway that will become as famous a landmark as the former twin towers, a fragment of the latter having also been encased in the aforementioned capsule.

OTHER RUGBY LEAGUE MATCHES AT WEMBLEY

18 Jan 1930: Australia 26 Wales 10 (attendance 16,000)
30 Dec 1933: Australia 51 Wales 19 (11,000)
12 Mar 1949: England 5 France 12 (12,382)
16 Oct 1963: Great Britain 2 Australia 28 (13,946)
3 Nov 1973: Great Britain 21 Australia 12 (9,874)
27 Oct 1990: Great Britain 19 Australia 12 (54,569)
24 Oct 1992: (World Cup Final):
Great Britain 6 Australia 10 (73,631)
16 Oct 1993: Great Britain 17 New Zealand 0 (36,131)
22 Oct 1994: Great Britain 8 Australia 4 (57,037)

PROFESSIONAL RUGBY LEAGUE CLUBS IN LONDON

London Highfield (1933–1934)
Acton & Willesden (1935–1936)
Streatham & Mitcham (1935–1937)
Fulham (1980–1991)/London Crusaders
(1991–1994)/London Broncos (1994–2005)/Harlequins RL
(2006 to date)
London Skolars (2003 to date)

2007 RUGBY LEAGUE CHALLENGE CUP FINAL
St Helens v Catalans Dragons

The much-anticipated Wembley return in 2007 was momentous in more ways than one with Catalans Dragons becoming the first overseas team to feature in the Rugby League Challenge Cup Final. The French club—which has played a significant role in reviving rugby league's profile in their homeland, and is, quite probably, the first foreign team to appear in the final of a 'domestic' British sporting competition—created a Challenge Cup record through reaching the final in only their second season of existence. Their appearance livened up what was already guaranteed to be a memorable occasion with virtually everyone who was not a supporter of opponents St Helens becoming an adopted son or daughter of France for the day!

The slick St Helens team, however, was not an outfit to dwell overlong on sentiment, retaining their prize with a thoroughly competent and professional display in a match that generally fell below expectations, to earn a 30–8 victory, their sixth success since 1996. St Helens took to the field without loose forward Paul Sculthorpe who had been absent with an Achilles injury since June and missed the remainder of the season, Keiron Cunningham taking over as captain, whilst Catalans stand-off Casey McGuire was missing due to a pectoral injury picked up earlier in the month. On a baking hot day, and with both team benches exposed to the sun, the substitutes 'warmed up' in the shade of the tunnel as the match progressed.

The Dragons made a positive start, trapping St Helens redoubtable full back Paul Wellens inside his own in-goal after 128 seconds of play, forcing a drop-out from under the posts. As the game settled both teams tested each other with kicks to their respective in-goal areas and there were close calls at both ends before, in the 19th minute, Matt Gidley

All eyes are fixed on the ball as Paul Wellens touches down for St Helens despite being tackled by Catalans Dragons' Stacey Jones. Other Saints players are Sean Long (on ground behind Jones), Leon Pryce (background) and James Graham, the Catalans defenders on the right being Remi Casty (standing) and Clint Greenshields (ground)

244

Catalans' New Zealand-born captain Stacey Jones gets the ball away from a scrum

The Rugby League again demonstrated its innovative qualities when two French Federation club sides participated in the 2000 Challenge Cup, increased to four for 2002, two Russian clubs being included from 2003. Apart from Super League club Paris St Germaine in 1997, the first overseas team to take part was the Dublin Blues, who did so in 1998. Closer to home Scottish Border Eagles became, in 1999, the first entry from Scotland, whilst Wales were represented as far back as 1908, Merthyr Tydfil winning 9–6 in a 'domestic' qualifying tie away to Ebbw Vale to gain entry to the first round proper. Another interesting 'first' came in 2000 when the armed services—The Army, Royal Air Force and Royal Navy—made debuts. The following is a list of overseas clubs to have taken part:

- 1997: Paris St Germaine (France)
- 1998: Dublin Blues (Ireland)
- 1999: Northside Saints (Ireland)
- 2000: Dublin Blues, St Gaudens (France), Villeneuve (France)
- 2001: Toulouse (France), Villeneuve
- 2002: Cork Bulls (Ireland), St Gaudens, Toulouse, Union Treiziste Catalane (France), Villeneuve
- 2003: Dublin City Exiles (Ireland), Lokomotiv Moscow (Russia), Pia (France), Strela Kazan (Russia), Toulouse, Union Treiziste Catalane, Villeneuve
- 2004: Dinamo Moscow (Russia), Limoux (France), Lokomotiv Moscow, Pia, Union Treiziste Catalane, Villeneuve
- 2005: Lokomotive Moscow, Pia, St Gaudens, Strela Kazan, Toulouse, Union Treiziste Catalane
- 2006: Catalans Dragons (France), Limoux, Lokomotiv Moscow, Pia, Strela Kazan, Toulouse
- 2007: Catalans Dragons, Limoux, Lokomotiv Moscow, Pia, Strela Kazan, Toulouse
- 2008: Catalans Dragons, Lezignan (France), Lokomotiv Moscow, Pia, Toulouse, Vereya (Russia)
- 2009: Carcassonne (France), Catalans Dragons, Lezignan, Lokomotiv Moscow, Pia, Toulouse

almost got in at the right corner for St Helens, losing the ball in a three-man tackle as he tried to reach over the line. Five minutes later it was Catalans' turn, the video referee being employed after their second-row Jason Croker, whilst challenged by Leon Pryce, dived spectacularly to retrieve and ground a ball kicked into the Saints in-goal by Stacey Jones. It was clear, though, that he lost control as he hit the dead-ball line. In the 30th minute Pryce beat three defenders on his way to

WINNING CAPTAIN

Keiron Cunningham (St Helens 2007, 2008)

Long-serving St Helens stalwart Keiron Cunningham signed for the club in late 1993 from Wigan St Judes, making his debut the following year. Originating from nearby Thatto Heath, the all-action hooker—a particular threat when running from acting-halfback—had made 437 appearances for the Saints prior to the 2009 season. To date he has won the Rugby League Challenge Cup (1996, 1997, 2001, 2004, 2006, 2007, 2008), Super League Grand Final (1999, 2000, 2002, 2006), Super League Championship (1996), League Leaders' Shield (2005, 2006, 2007, 2008) and World Club Challenge (2001, 2007). With Great Britain, he was a tourist in 1996 (Papua New Guinea, Fiji and New Zealand) and a member of the 1999 Tri-Nations squad (in Australia and New Zealand). To date, he has made 16 Test appearances and (due to a Welsh grandmother) represented Wales (9 times—including the 1995 and 2000 World Cups) and Lancashire (once). One of several brothers to play senior rugby league (Eddie winning the 1982 Lance Todd Trophy), he rejected a 2001 approach to move into Welsh rugby union.

the Dragons' try-line but was prevented from grounding.

Three minutes later, St Helens made the breakthrough, James Roby's brilliant 30-metre run from acting-halfback taking him through the first line of defence to the left of the posts after shaking off three assailants. Sean Long added the goal. In the 36th minute, Long had a kick charged down, the scramble for possession leading to Catalans claiming the ball and—in the following minute—their first try, slick passing from Jones and Adam Mogg (with a cut-out pass) sending Younes Khattabi diving over in the left corner. Jones' goal attempt was wide. In the final seconds of the half, St Helens scored a vital try that increased their lead to 12–4, after Long, Pryce and Gidley combined to send Ade Gardner on a powerful 20-metre run (although the final pass looked forward), beating Clint Greenshields and Alex Chan before crossing the try-line in the corner, Long adding an excellent goal.

Six minutes into the second half, Long—from 18 metres out—kicked towards the Catalans line. There appeared to be little danger but, somehow Greenshields misjudged it and Wellens picked up to dive over, the video referee confirming the score. Long converted. Five minutes later, Cunningham, from acting-halfback 20 metres out, transferred to Pryce who sent Paul Clough diving over the Catalans try-line for Saints' fourth try. Long was wide with the goal attempt but his side now held a decisive-looking 22–4 lead.

Justin Murphy doubled the Perpignan-based club's score, recovering the ball after Jon Wilkin's pass to Saints' colleague Lee Gilmour went to ground for a 35-metre dash down the left flank to touch down in the corner. Jones' goal effort was off-target. St Helens wrapped up the score with a 24-metre penalty from Long after a high tackle by Luke Quigley on Nick

Fozzard, and another Gardner try after Wellens broke two tackles before delivering an inside pass to the winger. The video adjudicator was called on to check for possible obstruction from Wilkin before the try was sanctioned, Long adding the goal.

STATS

St Helens 30 Catalans Dragons 8

Saturday 25 August at Wembley Stadium, London (3.00 pm)

St Helens (white with red chevron and trim): Wellens, Gardner, Gidley, Talau, Meli, Pryce, Long, Fozzard, Cunningham (captain), Cayless, Gilmour, Bennett, Wilkin. Substitutes: Roby, Graham, Clough, Fa'asavalu. Coach: D. Anderson

Catalans Dragons (blood red with gold chevrons and gold stripes down side): Greenshields, Murphy, Raguin, Wilson, Khattabi, Mogg, Jones (captain), Guisset, Quigley, Chan, Croker, Gossard, Mounis. Substitutes: Ferriol, Duport, Casty, Bentley. Coach: M. Potter

Referee: A. Klein Touch-judges: S. Marshall, J. Child Video referee: P. Bentham

Half-time: 12–4 Attendance: 84,241

Weather: sunny and hot

Lance Todd Trophy (joint winners): Wellens, Pryce (both St Helens)

Cup presentation: Sir Steven Redgrave CBE

Progressive score:

St Helens	score (min)	Catalans Dragons
Roby try, Long goal	6–0 (33)	
	6–4 (37)	Khattabi try
Gardner try, Long goal	12–4 (40)	
Wellens try*, Long goal	18–4 (46)	
Clough try	22–4 (51)	
	22–8 (58)	Murphy try
Long penalty	24–8 (67)	
Gardner try*, Long goal	30–8 (78)	

Route to the final:

Fourth round: St Helens 78 Batley Bulldogs 14, Catalans D 70 Featherstone R 12

Fifth round: St Helens 70 Rochdale Hornets 10, Whitehaven 14 Catalans Dragons 24

Sixth round: St Helens 25 Warrington Wolves 14, Hull FC 23 Catalans Dragons 26

Semi-finals: St Helens 35 Bradford B 14 (Galpharm Stadium, Huddersfield, 14,316),

Catalans D 37 Wigan W 24 (Halliwell Jones Stadium, Warrington, 10,218)

Head-to-head form guide:

St Helens 53 Catalans Dragons 10 (League)

Catalans Dragons 21 St Helens 0 (League)

Ade Gardner grabs his second St Helens try with two minutes left after outpacing the Catalans defence

2008 RUGBY LEAGUE CHALLENGE CUP FINAL
St Helens v Hull FC

Kirk Yeaman registers his second try to bring Hull back into contention despite the tackle from St Helens' Matt Gidley

St Helens defeated Hull FC 28–16 in the 2008 finale to emulate great rivals Wigan in winning the Challenge Cup for three successive years. As with their two earlier victories St Helens' opponents lay in the lower reaches of the Super League table, Hull belying their second-last position to mount a stirring second half recovery after a first quarter onslaught had given Saints a 10–0 lead. The hero of Humberside was Kirk Yeaman whose double try strike in the 44th and 62nd minutes—both goaled by Danny Tickle—sensationally propelled Hull 12–10 ahead and set the stadium on fire.

His first came through intercepting Keiron Cunningham's wide pass and sprinting 90 metres for the score. The second occurred after Saints' Paul Wellens was ruled to have knocked-on in diving to recover a ball kicked towards his right flank, just eight metres from his try-line. Despite protests that the ball went backwards, a scrum was ordered and Hull won possession. A few plays later the ball travelled through several pairs of hands towards the left, Yeaman taking Willie Manu's pass on the angle to go through a gap for the try. In between Yeaman's two efforts Saints twice came close; Sean Long's 54th minute 22-metre arcing run to the right

brought him a touchdown only for video evidence to highlight an obstruction by colleague Chris Flannery and, five minutes later, a neat chip kick into Hull's in-goal almost created a Lee Gilmour try, Tickle beating him to the ball.

Hull fans' euphoria after taking a two-point lead did not last long, St Helens' efficient machine slipping back into top gear, pressure on Hull's line bringing Francis Meli a try near the left corner off an inspired Leon Pryce delivery. Six minutes later Saints crossed again when Jon Wilkin, having charged down Danny Washbrook's attempted clearance, recovered the ball to race 40 metres, placing the ball beneath the posts. Video referee Ashley Klein declared Wilkin's action was legal and with Long tagging both conversions Saints were again in charge at 22–12.

Only six minutes remained when Gareth Raynor gave Hull a glimmer of hope, scoring in the left corner off Yeaman's pass to capitalise on a spirited mini-revival. Tickle missed the goal, the Black and Whites requiring six more points to force their third Challenge Cup Final replay (following 1910 and 1982). Hopes evaporated immediately after the restart when Jamie Thackray lost the ball 15 metres from his try-line in a tackle. St Helens won the resultant scrum, the ensuing play ending with Pryce virtually strolled over on the left off Cunningham's well-judged pass. Long's conversion closed the scoring.

St Helens had opened their account in the eighth minute although there was controversy in the build up; Wilkin's pass to Meli on the left wing looked forward, the latter hacking the ball forward, forcing a Todd Byrne knock-on. Saints won possession from the consequent scrum 20 metres from Hull's try-line, the ball moving rapidly to the right where Wellens sent Matt Gidley roaring in for the try. Long missed the goal. St Helens almost scored again six minutes later when James Graham was held short and, seconds afterwards, colleague Ade Gardner lost the ball in the act of diving over the try-line. Hull too, had their nearly moments; in the sixth minute Manu fumbled a difficult ball kicked towards the left corner flag and, in the 19th minute, Shaun Berrigan's delicate kick towards the Saints posts almost got Byrne in but the full back, having gathered, lost possession as he went over. The latter incident led to quick-thinking Saints' second try, Cunningham whipping the ball out to Graham from a hastily taken 20-metre tap-restart, the prop sending Meli racing through the

defence and down the left channel for a long-distance score. Long's goal made it 10–0.

In an opening half of near misses, Hull's Graeme Horne was held short in the right corner in the 23rd minute following a promising attack inspired by Matt Sing's 35-metre break, Saints being denied in the 29th

Francis Meli about to touch down for his second try in the 66th minute and regain the lead for St Helens

STATS

St Helens 28 Hull FC 16

Saturday 30 August at Wembley Stadium, London (2.30 pm)

St Helens (light blue with dark blue chevron and trim): Wellens, Gardner, Gidley, Talau, Meli, Pryce, Long, Hargreaves, Cunningham (captain), Graham, Wilkin, Flannery, Sculthorpe. Substitutes: Gilmour, Roby, Clough, Fa'asavalu. Coach: D. Anderson

Hull FC (black and white irregular hoops): Byrne, Sing, G. Horne, Yeaman, Raynor, Washbrook, Lee, Dowes, Berrigan, Cusack, Manu, Tickle, Radford (captain). Substitutes: R. Horne, Carvell, Briscoe, Thackray. Coach: R. Agar

Referee: S. Ganson   Touch-judges: J. Child, S. Wright (replaced by R. Hicks 46th minute) Video referee: A. Klein

Half-time: 10–0 Attendance: 82,821

Weather: sunny and hot

Lance Todd Trophy: Wellens (St Helens)

Cup presentation: The Rt Hon. Andy Burnham MP, Secretary of State for Culture, Media and Sport

Progressive score:

St Helens	score (min)	Hull FC
Gidley try	4–0 (8)	
Meli try, Long goal	10–0 (19)	
	10–6 (44)	Yeaman try, Tickle goal
	10–12 (62)	Yeaman try, Tickle goal
Meli try, Long goal	16–12 (66)	
Wilkin try*, Long goal	22–12 (72)	
	22–16 (74)	Raynor try
Pryce try, Long goal	28–16 (77)	

Route to the final:

Fourth round: St Helens 56 London Skolars 0, Rochdale Hornets 5 Hull FC 42

Fifth round: St Helens 40 Warrington Wolves 34, Widnes Vikings 18 Hull FC 32

Sixth round: Hull Kingston Rovers 18 St Helens 24, Bradford Bulls 16 Hull FC 22

Semi-finals: St Helens 26 Leeds Rhinos 16 (Galpharm Stadium, Huddersfield, 19,842), Hull FC 32 Wakefield Trinity Wildcats 24 (Keepmoat Stadium, Doncaster, 14,716)

Head-to-head form guide:

St Helens 30 Hull FC 29 (League)

Hull FC 8 St Helens 16 (League)

minute (Willie Talau's try ruled out by a forward pass) and 37th (Meli's dive into the left corner thwarted by Byrnes' tremendous tackle, the video referee ruling a double movement).

As the klaxon sounded to end the match, an altercation between Long and Thackray took place, the Saints scrum half taking exception to what looked a high tackle, players rushing from all sides to intervene. This was replaced by handshakes as they realised the match had concluded although it was not quite over! Referee Steve Ganson was obliged to give a penalty, awarded to Hull before amending his decision in St Helens favour on a touch judge's advice. The ball was kicked to touch and—one play later—Saints began celebrating, especially Wellens who entered the record books as the first to receive the Lance Todd Trophy in consecutive years.

Both teams were depleted. Knee injuries ruled out Saints' props Jason Cayless (incurred the previous weekend) and Nick Fozzard (still unfit after five months out), Hull being minus full back Motu Tony (knee) and halfback Adam Dykes (leg). St Helens were further handicapped after Paul Sculthorpe—absent most of the season with hamstring problems—left the field with a dislocated shoulder in making his side's first tackle after

58 seconds. The bench numbers were evened in the 43rd minute when Hull's 18-year-old Tom Briscoe was helped off with a bad ankle injury. The most unexpected casualty was touch judge Steve Wright who tore a calf muscle six minutes into the second half and was replaced by Robert Hicks. Meanwhile, Hull's Richard Horne returned after five months absence through a neck injury. Looking underweight he gave a brave display despite taking a heavy 18th minute tackle from Graham moments after coming off the bench.

As with the previous year, the sun was unforgiving, again baking everyone on the substitutes' bench, umbrellas being introduced to provide respite. Thirty minutes into the match Ganson halted play for a water break.

Hull had caused a furore earlier in the competition, playing unregistered Thackray in their opening matches against Rochdale Hornets and Widnes Vikings. Their punishment was a £100,000 fine, £40,000 of which was suspended, some scribes arguing they should have been disqualified. (The registration rules were subsequently tightened up for 2009.) Meanwhile St Helens-based Ganson became the first to referee his hometown club in a major final following a relaxation of the rule preventing match officials overseeing their local teams.

Leon Pryce seals St Helens' victory with a late try, much to the approval of team-mate Willie Talau (right)

2009 RUGBY LEAGUE CHALLENGE CUP FINAL
Warrington Wolves v Huddersfield Giants

Emotions are high as two of rugby league's longest serving players—Adrian Morley (left) and Lee Briers—lift the trophy for Warrington

Warrington Wolves ended their 35-year Challenge Cup famine, taking the 2009 spoils after a whirlwind opening 24 minutes that saw seven tries claimed—four of them endorsed—as they built an early 18–6 lead over Huddersfield Giants. The excitement began in the first minute, Warrington's Louis Anderson charging down Brett Hodgson's clearance kick to take possession and race for the posts. Somehow Hodgson recovered, tracking back to tackle the rampaging forward from behind when a try looked certain. But two plays later acting-halfback Michael Monaghan despatched Warrington colleague Richie Mathers through a gap to score under the posts. With 67 seconds gone it was the new Wembley's quickest score yet, Chris Bridge converting.

Huddersfield recovered, having a seventh minute 'try' by Shaun Lunt disallowed for a 'double movement' (an incorrect decision according to several observers). Undaunted, he made up for his disappointment two

minutes later, finishing off Brett Hodgson's break (from a David Faiumu offload that looked slightly forward) to race over the try-line. Brett Hodgson's goal levelled the score, 6–6. Warrington, though, were bossing the early stages and quickly added two tries to establish a 12-point lead. The first was by the irrepressible Monaghan (racing to the left of the posts from acting-halfback), Chris Hicks scoring the next three minutes later (racing down the right from close in after quick passing by Monaghan, Lee Briers and Bridge). Bridge appended both goals.

The drama continued, each team having a try overruled by video referee Phil Bentham (who had adjudicated for Mathers' early score and Lunt's disallowed try). The first unproductive effort was from Warrington's Matt King in the 19th minute, the ball judged 'stolen' during the melee to gain possession following Briers high kick to the in-goal. The second rejection went against the Giants' David Hodgson five minutes later, his try in the left corner nullified through

250

obstruction in the build up. Nine minutes before the interval, Huddersfield suffered a blow when key playmaker Kevin Brown limped out of the final with a knee ligament injury. A minute later Warrington's Vinnie Anderson retired with a deep cut to the forehead, requiring six stitches. (He resumed, to devastating effect, in the 56th minute.)

As Anderson departed, Lunt almost scored his second, being prevented from grounding behind the posts. Huddersfield kept up the pressure and a 36th minute Liam Fulton grubber kick into the corner almost produced a Leroy Cudjoe try, defender Chris Riley managing to smother the ball. One minute later, Brett Hodgson gave the Giants hope, scoring in the right corner off Cudjoe's inside pass although failing to augment his effort, the ball travelling just wide of the far post, leaving Warrington 18–10 up at the break.

Five minutes into the second half, officials failed to spot a Hicks knock-on when fielding a Fulton bomb, Warrington—aided by a tap penalty award—subsequently sweeping downfield. The end product was a near miss from Garreth Carvell whose 47th minute touchdown was denied by referee Steve Ganson, ruling him tackled three metres short before continuing his assault. Wolves, though, were relentless; Briers' neat chip kick to the left being rescued in the in-goal area by Cudjoe as Riley thundered in. A minute later Vinnie Anderson—complete with head bandage—burst through a big hole to go under the posts following a

scampering run and pass from acting-halfback Monaghan. The latter—involved in all Wolves' tries—deservedly took the Lance Todd Trophy, the third Australian honoured. Bridge's goal placed one hand on

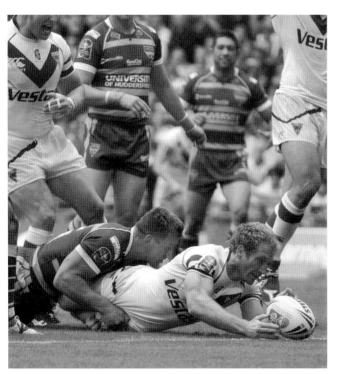

Man of the match Michael Monaghan dives over for Warrington's second try

---

STATS

Warrington Wolves 25 Huddersfield Giants 16

Saturday 30 August at Wembley Stadium, London (2.30 pm)

Warringon Wolves (white with blue and primrose chevron and trim): Mathers, Hicks, Bridge, King, Riley, V. Anderson, Briers, Morley (captain), Monaghan, Carvell, L. Anderson, Harrison, Westwood. Substitutes: Cooper, Johnson, Higham, McCarthy. Coach: T. Smith

Huddersfield Giants (claret with narrow gold hoops): B. Hodgson (captain), Cudjoe, Lolesi, Whatuira, D. Hodgson, K. Brown, Robinson, Lunt, Moore, D. Griffin, Fulton, Wild, Faiumu. Substitutes: Crabtree, Jackson, Moore, Aspinwall. Coach: N. Brown

Referee: S. Ganson Touch-judges: A. Martin, C. Sharrad
Video referee: P. Bentham

Half-time: 18–10   Attendance: 76,560

Weather: sunny and hot

Lance Todd Trophy: Monaghan (Warrington Wolves)

Cup presentation: The Rt Hon. Gerry Sutcliffe MP, Minister for Sport

Progressive score:

Warrington Wolves	score (min)	Huddersfield Giants
Mathers try*, Bridge goal	6–0 (2)	
	6–6 (9)	Lunt try, B. Hodgson goal
Monaghan try, Bridge goal	12–6 (12)	
Hicks try, Bridge goal	18–6 (15)	
	18–10 (37)	B. Hodgson try
V. Anderson try, Bridge goal	24–10 (60)	
	24–16 (77)	D. Hodgson try*, B. Hodgson goal
Briers drop-goal	25–16 (79)	

Route to the final:

Fourth round: Warrington W 56 York City Knights 10, Harlequins RL 16 Huddersfield G 42

Fifth round: Featherstone R 8 Warrington W 56, Huddersfield G 38 Rochdale H 12

Sixth round: Hull KR 24 Warrington W 25 (after extra time), Huddersfield G 16 Castleford T 14

Semi-finals: Warrington Wolves 39 Wigan Warriors 26 (Stobart Stadium, Widnes, 12,975), Huddersfield Giants 24 St Helens 14 (Halliwell Jones Stadium, Warrington, 10,638)

Head-to-head form guide:

Warrington Wolves 40 Huddersfield Giants 18 (League)

Huddersfield Giants 28 Warrington Wolves 10 (League)

Huddersfield captain Brett Hodgson scores a dramatic try just before half-time

the trophy, although missing a 28-metre penalty five minutes later, the ball going well wide.

Briers again caused panic when a high 66th minute kick almost brought King a try, the tall centre jumping to retrieve the ball a few metres from the try-line, being held short by sterling defence. With ten minutes remaining, Huddersfield produced a wonderful attacking move but it came to nought when Luke Robinson's deft kick into the right corner just escaped Cudjoe's grasp. With three minutes left, David Hodgson gave the Giants' supporters some joy, beating three

defenders on a thrilling 22-metre sidestepping run down the left before reaching out to place the ball on the line, Bentham confirming the score. Brett Hodgson converted, but Briers added a 'trademark' drop-goal from in front of the posts with just over a minute left, closing the scoring at 25–16.

Warrington's outstanding pack led the way to victory, particularly in the first and third quarters, Huddersfield producing a below-par performance. Wolves captain Adrian Morley, having tasted success at the old Wembley and in the Australian Grand Final, declared it 'the highlight of my career without a doubt'. In an emotion-charged gesture, he insisted on lifting the trophy with Briers, who had served Warrington without reward for 12 years, having helped St Helens reach Wembley in 1997 only to miss the big match.

Warrington triumphed without injured hooker Jon Clarke (ankle), halfback Simon Grix (shoulder), prop Paul Wood (broken leg) and wing Brian Carney (the recent signing breaking an arm during his fourth appearance in July). A back injury to forward Paul Rauhihi opened the way for 21-year-old Tyrone McCarthy's third senior appearance, whilst Mick Higham returned after a 12-week injury absence. For Huddersfield, forwards Danny Kirmond (knee injury) and Andy Raleigh (not fully fit after being out with an Achilles injury) also missed out.

Curiously, the semi-final draw (including the venues) replicated that of 2004, the two previous losers turning the tables to set up the first final since 1986 without one of the so-called 'big four' of Bradford, Leeds, Wigan or St Helens.

WINNING CAPTAIN

Adrian Morley (Warrington Wolves 2009)

Salford-born Adrian Morley signed for Leeds from the Eccles club in 1994, making the last of his 149 appearances for the Headingley outfit in 2000, having won the Rugby League Challenge Cup in 1999. Noted as a tough, uncompromising front or second row forward, he subsequently joined Sydney Roosters (2001–06) playing 113 times and being a winner in the NRL Grand Final (2002). Returning to England he signed for Warrington Wolves from 2007, the 2009 Challenge Cup Final win being his 72nd match for the club. A tourist to New Zealand, Fiji and Papua New Guinea in 1996, he has represented Great Britain in 30 Tests and made his ninth appearance for England (including the 2000 and 2008 World Cup) in June 2009 (against France). In 2007 he captained the 'Northern Union' against the (New Zealand) 'All Golds', commemorating 100 years since the first tourists came to Britain. At the end of the 2005 season he played six times for Bradford Bulls on a short-term contract, earning success in the Super League Grand Final. His elder brother Chris, also a forward, was a Wembley Challenge Cup winner with St Helens in 1997.

Graham Morris

IT'S STILL A GREAT OCCASION, BUT ...

The Rugby League Challenge Cup Final is the biggest day out in the code's calendar, attracting the highest crowd of the season. However, one aspect causes concern—poor attendances at earlier rounds. In the past, opening ties were eagerly anticipated, drawing bigger support than corresponding League fixtures and often setting attendance records. They now have some of the poorest turnouts, particularly at Super League grounds. The accompanying table ('50-year attendance review') gives a 'snapshot' of pre-final attendances on a 10-year cycle (1956 until 2006). It makes depressing reading, 2006 being over 70% down on 1956.

Many theories have been advanced as to the cause, the following being some to appear in the press in recent years:

* The creation of Super League with full-time playing staff makes the outcome predictable, lower placed clubs unable to 'dream' of Wembley.
* Switching to summer was disruptive, the Challenge Cup, initially, becoming an early season event rather than a climactic end to the campaign.
* Having already purchased season tickets, supporters (at Super League clubs especially) are unwilling to pay extra to see the ties.
* The temporary loss of Wembley after 1999 made early rounds less appealing.
* The eight-year dominance of Wigan (1988–1995) killed interest.
* Sky Television's promotion of Super League overshadows the appeal of the Challenge Cup.
* Increased BBC coverage in 1998 from one to two ties in the three rounds preceding the semi-finals creates a counter-attraction.
* The scheduling of approximately one round per month (since the final transferred to August in 2005) does not sustain public interest.

None of the above provides a definitive answer although 2009's experiment (see below) implies an issue exists for season tickets holders. Also, since moving to a summer schedule in 1996, pre-final crowds often average below 5,000, as illustrated in a second table ('25-year attendance review'). (It should be noted overall attendances fluctuate based on progression of best supported clubs, attractiveness of ties and the weather.)

The Rugby Football League recognises there is a problem to be remedied and, in 2009, Super League season ticket holders received free admission to their club's fourth round tie. The resultant aggregate 66,497 was the highest for that stage since 1995, the Leeds-St Helens tie generating the largest pre-semi-final crowd (17,589) since 1994's Leeds-Bradford quarter-final (22,615) and best 'last 32' attendance since 1967's Wigan-Warrington replay (25,133). However, all-pay crowds at subsequent rounds varied little to previous years; the fifth round total (30,822) was probably the lowest ever for the 'last 16', the semi-final aggregate (23,613) the smallest since 1998. Clearly, fans will turn out in numbers if they are not adding to their season ticket cost but can the RFL discover a workable solution for a resurgence of spectator interest at all opening rounds? Only time will tell!

50-YEAR ATTENDANCE REVIEW

1956: 457,960 (15,265)	1986: 175,593 (5,853)
1966: 293,508 (9,784)	1996: 137,550 (4,585)
1976: 184,715 (6,157)	2006: 125,770 (4,192)

(Note: Figures included in both tables produced on this page are the aggregate attendance calculated from the round of the last 32 onwards. They exclude the final and, for consistency, any replays, each year covering 30 matches in all. Figures in brackets are the average per match.)

25-YEAR ATTENDANCE REVIEW

1985: 175,306 (5,844)	1998: 133,381 (4,446)
1986: 175,593 (5,853)	1999: 156,405 (5,214)
1987: 153,747 (5,125)	2000: 160,317 (5,344)
1988: 199,854 (6,662)	2001: 160,704 (5,357)
1989: 223,444 (7,448)	2002: 144,808 (4,827)
1990: 169,945 (5,665)	2003: 154,788 (5,160)
1991: 161,076 (5,369)	2004: 143,004 (4,767)
1992: 182,251 (6,075)	2005: 156,739 (5,221)
1993: 171,620 (5,721)	2006: 125,770 (4,192)
1994: 185,774 (6,192)	2007: 134,055 (4,469)
1995: 175,336 (5,845)	2008: 133,939 (4,464)
1996: 137,550 (4,585)	2009: 148,753 (4,958)
1997: 167,482 (5,583)	

SUMMARY OF RESULTS

Year	Winner	Runner-up	Venue	Year	Winner	Runner-up	Venue
1897	Batley 10	St Helens 3	Headingley	1955	Barrow 21	Workington T 12	Wembley
1898	Batley 7	Bradford 0	Headingley	1956	St Helens 13	Halifax 2	Wembley
1899	Oldham 19	Hunslet 9	Fallowfield	1957	Leeds 9	Barrow 7	Wembley
1900	Swinton 16	Salford 8	Fallowfield	1958	Wigan 13	Workington T 9	Wembley
1901	Batley 6	Warrington 0	Headingley	1959	Wigan 30	Hull 13	Wembley
1902	Broughton R 25	Salford 0	Rochdale	1960	Wakefield T 38	Hull 5	Wembley
1903	Halifax 7	Salford 0	Headingley	1961	St Helens 12	Wigan 6	Wembley
1904	Halifax 8	Warrington 3	Salford	1962	Wakefield T 12	Huddersfield 6	Wembley
1905	Warrington 6	Hull KR 0	Headingley	1963	Wakefield T 25	Wigan 10	Wembley
1906	Bradford 5	Salford 0	Headingley	1964	Widnes 13	Hull KR 5	Wembley
1907	Warrington 17	Oldham 3	Broughton	1965	Wigan 20	Hunslet 16	Wembley
1908	Hunslet 14	Hull 0	Huddersfield	1966	St Helens 21	Wigan 2	Wembley
1909	Wakefield T 17	Hull 0	Headingley	1967	Featherstone R 17	Barrow 12	Wembley
1910	Leeds 7	Hull 7	Huddersfield	1968	Leeds 11	Wakefield T 10	Wembley
Replay	Leeds 26	Hull 12	Huddersfield	1969	Castleford 11	Salford 6	Wembley
1911	Broughton R 4	Wigan 0	Salford	1970	Castleford 7	Wigan 2	Wembley
1912	Dewsbury 8	Oldham 5	Headingley	1971	Leigh 24	Leeds 7	Wembley
1913	Huddersfield 9	Warrington 5	Headingley	1972	St Helens 16	Leeds 13	Wembley
1914	Hull 6	Wakefield T 0	Halifax	1973	Featherstone R 33	Bradford N 14	Wembley
1915	Huddersfield 37	St Helens 3	Oldham	1974	Warrington 24	Featherstone R 9	Wembley
1916 to 1919—no competition due to First World War				1975	Widnes 14	Warrington 7	Wembley
1920	Huddersfield 21	Wigan 10	Headingley	1976	St Helens 20	Widnes 5	Wembley
1921	Leigh 13	Halifax 0	Broughton	1977	Leeds 16	Widnes 7	Wembley
1922	Rochdale H 10	Hull 9	Headingley	1978	Leeds 14	St Helens 12	Wembley
1923	Leeds 28	Hull 3	Wakefield	1979	Widnes 12	Wakefield T 3	Wembley
1924	Wigan 21	Oldham 4	Rochdale	1980	Hull KR 10	Hull 5	Wembley
1925	Oldham 16	Hull KR 3	Headingley	1981	Widnes 18	Hull KR 9	Wembley
1926	Swinton 9	Oldham 3	Rochdale	1982	Hull 14	Widnes 14	Wembley
1927	Oldham 26	Swinton 7	Wigan	Replay	Hull 18	Widnes 9	Elland Rd, Leeds
1928	Swinton 5	Warrington 3	Wigan				
1929	Wigan 13	Dewsbury 2	Wembley	1983	Featherstone R 14	Hull 12	Wembley
1930	Widnes 10	St Helens 3	Wembley	1984	Widnes 19	Wigan 6	Wembley
1931	Halifax 22	York 8	Wembley	1985	Wigan 28	Hull 24	Wembley
1932	Leeds 11	Swinton 8	Wigan	1986	Castleford 15	Hull KR 14	Wembley
1933	Huddersfield 21	Warrington 17	Wembley	1987	Halifax 19	St Helens 18	Wembley
1934	Hunslet 11	Widnes 5	Wembley	1988	Wigan 32	Halifax 12	Wembley
1935	Castleford 11	Huddersfield 8	Wembley	1989	Wigan 27	St Helens 0	Wembley
1936	Leeds 18	Warrington 2	Wembley	1990	Wigan 36	Warrington 14	Wembley
1937	Widnes 18	Keighley 5	Wembley	1991	Wigan 13	St Helens 8	Wembley
1938	Salford 7	Barrow 4	Wembley	1992	Wigan 28	Castleford 12	Wembley
1939	Halifax 20	Salford 3	Wembley	1993	Wigan 20	Widnes 14	Wembley
1940—no competition due to Second World War				1994	Wigan 26	Leeds 16	Wembley
1941	Leeds 19	Halifax 2	Bradford	1995	Wigan 30	Leeds 10	Wembley
1942	Leeds 15	Halifax 10	Bradford	1996	St Helens 40	Bradford B 32	Wembley
1943	Dewsbury 16	Leeds 15	Over two legs	1997	St Helens 32	Bradford B 22	Wembley
1944	Bradford N 8	Wigan 3	Over two legs	1998	Sheffield E 17	Wigan W 8	Wembley
1945	Huddersfield 13	Bradford N 9	Over two legs	1999	Leeds R 52	London B 16	Wembley
1946	Wakefield T 13	Wigan 12	Wembley	2000	Bradford B 24	Leeds R 18	Murrayfield
1947	Bradford N 8	Leeds 4	Wembley	2001	St Helens 13	Bradford B 6	Twickenham
1948	Wigan 8	Bradford N 3	Wembley	2002	Wigan W 21	St Helens 12	Murrayfield
1949	Bradford N 12	Halifax 0	Wembley	2003	Bradford B 22	Leeds R 20	Cardiff
1950	Warrington 19	Widnes 0	Wembley	2004	St Helens 32	Wigan W 16	Cardiff
1951	Wigan 10	Barrow 0	Wembley	2005	Hull FC 25	Leeds R 24	Cardiff
1952	Workington T 18	Featherstone R 10	Wembley	2006	St Helens 42	Huddersfield G 12	Twickenham
1953	Huddersfield 15	St Helens 10	Wembley	2007	St Helens 30	Catalans D 8	Wembley
1954	Warrington 4	Halifax 4	Wembley	2008	St Helens 28	Hull FC 16	Wembley
Replay	Warrington 8	Halifax 4	Bradford	2009	Warrington W 25	Huddersfield G 16	Wembley

CLUB FACTS AND FIGURES

Club Records

Most wins in all finals:
17 by Wigan/Wigan Warriors

Most wins at Wembley:
15 by Wigan

Most appearances in all finals:
28 by Wigan/Wigan Warriors

Most appearances at Wembley:
22 by Wigan/Wigan Warriors

Most consecutive wins in all finals (and at Wembley):
8 by Wigan (1988, 1989, 1990, 1991, 1992, 1993, 1994, 1995)

Most consecutive appearances in all finals (and at Wembley):
8 by Wigan (1988, 1989, 1990, 1991, 1992, 1993, 1994, 1995)

Highest score in all finals (and at Wembley):
52 by Leeds Rhinos (1999)

Highest score by losing team in all finals (and at Wembley):
32 by Bradford Bulls (1996)

Widest marginal win in all finals (and at Wembley):
36—Leeds Rhinos 52 London Broncos 16 (1999)

Highest aggregate score in all finals (and at Wembley):
72—St Helens 40 Bradford Bulls 32 (1996)

Lowest aggregate score in all finals:
4—Broughton Rangers 4 Wigan 0 (1911)

Lowest aggregate score at Wembley:
8—Warrington 4 Halifax 4 (1954)

Best recovery in all finals (and at Wembley):
St Helens recovered a 14-point deficit (12–26) to defeat Bradford Bulls 40–32 (1996)

Miscellaneous Records
(Excludes 1941 to 1945 wartime finals and drawn finals unless stated)

First to score:
The eventual winners scored first in 71 finals (out of 103)

Ahead at half-time:
The eventual winners led at half-time in 76 finals (out of 103—12 were level)

Losers ahead:
The eventual losers led at some stage in 41 finals (out of 103)

Most tries scored in final:
12 in 1996 (St Helens v Bradford Bulls) and 1999 (Leeds Rhinos v London Broncos)

Most tries scored by one team:
9 by Huddersfield (1915) and Leeds Rhinos (1999)

Fewest tries scored in final:
0 in 1911 (Broughton Rangers v Wigan) (also 1954 Warrington v Halifax drawn final at Wembley)

Most goals scored in final:
13 in 1973 (Featherstone R v Bradford Northern)

Most goals scored by one team:
9 by Leigh (1971), Featherstone R (1973) and Warrington (1974)

Fewest goals scored in final:
0 in 1901 (Batley v Warrington), 1905 (Warrington v Hull KR) and 1914 (Hull v Wakefield T)

Most overseas players in final:
15 in 1999 (Leeds R v London Broncos)

Most overseas players in one team:
11 by London Broncos (1998—excludes Tulsen Tollett, raised in Australia but born in England) (Note: In 2007 Catalans Dragons included 8 French players and 9 'overseas' players)

Challenge Cup finalists by final League position
(Excludes 1897–1901 when separate county leagues operated and Second World War period of 1941–1945 when not all clubs competed)

Highest placed winners:
1st position on 21 occasions, most notably Wigan who achieved the feat six consecutive times (1990–1995)

Lowest placed winners:
20th position (Leigh 1921, Widnes 1937, Featherstone Rovers 1967)

Lowest placed finalist:
25th position (Halifax, 1949 runners-up)

Breakdown of wins by final League position:
The team finishing first in the League won 21, second won 11, third won 13, fourth won 8, fifth won 11, sixth won 7, seventh won 2, eighth won 8, ninth won 4, tenth won 1, eleventh won 2, twelfth won 3, thirteenth won 1, fifteenth won 1, eighteenth won 1, twentieth won 3 (Note: Excludes 2009 winners)

PLAYERS FACTS AND FIGURES

Players Records

Most wins in all finals (and at Wembley):
9 by Shaun Edwards (Wigan 1985, 1988, 1989, 1990, 1991, 1992, 1993, 1994, 1995)

Most appearances in all finals (and at Wembley):
11 by Shaun Edwards (Wigan 1984, 1985, 1988, 1989, 1990, 1991, 1992, 1993, 1994, 1995, London Broncos 1999)

Most consecutive wins in all finals (and at Wembley):
8 by Shaun Edwards (Wigan 1988, 1989, 1990, 1991, 1992, 1993, 1994, 1995)

Most consecutive appearances in all finals (and at Wembley):
8 by Shaun Edwards (Wigan 1988, 1989, 1990, 1991, 1992, 1993, 1994, 1995)

Most tries in a match in all finals (and at Wembley):
4 by Leroy Rivett (Leeds Rhinos 1999)

Most goals in a match in all finals (and at Wembley):
8 by Cyril Kellett (Featherstone Rovers 1973) and Iestyn Harris (Leeds Rhinos 1999)

Most drop-goals in a match in all finals (and at Wembley):
3 by Neil Fox (Wakefield Trinity 1962)

Most points in a match in all finals (and at Wembley):
20 by Neil Fox (Wakefield Trinity 1960) and Iestyn Harris (Leeds Rhinos 1999)

Most successful captains:
3 wins by Harold Wagstaff (Huddersfield 1913, 1915, 1920), Derek Turner (Wakefield T 1960, 1962, 1963), Eric Ashton (Wigan 1958, 1959, 1965), Alex Murphy (St Helens 1966, Leigh 1971, Warrington 1974), Ellery Hanley (Wigan 1989, 1990, 1991), Dean Bell (Wigan 1992, 1993, 1994) (Note: Ernest Ward led Bradford N in their 1947 and 1949 wins and was captain in first leg of successful 1944 final)

Most appearances as captain:
6 by Eric Ashton (Wigan, 1958, 1959, 1961, 1963, 1965, 1966)

Youngest player to appear at Wembley:
Francis Cummins aged 17 years 200 days (Leeds 1994).

Oldest player to appear at Wembley:
Gus Risman aged 41 years 29 days (Workington T 1952)

Earliest try scored (1929 to date):
26 seconds by Graham Rees (St Helens 1972)

Earliest goal scored (1929 to date):
54 seconds by Laurie Gilfedder (Wigan 1965)

Lance Todd Trophy

Most wins:
3 by Sean Long (St Helens 2001, 2004, 2006)

Most consecutive wins:
2 by Paul Wellens (St Helens 2007—joint winner, 2008)

Youngest winner:
Peter Ramsden, aged 19 years exactly (Huddersfield 1953)

Oldest winner:
Frank Whitcombe, aged 34 years, 337 days (Bradford Northern 1948).

Players that missed the Final

Tourists:
(Players on sea voyage to Australia before air travel introduced from 1954 tour. Only affected 1946 and 1950 tourists as earlier Challenge Cup Finals were brought forward ahead off the tourists departure)
1946: Harry Murphy (Wakefield T), Joe Egan, Ken Gee, Martin Ryan, Ted Ward (all Wigan)
1950: Jim Featherstone, Bob Ryan (both Warrington), Fred Higgins, Danny Naughton (both Widnes)

Suspended:
(Players not available for final due to suspension)
1899: Tom Gillings (Hunslet)
1964: John Taylor (Hull Kingston Rovers)
1966: Colin Clarke (Wigan)
1971: David Chisnall (Leigh)
1991: Kelvin Skerrett (Wigan)
2003: Stuart Fielden (Bradford Bulls)

Players sent off
Red cards:
(Players dismissed from the game during final)
1900: Billy Brown (Salford)
1901: George Maine (Batley)
1906: Harry Feather (Bradford), Silas Warwick (Salford)
1912: Bert Avery (Oldham)
1914: Herbert Kershaw (Wakefield Trinity)
1971: Syd Hynes (Leeds)
1993: Richie Eyres (Widnes)

Yellow cards:
(Players sent to the 'sin bin'—introduced in 1983 initially for 5 or 10 minutes and later standardised at 10. Those listed were for 10 minutes)
1983: Paul Rose (Hull), Terry Hudson (Featherstone Rovers)
1991: Steve Hampson (Wigan)
2001: Shane Rigon (Bradford Bulls)

COACHES/REFEREES/ATTENDANCE FACTS AND FIGURES

Coaches Records

Most wins in all finals (and at Wembley):
4 by John Monie (Wigan 1990, 1991, 1992, 1993)

Most appearances in all finals (and at Wembley):
6 by Alex Murphy (Leigh 1971, Warrington 1974, 1975, Wigan 1984, St Helens 1987, 1989)

Most consecutive wins in all finals (and at Wembley):
4 by John Monie (Wigan 1990, 1991, 1992, 1993)

Most consecutive final appearances in all finals (and at Wembley):
4 by John Monie (Wigan 1990, 1991, 1992, 1993)

Referees Records

Most appointments in all finals:
7 by George Phillips (1939, 1943—1st leg, 1943—2nd leg, 1945—2nd leg, 1948, 1949, 1953). Note: The most peacetime finals (excluding 1941–1945) is 5 by Ron Gelder (1954, 1954 replay, 1955, 1956, 1958), Fred Lindop (1979, 1980, 1982, 1982 replay, 1988) and Russell Smith (1993, 1995, 1999, 2001, 2003)

Most appointments at Wembley:
4 by George Phillips (1939, 1948, 1949, 1953), Ron Gelder (1954, 1955, 1956, 1958) and Fred Lindop (1979, 1980, 1982, 1988)

Most consecutive appointments in all finals:
4 by Ron Gelder (1954, 1954 replay, 1955, 1956)

Most consecutive appointments at Wembley:
3 by Ron Gelder (1954, 1955, 1956) and Stuart Cummings (1996, 1997, 1998)

Attendance and Receipt Records

Highest attendance in all finals:
102,569—Warrington 8 Halifax 4 (replay at Odsal Stadium, Bradford, 1954)

Highest attendance at Wembley:
99,801—Wigan 28 Hull 24 (1985) (Note: Until recently this attendance was believed to be 97,801, with the record previously acknowledged as 98,536 for St Helens v Wigan in 1966. The author is grateful to Ray Fletcher, former co-editor of the Rothman's Rugby League Yearbook for providing this new information)

Highest receipts in all finals (and at Wembley):
£2,040,000—Wigan 30 Leeds 10 (1995). Note: This was the highest up to 1998, no receipts having been reported from 1999. (The 1995 receipts, when 78,550 paid ticket prices ranging from £12 to £50, has undoubtedly been exceeded. In 2007, 84,241 paid from £21 to £76.)

Terry Hudson: Fea 1983W

Arthur Hughes: Wid 1964W

Eric Hughes: Wid 1975W, 1976L, 1977L, 1979W, 1981W, 1982D, 1982rL, 1984W

Harry Hughes: Bar 1967L

David Hull: StH 1976W, Wid 1979sW

David Hulme: Wid 1984sW, 1993L

Fred Hulme: Fea 1952L

Paul Hulme: Wid 1993L

Alan Hunte: StH 1991L, 1996sW

John Hunter: Hud 1953W

Danny Hurcombe: Wig 1920L, 1924W

Fred Hurst: Lei 1921W

Wally Hurstfield: Wid 1964W

Billie Hutchinson: Bra 1944(1+2)W, 1945(1+2)L

Lou Hutt: StH 1930L

Colin Hutton: Wid 1950L

Gary Hyde: Cas 1986W

Syd Hynes: Lee 1968W, 1971L, 1972L

Graham Idle: Wak 1979L

Craig Innes: Lee 1994L, 1995L

Kevin Iro: Wig 1988W, 1989W, 1990W, 1991W, Lee 1994L, 1995L, StH 2001W

Tony Iro: Wig 1988W, 1989W

Sam Irvin: Old 1907L

Hudson Irving: Hfx 1939W, 1941L, 1942L

Iorwerth Isaac: Lee 1936W

Danny Isherwood: War 1901L, 1904L, 1905W, 1907W

Billy Ivison: Work 1952W, 1955L

Edward Jackett: Dew 1912W

Percy Jacks: Wid 1934L

Bob Jackson: War 1990L

George Jackson: Lee 1923W

Lee Jackson: Lee 1999sW, 2000sL

Michael Jackson: Shef 1998sW

Paul Jackson: Sfd 1969L

Paul Jackson: Hud 2006L, 2009sL

Phil Jackson: Bar 1951L, 1955W, 1957L

William Jackson: StH 1915L

Billy Jacques: StH 1897L

Kevin James: Hull 1985L

Mel James: StH 1976sW, 1978L

Neil James: Hfx 1987sW, 1988L

Sam James: Bro 1902W

Willie James: Bro 1902W

Billy Jarman: Lee 1910D, 1910rW

David Jeanes: Wak 1968L

Bert Jenkins: Wig 1911L

Dai Jenkins: Lee 1941W, 1942W, 1943(1+2)L, 1947L

David Jenkins: Wid 1976L

Griff Jenkins: War 1936L

Sid Jerram: Wig 1920L, 1924W

Dai John: Sfd 1906L

Abe Johnson: Old 1927W

Albert Johnson: War 1950W

Barry Johnson: Cas 1986W

Bill Johnson: York 1931L

B. Johnson: Wak 1914L

David Johnson: Hull 1960L

Paul Johnson: Wig 2002W, War 2009sW

Peter Johnston: HKR 1986L

Ben Jolley: War 1913L

Bill Jolley: Wig 1920L

G. Jolley: War 1904L, War 1905W

Stan Jolley: Wig 1946L

Dick Jones: Swi 1900W

E. 'Ned' Jones: Bro 1911W

Glyn Jones: Hfx 1942L

Harold Jones: Kei 1937L

Jimmy Jones: Wid 1934L, 1937W

Joe Jones: Wig 1944(2)L

Johnny Jones: Wak 1946W

Keri Jones: Wig 1970L

Les Jones: StH 1972W, 1976W, 1978L

Leslie Jones: War 1950W

Lewis Jones: Lee 1957W

Reg Jones: Old 1926L, 1927W

Stacey Jones: Cat 2007L

Stuart Jones: Hud 2006sL

Jamie Jones-Buchanan: Lee 2005sL

Tim Jonkers: StH 2001sW, 2002L

Gary Jordan: Fea 1967W

Graham Joyce: Bra 1973L

John Joyner: Cas 1986W

Chris Joynt: StH 1996W, 1997W, 2001W, 2002L, 2004W

Ken Jubb: Lee 1936W, 1943(1+2)L

Patrick 'Paddy' Judge: Bat 1901W

Bill Jukes: Hun 1908W

Brian Juliff: Wak 1979L, Wig 1984sL, Hfx 1987sW

Tony Karalius: StH 1976W, 1978*L

Vince Karalius: StH 1956W, 1961W, Wid 1964W

Stephen Kearney: Hull 2005W

Arthur Keegan: Hull 1959L

Ivor Kelland: Bar 1967L

Cyril Kellett: HKR 1964L, Fea 1973W

Ken Kellett: Fea 1973W, 1983W

Andy Kelly: HKR 1986L

Ken Kelly: StH 1972W

Fred Kelsall: Wid 1930W

E. Kelsey: Bra 1898L

Gary Kemble: Hull 1982D, 1982rW, 1983L, 1985L

George Kemel: Wid 1964W

Albert Kemp: HKR 1905L

Jim Kennedy: Hull 1922L, 1923L

Brett Kenny: Wig 1985W

George Kenny: Hfx 1949L

Jack Kenny: Swi 1932L

Tom Kenny: Sfd 1939L, Dew 1943(1+2)W

T. Kenyon: War 1905W

George Kershaw: Dew 1943(1+2)W

Herbert Kershaw: Wak 1909W, 1914L

Jack Kershaw: Hull 1960L

Martin Ketteridge: Cas 1986W, 1992L

Andy Key: Work 1955L, 1958L

Younes Khattabi: Cat 2007L

Stan Kielty: Hfx 1949L, 1954D, 1954rL, 1956L

George Kilburn: Hull 1908L

Len Killeen: StH 1966W

Matt King: War 2009W

Paul King: Hull 2005sW

Roy Kinnear: Wig 1929W

Terry Kirchin: Bar 1967*L

Billy Kirk: War 1928L

Bill Kirkbride: Cas 1970W

Nicky Kiss: Wig 1985W, 1988W, 1989W

Jack Kitching: Bra 1944(2)W, 1945(1+2)L, 1947W, 1949W

Ernie Knapman: Old 1924L, 1925W, 1926L

Bryn Knowelden: War 1950W

Simon Knox: Bra 1996L, 1997sL

Milan Kosanovic: Wak 1963W, Fea 1967*W

Dicky Kynan: Roc 1922W

Alex Laidlaw: Bra 1906W

Trevor Lake: Wig 1965W, 1966L

Adrian Lam: Wig 2002W, 2004L

Mike Lamb: Bra 1973L

Cliff Lambert: Fea 1952L

Mike Lampkowski: Wak 1979L

Leonard Land: Wak 1914L

George Langfield: StH 1953L

George Langhorn: Hfx 1904W

John Langley: Lee 1968*W, 1971L, 1972sL

Billy Langton: Hun 1965L

Jack Large: Hud 1953W

Ken Large: StH 1961W

Dale Laughton: Shef 1998W

Doug Laughton: Wig 1970L, Wid 1975W, 1976L, 1977L, 1979W

Jerry Laughton: Wid 1930W

Ali Lauitiiti: Lee 2005L

Dean Lawford: Lee 2000L

Johnny Lawless: Shef 1998W

Johnny Lawrenson: Lee 1941W, Wig 1944(1+2)L, Work 1952W

David Laws: HKR 1986L

Joe Lawton: Old 1899W

Ted Layhe: York 1931L

Tommy Leach: Hun 1899L

Bill Leake: Hud 1945(1+2)W, Bra 1948L,

1949W

Andy Leathem: StH 1996W

Danny Leatherbarrow: Work 1958L

Barry Ledger: StH 1987L

Aaron Lee: Hud 1913W, 1915W

Barry Lee: Hun 1965L

Tommy Lee: Hull 2008sL

Arthur Lees: Old 1899W, 1907L

Joe Lees: Old 1899W

Sam Lees: Old 1899W,

Sammy Lees: War 1907W

Elwyn Leigh: Swi 1927L

Fred Leigh: Wid 1950L

Jack Lendill: Lee 1957W

Roy Lester: Lei 1971*W

James Leuluai: Hull 1982*D, 1982rW, 1983L, 1985L

George Lewis: StH 1930L

George Lewis: Cas 1935W

Ike Lewis: Sfd 1906L

Jack Lewis: Swi 1900W

Randall Lewis: Hud 1945(1+2)W

Jim Lewthwaite: Bar 1951L, 1955W, 1957L

Jimmy Leytham: Wig 1911L

Graham Liptrot: StH 1978L, 1987L

R. 'Bert' Lister: Old 1926L

Billy Little: Hfx 1903W, 1904W

Billy Little: Bar 1938L

Freddie Little: StH 1897L

J. Littlewood: Bat 1897W

Stewart 'Steve' Llewellyn: StH 1953L, 1956W

Arthur Lloyd: York 1931L

Bobby Lloyd: Hfx 1921L

Geoff 'Sammy' Lloyd: Hull 1980L, 1982D

Ian Lloyd: Bar 1938L

Reg Lloyd: Kei 1937L, Dew 1943 (1+2)W

Brian Lockwood: Cas 1969W, 1970W, HKR 1980W, Wid 1981W, 1982D, 1982rL

Hubert Lockwood: Hfx 1939W, 1942L

Jamahl Lolesi: Hud 2009L

James Lomas: Sfd 1902L, 1903L, 1906L, Old 1912L

Arnold 'Arnie' Long: Bra 1973sL

Sean Long: StH 2001W, 2002L, 2004W, 2006W, 2007W, 2008W

Frank Longman: Bar 1951L

Fred Longstaff: Hud 1913W, 1915W

Gary Lord: Cas 1986W

Paul Loughlin: StH 1987L, 1989L, 1991L, Bra 1996L, 1997L

Gerald Lowe: War 1950W, 1954D, 1954rW

Gerard Lowe: Wid 1964W

Jimmy Lowe: Wig 1920L

John Lowe: Lee 1932W

Phil Lowe: HKR 1980W, 1981L

James Lowes: Lee 1994L, 1995L, Bra 1997L,

2000W, 2001L, 2003W

Alan Lowndes: Cas 1969W, 1970W

Reg Lowry: Wig 1946L

Ian Lucas: Wig 1989W, 1991W

Ernie Lunt: War 1904L

Shaun Lunt: Hud 2009L

John Lydiat: HKR 1986sL

Joe Lydon: Wid 1984W, Wig 1988W, 1989W, 1990W, 1992W, 1993W

Joe Lyman: Dew 1929L

Paul Lyman: Fea 1983sW

Bill Lymer: Work 1955L

Billie Lynch: Wak 1909W, 1914L

Tommy Lynch: Hfx 1954D, 1954rL, 1956L

David Lyon: War 1990L

Geoff Lyon: Wig 1961L, 1963L, 1965*W, 1966*L

Jamie Lyon: StH 2006W

Billy Lyons: Lee 1923W

John 'Jock' McAvoy: Work 1958L

Nathan McAvoy: Bra 2000W

Seamus McCallion: Hfx 1987W, 1988L

Tyrone McCarthy: War 2009sW

Kevin McCormack: StH 1987L

Robbie McCormack: Wig 1998L

Stan McCormick: StH 1953L, Warr 1954D, 1954rW

Tommy McCue: Wid 1934L, 1937W, Hfx 1941L, 1942L

Alan McCurrie: Wak 1979L

Steve McCurrie: Wid 1993sL

Barrie McDermott: Lee 1999W, 2000L, 2003L

Brian McDermott: Bra 1996L, 1997L, 2000W, 2001L

Johnny MacDonald: Hfx 1949L

Wayne McDonald: Lee 2003sL, Hud 2006sL

Des McDonnell: Bar 1938L

Hughie McDowell: Wid 1934L, 1937W

Brian McGinn: StH 1961W

Billy McGinty: War 1990sL, Wig 1992W

Hugh McGregor: Bar 1951L

Danny McGuire: Lee 2005sL

Bernard McGurrin: Wig 1958W

John 'Paddy' McIntyre: HKR 1925L

Len McIntyre: StH 1956W

Brad Mackay: Bra 2000W

Danny McKeating: Bar 1938L

Vince McKeating: Work 1952W, Bar 1955W

Chris McKenna: Lee 2003L, 2005L

John McKinnell: Bar 1951L

Keith McLellan: Lee 1957W

Matt McLeod: Wak 1968L

Stan McLeod: Wig 1963L

Eddie McLoughlin: Roc 1922W

J. McLoughlin: Bra 1898L

Pat McManus: Cas 1935W

Shayne McMenemy: Hull 2005W

Steve McNamara: Bra 1997L

Brian McTigue: Wig 1958W, 1959W, 1961L, 1963L, 1965W, 1966L

Derek McVey: StH 1997W

Harry McWhirter: Sfd 1906L

W. Madley: HKR 1905L

George Maine: Bat 1897W, 1898W, 1901W

Harry Major: Wig 1966L

Terry Major: HKR 1964L

Joe Malkin: Dew 1929L

Fred Mallinson: Hfx 1903W, 1904W

Ken Mallinson: Hud 1945(1+2)W

Austin 'Gus' Malone: Wid 1950L

Jack Maloney: Wig 1944(1+2)L

Duane Mann: War 1990L

George Mann: StH 1991L, Lee 1995sL

John Mantle: StH 1966W, 1972W, 1976W

Willie Manu: Hull 2008W

Alan Marchant: Hun 1965L

Tony Marchant: Cas 1986W

Ray Markham: Hud 1933W, 1935L

Alf Marklew: Bar 1938L, Bra 1944(1)W, 1945(1)L

Rothwell 'Rod' Marlor: Old 1925W, 1926L, 1927W

George Marsden: Bra 1906W

John Marsden: Fea 1983W

Len Marson: Wak 1946W

Tommy Martyn: War 1975L

Tommy Martyn: StH 1996sW, 1997W, 2001W, 2002L

Keith Mason: StH 2004W, Hud 2009L

Len Mason: Wig 1929W

Mel Mason: Fea 1973W

Vila Matautia: StH 1996sW, 1997sW, 2001sW

Barrie-Jon Mather: Wig 1994W

Billy Mather: Hfx 1954rL

Richard 'Richie' Mathers: Lee 2005L, War 2009W

Roy Mathias: StH 1976W, 1978L

James Mathiou: Lee 1999sW, 2000sL

George Matthews: Hull 1959L

Frank Mawson: Hfx 1949L

Jim Measures: Wid 1964W

Paul Medley: Bra 1996sL, 1997sL

Mel Meek: Hfx 1941L, 1942L

Francis Meli: StH 2006W, 2007W, 2008W

Brian Mennell: HKR 1964L

Billy Mercer: StH 1930L

Gary Mercer: War 1990L, Lee 1994L, 1995L

Jesse Meredith: War 1928L

Martin Meredith: Hfx 1988L

Bob Messer: Swi 1900W, Sfd 1903L

Tony Mestrov: Wig 1998L

Don Metcalfe: Fea 1952L

Jimmy Metcalfe: Wak 1909W

J. 'Pop' Midgley: Bat 1901W

Trevor Midgley: Wak 1979*L

Gene Miles: Wig 1992W

Shane Millard: Lon 1999L

Fred Miller: Fea 1952L

Gavin Miller: HKR 1986L

Jack 'Cod' Miller: War 1928L, 1933L, 1936L, Hud 1945(1+2)W

Joe Miller: Wig 1911L

Sammy Miller: Sfd 1939L

W. Millican: Wak 1914L

Harry Millington: Wid 1930W, 1934L, 1937W, Hfx 1941L, 1942L

John Millington: KKR 1980sW, 1981sL

Ernie Mills: Hud 1933W

Jim Mills: Wid 1975W, 1977L, 1979W

Roger Millward: HKR 1980W

Tommy Milner: Dew 1912W

Alf Milnes: Hfx 1921L

Jack Mitchell: Hun 1899L

Norman Mitchell: Fea 1952L

James Moffatt: Old 1899W

Adam Mogg: Cat 2007L

Michael Monaghan: War 2009W

Walt Mooney: Lei 1921W

Danny Moore: Wig 1998L

Scott Moore: Hud 2009sL

Jeff Moores: Lee 1932W

Stanley Moorhouse: Hud 1913W, 1915W

Arnold 'Arnie' Morgan: Fea 1967W

Edgar Morgan: Hull 1922L, 1923L

Joe Morgan: Swi 1900W

Adrian Morley: Lee 1999W, 2000L, War 2009W

Chris Morley: StH 1997sW

Johnny Morley: Hfx 1903W, 1904W

Cyril Morrell: Hun 1934W

Bert Morris: 1926W, 1927L, 1928W

Oliver Morris: Lee 1941W, 1942W

D. Morrison: War 1901L, 1904L

Andy Morton: Hull 1910D, 1910rL

Walter Morton: Hfx 1903W, Hfx 1904W

Glyn Moses: StH 1953L, 1956W

Gregory Mounis: Cat 2007L

Stanley Mountain: Hud 1935L

Cec Mountford: Wig 1948W, 1951W

Johnny Mudge: Work 1952W, 1955L

John Muggleton: Hull 1985L

J.T. 'Paudy' Munns: Bat 1897W, 1898W

Frank Murgatroyd: Bra 1898L

Willie Murgatroyd: Bra 1898L

Alex Murphy: StH 1961W, 1966W, Lei 1971W, War 1974W

Ben Murphy: Swi 1900W

Cornelius 'Con' Murphy: Lee 1941W, 1942W,

1943(1+2)L, 1947L

Justin Murphy: Cat 2007L

Mike Murray: Bar 1967L

Brian Murrell: Lee 1977W

Peter Muscroft: HKR 1981L

David Myers: Wig 1991W, Wid 1993L

Eddie Myers: York 1931L

William Myers: StH 1915L

A. 'Tony' Myler: Wid 1982sD, 1982r*L

Frank Myler: Wid 1964W

John Myler: Wid 1981sW

Steve Nash: Fea 1973W, 1974L

Albert 'Ally' Naughton: War 1950W

Danny Naughton: War 1954D, 1954rW

Johnny Naughton: Wid 1950L

Arthur Naylor: War 1904L, 1905W, 1907W

George Naylor: Hud 1920W

Scott Naylor: Bra 2000W, 2001L, 2003W

J. Nearey: Dew 1912W

Jonathan Neill: StH 1991L

Keith Neller: Hfx 1987W, 1988L

David Nelson: Cas 1992L

Nick Nelson: Wid 1975*W, 1976L

Chris Nero: Hud 2006L

Arnold Nettleton: Hfx 1904W

Tommy Newbould: Wak 1909W

Jim Newcombe: War 1936L

John Newlove: Fea 1973W, 1974L, Hull 1980L

Paul Newlove: StH 1996W, 1997W, 2001W, 2002L

Terry Newton: Lee 1999W, Wig 2002W, 2004L

Mike Nicholas: War 1974W, 1975sL

Syd Nicholas: War 1913L

George Nicholls: StH 1976W, 1978L

Sonny Nickle: Bra 1996L, 1997L, StH 2001W

Tawera Nikau: Cas 1992L

Ken Noble: Hud 1962L

Derek Noonan: War 1974W, 1975L, StH 1976W, 1978L

Ernest Norcliffe: Hfx 1931W

Brian Nordgren: Wig 1946L, 1951W

A. Norris: Sfd 1903L

Andy Northey: StH 1996W, 1997sW

Steve Norton: Cas 1970*W, Hull 1980L, 1982D, 1982rW, 1983L, 1985L

Geoff Oakes: Wak 1960W, 1962W

Joe Oakland: Bat 1897W, 1898W, 1901W

Michael O'Connor: StH 1989L

Terry O'Connor: Wig 1998sL, 2002W, 2004sL

Martin Offiah: Wig 1992W, 1993W, 1994W, 1995W, Lon 1999L

Terry Ogden: Sfd 1969L

Terry O'Grady: Wig 1958W

Dane O'Hara: Hull 1982D, 1983L, 1985L

Richard O'Hara: StH 1897L

George Oliver: Hull 1922L, 1923L

Keiron O'Loughlin: Wid 1982D, 1982rL, 1984W

Kevin O'Loughlin: Wig 1965*W, 1970L

Sean O'Loughlin: Wig 2004L

Dennis O'Neill: Wid 1976sL, 1977L

Jimmy O'Neill: Wid 1975*W

John O'Neill: Work 1958L

Julian O'Neill: StH 1997W

Julian 'Jules' O'Neill: Wid 1993sL, Wig 2002W

Mike O'Neill: Wid 1979sW, 1981W, 1982D, 1982rL, 1984W, Lee 1994sL

Patrick 'Paddy' O'Neill: Dew 1912W

Steve O'Neill: Wid 1982sD, 1984W

Billy Oram: Bro 1902W

Frank O'Rourke: Lee 1932W

Danny Orr: wig 2004L

Harold Osbaldestin: Sfd 1938W, 1939L

F. Osborne: Hfx 1941L

Will Osborne: HKR 1905L, Hull 1910D, 1910rL

Laurie Osbourne: HKR 1925L

Jack Oster: War 1933L

Willie Oulton: Lee 1978W

Harry Owen: Wid 1930W, 1934L

James Owen: Hull 1908L

Ray Owen: Wid 1964W, Wak 1968L

Ted Owen: York 1931L

Ike Owens: Lee 1947L

Dicky Padden: Roc 1922W

Richard Paley: Wak 1968*L

Harold Palin: War 1950W

Eric Palmer: HKR 1964L

Geoff Palmer: Hfx 1956L

Sam Panapa: Wig 1993sW, 1994sW

Jack Pansegrouw: Hfx 1949L

Gwyn Parker: Lee 1936W, Kei 1937L

Reg Parker: Bar 1955W, 1957L

Robert Parker: Bra 2003sW

Tommy Parker: Wig 1924W, 1929W

John Parkes: Wid 1950L

Ernest Parkin: Wak 1914L

Jonathan ' Jonty' Parkin: Wak 1914L

Billy Parkinson: Lei 1921W

Frank Parr: Wig 1965W, 1966L, 1970L

George Parr: StH 1953L

Laurie Parry: Hull 1908L

George Parsons: StH 1953L, 1956W

Dan Pascoe: York 1931L

Tony Paskins: Work 1952W, 1955L

B. Patrick: Bra 1898L

Shaun Patrick: Hull 1985L

Bill Pattinson: Bra 1973L

Graham Paul: HKR 1964L

Henry Paul: Wig 1995W, 1998L, Bra 2000W, 2001L

Robbie Paul: Bra 1996L, 1997L, 2000W, 2001L, 2003W, Hud 2006L

Alfred Peacock: War 1928L

Danny Peacock: Bra 1997L

Jamie Peacock: Bra 2000W, 2001L, 2003W

Ossie Peake: Hud 1945(1+2)W

Les Pearce: Hfx 1956L

Roger Pearman: Wak 1963W

Arthur Pearson: Sfd 1900L

Ben Pearson: Lee 1941W

Jack Pearson: Swi 1926W

John Pendlebury: Wig 1984L, Hfx 1987W, 1988L

Albert Pepperell: Hud 1945(1+2)W, Work 1952W

Russell Pepperell: Hud 1953W

Apollo Perelini: StH 1996W, 1997W

Les Perkins: War 1928L

Barry Philbin: War 1974W, 1975L

Mike Philbin: War 1974W, 1975L

Billy Phipps: HKR 1905L

Ian Pickavance: StH 1996sW, 1997sW

Clive Pickerill: Hull 1980L

Billy Pickup: War 1974sW

Geoff Pimblett: StH 1972W, 1976W, 1978L

Nick Pinkney: Shef 1998W

Harry Pinner: StH 1978L

Frank Pitchford: Wig 1963L

Steve Pitchford: Lee 1977W, 1978W

Herbert Place: Hun 1908W

David Plange: Cas 1986W

Andy Platt: StH 1987L, Wig 1989W, 1990W, 1991W, 1992W, 1993W, 1994W

Willie Poching: Lee 2003sL, 2005sL

Hubert Pogson: Hud 1920W

Charlie Pollitt: Swi 1900W

Quentin Pongia: Wig 2004L

Bernard Poole: Lee 1957W

Harry Poole: HKR 1964L

Ian Potter: Wig 1985W, 1988W, 1989W

Daryl Powell: Lee 1999W, 2000L

Harold Poynton: Wak 1962W, 1963W, 1968L

Tommy Poynton: Wak 1914L

Karl Pratt: Bra 2003sW

Alan Preece: Hun 1965L

Paul Prendiville: Hull 1980L, 1982D, 1982rW, 1983L

Alan Prescott: StH 1953L, 1956W

Alan Prescott: Wid 1975W, 1976L

Eric Prescott: Wid 1981W, 1982D, 1982rL

Frank Prescott: Wig 1920L, Roc 1922W

Steve Prescott: StH 1996W, 1997W

Tom Prescott: Wig 1920L

Dave Preston: Sfd 1906L

Jack Preston: Swi 1900W

Mark Preston: Wig 1990W

Gareth Price: Lee 1947L, Hfx 1949L

Horace Price: Sfd 1902L

Jack Price: Wig 1924W

Ray Price: War 1954D, 1954rW

Bernard Prior: Lee 1957W, Hun 1965L

Paul Proctor: HKR 1981sL

Gary Prohm: HKR 1986L

Harry Prole: Bra 1898L

Bob Prosser: Sfd 1969*L

Dai Prosser: Lee 1941W, 1942W, 1943(1+2)L, 1947L

Jack Prosser: Lei 1921W

Stuart Prosser: Hfx 1921L

Leon Pryce: Bra 2000sW, 2001L, 2003W, StH 2006W, 2007W, 2008W

Neil Puckering: Hull 1985L

Luke Quigley: Cat 2007L

Pat Quinn: Lee 1957W

Steve Quinn: Fea 1983W

Les Quirk: StH 1989L, 1991L

Lee Radford: Bra 2003W, Hull 2008L

Kris Radlinski: Wig 1998L, 2002W, 2004L

Sebastien Raguin: Cat 2007L

Andy Raleigh: Hud 2006L

Dicky Ralph: Lee 1936W

Jimmy Ramage: Hun 1899L

Denis Ramsdale: Wig 1984L

Dick Ramsdale: Wig 1911L, 1920L

Peter Ramsden: Hud 1953W, 1962L

Bill Ramsey: Hun 1965L, Lee 1968W, 1971L, 1972L, Wid 1977L

Bob Randall: Wid 1964W

Jack Randall: Hun 1908W

Albert Ratcliffe: Wid 1930W, 1934L

Gordon Ratcliffe: Wig 1946L, 1948W

Gordon Rawlings: Bar 1938L

Albert Rawnsley: Hfx 1931W

Keith Rayne: Wak 1979L

Kevin Rayne: Wak 1979*L

Gareth Raynor: Hull 2005W, 2008L

John Raynor: HKR 1925L

John Rea: Bar 1957L

Jack Read: Old 1926L, 1927W

David Redfearn: Bra 1973L

Mick Redfearn: Cas 1969W, 1970W

Maurice Redhead: Bar 1957L, 1967L

Dai Reed: HKR 1905L

Dai Rees: Sfd 1906L

Dai Rees: Hfx 1931W

Graham Rees: StH 1972W

William 'Billo' Rees: Swi 1926W, 1927L, 1928W, 1932L

Patrick 'Paddy' Reid: Hfx 1949L

Tahi Reihana: Bra 1997L

Macolm Reilly: Cas 1969W, 1970W

Paul Reilly: Hud 2006L

Arthur Render: Hun 1965*L

Bill Renton: Hfx 1931W

Bert Renwick: War 1913L

Steele Retchless: Lon 1999L

Charlie Reynolds: Wid 1950L

Frank Reynolds: War 1975L

Tom Reynolds: StH 1897L

Jack Rhapps: Sfd 1900L, 1902L, 1903L, 1906L

Alan Rhodes: Fea 1973W, 1974L

Austin Rhodes: StH 1956W, 1961W

Billy Rhodes: Dew 1912W

Billy Rhodes: War 1928L

William Rhodes: Dew 1929L

Gwyn Richards: Hud 1933W, 1935L

Fred 'Cosh' Richardson: Dew 1912W

J. Arthur 'Archie' Rigg: Hfx 1903W

Shane Rigon: Bra 2001L

Chris Riley: War 2009W

Jack Riley: Hfx 1903W, 1904W

Joe Riley: Hfx 1903W, 1904W

Sam Rimmer: StH 1897L

Johnny Ring: Wig 1924W, 1929W

Augustus J. 'Gus' Risman: Sfd 1938W, 1939L, Lee 1942W, Work 1952W

Bev Risman: Lee 1968W

Leroy Rivett: Lee 1999W, 2000L

Grant Rix: Hfx 1987W

Sid Rix: Old 1924L, 1925W, 1926L, 1927W

Bert Roberts: StH 1915L

Bob Roberts: Wid 1937W

Laurie Roberts: Bra 1944(1+2)W, 1945(1+2)L

Reginald Roberts: Hud 1935L

Bob Robertson: Bra 1898L

A.W. Robinson: HKR 1905L

David Robinson: Wig 1970L

Don Robinson: Lee 1957W

Herbert Robinson: Hun 1899L

Jason Robinson: Wig 1993W, 1995W, 1998L

Jimmy Robinson: Dew 1943(1+2)W

Luke Robinson: Hud 2009L

Roy Robinson: StH 1956W

Steve Robinson: Hfx 1988L

James Roby: StH 2006sW, 2007sW, 2008sW

Jack Rodgers: Bat 1898W, 1901W

Fred Roffey: Wig 1924W

E. 'Ned' Rogers: Hull 1908L, 1909L, 1910D, 1910rL, 1914W

Greg Rogers: Hull 1910rL

Johnny Rogers: Hud 1915W, 1920W

Ken Rollin: Wak 1960W

David Roockley: Cas 1986sW

Sid Rookes: Lee 1943(1)L

Tea Ropati: StH 1991L

John 'Sol' Roper: Work 1955L, 1958L

Paul Rose: HKR 1980W, Hull 1983L, 1985L

Albert Rosenfeld: Hud 1913W, 1915W

Mel Rosser: York 1931L

John Rothwell: Hfx 1949L

George Roughley: Wig 1951W

Gerry Round: Wak 1960W, 1962W, 1963W, 1968*L

Paul Round: StH 1987sL

Ron Rowbottom: Wid 1950L

Harold Rowe: Lee 1910rW

Peter Rowe: Wig 1970L

Harry Royal: Dew 1943(1+2)W

Dick Rubrey: Hun 1899L

Jim Rudd: Dew 1929L

George Ruddick: Bro 1911W

Fred Rule: Hfx 1941L, 1942L

Bob Ryan: War 1954D, 1954rW

Chris Ryan: Lon 1999sL

Martin Ryan: Wig 1944(1+2)L, 1948W

Ron Ryder: War 1950W, 1954rW

Ron Rylance: Wak 1946W

Ted Sadler: Cas 1935W

Tommy Sale: Wid 1950L

Matt Salter: Lon 1999L

Dean Sampson: Cas 1992sL

Malcolm Sampson: Wak 1963W

Fred Samuel: Hull 1923L

Jimmy Sanders: Lee 1910D

Gary Sanderson: War 1990L

John 'Sammy' Sanderson: Lee 1978W

Mike Sanderson: Bar 1967L

Jamie Sandy: Cas 1986W

Stan Satterthwaite: Lee 1936W, 1941W, 1942W, 1943(1+2)L

Brian Saville: Hull 1959L

Tom Saxton: Hull 2005sW

Bill Sayer: Wig 1958W, 1959W, 1961L, 1963L, StH 1966W

Jack Scaife: Old 1927W

Jon Scales: Bra 1996L

Derrick Schofield: Hfx 1954D, 1954rL

Garry Schofield: Hull 1985sL, Lee 1994L, 1995L

Tom Schofield: Hfx 1921L

J. Scholtze: War 1901L

Bob Scott: Swi 1932L

Mick Scott: Hull 1959L, 1960L

Mick Scott: Wig 1984L, Hfx 1987W, 1988sL

Walter Scott: Bro 1911W

Tom Scourfield: Hud 1933W, 1935L

Danny Sculthorpe: Wig 2004sL

Paul Sculthorpe: StH 2001W, 2002L, 2004W, 2006W, 2008W

Barry Seabourne: Lee 1968W, 1971L, Bra 1973L

Charlie Seeling: Wig 1911L, 1920L

Charlie Seeling: War 1928L, 1933L, Dew 1943(1+2)

Keith Senior: Shef 1998W, Lee 200L, 2003L, 2005L

Mark Shackleton: Bat 1897W, 1898W

James Shallcross: StH 1915L

Bill Shankland: War 1933L, 1936L

Tommy Shannon: Wid 1934L, 1937W

George Sharples: Dew 1912W

Bert Sharratt: Bra 1906W

Jim Sharrock: Wig 1911L

Darren Shaw: Shef 1998W

Ernie Shaw: Wig 1920L

Glyn Shaw: Wid 1979W, 1981sW

Ike Shaw: Bat 1897W

Robert Shaw: Sfd 1900L, 1902L, 1903L

Les Sheard: Wak 1979L

Adrian Shelford: Wig 1988W, 1989W, 1990W

Geoff Shelton: Hun 1965L

George Shepherd: Wak 1968L

Joe Sherburn: Kei 1937L

Barry Sheridan: Wid 1975W, 1976sL

Ryan Sheridan: Lee 1999W, 2000L

John Sherrington: Wig 1929W

Arthur Sherwood: Hud 1920W

Herbert Sherwood: Hud 1933W, 1935L

Peter Shiels: StH 2001W, 2002L

Mick Shoebottom: Lee 1968W

Hugh Shore: Sfd 1900L, 1903L

Frank Shugars: War 1905W, 1907W

Gary Siddall: Fea 1983sW

E. Sidwell: Wak 1909W

Dick Silcock: Wig 1911L

Nat Silcock: Wid 1930W, 1934L, 1937W

Nat Silcock: Wig 1951W, StH 1956W

Billie Simpson: Wak 1909W

Robbie Simpson: Lon 1999L

Herbert Sinclair: HKR 1905L

Kevin Sinfield: Lee 2003L, 2005L

Matt Sing: Hull 2008L

Bill Sinton: Bra 1906W

Arthur Skelhorne: War 1913L

Bill Skelly: Bar 1938L

Alan Skene: Wak 1960W, 1962W

Kelvin Skerrett: Wig 1992W, 1993W, 1994W, 1995W

Trevor Skerrett: Wak 1979L, Hull 1982D, 1982rW, 1983L

Harry Slater: Wak 1909W

Tim Slatter: Fea 1983W

Ted Slevin: Wig 1951W, Hud 1953W, 1962L

Bob Sloman: Old 1924L, 1925W, 1926L, 1927W

Benny Smales: Bra 1906W

Tom Smales: Fea 1967W

Tommy Smales: Hud 1962L

Peter Smethurst: Sfd 1969*L, Lei 1971W

Alan Smith: Lee 1968W, 1972L, 1977W

Arthur Smith: Old 1907L, 1912L

Bob Smith: Lee 1932W, War 1933L

Charlie Smith: Hfx 1939W, 1941L, 1942L

Cliff Smith: Dew 1929L

Craig Smith: Wig 2002W, 2004L

Dan Smith: Sfd 1900L, 1902L, 1903L

David Smith: Lee 1977sW, 1978W

Frank Smith: Cas 1935W, Dew 1943(1+2)W

Fred Smith: Hun 1908W

Fred Smith: Wak 1960W, 1962W

Gerald Smith: Bar 1967L

Gordon Smith: HKR 1986sL

Herbert Smith: Bra 1945(2)L, Bra 1947W, 1948L

Keith Smith: Wak 1979L

Len Smith: Hun 1934W

Mark Smith: Wig 2002sW

Mick Smith: Fea 1967W, 1973W, 1974L

Mike Smith: Hull 1960L

Mike Smith: HKR 1980W, 1981L, 1986L

Paul Smith: Hud 2006sL

Peter Smith: Fea 1983W

Tony Smith: Cas 1992sL, Wig 198L

Vince Smith: Wig 1920L

Wilf Smith: StH 1961W

Rob Smyth: Lon 1999L

Steve Snitch: Hud 2006sL

Kurt Sorenson: Wid 1993L

Graham Southernwood: Cas 1992L

Ike Southward: Work 1955L, 1958L

Waisale Sovatabua: Shef 1998W

Alf Spackman: HKR 1905L

Jack Spencer: Sfd 1906L

Stuart Spruce: Wid 1993L, Bra 1997L, 2000W

Bob Spurr: Bat 1897W, 1898W, 1901W

Marcus St Hilaire: Lee 1999sW, 2000sL

Cyril Stacey: Hfx 1921L

John Stankevitch: StH 2002sL

Anthony Starks: HKR 1905L

John Stead: Bro 1902W

Graham Steadman: Cas 1992L

Ian Stenton: Cas 1970W

A. 'Tony' Stephens: Wig 1965W, 1966L

David Stephens: Wig 1966L

Frank Stephens: Wig 1929W

Gary Stephens: Wig 1984L, Hfx 1987W

John Stephens: StH 1972W

David Stephenson: Wig 1984L, 1985W

Peter Sterling: Hull 1985L

Arnold Stevens: War 1954D

George Stevens: Wid 1930W

Jeff Stevenson: Lee 1957W

Anthony Stewart: StH 2001*W, 2002L

David Stockwell: Bra 1973L

Billy Stone: Hull 1922L, 1923L

Richard 'Charlie' Stone: Fea 1973W, 1974sL, Hull 1980L, 1982D, 1982rW, 1983L

Billy Stott: Wak 1946W

Lynton Stott: Sheff 1998*W

Harry Street: Lee 1957W

Harry Stretch: Bar 1951L

Miller Strong: Swi 1926W, 1927L, 1928W, 1932L

Charlie Stubley: Bat 1897W, 1898W, 1901W

Anthony Sullivan: StH 1996W, 1997W, 2001W

Clive Sullivan: HKR 1980W, Hull 1982rW

Jim Sullivan: Wig 1924W, 1929W, 1944(1)L

Mick Sullivan: Wig 1958W, 1959W, StH 1961W

Wilf Sulway: Swi 1926W

Tom Sutton: Hull 1960L

Richard Swain: Hull 2005W

J. Swift: War 1901L

W. 'Bill' Swift: War 1905W

Jack Swinbank: Hfx 1903W, 1904W

Arthur Swinden: Hud 1920W

Cyril Sykes: Hull 1959L

Whetu Taewa: Shef 1998W

Alan Tait: Lee 1994L, 1995L

Willie Talau: StH 2004W, 2006W, 2007W, 2008W

Fred Talbot: Hud 1933W, 1935L, Kei 1937L

Howie Tamatai: Wig 1984L

Kevin Tamati: Wid 1984W

Ted Tattersfield: Lee 1941W, 1942W, 1943(1+2)L

Bob Taylor: Hull 1922L, 1923L

George Taylor: Wak 1909W

Ike Taylor: War 1907W

R. 'Dick' Taylor: Hull 1910D, 1910rL, 1914W

Tommy Taylor: Cas 1935W

W.H. 'Harry' Taylor: Hull 1908L, 1909L, 1910D

Billy Teall: Wak 1946W

Eddie Tees: Bar 1967L, Bra 1973L

E.W. 'Jim' Telfer: Old 1899W

Alan Tennant: Fea 1952L

Albert 'Abe' Terry: StH 1961W

Jamie Thackray: Hull 2005sW, 2008sL

Emlyn Thomas: Lei 1921W

E.J. 'Evan' Thomas: Sfd 1906L

George Thomas: War 1904L, 1905W, 1907W, 1913L

Harold Thomas: York 1931L

Harold Thomas: Sfd 1938W, 1939L

Jack Thomas: Work 1952W

Johnny Thomas: Wig 1911L

Mark Thomas: War 1990sL

Rees Thomas: Wig 1958W, 1959W

Richard Thomas: War 1913L

R.L. 'Dicky' Thomas: Old 1899W, 1907L

Tony Thomas: Cas 1969W, 1970W

Vaughan Thomas: Fea 1967W

W. 'Billie' Thomas: York 1931L

W.S. 'Willie' Thomas: Sfd 1906L

Bill Thompson: Wid 1964W

Cec Thompson: Work 1958L

Charlie Thompson: Bro 1902W

Jim Thompson: Fea 1967W, 1973W, 1974L

Joe Thompson: StH 1897L

Joe Thompson: Lee 1923W, 1932W

Tommy Thompson: War 1933L

John Thorley: Hfx 1954D, 1954rL

Chris Thorman: Hud 2006L

Jim Thornburrow: Bar 1938L

Billy Thornton: Hun 1934W

Danny Tickle: Wig 2004L, Hull 2008L

Henry Tiffany: Hud 1933W, 1935L

Jimmy Tilley: War 1907W

John Timu: Lon 1999L

Keith Tindall: Hull 1980L, 1982rW

Frank Todd: Hfx 1921L

George Todd: Hud 1920W

George Todd: Hun 1934W, Hfx 1939W, 1941L, 1942L

Lance Todd: Wig 1911L

Peter Todd: Hfx 1954D

Tulsen Tollett: Lon 1999L

Mark Tolson: Hun 1934W

Alf Tomkins: Old 1924L, 1925W

Glen Tomlinson: Bra 1997sL

Les Tonks: Fea 1967W, 1973W, 1974L

Motu Tony: Hull 2005W

Ted Toohey: Bar 1951L, 1955W

Jack Toothill: Bra 1898L

Harry Topham: Old 1907L, Lee 1910D, 1910rW

David Topliss: Wak 1979L, Hull 1982D, 1982rW, 1983L

Peter Topping: Wid 1930W, 1934L, 1937W

Matt Toshack: Lon 1999sL

Idris Towill: Hud 1935L, Kei 1937L

Jim Traill: Kei 1937L

Ken Traill: Bra 1948L, 1949W, Hfx 1956L

Jimmy Tranter: War 1913L, 1928L

David Traynor: StH 1897L

David Treasure: 1973sL

Jack Treen: Hfx 1939W

Fred Trenwith: StH 1915L

Jim Trotter: Bro 1902W

Alec Troup: Bar 1938L

Henry Trusler: Lee 1923W

Va'aiga Tuigamala: Wig 1994W, 1995W

Pat Tunney: Sfd 1900L, 1902L, 1903L

Reggie Turnbull: Hfx 1921L

Darren Turner: Shef 1998sW

Derek 'Rocky' Turner: Wak 1960W, 1962W, 1963W

J. Turner: Bra 1906W

Barry Tyler: Bra 1947W, 1948L, 1949W

Colin Tyrer: Wig 1970L

Brian Tyson: HKR 1964L

George Tyson: Old 1907L

Joe Vagana: Bra 2001L, 2003W

Tevita Vaikona: Bra 2000W, 2001L, 2003W

Lesley Vainikolo: Bra 2003W

Dave Valentine: Hud 1953W

Jim Valentine: Swi 1900W

R. 'Bob' Valentine: Swi 1900W

Adriaan 'Attie' van Heerden: Wig 1924Wa

George van Rooyen: Wig 1924W, Wid 1930W

Tom van Vollenhoven: StH 1961W, 1966W

Marcus Vassilakopoulos: Lee 1994sL

Paul Vautin: StH 1989L

Phil Veivers: StH 1987L, 1989L, 1991L

Joe Vickers: Work 1955L

Evan Vigors: Swi 1900W

Don Vines: Wak 1960W, StH 1961W, Wak 1963W

Harry Vowles: Old 1907L

Harold Wagstaff: Hud 1913W, 1915W, 1920W

Tony Wainwright: Lee 1971L

Chev Walker: Lee 2003L, 2005L

Jack Walkington: Hun 1934W, Lee 1943(1+2)L

Harry Wallace: Hull 1908L, 1909L, 1910D, 1910rL

Syd Walmsley: Lee 1923W

Joe Walsh: Lei 1971W

John Walsh: StH 1972W

Owen Walsh: Hun 1899L

Tom Walsh: Hun 1899L, 1908W

Emlyn Walters: Bra 1944(2)W, 1947W

Graham Walters: Hull 1980L

Harry Walton: Hull 1910D, 1910rL

Jack Walton: Wak 1909W

Bob Wanbon: War 1974sW, 1975L

Shaun Wane: Wig 1988sW

Barry Ward: StH 2002sL

Billy Ward: Lee 1910D, 1910rW

Danny Ward: Lee 2003sL, 2005L

David Ward: Lee 1972*L, 1977W, 1978W

Donald Ward: Bra 1944(1+2)W, 1945(1+2)L, 1947W, 1948L, 1949W

Ernest Ward: Dew 1912W

Ernest Ward: Bra 1944(1+2)W, 1945(1+2)L, 1947W, 1948L, 1949W

E. 'Ted' Ward: Wig 1948W

Fred Ward: Hun 1965L

Johnny Ward: Cas 1969W

Kevin Ward: Cas 1986W, StH 1991L

Ernest Ware: Lee 1910D, 1910rW, Dew 1912

Jim Wareing: Work 1952W

Douglas 'John' Warlow: StH 1966W
Dennis Warrior: Lee 1943(1+2)L
Silas Warwick: Sfd 1906L
Danny Washbrook: Hull 2008L
Billy Watkins: Sfd 1938W, 1939L
David Watkins: Sfd 1969L
Eddie Watkins: Wig 1944(1+2)L, 1946L
David Watkinson: HKR 1980W, 1981L, 1986L
Alf Watson: Lee 1947L
Bernard Watson: Lee 1968W, Bra 1973L
Cliff Watson: StH 1961W, 1966W
Dave Watson: Shef 1998W
Mike Watson: Bar 1967L
William Watson: Hud 1935L
Derek Watts: Lei 1971W
Ivor Watts: Hull 1959L
Bob Wear: Bar 1967*L
Bert Webster: Wig 1924W
Fred Webster: Lee 1910D, 1910rW
William Wedgewood: Hfx 1903W
Ken Welburn: Fea 1952L
Paul Wellens: StH 2001W, 2002L, 2004W, 2006W, 2007W, 2008W
George 'Tich' West: HKR 1905L
Graeme West: Wig 1984L, 1985W
Billy Westerdale: HKR 1925L
Ben Westwood: War 2009W
Paul Whatuira: Hud 2009L
Sam Whitaker: Lee 1910rW
Frank Whitcombe: Bra 1944(1+2)W, 1945(1+2)L, 1947W, 1948L, 1949W
Les White: Wig 1948W
Leslie White: Hun 1934W
Tom White: Old 1907L
Tom White: StH 1915L
Derek Whitehead: War 1974W, 1975L
Ernest Whitehead: Lee 1947L
George Whitehead: Bro 1902W
Harold Whitehead: Hud 1945(1+2)W
Stuart Whitehead: Sfd 1969L
Billy Whiteley: StH 1897L
Johnny Whiteley: Hull 1959L, 1960L
Selwyn Whiteley: Hfx 1921L
Colin Whitfield: Wig 1984L, Hfx 1987W, 1988L
Fred Whitfield: Wid 1982r*L, 1984sW
Richard Whiting: Hull 2005W
Tom Whittaker: Wig 1911L
Alan Whittle: StH 1972*W, War 1974W, 1975L
Stan Whitty: Hull 1923L
Frank Whyte: Wid 1937W
Mike Wicks: Hud 1962L
Arthur Widdeson: Bro 1902W
Tim Wilby: Hull 1980L
Charlie Wilcox: Wid 1950L
Alfred Wild: Bro 1911W
Hughie Wild: Roc 1922W

Stephen Wild: Wig 2004sL, Hud 2006L, 2009L
Ron Wileman: Hull 1980L, 1982D
Jon Wilkin: StH 2004sW, 2006W, 2007W, 2008W
Harry Wilkinson: Wak 1946W
Ian Wilkinson: Hfx 1988L
Jack Wilkinson: Hfx 1954D, 1954rL, 1956L, Wak 1960W, 1962W, 1963W
Joe Wilkinson: Old 1907L
John Henry 'Jack' Wilkinson: HKR 1925L
John Robert 'Bob' Wilkinson: HKR 1925L
Billy Williams: Sfd 1938W
Evan Williams: Lee 1932W, 1936W
Frank Williams: War 1928L
Jack Williams: Sfd 1900L, 1902L, 1903L
Leslie Williams: Lee 1947L
Percy Williams: Wig 1911L
R. 'Dicky' Williams: Lee 1947L
Sam Williams: Old 1899W
Tom Williams: Sfd 1900L, 1902L
Tom Williams: Old 1912L
W. 'Billy' Williams: Hfx 1903W, 1904W
Denis Williamson: Wak 1962W
Bevan Wilson: Work 1952W
Bob Wilson: Bro 1902W
Don Wilson: Bar 1957L
Frank Wilson: StH 1972W
George Wilson: Work 1952W
Harry Wilson: Hun 1899L, 1908W
Justin Wilson: Cat 2007L
Scott Wilson: Hfx 1987W
Jack Wiltshire: Old 1912L
A. Windle: HKR 1905L
Billy Winskill: Bro 1902W, 1911W
Bob Winskill: Hfx 1903W, 1904W
Jim Winstanley: Lei 1921W
Tom Winstanley: StH 1897L
William Winstanley: StH 1897L
Ernest Winter: Hun 1934W
Fred Wise: Old 1912L
Michael Withers: Bra 2000W, 2001L
Alf Wood: Old 1912L
Bob Wood: Bra 1898L
John Wood: Wid 1976L
Martin Wood: Shef 1998sW
Harry Woodhead: Bro 1902W
Paul Woods: Hull 1980L
Tommy Woods: Roc 1922W
Alan Woodward: Old 1924L
Bill Wookey: Work 1955L, 1958L
John Woolmore: Dew 1929L
George Woosey: Bar 1957L
Tom Woosey: Wig 1966L
Jon Wray: Cas 1992L
Brian Wrigglesworth: Fea 1967W
Darren Wright: Wid 993L

David Wright: War 1974W
Frank Wright: War 1954D, 1954rW
Jack Wright: Hun 1899L
Jim Wright: Old 1912L
Joe Wright: Swi 1932L
Stuart Wright: Wid 1977L, 1979W, 1981W, 1982D, 1982rL, 1984W
J.E. 'Danny' Wyburn: Hull 1922L

Kirk Yeaman: Hull 2005W, 2008L
Michael Yewlett: Old 1907L
Billy Young: Swi 1928L
Frank Young: Lee 1910D, 1910rW
Tommy 'Boxer' Young: Hun 1899L

INDEX OF COACHES

(Abbreviations: W—won, L—lost)

Allan Agar: Featherstone Rovers 1983W

Richard Agar: Hull FC 2008L

Chris Anderson: Halifax 1987W, 1988L

Daniel Anderson: St Helens 2006W, 2007W, 2008W

Eric Ashton: Wigan 1965W, 1966L, 1970L, St Helens 1976W, 1978L

Albert Atkinson: Halifax 1949L

Eric Batten: Featherstone Rovers 1952L

Arthur Bennett: Huddersfield 1913W, 1915W

Fred Bennett: Batley 1897W, 1898W

W. 'Billy' Bennett: Warrington 1933L, 1936L, Halifax 1939L, 1941L, 1942L

Joseph Briscoe: Leigh 1921W

Chris Brockbank: Huddersfield 1933W, 1935L, Warrington 1950W

Ian Brooke: Bradford Northern 1973L

Jim Brough: Workington Town 1955L, 1958L

Nathan Brown: Huddersfield Giants 2009L

Arthur Bunting: Hull 1980L, 1982W, 1983L, 1985L

Jim Challinor: Barrow 1967L, St Helens 1972W

Colin Clarke (joint-coach): Wigan 1985W

Joe Coan: St Helens 1966W

Tom Coates: Hull 1908L

George Cook: Salford 1902L, 1903L

J. Cooper: Swinton 1900W

Jim Croston: Wakefield Trinity 1946W

Ken Dalby: Leeds 1957W

J.E. Davies: Dewsbury 1912W

Frank Dawson: Leeds 1947L, Halifax 1954L, 1956L

John Dorahy: Wigan 1994W

Joe Egan: Wigan 1958W, 1959W, 1961L, Widnes 1964W

Matthew Elliott: Bradford Bulls 1997L, 2000W

J. Farrell: Bradford 1906W

Jack Fish: Warrington 1928L

E. 'Ted' Forber: St Helens 1930L

Peter Fox: Featherstone Rovers 1973W, 1974L

Roy Francis: Hull 1959L, 1960L, Leeds 1968W

Laurie Gant: Featherstone Rovers 1967W

Alf Glover: St Helens 1915L

Mike Gregory: Wigan Warriors 2004L

I. Hackett: Warrington 1905W, 1907W, 1913L

Hector Halsall: Barrow 1938L

A. Hannah: Leeds 1923W

W. 'Billy' Hannah: Hunslet 1908W, 1934W

Ernest Hayley: Wakefield Trinity 1909W

Jack Hesketh: Wigan 1911L

Bright Heyhirst: Halifax 1921L, Leeds 1932W

W.J. Hobbs: Dewsbury 1929L

Jesse Hodgkinson: Rochdale Hornets 1922W

Willie Horne: Barrow 1955W, 1957L

Maurice Hughes: Barrow 1951L

Colin Hutton: Hull Kingston Rovers 1964L

Syd Hynes: Leeds 1977W, 1978W

W. 'Billy' Jacques: Hull Kingston Rovers 1925L

Dai Jenkins: Leeds 1931W

Griff Jenkins: Wigan 1963L, Salford 1969L

Brian Johnson: Warrington 1990L

Vince Karalius: Widnes 1975W, 1984W

John Kear: Sheffield Eagles 1998W, Hull FC 2005W

W. 'Billy' Kearns: Swinton 1926W, 1927L, 1928W, 1932L

Robert King: St Helens 1897L

W. 'Bill' Kirkbride: Wakefield Trinity 1979L

H.J. Knutton: Bradford 1898L

Dean Lance: Leeds Rhinos 2000L

Phil Larder: Widnes 1993L

Doug Laughton: Widnes 1979W, 1981W, 1982L, Leeds 1994L, 1995L

J. Lewis: Hull 1909L, 1910L

Graham Lowe: Wigan 1988W, 1989W

Peter Lyons: Widnes 1930W, 1934L, 1937W

Tommy McCarty: Wigan 1920L, 1924W, 1929W

Alan McInnes (joint-coach) Wigan 1985W

Mike McLennan: St Helens 1991L

Shaun McRae: St Helens 1996W, 1997W

Jim Mallalieu: Oldham 1912L

Charles R. Marsden: Oldham 1924L, 1925W, 1926L, 1927W

Sid Melville: Hull 1914W, 1922L, 1923L

J. Midgley: Halifax 1903W, 1904W

Ian Millward: St Helens 2001W, 2002L, 2004W

Roger Millward: Hull Kingston Rovers 1980W, 1981L, 1986L

John Monie: Wigan/Wigan Warriors: 1990W, 1991W, 1992W, 1993W, 1996L

W. Morn: Leeds 1910W

Cec Mountford: Warrington 1954W

Alex Murphy: Leigh 1971W, Warrington 1974W, 1975L, Wigan 1984L, St Helens 1987L, 1989L

Graham Murray: Leeds Rhinos 1999W

Frank Myler: Widnes 1976L, 1977L

Brian Noble: Bradford Bulls 2001L, 2003W

E. 'Teddy' Parkes: Wigan 1944L

Russ Pepperell: Huddersfield 1953W

Mick Potter: Catalans Dragons 2007L

Daryl Powell: Leeds Rhinos 2003L

Alan Prescott: St Helens 1961W

Stuart Raper: Wigan Warriors 2002W

Dai Rees: Bradford Northern 1944W, 1945L, 1947W, 1948L, 1949W

George Rees: York 1931L

Malcolm Reilly: Castleford 1986W

W. 'Billy' Rhodes: Castleford 1935W

A.J. 'Gus' Risman: Workington Town 1952W

Jack Roberts: Salford 1900L

Tom Royle: Broughton Rangers 1901W

Mark Shackleton: Batley 1901W

H. Shann: Hull Kingston Rovers 1905L

Tommy Shannon: Widnes 1950L

Jon Sharp: Huddersfield Giants 2006L

Herbert Slater: Keighley 1937L

Tommy Smales: Castleford 1970W

Brian Smith: Bradford Bulls 1996L

Tony Smith: Leeds Rhinos 2005L, Warrington Wolves 2009W

W. 'Billy' Smith: Leeds 1936W, 1941W, 1942W, 1943L

Stanley Spencer: Huddersfield 1945W

Dan Stains: London Broncos 1999L

Jim Sullivan: Wigan 1946L, 1948W, 1951W, St Helens 1953L, 1956W

H. Taylor: Broughton Rangers 1911W

Lance B Todd: Salford 1938W, 1939L

Ken Traill: Wakefield Trinity 1960W, 1962W, 1963W, 1968L

Derek Turner: Castleford 1969W, Leeds 1971L, 1972L

Dave Valentine: Huddersfield 1962L

Darryl van de Velde: Castleford 1992L

Harry Varley: Oldham 1899W

Fred Ward: Hunslet 1965L

Eddie Waring: Dewsbury 1943W

Graeme West: Wigan 1995W

Joe White: Salford 1906L

(Note: The above list includes whoever is deemed responsible for the team, whether trainer, coach or team manager. Trainers, who were responsible for players' fitness rather than tactics, gave way to coaches and team managers during the 1930s/1940s)

(Note: The author regrets he has been unable to confirm the coach/trainer for the following teams: Huddersfield 1920, Hunslet 1899, Oldham 1907, Wakefield Trinity 1914, Warrington 1901, 1904)

INDEX OF REFEREES

(Abbreviations: Bar—Barrow, Bat—Batley, Bra—Bradford/Bradford Northern/Bradford Bulls, Bro—Broughton Rangers, Cas—Castleford, Cat—Catalans Dragons, Dew—Dewsbury, Fea—Featherstone Rovers, Hfx—Halifax, HKR—Hull Kingston Rovers, Hud—Huddersfield/Huddersfield Giants, Hull—Hull/Hull FC, Hun—Hunslet, Kei—Keighley, Lee—Leeds/Leeds Rhinos, Lei- Leigh, Lon—London Broncos, Old—Oldham, Roc—Rochdale Hornets, Sfd—Salford, Shef—Sheffield Eagles, StH—St Helens, Swi—Swinton, Wak—Wakefield Trinity, War—Warrington/Warrington Wolves, Wid—Widnes, Wig—Wigan/Wigan Warriors, Work—Workington Town, York—York, r—replay, 1—1st leg, 2—2nd leg)

S. Adams (Hull): 1944(1) Wig v Bra

C.F. 'Charlie' Appleton (Warrington): 1952 Fea v Work, 1957 Bar v Lee, 1959 Hull v Wig

Arthur Brown (Wakefield): 1926 Old v Swi

D.S. 'Deryk' Brown (Preston): 1969 Cas v Sfd

J. Bruckshaw (Stockport): 1903 Hfx v Sfd, 1905 HKR v War

David Campbell (Widnes): 1994 Lee v Wig

Ron Campbell (Widnes): 1985 Hull v Wig

Reverend F.H. 'Frank' Chambers (Huddersfield): 1924 Old v Wig

Eric Clay (Leeds): 1960 Hull v Wak, 1967 Bar v Fea

Matt Coates (Pudsey): 1951 Bar v Wig

Paul Cowell (Warrington): 1937 Kei v Wid, 1941 Hfx v Lee, 1942 Hfx v Lee, 1944(2) Bra v Wig, 1947 Bra v Lee

Stuart Cummings (Widnes): 1996 Bra v StH, 1997 Bra v StH, 1998 Shef v Wig, 2002 StH v Wig

D.T.H. 'Dennis' Davies (Manchester): 1962 Hud v Wak, 1963 Wak v Wig

A.S. 'Albert' Dobson (Featherstone): 1936 Lee v War, 1950 War v Wid

Jack Edden (Swinton): 1931 Hfx v York

Ben R. Ennion (Wigan): 1912 Dew v Old

Frank Fairhurst (Wigan): 1933 Hud v War, 1945(1) Hud v Bra

Steve Ganson (St Helens): 2005 Hull v Lee, 2008 Hull v StH, 2009 Hud v War

Ron Gelder (Wakefield): 1954 Hfx v War, 1954(r) Hfx v War, 1955 Bar v Work, 1956 Hfx v StH, 1958 Wig v Work

Paul Geraghty (York): 1975 War v Wid

A.E. 'Albert Harding (Manchester): 1935 Cas v Hud

J.P. 'John' Hebblethwaite (York): 1968 Lee v Wak

Alf Hill (Leeds): 1946 Wak v Wig

Andy Holbrook (Warrington): 1934 Hun v Wid

John Holdsworth (Kippax): 1987 Kfx v StH, 1990 War v Wig

H. Horsfall (Batley): 1928 Swi v War

H.G. 'Harry' Hunt (Warrington): 1966 StH v Wig

J.E. 'Joe' Jackson (Pudsey): 1979 Wak v Wid

R.A. 'Dick' Jones (Widnes): 1922 Hull v Roc, 1925 HKR v Old

D.G. 'Gerry Kershaw (York): 1981 HKR v Wid

J. Kidd (Millom): 1901 Bat v War

Karl Kirkpatrick (Warrington): 2004 StH v Wig

Ashley Klein (Keighley): 2007 Cat v StH

Eric Lawrenson (Warrington): 1972 Lee v StH

G.F. 'Fred' Lindop (Wakefield): 1970 Cas v Wig, 1980 Hull v HKR, 1982 Hull v Wid, 1982(r) Hull v Wid, 1988 Hfx v Wig

W. 'Billy' McCutcheon (Oldham): 1906 Bra v Sfd

Joe Manley (Warrington): 1965 Hun v Wig

T.H. Marshall (Bradford): 1899 Hun v Old

J.F. 'Jimmy' May (St Helens): 1911 Bro v Wig, 1913 Hud v War, 1914 Hull v Wak

F. Mills (Oldham): 1920 Hud v Wig, 1923 Hull v Lee

Ron Moore (Wakefield): 1976 StH v Wid

Vince Moss (Manchester): 1977 Lee v Wid

M.J. 'Mick' Naughton (Widnes): 1973 Bra v Fea

Frank Peel (Bradford): 1930 StH v Wid, 1932 Lee v Swi, 1938 Bar v Sfd

G.S. 'George' Phillips (Widnes): 1939 Hfx v Sfd, 1943(1) Dew v Lee, 1943(2) Lee v Dew, 1945(2) Bra v Hud, 1948 Bra v Wig, 1949 Bra v Hfx, 1953 Hud v StH

Steve Presley (Castleford): 2000 Bra v Lee

Joseph Priestley (Salford): 1910 Hull v Lee, 1910(r) Hull v Lee

Frank Renton (Hunslet): 1900 Sfd v Swi, 1907 Old v War, 1921 Hfx v Lei

R. 'Bob' Robinson (Bradford): 1915 Hud v StH, 1927 Old v Swi, 1929 Dew v Wig

W. Robinson (Manningham): 1902 Bro v Sfd

Sam Shepherd (Oldham): 1974 Fea v War

Richard Silverwood (Dewsbury): 2006 Hud v StH

E.H. 'Ted' Smirk (Wigan): 1909: Hull v Wak

J.H. 'Jack' Smith (Widnes): 1897 Bat v StH, 1898 Bat v Bra, 1904 Hfx v War, 1908 Hull v Hun

Jim Smith (Halifax): 1991 StH v Wig

Russell Smith (Castleford): 1993 Wid v Wig, 1995 Lee v Wig, 1999 Lee v Lon, 2001 Bra v StH, 2003 Bra v Lee

Ray Tennant (Castleford): 1989 StH v Wig

R.L. 'Dickie' Thomas (Oldham): 1964 HKR v Wid

W.H. 'Billy' Thompson (Huddersfield): 1971 Lee v Lei, 1978 Lee v StH, 1984 Wid v Wig

T.W. 'Tom' Watkinson (Swinton): 1961 StH v Wig

Robin Whitfield (Widnes): 1983 Fea v Hull, 1986 Cas v HKR, 1992 Cas v Wig

Index of Video Referees

David Asquith (York): 1999 Lee v Lon

Phil Bentham (Warrington): 2007 Cat v StH, 2009 Hud v War

Geoff Berry (Batley): 2003 Bra v Lee

David Campbell (Widnes): 2004 StH v Wig

Robert Connolly (Wigan): 2005 Hull v Lee

Steve Cross (Hull): 2001 Bra v StH

D.G. 'Gerry' Kershaw (York): 2000 Bra v Lee

Ashley Klein (Keighley): 2008 Hull v StH

Ian Ollerton (Wigan): 2006 Hud v StH

Ray Tennant (Castleford): 2002 StH v Wig

(Note: Excepting the earlier years, when referees place names were listed according to the clubs they were attached to, the city/town name is based on their place of residence)